RIGGER 5.0

CONTENTS & CREDITS

First Printing by Catalyst Game Labs, an imprint of InMediaRes Productions, LLC
PMB 202 • 303 -91st Ave. NE, E-502
Lake Stevens, WA 98258

Find us online:
info@shadowruntabletop.com
(*Shadowrun* questions)
http://www.shadowruntabletop.com
(Catalyst *Shadowrun* website)
http://www.shadowrun.com
(official *Shadowrun Universe* website)
http://www.catalystgamelabs.com
(Catalyst website)
http://shop.catalystgamelabs.com
(Catalyst/Shadowrun orders)

INTRODUCTION

If you know what a rigger can do for your shadowrunning team, you know how badly you need one on your side. And if you don't know, you'd better find out, because someone else is going to come in with their rigger doing all sorts of fancy drek, and you're going to look very foolish. And maybe dead.

There are obvious uses for riggers that everyone knows about—getaway drivers, border crossers, that sort of thing. Those tasks are plenty useful, and often reason enough on their own to make sure you sign up a rigger. But there's more than that. Any rigger worth their salt has a squad of drones they can bring to the party, and those drones are a miniature army waiting for your command. They're spies, force multipliers, decoys, even one-person transportation, if they're big enough. They are the ultimate stealth teammate, one that won't set off heat sensors and won't show up on astral overwatch. Keep them hidden, wait for the right moment to bring it out, and you'll have an ambush that will catch all but the most alert teams by surprise. Or you'll have the chance to sneak around and see or hear information you were never supposed to know. The things a rigger can do with their drones to help out a team is only limited by shadowrunners' imagination—which is one thing they should never be short on.

But it's not just about drones once the job starts. A rigger has vehicle options during the run, too. From air vehicles that can hover over the job site and provide much-needed cover fire to vehicles that can provide a little extra speed and heft even in corporate office halls, a fully equipped rigger knows how to select the right option for the job. They also know how to trick their vehicles and drones out right, to give just the right advantage at the right time.

This book is what a fully equipped rigger needs. It starts with **Hot Rubber and Cold Steel**, which gives an overview of the different types of riggers and vehicles there are out there, as well as details on the absolute rush riggers feel when fully jacked into one of their toys. **All the Angles** gets tactical, discussing how riggers can use all their tools in harmony to make vehicle magic happen, while also giving rules to support what they do. **On the Bleeding Edge** helps players make a rigger as customized as their vehicles, with qualities and life modules made with rigging in mind. Then we get to the gear—**Demolition Derby** brings the ground craft, **Ruling the Waves** details watercraft, **Air Superiority** lists off the aircraft, and **The Automated Army** rolls out the drones. **Building the Perfect Beast** has all sorts of vehicle accessories and modifications, and **Maximum Pursuit** offers advanced chase rules. Finally, you'll find tables of vehicles from this book as well as *SR5* for easy reference.

So burn rubber, break the waves, push the envelope, and head for the skies! Riggers are not happy to sit still for very long, so get up to speed with all the gear and rules and start leaving the slugs of the Sixth World in your dust.

RIGGER 5.0 CREDITS

Writing: Mark Dynna, Jeff Halket, Jason M. Hardy, Adam Large, Aaron Pavao, Scott Schletz, R.J. Thomas, Malik Toms, Thomas Willoughby

Proofing: Chuck Burhanna, Bruce Ford, Mason Hart, Francis Jose, David Silberstein, Jeremy Weyand

Playtesting: Jackson Brunsting, Jacob Cohen, Derek Doktor, Bruce Ford, Eugen Fournes, Joanna Fournes, Tim Gray , Kendall Jung, Richard Riessen, Matt Riley, Leland Zavadil

Art Direction: Brent Evans

Development Assistance: Peter M. Andrew, Jr., Robert Volbrecht

Cover Art: Echo Chernik

Art: Bruno Balixia, Igor Fiorentini, Andre Garcia, Benjamin Giletti, David Hovey, Ian King, David Lecossu, Marco Mizzoni, Victor Moreno, Mauro Peroni, Chris Peuler, Erich Schriner, Takashi Tan, James Cory Webster, and Iwo Widulinski

Cover Layout: Matt "Wrath" Heerdt

Iconography: Nigel Sade

Interior Layout: Matt "Wrath" Heerdt

Shadowrun Line Developer: Jason M. Hardy

HOME SECURITY

Fetch was in the truck .029 seconds before he realized he was the decoy. They had to know he'd figure it out. He felt the weight differential against his chassis and calibrated his active suspension so the change wouldn't hinder performance.

Decoy meant demotion, which meant he'd screwed up at some point, but Fetch couldn't figure how. It wasn't about his performance in the truck. The last three deliveries had gone smoothly. This decoy job was no different. So far the drive east was uneventful. He breathed a sigh of relief as his truck and drones cleared the most heavily gang-controlled portion of the road without incident. It was all corp-secured freeway to the finish line. The rigger took a moment to breathe it all in. Slipping into the skin of his Cyberspace Designs Dalmatian, Fetch climbed to six hundred feet, tilted his nose, and took in the sight of the freeway. Ahead, twelve lanes of silicon-pressed blacktop were fat with the husks of insectoid automobiles flashing brake lights. Fetch couldn't imagine a situation where his Mack Hellhound would be attacked here.

In truth, the ordnance the run required could laughingly be called an overreaction—even as a decoy. Every combat drone Fetch owned, save the X2, was either inside or flying above the monstrous big rig. The truck itself carried a bristling arsenal of mounted assault weapons. At a per drone cost, he was making more today as a decoy than shadowrunners made in a dozen runs. Fetch could only guess how many in the sprawling corporate mess of Maersk knew what kind of nuyen his handler was

paying out for these simple transport jobs, or worse, how many department heads were just like him.

Fetch wondered idly if the demotion order came from Mr. Brinkley or someone else. He didn't like Brinkley. The man had a rat face, and when he smiled, his mustache took on the curious appearance of whiskers. They'd met through a broker who helped freelance tech workers secure corporate jobs. They'd found camaraderie in the trid shows they watched. It seemed like the fixer cared more about whether they got along than Fetch's bonafides. Maybe he could lean on that camaraderie to figure out how and why he got demoted.

The rigger supposed he could take it easy now, slave the drone set to autopilot, disconnect, and slot that new Magestone trid he'd been meaning to watch. He'd earned it. At this point, what would be the harm? The company only monitored the truck's camera feeds. They'd have no way to know he'd completely slacked off on the job. Still, Fetch wasn't the type to sandbag a run. No, he'd do the work and check in with Mr. Brinkley in the morning, chat him up, maybe remind him how much he appreciated the opportunity to work for Maersk. Runners acted like it was tough living in the shadows, but it took a lot more finesse and effort to break into corporate life. It took Fetch ten years to find his way into the corporate system, and he was not ready to be unplugged.

Near exit 347, a LoneStar AR security routine scanned his big rig and the aerial drone marking its progress. His drones came up with the RFID markings of Eastern Tiger Transport, a

BY MALIK TOMS

convenient lie in case he was pulled over. Like he did every time a scan hit, he wondered if this was the time when he'd finally be exposed as a gutterpunk climber living the good life on a stolen SIN.

All of this—the life, the history, even the job—felt like lie piled on top of lie. Lately he'd gotten in the habit of telling people he'd done two military tours, and none of that commercial Desert Wars shit either. The brass would tell him go fetch this, go fetch that, and eventually the name just stuck. That was the lie he told. And that lie led to the next one. Now here he was, out on the road to nowhere hauling the illusion of something worth taking.

Except that was a lie too.

Fetch's meat body wasn't in the truck at all. Twenty years ago he would have been riding a Kensai rig, his body buried somewhere inside the tractor trailer, four gleaming ports wired to four SOTA datajacks pumping hot feed straight to his cerebral cortex. Twenty years ago he could've gotten around on his own, run the op the way he had to—line of sight. Nowadays he spent his hours laid up in a suburban split level wrapped in the couture of near-do-wells and thought-I'd-do-much-better's, and relying on a double-insulated WAN to rig on a low-noise bandwidth. *The corporate life.* Well, Auburn's Valencia Hills community was not quite corporate turf but it was close enough to smell the LTG.

The more he thought about the demotion, the angrier he grew. Fetch wasn't about to go backwards. He'd built a comfortable life. Before Valencia, he had to worry about protecting his doss through the night. Now the only thing he worried about was, "Where's my fracking pizza?"

He said it out loud, the words slurring through chapped lips. His hydration tube slipped free and slithered earthwards. He cursed again and then a third time when he realized he couldn't reach it without sitting up. So the fat elf heaved himself forward, his tactical chair squealing and twisting in the process. He almost wrenched the single remaining datajack out of his skull and had to force himself under control, wheezing. Fetch's condition was far past the point of a gym membership—the better option was to save up for muscle toner bioware that would force his body to stay fit. Too bad he'd gone and blown that nuyen on a new truck.

The doorbell rang.

Fetch called up a panel of camera images and enlarged the panel labeled "front door." On the virtual screen was a punk kid with a Knights of Rage t-shirt and a pizza wrapped in a urethane foam sleeve. Fetch sighed with relief. He fired up an Aztech Crawler—his mobile plate bot—and sent it toward the front of the house. He moved to activate the front door, but then froze. Something nagged at him.

He refocused on the door cam again. Definitely the kid from the last few times he ordered. Fetch tipped well, so the kid kept coming back. Liked it. But now the kid was tapping his foot impatiently, and he kept looking back to the car. Maybe he had a girl there. The kid's eyes then flicked to the right, off along the front edge of the house.

Fetch switched to a camera on the side of the house. He couldn't see anything out of the ordinary—only lawn, unused porch, and the Anderson's lawn just beyond. He flipped back to the pizza boy, prepared to chalk the whole thing up to paranoia inspired by a sudden demotion and too many hours in the chair. The kid's eyes flicked right again.

Fetch raised his eyebrows and switched back to the side view camera. That's when he noticed a ripple of fabric. It blended so perfectly with the evening shadows that he almost missed it. The pizza boy was not alone.

A throb of fear burned through Fetch's chest. He could barely make out the form of a man wearing a black balaclava and carrying an uzi. Out front the kid rang a third time, nervous now. Fetch was taking too long to answer.

The masked man stepped from the blind at the corner of the house. A second emerged from the pizza kid's Opel Luna. This second man put a finger to his ear, muttered something, and an American squealed into the driveway behind the tiny delivery vehicle. Fetch immediately checked in on his drone set. It had to be a two-site attack. Hit the truck on the road and hit the rigger at home, so the vehicular weapons systems couldn't respond fast enough. Back in the Puyallup days he would have been ready for this, but these kinds of things didn't happen in Valencia. They happened to shadowrunners, not to regular people like him.

The Maersk run was fine. Beyond too-heavy traffic, there was nothing his spotter drone or Hellhound could see out of the ordinary. Was it a corporate action? They could be trying to take him out from the home. Hit his WAN with a good enough hacker, and you could take control of the whole drone set. It took every ounce of courage he could muster to stop himself from firing up the exterior speakers and screaming, 'I'm just the decoy!'

He studied the two operators on the street and the other two who'd just pulled up in the car. If they wanted to disrupt his WAN and steal the Maersk load they'd need a hacker—maybe a rigger too. These men were shooters, not hackers. So, what the hell were they doing in his driveway?

Fetch's hand hovered over the AR command string for 911. Local security response time was under four minutes in Valencia Hills. He could hold out for that long on the strength of his home security system. Still, it didn't stop his heart from climbing up his throat. Then the last man out of the vehicle tore away a strip of black sheeting on the driver door, revealing the KE insignia beneath. Fetch yanked his hand away from the command string like he'd touched something hot.

They weren't really Knight Errant Security, he was certain of that, but a quick scan proved the RFID signatures coming off the American looked real enough to back down the local security response. Valencia Hills residents were climbers by nature. They all want into that enclave world—even the cops want the uniform upgrade and the pension it brought. They weren't going to question a corporate security action. Even if Fetch knew that wasn't what this was.

The shooters were armed with uzis. They split into pairs, two hopping the fence and moving into the backyard. The pair from the car advanced quickly on the delivery driver. They bound his hands and feet with zip ties and left him there, hogtied, in plain view of the front door.

"Come on, Fetch. You have to think of something." The rigger muttered aloud, flipping through his drone manifest and scanning the capabilities of everything in his arsenal. He had a trio of Steel

Lynxes armed to the teeth and sleeping in the back of his Mac Hellhound almost two hundred miles away. The Dalmatian dron providing air cover for that run was fast, but there was no way could make it back here in time. Nothing else on his list was comba capable. Maybe the Optic-X2 in the garage, but it was still damage and ammo dry from that side job he'd covered for his old frien Ellida a week back. Desperate, Fetch ran diagnostics on it anyway A moment after rebooting its system, he was convinced it woul never fly again. A waste. He hadn't even been paid for that side job All he got for his trouble was a drone full of bullet holes and a har drive's worth of surveillance data he hadn't had time to analyze.

Beneath the list of unavailable combat drones were a half-doz en local signals, but they were all useless—worker bees servin the one true king. The aforementioned plate bot, an Ares Dueli stripped and modded to look like a butler he jokingly named Fri day, a Frisbee-sized Sikorsky-bell microskimmer, a Horizon flyin eye no larger than an actual eye, and his BMW convertible in th garage. He cursed out loud and beat his fist against the arm of hi command chair.

Fetch had no way to defend himself. He didn't even own a gun He had once, a Ruger Super Warhawk big enough that it felt like blow dryer in his hands. The day he got it, he drove to the wood for target practice. He turned it sideways like they did in the tride flicks, fired it at a tree, and the kickback snapped his wrist so har that he was in a brace for a month. He didn't even know what hap pened to the gun. It might still be in the dirt where he dropped it.

The two operators in the back were checking the windows an French doors for a way in, but this rigger's nest was very hard t break into. With a wave of his hand, metal shutters slammed shu over all of the windows and doors. Fetch cursed himself for no adding offensive hardpoints to the house. At the time he'd ratio nalized that the hardpoints were too conspicuous in the wageslav world. Besides, when you worked with combat drones, you didn' need the extra offense.

He sure needed it now.

Fetch extended his digital web. He sent out feelers into th Matrix to ping any other drones out there. It was a risk. Without hacker running overwatch, his WAN was only as safe as it was in visible to intruding hackers. Fortunately, these guys hadn't brough one along—another clear sign they weren't Knight Errant.

The residents of Valencia were PTO members and weeken golfers with "my kid is on the honor roll" stickers plastered o the back of their minivans. Fetch wasn't expecting to find a full armed Roto-Drone lying around, so it wasn't a surprise when th only useful wi-fi signal came from next door. The Andersons ha bought their sixteen-year-old brat a used Strato-9 that was rust ing away in the backyard. They told him about it over dinner once asking if he could teach the boy something about being a dron hobbyist, which is what they clearly thought Fetch was. The dron had no weapons to speak of, but with a 2700 engine RPM, th rotors could be useful.

A plan started to take shape. Even though his drones weren' rated for use in this fashion, Fetch didn't have a lot of choices. H checked the position of the four operators one last time. The tw in the front were spread out on either side of the driveway. At th back of the house, the men were still clumped together studying the metal shutter on the back door.

He unshuttered a slit of a window in the upstairs bathroom The flying eye and microskimmer went through in quick succes sion. It took a hard reboot to get the Strato-9 going, but the dron was airborne in a matter of seconds. The rigger already had the drone's protocols, from when he showed the teen how to fly the outdated machine. He triggered his silent alarm, marked the time at four minutes, and prayed God had a soft spot for elves.

Fetch jumped into the skin of the Flying Eye. He had more control when he was fully immersed in the drone, and for what he was attempting control was everything. He moved around to the side of the house, keeping to the shade of the high trees. The operator on the far side of the driveway was making his way around the side of the house, looking for any weak spot in the home's defenses. That distraction made him the target. Fetch lined himself up with the man and zoomed the camera, searching the balaclava-covered face for any sign that the man noticed him. Then abruptly the rigger flung himself at the man, internal propulsion unit straining to break 25 KPH. He tilted slightly, mentally bracing for impact, and collided with the side of the man's head. The impact sent a jolt of pain feedback up through wire into the rigger's real arms and legs, and he reflexively pulled back out of the drone. The eye fell backwards and rattled to the ground. On the eye's camera, Fetch saw the man yowl and take a step back, training his weapon on the tiny drone. The man leaned in closer, focused on trying to figure out what had just hit him. It was only a moment, but it was the moment Fetch needed.

The Strato-9 sliced out of the sky. The man heard it just before it hit and jumped back, but the rotors connected with a wet chop and stopped spinning. The drone hung there in mid air a moment before crashing to the ground on top of the dead operator.

His partner screamed, "Man down. East side of the house!" Fetch exhaled a quick sigh. He tried to raise the Flying Eye off the ground, but a heavy boot slammed into the camera. Fetch winced, watching several grand of mods and a lot of history grind into dust on the pavement of his driveway. He couldn't worry about that. Living through this meant letting go of a lot more than an Eye.

Fetch switched over to the BMW. He powered up and closed the ragtop and mirrored windows. He gassed it, holding the break until the tires spun fast enough to squeal, leaving smoking rubber marks on the garage floor. He threw up the garage shutter, flipped into drive, and tore into the driveway at close to 47 KPH. His prized car smashed into the Opel Luna, knocking the smaller car backwards. Smoke and sparks puffed out from each vehicle. From the cameras of the microskimmer, he could see the initial hit hadn't cleared enough room for his car to escape the driveway. Fetch mentally backed the car up until he was touching the back of his garage and then rammed the Luna again. That's when the three operators raced around the corner, leveled their guns on the car, and unloaded their weapons.

They spread out in overlapping fields of fire, as he predicted. As the bullets tore his prized car to shreds, he felt his heart beat faster, fear seizing control. Now for the real risk. He jumped into the microskimmer, taking careful aim. He spun toward them, isolating the guard farthest from the other two and crashed into his gun arm, pushing the weapon and the live fire toward the other two men. The force of impact against the man's arm sent pain down the wire like a bat to the side of the head. His cameras went dark for a moment. When they came back online, a second gunman was down, clutching his shoulder. Fetch barely had time to back out of the microskimmer before gunfire tore it to shreds. Echoes of dumpshock left him painfully disoriented. He tried desperately to clear his head and focus on the garage-side cameras. He came to his senses just in time to see the two remaining operators running toward the open garage door. He lashed out in AR, mashing the close button. As the door started to fall, the closer of the two men dove through the entrance. Desperate, Fetch urged the bullet-riddled sports car into reverse. It lurched backwards on dying cylinders, catching the second operator in the legs and knocking him off balance before he could start his own dive. The armored garage door rattled shut.

"What the hell do you want with me?!" Fetch screamed. Outside, none of his neighbors dared to come out of their homes. Fetch could see faces in the windows lit by their commlink screens as they nervously keyed 911 or tried to film the event to share with friends later when their safety was no longer at risk. In the distance, police sirens warned of their arrival. The operator outside banged his fists against the garage door in frustration. He knew his Knight Errant car was meaningless now. It was one thing to be told this was a police action, but a full-fledged firefight couldn't be fast-talked away.

A warning flash in Fetch's AR display reminded him that he had an intruder. The other operator was still in the garage, crouched by the X-2 drone, fishing around inside the hardware access panel. He yanked something out and secured it in one of the pockets on his combat vest. It might have been the memory core.

Fetch said, "Is that what this is about?" But it didn't matter why they were here anymore. The operator moved forward, slowly sweeping his gun from left to right until he moved out of the garage, out of camera range, and into the house proper. He could hear the man moving steadily through his home, coming to kill him. The rigger only had one card left to play. He fed a command string to his plate bot and then jumped into his Ares Duelist.

The drone was sheathed in a black suit. It clomped awkwardly down the hall, pausing just inside the doorway to the bedroom Fetch used as his command center. At this distance, Friday almost looked like a man. The traditional bulky samurai-styled armor plating of the original model was gone, along with the sword hands. These were replaced by one blunted tray arm and second dual-jointed appendage with a fully articulated hand tuned for fine manipulations. Fetch hoped they'd be enough to save his life.

The operator stepped into the long hallway leading to Fetch's command room. He cautiously moved forward, staying low, weapon raised and ready. Suddenly, plate bot skittered around the corner and charged the gunmen. The man spun and fired. As he did, Friday charged out of the command room on stumpy black legs and crashed headlong into the operator. The man struggled to get clear, but Friday's articulated arm clamped down on his gun, wrenching the weapon away. Then the heavy drone tipped and fell on top of the man, pinning him to the ground.

Nearby, Fetch let out a cry of joy. It was over. He unhooked his RCC cord and stood on legs wobbly from disuse. Fetch could hear sirens right outside now. He walked toward the man slowly, using the doorframe to steady himself. If this were the trids, he would stride out and stand over the fake cop, peel the gun from his fingers and turn it on him. He'd be in control, because he had won.

As soon as Fetch stepped through the door, the fallen man struggled to get his hand free to reach for a weapon. Fetch flinched backwards into the room. He wasn't a shadowrunner or a trid character. He was a suburbanite who opened the door when the cops knocked. As the local police flooded the hallway, Fetch sighed and made sure his drones remained on mission. Tomorrow he'd call into his handler and try to fix things—right after he upgraded his home security.

HOT RUBBER AND COLD STEEL

Stitcher jumped through the empty frame of the long-ago broken window and tucked into the nearest shadowy corner. He could hear the thwupping of the rotors outside, but he was sure he wasn't spotted.

From his dark corner he began to scan around the empty room for the slightest sign of movement or glint of metal. The rigger on his tail was good. Whoever was behind this drone armada that had been running him ragged for the past six hours must have known the area well. Every hideout and bolthole Stitcher knew was quickly discovered by the mysterious being behind the machines.

It all started with a trio of little tracked Crawlers. Whoever was behind this had mounted some kind of machine pistol on the Aztechnology drones. They rolled out from behind some dumpsters in an alley and very politely asked him to come with them. They opened fire when Stitcher bolted into a nearby doorway.

Five minutes later, when he thought he was totally clear, something landed on his back and crawled up his jacket. It kept dodging his attempts to swing at it, and it repeated the same polite surrender message of the Crawlers. He was well aware that whoever was controlling the little bug drone would be able to keep tracking him and eventually bring in something bigger. While he wasn't a fan of angering the rigger by trashing his drones, he also wasn't a fan of getting dragged in for whatever this rigger wanted, so the decision to slam his back against a wall took some time to make. When the shattered remains of the drone fell to the concrete, Stitcher decided to go dark and head for the hills.

He hailed a cab, paid upfront for the trip, and then shut down his commlink while the cabbie took him out to the edge of the Barrens. From there he popped into a local bar he knew, slipped a local driver a hundred nuyen and got a ride out of Touristville and over to Fall City.

Even though it was dark, whoever was after him kept finding him. Under Construction, a skeevy bar in Fall City, held a pesky little Spyball that tried to gas him. The rundown apartment over Yang's Grocery had a little cockroach drone creeping under the door. The warehouse office he'd first found when he was a teenager running from a mom who drank too much and had way too many boyfriends was discovered by a trio of those flying trash can lids. His last bolthole, a squatter den where the floor crunched from the layer of used up BTLs, was where the Roto-Drone had found him.

Despite his exhaustion, he knew he had to move on. But he was quickly running out of hiding spots.

Lynx swore as he lost sight of the target again. Mr. Johnson was going to be pissed if this guy got aced, but every time Lynx made an effort to communicate, this Stitcher twit freaked out and ran. Lynx had taken the gig solo because he knew he had the tools, but now he was down several of those tools. He lost three Crawlers after saving the twit target's hide from gunners that Lynx still wasn't sure how the guy had spotted; he lost his Fly-Spy when the guy crushed it against a wall; his SpyBall got bricked by a hacker in Under Construction after Lynx tried to just KO the target for an easy pick-up; his Kanmushi was still stuck under the heavy sweatshirt the target had tossed on it; and now his Roto-Drone was under attack by some Barrens hacker.

It was days like this Lynx actually considered getting some meat teammates.

Maybe this Stitcher guy would be available once Mr. Johnson was done with him.

RIGGING 101

I don't care what you've seen on the trid or heard from a friend of a friend. Sliding into a fully rigger-ready ride is like no other experience you will ever have. It's better than Better-Than-Life, it's hotter than novacoke, it's calmer than zen, it's more visceral than even the most UV simfeed. Rigging is living. If you've never rigged, you've never lived.

Two millennia ago, the Romans conquered over 2.7 million square kilometers by understanding the value of mobility. Roads were referred to as the arteries of the empire. The Sixth World doesn't limit mobility to roads, but the value hasn't changed. Now, it's not about the roads, but about the riggers. Riggers make the world go 'round.

Dramatic, I know, but it's the truth these days. Whether it's operating the drones that patrol the borders or the ones delivering your take-out, riggers are all around you. I know trid shows skew the public view. They make every rigger look like some hot-shot rig-jock breaking all the rules for the forces of good or maniacal terrorist flying an army of drones to take over the world. They occasionally gloss over the security rigger as he gets trumped by the slick decker or runner rigger. They don't take into account the guy running the construction site, the dock, the freighter, or the one covering all the pizza-delivery drones. For every hotshot out there, there are a score of Everyday Joes.

But the wisest of those Everyday Joes know something most people don't. They know the truth of that opening paragraph. Rigging is being your ride. It's not steering, piloting, shifting, pushing buttons, or pressing the pedals. It's running, flying, swimming, pushing your limits, and feeling everything like it's your own flesh and blood out there. Those Everyday Joes chose to trade a little piece of themselves and a big chunk of nuyen so that they can control their vehicles with the same precision that they control their thoughts. On top of that, every one of them has a sim system like no other, and plenty of them have slipped the doc a little on the side to make sure the feeds go nova hot. It's a job, a rush, and—usually—an addiction all wrapped into one.

While drones are the most common vehicle for a rigger to jump into, every vehicle out there can be outfitted with the electronics needed for a rigger to take precise control. Most of the time they let the vehicle operate on its regular pilot program because there just aren't enough riggers in the world to be jumped into every drone, all the time. They only hop in when something really spectacular is needed. Or they feel like. A lot of riggers feel much more comfortable in their ride than in their own skin. If you see a drone that was built after the '40s, you can expect there's a rigger somewhere on its network. If there's a vehicle that does anything dangerous, menial, demanding, precise, or extraordinary, you can expect a rigger there too.

Besides the perpetual access to unique sim feeds, the riggers of the world are usually gearheads or techheads at heart. They may have started out life fiddling with their parents' car or taking apart every drone toy they got for their birthday. They don't just want to fix, drive, or make it better, they want to be it. They chose the life of a rigger because they were called to get inside their ride. Not just in the seat or under the hood, but in its heart. Riggers know that vehicles have souls. There is the rare case that simply took it on as a job because it was available. Corporations offer big incentives to riggers beyond just the expensive augmentations because they know their true value. But even when this is the case, it doesn't take long for the rigger to get hooked. It's the ultimate level of control.

That control comes from three pieces of equipment working in perfect tandem. One in the rigger, one with the rigger, and one wherever the hell the rigger wants it to go. The control rig is what makes a rigger a rigger and not just a remote operator. It's the headware that allows the rigger out of their meat body and into the vehicle's metal. Sensations are translated into something the mind is used to feeling, and the rigger gets to *be* the vehicle. The control rig connects to one of two things, either straight into whatever the rigger is controlling or into the rigger command console (RCC). That straight connection makes it only two pieces of equipment, the rigger and their ride, but it's good to point out the ride needs the right equipment. Most riggers run the other way, through the RCC, because that way they aren't limited to just one ride. The RCC creates a wireless network where the rigger can hop into any of the vehicles he's got connected. Then there's

the vehicles themselves. Cars, trucks, tanks, and other vehicles that are normally manually operated need special equipment for riggers to truly use them. They can drive them via remote, but to jump in they need to be rigger adapted. A rigger adaptation kit consists of special sensors and equipment that lets the rigger feel the ride and the ride respond to the rigger. It's standard on drones, because nobody can climb inside most of those. When that trio of gear is operating smoothly, riggers make their rides do the improbable.

The expense of equipment, programs, augmentations, and drones means most riggers work for the corporations. Some big governments have riggers on staff, too, but more often than not they're renting a rigger from a corporation. The only place to consistently find them is the military or national security agencies. With the corps, it could be a construction company, a security firm, a public or private transportation service, a police force, or a myriad of other areas that rely on drones or specialized vehicles or that deal with hazardous situations, because it's cheaper to lose a drone than a trained tech. Riggers work for whoever will give them

the chance to play with the latest tech, jump into the hottest machines, or just look the other way when they spike their feeds to get a little rush.

Riggers work on every continent and in every body of water on Earth. They work in orbit and on the Moon. They work on Mars and even out in space. Riggers work in every condition. They swim into volcanoes and deep beneath the Arctic ice. They fly nape-of-the-earth trips, launch into orbit, and zip along everywhere in between. They rip up the earth with tracks, treads, tires, and turbofans. They walk the world on mechanical legs to reach the highest peaks, the deepest chasms, and the darkest forests. There is nowhere a rigger can't—or won't—go.

THE RIGGER EXPERIENCE

Now that you've gotten my view of rigging, I'd like to toss out the views of some friends with very specific experiences. They've introduced themselves in each piece, but I'd like to remind everyone here that none of these guys are runners. These are real-world riggers. Rigging the shadows is a whole different animal that I'll cover later.

MY NAME IS ALLEN WALTERS, and I'm a CAS Navy rigger. That's what we call ourselves. We have an official title that breaks down into a bunch of letters, but based on what I heard from the guy who asked me to do this, the readers don't care. They want to know what it's like to be one with the machines, especially the hottest milspec tech machines out there. I'll tell you, it's like nothing you've ever felt before. Each type of rigging is different. I've flown drones, planes, helicopters, and VTOLs; sailed skiffs, tugs, cruisers, and subs; and every one brings a different rush. And not just the different types, each different craft has its own feel. They all make you feel like a superhero. Sometimes you're flying faster than sound, other times you're hovering over a scene and blasting away at the enemy or diving beneath the surface to creep up undetected.

I handle air and water myself. I don't do much land time except for the occasional duck, but those are never dirtdigging for long.

Water's my favorite. There's just something about the peace of the depths or the roll of the waves as you glide along. The freedom of life without roads or lanes. Feeling the coolness of the water like it's gliding over your whole body or knowing when you're hiding under the thermocline because you can feel it as you pass. All that keeps me coming back. The sky has its freedoms as well, but it's not peaceful. The ever-present battle with gravity tinges everything, but it also tweaks the rush just a little more. One wrong move and gravity's got you, pulling you down, but I'm a rigger. Falling doesn't mean hitting the ground. The rush is there, but I've got tricks that channel th rush for my good. I can let gravity take me and drop like a rock. It's a move that would have stick-jockeys pulling the ejector cord, but I can hold out and then pop right back up in the fight.

Rigging is a rush, rigging is peace.

Rigging is living.

I'M RICHARD LINCOLN, but people call me Goggles. I'm not a combat pilot or a police rigger, I'm just a guy with a control rig. I like to call myself a freelance rigger. I'm not a shadowrunner or anything. I just work for lots of different people rigging lots of different rides. I'm kind of the jack-of-all-trades rigger. I often operate several different vehicles in one day. Most people get what I do confused with simple remote commanding but I only offer my services to people who want me jumped in. Sometimes it's a rich executive who wants me as his car or plane because he likes that extra feeling of security. I've worked as a camera

drone for a famous trid star who wanted a real person snapping her photos for the red carpet walk. I've handled cargo runs for drone delivery services because they need to use different routes to avoid trouble. I've handled taking out a billionaire's yacht filled with drones and spent the whole time in the engine room because he didn't want his guests to see any staff but he wanted his drones to be extra responsive. I like doing recovery dives in subdrones for people who've lost valuables overboard or who like hunting for imaginary treasure but don't know how to drive a submersible.

I do it all. Rigging is my life and my living.

I'M DESIKA "DIZZY" MONTGOMERY, a rigger for DocWagon's High Threat Response teams. Being a rigger for DocWagon is a special gig. I can be the angel of mercy or the angel of death, depending which side of the bracelet you're on. I started the same way we all do, on a rig. In this case a regular old Ford ambulance. Nothing special. I was an EMT rolling in and checking on our "Golden Oldies," as we call them. I grew up working on my dad's old truck, and it only took six months before the garage stopped sending me on runs and kept me back slapping duct tape on the rigs to keep them running. For all you who don't know, medical folks call ambulances "rigs." Got nothing to do with rigging like a rigger—it's just a nickname. Time in the garage gives you a chance to see "them," those clean-dressed, slicked-hair gods that run the Ospreys and Black Mariah's. They give you a little nod as they pass, and you want to just scream and ask for an autograph.

That was then. I am one now, and I'm not sure where the glamour went. I just know can't find it. Might be that I run an HTR team on the edge of hell and they were working the downtown

beat but the point is the awe. And the start. I applied for my control rig before my first year was up and I got it during my third. I thought I was ready to go then, but boy was I a dim bulb. Training took me out of the field for almost another year, but by the end I was certified in everything. But understand, certified doesn't mean squat. When I finished training I could operate DocWagon's vehicles. Now that I've had a decade on the streets, I can make a Black Mariah dance the tango, while running a perimeter with a quad of rotos, and bringing in a Osprey for a hot scoop.

I can fly in, roll in, or buzz in and every one feels just a little different. Every one has its little perks. Whether I'm chuffing along as a big Osprey and feel like the biggest beast on the block or zipping down an alley as a Roto-Drone to run off a hostile, I can get whatever feeling I want from the range of rigs DocWagon has to offer.

Do I miss patching them up? Maybe a little. But I can save dozens of lives at once by handling my rigs. I wouldn't give up rigging for anything. It's the reason I get up every night with a smile and a bounce in my step.

MY NAME IS SGT. GUTHRIE MICHAELSON, but my squadies call me Gunmetal. I operate close-quarters mechanized support for the CAS Army. That means I'm an Army rigger, but I specialize in close-quarters drone operations. I'm not the Wandjina Vagina dropping ordnance from a few klicks up, or the MPUV driver dropping the squad in a hotzone, or the Stonewall rigger popping off ordnance into random buildings to make myself feel useful. I'm the guy who's right there with my squad as they kick in doors and clear a room. I'm their eyes in the sky, making sure they've got a clean way out. And if the way gets dirty, I'm the first one there with the broom to sweep it clean.

I run everything from the SpyBall they're each hauling to the Condor overhead, keeping an eye on everything. They especially love when I run the Lynx and kick in doors right by their side, or run the Dalmatians through their paces to keep the whole zone clean. Being a rigger is being part of the team—a big part of the team. My drones pack more ordnance than the whole squad combined and when they get hit, they don't bleed. I make the sacrifices if I can. But if I do my job right, it's a moot point. Nobody gets hurt. Well, nobody on my side.

I always have a tough time describing what it actually feels like, because it feels just like how it feels. The rig and the adaptations make it all feel natural. Take the Fly-Spy. I could describe it as flying and that seems obvious, but that only works for me. Problem is, it's the only way I can describe it. It feels totally natural, as if I'm an insect with wings and little legs, and I'm flying. I think "up," but what I really mean is "increase wing flap speed, alter wing angle, shift head and thorax angle, tuck back legs," and dozens of other things that we don't really think about; they're just things we do when we move. It's like having a whole new body every time. Roto-Drones give you the strange sensation of being upside down but right-side up all at once, like your legs are above your shoulders and your head is upright—but it's located at the bottom of your torso. It sounds completely unnatural, but it feels totally normal while you're jumped in. I like the Steel Lynx best. It makes me feel like I'm right in there with my guys, and I'm one tough SOB. It's the posture that really does it, though. I feel like I'm prowling and spitting fire.

I can't make it all sound good. I've been dropped off duty for detox plenty of times when I get addicted to the feeds. A little physical activity never killed anybody, but you sure feel like it will after a few months of doing all your rocking and rolling with your brain. It's a balance, but at least they let us go back to getting our fix on after a little while off. They'd lose too many of us, too quickly if we washed out every time we got addicted to the sim. Best to just accept it. We do.

FIRST OFF, I'M DALE EARNHARDT V. If ya ain't never heard of me I'm the great-great-grandson of the famous "Intimidator." Also, you've been livin' under a rock. Bein' the sixth generation of racer in NASCAR was all I wanted when I was young, and my early success was nice. It just wasn't enough. While NASCAR kept a lot of the same rules for over a century, lots of thangs have changed elsewhere in racing. That's why I got my SpIntimidator control rig and moved over to the Formula 1 circuit. Now I'm not just a driver—I am the car. I'll admit, the crashes hurt more, but the rush of the speed and control I have when rocketing around Monaco makes the 220 curve at Talladega feel like your sittin' at home on the couch in Louisiana watchin' paint dry.

It's not just the speed. Everyone's seen my '75 French GrandPrix finish where I dropped back, clipped Gerhardt's wheel, did a 360 spin and twist over the finish line, and landed flat on all four wheels. Some call me a liar, but that was on purpose. I took the fine just to prove a point to the world of why F1 racing makes any oval-rolling meat drive race look like kids play. Those are the tricks we can pull off. Had to wait to the finish, because I didn't even make a victory lap on those busted spindles, but that's the next evolution. Give me a ride that can take that beating, and I'll give you the ultimate race.

Riggin' changed the world. Some parts just ain't caught up yet.

YOU DON'T KNOW ME, BUT YOU WILL KNOW MY NAME. I'm Aleksya "Spider" Watada, and being a rigger is all I've ever known. I was born with no arms or legs and too much nerve damage to get cyberlimbs. I was born into the Watada-rengo, and while I was born the double negative of a girl and a gimp, I was cherished by my mother who had lost many before me. My state is a compromise between a father who wanted resources and a mother willing to do anything to have a child. What is that state? I had my first control rig implanted before I'd lived a year. I'm sure my father had figured I wouldn't survive, but I did. I've cost him hundreds of thousands of nuyen over the years, but I've made him millions.

Rigging for me is more than just controlling vehicles—it's my natural state of motion. I've adapted over the years, and while I have no arms or legs I have a mind that doesn't stop. I earned my name, not by being the security spider for some corporation, but for the legs and arms I built for myself. Yes, I am that Spider.

I drive for the Watada-rengo, and I am their best. I'll admit others are better with many of the drones we use, but my skills there are adequate, and I know how to command them to best serve my driving. When I'm in control, I am a prima-ballerina no matter how bulky the armored limo that is my metal flesh. I've never done ballet, obviously, but I've stood in awe at its grace. I know what it looks like, and that's what I see on the faces of those who see me drive.

NAME'S JOE MANIAITIS, and I work for Mitsuhama Construction as an industrial site rigger. Most people hear rigger and think about crazy flying and driving tricks. That's not me. I rig for precision. It's actually quite funny, because I'm usually operating 100 tons of machine clinging to the side of a mining or construction operation using connectors you could fit in the palm of your hand, but that's my job. Well, part of my job. The other part is the opposite end where I'm running the demo-drone setting up a blast, or buzzing into a shaft to check stability and air quality.

I'm not what most expect of a rigger. Nothing I do is fancy, and my drones are just tools. I use them like extra bodies to get me to places it isn't safe to hang out, sometimes literally. They're an extension of me, and full of tools to put my skills to use. I've only run the sim feed over the redline once, and it was to make sure my weld was perfect. I spend too much time in dangerous places where anything can go wrong to risk frying my brain.

TRYING TO DESCRIBE RIGGING IS LIKE TRYING TO DESCRIBE SEX. It's always good, but it's the inexplicable nuances of each partner that make it unique. Each car is like a new partner. I'm Everett Holtun, Transportation Security Specialist with SecureTech, Inc. I operate primarily around the Chicago sprawl, so I've seen some crazy things in my time but being a rigger gives you a special set of skills and abilities one doesn't have when they operate a vehicle manually or even via standard remote control.

Let me clear a few points up early on. I don't use an RCC, because I do one thing and one thing only: I drive. I'd like to claim I'm the best at what I do, but I'm smart, not cocky. I know I'm good, but I also know someone else could be better, and keeping that in mind is one of my cardinal rules. I only drive two cars. A slightly modified 2075 Saab Dynamit and a heavily modified Mitsubishi Nightsky. The Saab is for those single clients willing to forsake the spacious back of a limo, while the Nightsky is for everybody else. I've driven others over the years and I'm eye-balling the Gladius and some new security vehicles that are coming out, but right now these two are my girls. I know every inch of them.

These two points give me a very focused perspective on rigging. I'm always about putting the rubber to the road when the time comes. I feel the grip of the tires like pressure on my palms and feet. I know how far I can tip it before I go on two wheels and how far before I flip clean over. I can pop a door or push my shocks to make sure I roll back onto my wheels and keep moving. I can skim through an alley at a 100 kph while aggressively diverting pursuit with onboard weapons or just keep rolling in traffic while I spot a sniper and call in support. All done as naturally as walking and talking.

RIGGING THE SHADOWS

Something that is very important to know—riggers can do it all, even magic! They have such a wide array of tech and systems to control and command it all, and they can act as a one-man runner team. Is it ever that easy? Not usually. Do they need the skillset of a trid-show spy? Probably. But they could if they put their mind to it. However, what they usually do is select a particular area of rigging and get really good at that. They'll have some other skills and usually a decent understanding of everything a rigger could do, but these are the real shadows, not some made-up game or trid show. Riggers can fill in or back-up just about any spot on a runner team. They aren't just the transport, and sometimes aren't the transport at all, but let's take a look at what having a rigger around is going to do for your team.

Transportation is the first thing that always comes to mind when vetting good riggers for a job. The key is remembering that riggers aren't all wheelmen. When you see your rigger roll up to the meet in a tricked-out Bulldog, your first thought is probably about how chill it is that you can all stick together, but the reality is probably a cargo area with enough space to fix the drones that are racked and stacked. If you want your rigger to help with transport, get your ride adapted for them so they can make the best use of it.

I can hear the response already from that last line. "But we hire the rigger so we can trash their vehicle because they can fix it!" Don't be that runner. Riggers aren't all mechanics, and even the ones that are don't like spending all their spare nuyen patching bullet holes and painting over scorch marks and scratches. They can also do the same for your ride, too. And your car probably isn't full of expensive electronics and gear that doesn't respond well to ricocheting lead.

Riggers trained in this area are great to have around for transportation, but remember, I said "trained," and remember to check what modes of transportation they operate. Riggers can specialize or be a jack of all trades, and it's important to know what they operate and what they don't. If you're looking for someone good at handling tight urban streets, make sure they drive an Americar, not a Vista. If you happen to be looking for a rigger to do a rooftop extract, make sure they've got an Osprey and not a Banshee. If your team needs a ride from the Emerald City to Bug City, make sure they're using a Bergen and not a Xenon. Transport is one of the easiest jobs for a good rigger if they have the right equipment.

Riggers aren't a one-size-fits-all group of guys and gals. They're as varied and specialized as the muscle you're running with. The only thing every rigger has in common is that control rig. Like everything else, you have to know who you're talking to and what you're looking for to get the right ride at the right time. Let's move on and look at a few other roles the rigger can flesh out for a team.

Surveillance is often confused with reconnaissance. I cover the second one later, but riggers are especially well equipped to perform surveillance. They're good at reconnaissance, too, don't get me wrong, but I'll cover that later as I said.

See what I did there? I repeated something just to get you to think about it, and possibly distract you. That's how a mark throws off a tail or gets them to reveal themselves, but a rigger isn't limited to just one tail. A rigger will run several tails at once so that when one would be burned by a double-back, another can pick up the trail. A regular surveillance team could consist of half a dozen people trying to work in coordination to pull that off, while one rigger can have a dozen drones that he's jumping between and keeping on a rotation. Half a dozen people trying to coordinate, or one person running the whole show. Advantage rigger.

A rigger brings a wide range of surveillance options to a runner team. In urban environments, there are very few places that a drone or a vehicle won't blend in with the background, given it is the right kind. Using a series of them, spread all around, is the advantage a rigger has over traditional surveillance. Drones are easy to deploy, leave stationed on a rooftop, flow within the dronestream, float among the other advertisements, or sit so high up they are indistinguishable from the sky. In rural areas, the options are different. Riggers will trade the usual, one among many, method of blending in for being unseen or blending in in a different way. Out here they can use smaller drones to stay hidden or disguised within nature. They can use camouflage in the form of traditional shape-breaking methods or more advanced ruthenium polymer or ElectroPaint options to hide almost anywhere. The most common change a rigger will make with rural surveillance is distance. With advanced optics and microphones, their drones can be a kilometer away and still see and hear everything going on with a target. Distance combined with the right paint job and the rigger is golden. Traditional methods can do similar things, but again require large amounts of personnel coordination over even longer distances. Once again, advantage rigger.

Not only can riggers take on the role of surveillance, but they tend to be the superior option to traditional methods. Now, hackers can work a lot of similar areas by snagging camera feeds or taking over drones from their standard users, but hackers have the issue of GOD. A rigger operates without the coding designed to draw the attention of authorities. Not that GOD has never blasted a rigger out of the Matrix—it has happened—but at nowhere near the frequency of hackers getting the boot and scoop.

Next up, **combat rigging**. Who needs an angsty, anti-social, over-cybered street samurai, or prissy, hy-

per-zen adept when you can have an army of drones with no anger issues, the ability to follow orders and execute a plan, no drama, and best of all, no itchy trigger fingers. Riggers can easily replace the muscle on a runner team with drones that lack the chemical miasma that is the human psyche. They may not be able to solve some problems that require lateral thinking, but they can quickly be commanded to execute whatever solution the rest of the team or the rigger decides on.

With drones of all shapes, sizes, and combat potential, riggers also have the potential of bringing a much wider range of options to the solutions table. A microdrone, or even a small swarm of them, with small gas payloads, a dart, electrical discharge, or chemical syringe stinger can go in quiet to take out guards just like that former corporate operative who no one trusts because he lives a life of secrecy. Minidrones pack a little more punch or versatility in the same role. Larger drones often become more specialized, but riggers do a lot of customizations that blend into the original design but add features that are useful to the specific job. These can often be snuck in as service drones for a building or personal assistants, and then they deploy their hidden talents once inside the facility. These talents can be quite exceptional when they are directly inhabited by the rigger.

The most obvious advantage the rigger brings in terms of being the team's combat support is numbers in a **direct assault**. While we are called shadowrunners, insinuating some level of stealth in our activities, open and obvious violence is often the only solution some people see. Here riggers are like military fire support. They can bring in several drones with commands for suppression or specific targeting. They can arm them with a range of weapons and ammunitions to cover several contingency plans. They can be commanded to stop firing, switch targets, move, cover a new area, charge straight in, and even self-destruct without any argument, attitude, delay, or hesitation, all with a single thought from the rigger.

The single greatest thing a rigger brings to any runner team in terms of combat prowess is the ability to sacrifice without regret. Yes, there are some riggers out there who grow very attached to their drones and would never let anyone send them in on a suicide mission, but most riggers understand that drones are expendable assets that can easily be replaced, unlike metahuman lives. The team that uses the rigger as their combat support will rarely know that moment of saying tearful goodbyes to the one member who needs to stay back and hold off the oncoming wave while the rest of the team escapes, because the rigger will happily wade into the maelstrom in his synthetic shell to hold off the opposition. Even if they "die," it's an unpleasant, but rarely fatal, case of dumpshock and they're back in action. Again, I have to say, advantage rigger.

I moved **reconnaissance** down here, though it was mentioned above, because I'm trying to progress down the order of what riggers tend to be best at handling versus other team members. When it comes to reconnaissance, riggers are great. They have a range of drones with an abundance of sensor systems that can get every drop of intel on a target person or site. I move it down here because, I'll admit, this is often just as easily done by others with similar sensors and equipment as you'd find on the drone. And since most reconnaissance requires getting somewhere and then watching or recording, drones and metahumans both have their strengths and weaknesses.

Riggers are perfect for stealthy flybys with an aircraft or drone. They can record the data they take in and either feed it back instantly or bring it back after they're done. Long-range sensor systems make this easier, but those same systems can be employed by the opposition. Drones offer a way to feed the data back right up to the point that the target notices and hides or destroys the drone. Loss of a drone is better than loss of a life inside an aircraft.

On the ground, a rigger can get a drone into place and watch, but they are limited to the power life of the drone. People may get cold, uncomfortable, or cranky, but they can bring something along to easily replenish their energy in the field. Yes, they may have to sleep, but hiding and sleeping is a better option than needing to travel back and recharge or refuel, especially when it comes to long-term reconnaissance, because spotting something that is out of place is all it takes to blow the recon—especially if the thing is seen more than once.

When it comes to going into a facility for reconnaissance, drones cannot always replace people, but they always offer the less costly option for failure. If a person is caught in the wrong place at the wrong time, the recon is blown and the person needs to get out. If a drone falls into the same situation, the recon is still blown, but the drone can be abandoned. Yes, people can talk their way out, but that's why this is down here. It's a job a rigger can cover for the team, but it isn't the best option when considering which area of the team to leave in the hands of the rigger and which part you're going to need to split the payday on.

Much like reconnaissance, **infiltrating a site** to get someone or something can be handled by a rigger with the right tools. That's important to mention again, that it's all about the right rigger with the right tools. The wrong rigger or the wrong tools means they aren't going to cover the gap.

Infiltrating for a data steal is the best option for a rigger. They can take in a micro or minidrone that can get wherever the team needs and get access for the hacker to do their part. Move up to larger drones to impersonate (or would it be imdroneate?) a drone on site, and it's again just a matter of getting the drone to the right place for the right access. Doors and other passage barriers are often an issue for a drone, but small drones can hide on the person or within the briefcase of someone going into the building. Options like this could involve plant-

ing the drone on an employee or the cooperation of the team's infiltration specialist and the rigger to get in and use the drone to keep the access inconspicuous.

Infiltrating in order to grab something physical is tougher. The imposter drone method above might work if some method of getting the drone in and out can be developed. A mixed method with rigger and infiltration specialist to get the item and then plant it in a drone to head out, especially in the case of a rapid, non-standard exit, like out a window or quickly from a rooftop is ideal to keep the meat partner from walking out with the package. Special consideration should be given to a rigger skilled with anthroform drones, especially some of the lighter and stealthier models, that can be used to sneak around just like a metahuman, but again cost no loss of life if they are caught. Expense of these drones is something to consider, and the need for the rigger to possess, or be guided by someone with, appropriate training in infiltration techniques makes it more rare and expensive. Which is another reason infiltration is so low in this list. This would be one of those no-advantage calls.

Riggers are not hackers. They may occasionally partake in a little warfare on the airwaves, but their normal equipment, the RCC, is not configured to be a cyberdeck. That's what cyberdecks are for. Of all things. That said, a rigger can manage to fill in a few of the aspects your hacker handles and can convincingly work to stymie the efforts of opposing hackers, though often at a cost. Let's look at the two instances and try to help you develop an understanding of when your team's rigger can cover a job and when you need to just cough up the cash for a real hacker.

Hackers are often asked to obstruct the communications of the opposition, handle the monitoring and securing of the team's communications, gain and provide access to video or audio feeds from nearby or inside a facility, and help in accessing and bypassing electronic locks and security measures. The order above is intentional. The four areas are in the order in which a rigger tends to best be able to cover in some capacity.

The easiest is **obstructing communications**. Due to the nature of modern communications and the processing and bandwidth needs for accessing the Matrix, turning a commlink into a jammer is relatively easy. Riggers do it all the time in order to reduce the effectiveness of other riggers and hackers communicating in their vicinity. Have a burner handy and kick up the squelch. The move jams up the rigger along with everyone else, but the good ones have ways around that, especially if they know it's coming. The standard jammer works in anyone's hands, but it's a jammer and becomes the instant target for opposing gun bunnies to clear the airwaves for their hacker. Harder to tell what's muddling the airwaves when it's a commlink just like everyone else has.

Securing the team's communications can be like second nature to a rigger. Riggers are not huge fans of having their drones hacked and therefore tend to have a solid firewall on their RCC network to prevent it from happening. This same firewall can protect the team's communications via their commlinks, if the rigger wants to slave those commlinks in place of some drones. The big potential downfall is the replacement of drones with commlinks, but in a pinch it's something to do. Riggers also tend to have the technical know-how to make a pretty secure network with a decent commlink as well, as long as someone on the team didn't skimp and is willing to be a bullseye for potential hackers. As a note, skimping on a 'link is getting a lot more common as SINs are getting harder to come by, and more and more megacorporations are having them hardwired onto commlinks.

A high priority for hackers on a runner team is providing intel, especially up to date visual and audio data by hacking into local camera feeds. Riggers can't hack local feeds. What they can do is **piggyback microdrones in places where there are cameras and match the feed**. They can't edit it, but at least they know what's going on in a given location. This piggy-backing can also be quite handy if a rigger and hacker team up and while duplicating the video feed; in this instance, the drone also taps into the camera's wiring for the hacker to get in. Remember, shadowrunners work in teams for a reason.

Last point is **bypassing electronic locks**. Hackers often do this with a simple wave of their hand. What goes on in the Matrix is a whole other ballgame, but you get the point. Riggers, most of them anyways, tend to have a decent understanding of electronics that they can use to take apart electronic locks and bypass them manually, rather than in the Matrix. It's never as easy or quick as how hackers would do it, but it's a place for riggers to back them up—or take the lead if necessary.

Time for the one everyone's been waiting to jump on and cry foul: **Magic**! Now I don't mean a rigger can cast spells or summon spirits, but they've got some countering and detecting tricks up their greasy sleeves. Plus, with flamethrowers, lasers, Stick 'n' Shock rounds, and grenades, I don't think they're lagging behind in the combat options field anyway. But let's get specific on what I'm talking about here.

First, let's discuss the countering options riggers provide against magic. The biggest of which is plain, old-fashioned line of sight. Riggers can deploy smoke, tint windows, cut off sight lines, and use lights to blind opposing spellcasters and prevent or hinder spellcasting, all through mundane means. Thanks to the great research & development departments at most of the major megacorporations, there are also a number of magic-inhibiting options that are not so mundane. Gas grenade loads that contain FAB (fluorescing astral bacteria) can be used to detect spellcasting or hinder astral movement depending on whether the FAB-I or FAB-II strain is used. One of the best tricks riggers have developed lately to help out in the arcane arena is the AP grenade, usually called a dust bomb. AP doesn't stand for armor piercing, but rather astral powder, a substance that is drawn to magically active items, including people. It's the ultimate way to identify the opposition's magical resources when you don't have your own arcane specialist handy. Once those resources are identified, the rest of the team can decide how to apply the principles of "geek the mage first."

Last in line here is a look at riggers **taking over for the team's face**. Or at least, a drone taking over, if not the rigger. The move is not always the best option and sometimes considered in poor taste by Mr. Johnson, but if it gets the team more money when their negotiator is currently out of the picture, all that matters is that the Johnson goes with the deal. First off, even the cockiest rigger would never suggest sending in just a drone. Some other member of the team needs to go in, preferably the muscle (as long as they are the type of muscle that knows not to talk during negotiations). Whoever goes in, it is their job to sit back, be quiet, and let the best talker left on the team communicate through the drone with Mr. Johnson. The benefits of this are two-fold. The negotiator doesn't feel the same personal pressure when talking through a drone. Much like "trolls"— the Matrix kind, not the big metahumans—that level of personal separation often frees one to say things they would never say to someone's face. The second benefit is the lack of olfactory or any other form of hormone analyzing and processing systems, making implants designed to sway people via subconscious chemical cues completely ineffective. The team members in the room may start wondering why their negotiator is such a dick to their new best friend, but as long as the negotiation is defined at the beginning as between the corp drone and the real drone, those runners who catch feelings for Mr. Johnson shouldn't be a problem. Kane once told me of a rigger he knows down in the Carib League who will run solo jobs but hires local gangers or squatters to go into the meet and stand with the drone. He said the move has become such a common occurrence that area Johnsons have told the rigger not to bother bringing in the local. Kane said the rigger sticks with it to help out locals without making it look like a handout.

Hope that helps everyone understand that riggers aren't just your wheelman. They may play that role, but if you find the right one they can be so much more beneficial to the team than just a driver. But the trick, of course, is finding the right one.

THE WHEELS ON THE BUS

It's not just about the wheels. It's about the wings, the rudders, the rotors, the tracks, the turbofans, the thrusters, the props, the legs, the sails, and the basic laws of physics. The vehicles and drones of the 2070s cover the gamut of drives and guidance. The mundane, the insane, and everything in between is available to move

you around the Sixth World as long as you've got the nuyen. No matter whether it drives, flies, floats, runs, or dives, riggers handle them all. Let's take a peek under the hood of the various types of vehicles and drones available these days and see what they're intended for, and what they're really used for in the shadows.

PERSONAL MOTORIZED VEHICLE (PMV)

These are small, single-person vehicles usually used by commuters for work or solo drivers to just putter around town. Runners use them for much the same thing. When taking a PMV to a meet or a job, runners usually park far away to avoid embarrassment or detection. PMVs are also good for blending in with a crowd while conducting surreptitious surveillance or reconnaissance. A few select riggers or tuners have turned their PMV into something fast and furious, but those are rare oddities.

MOTORCYCLES

The world of monocycles, standard two-wheel bikes, and the three-wheel trikes is the place for more of the speed junkies, but some of the smaller mopeds and scooters are used for commuting and regular urban transit. The development of gyro-stabilization systems also boosted the use and modification of motorcycles. The newest cycles, the monocycles, are still catching on, but as more and more people become accustomed to AR in everything, monocycles will definitely move up in the market share. Bikes is a broad category stretching from the dirtbikes of youth to the fastest racing bikes on the market to the big comfortable cruisers with many of the amenities of a car.

On the streets and in the shadows, motorcycles are everyday transportation, assault vehicles, and fast getaway machines. Riggers can tweak the motors for speed or add armaments for some offensive capability. The gyro stabilization revolution also allows motorcycles to be remote operated or modified to function as drones. Trikes tend to be big, comfortable cruisers with some extra seating, but modifications for weapons, bigger engines, off-road capabilities, or storage capacity can be added or the main reason for the extra wheel. The trike design varies, with some designs pairing up the front wheels, while the classic design is for two wheels in the rear.

CARS

The massive world of cars has been filling datastores for years. I can't cover everything out there, so I'll just give an overview. At their most basic, cars are enclosed conveyances for personal transportation controlled by the user. The controlled part can be a little muddled these days, but at least the user gets to program in where they're headed. The purpose of a car is to get someone from one place to another while protecting them from the elements. They come in a wide variety of shapes and sizes, usually to fulfill a certain purpose or class of transportation. Smaller cars for efficiency or speed, mid-size cars for comfort and versatility, big sedans for luxury, and all the way up to limousines for opulence to share.

In the shadows, cars are used for just about any purpose imaginable. They can go from cover, to transportation, to a weapon, and finally to an escape vehicle in a matter of seconds. And they can end up as a massive flaming wreck just as quick. Riggers and gearheads modify and upgrade their cars to be the strongest, fastest, and toughest, but they also strip them down to bare bones to minimize loss when they use them for something not-so-legal and have to leave them behind.

TRUCKS

For those who find cars underpowered or need something with more hauling capacity, there are trucks. Like cars, they range in size, usually based on how big of a load they're intended to haul, and they fall into three general categories; on-road, off-road, and luxury. On-road and luxury are similar; one just has more amenities and comfort, though they are often based off the same chassis. Off-road trucks have rougher suspension, and lift kits to give them more clearance. Some have alternate air intakes and exhaust so their engine can be submerged, light kits to operate at night, or additional armor to deal with things they might run across off the beaten path.

In the shadows, trucks are just like cars. The purpose is often determined more by the user than by the original design, with luxury trucks being used to go off-road without the added features of an off-roader. The additional cargo and carrying capacity of trucks is a big deal for runners who work heavily out of their vehicle because they can't be running back to their slumhovel every time they need a piece of gear. The extra roomy interiors are also favorites of orks for the extra legroom and trolls for the extra space to customize for their bulk.

BIG BOYS

This categories fits all the big vehicles, like RVs, busses, tractors, and construction vehicles. These are too big to park in the garage at home, but their size is intended for a specific purpose. Whether it's hauling all the comforts of home or hauling all the crew in Compton, these big vehicles are built with a job in mind. For regular folks this means they tend to know what it means when something shows up. A bus means lots of people, a motorhome means mobile living, and a tractor means cargo being moved across the country.

To a runner, these vehicles can mean exactly the same thing, or something very different. A bus could be hauling a go-gang or smuggling people across a border.

A motorhome is a portable place to live. It could be a place to lie low or provide some semblance of comfort when they need to hide out in the wilderness. A tractor could be hauling their target, could be full of dangerous chemicals, could be smuggling people, or it could be hiding all sorts of unpleasant surprises, like weapon mounts or anti-personnel devices.

PERSONAL WATERCRAFT

These are basically the motorcycles of the water. They're built for fun and excitement. They are sometimes repurposed by shadowy types, especially in places with a lot of water, like Amazonia or Los Angeles. Here they can be small transports or attack vehicles that are maneuverable and quick. Their smaller size makes them ideal for moving up and down small rivers or streams that might have shallow water or tight spaces.

POWERBOATS

Unless a person lives on an island and needs their boat to get to the mainland, the main reason anyone owns a powerboat is for recreation. From the small fishing boats all the way up to the massive ocean-going cruisers, powerboats are almost always a luxury item. And honestly, if you live on an island and have your own boat to get to the mainland, it's probably a luxury for you too. There are some people who use their powerboats to earn a living or gather sustenance, but it's not the norm. To be frank, powerboats are something the rich and powerful use to show off that they're rich and powerful.

Now, wherever there are rich and powerful people, you will find runners skulking around in the shadows. When that's out on the water, runners use their boat as a means to access someone else's craft or get close enough to keep an eye on their quarry. They're used for smuggling and escape, since water routes are more open and land can be accessed from almost anywhere with enough ingenuity. And just like using a boat to get to someone else's boat, runners use boats to access corporate facilities on the water. Finally, rich and successful runners use them to show off that they are rich and successful. We don't always have to be different.

SAILBOATS

Sailboats and some of their hybrid relatives have no commercial applications anymore other than using yours to ferry around people who want to go out on a sailboat. Yes, there are some massive cargo liners that use a wing-sail to decrease their fuel consumption, but if those things relied on that sail alone it would take about fifteen years to reach their destination. Sailboats run a wide size range, with smaller ones being relatively inexpensive, stable on rougher waters, and cheap to operate without fuel costs. Don't get me wrong, sailboats are expensive if you have a slip and need to fix things often, but they aren't limited to the ultra-rich in the same way as big powerboats.

Shadowrunners don't find themselves involved with sailboats very often. Maybe during smuggling runs or working as a bodyguard, but the lack of speed tends to keep runners away. But when they need something stealthy for a night operation or a quiet sail down a coast, these are ideal. The secret of a sailboat in the shadows is to look innocent.

As a small point of clarification, there are wing-sail racing sailboats that can get up in the seventy knot range but this is the exception to the norm, not the norm.

YACHTS

If regular powerboats are just rich people showing off being rich, yachts are rich people showing those rich people they aren't really fully rich and employing some average people with jobs serving them on their yachts. Once you get this big, the boats have cabins and regular size rooms and beds, along with amenities like hot tubs, additional smaller boats and personal watercraft to take out, and an obscene amount of money to burn on maintenance and operations.

For runners, these are targets, sometimes targets to be sunk and sometimes to be infiltrated. If a runner owns a yacht, they aren't a runner. They're an adrenaline junkie with criminal tendencies because they could sell off their yacht and retire, rather than continuing to sail the world. They could also be a pirate, like Kane. Though he is the perfect example of that first characterization, the adrenaline-junkie criminal.

SUBMERSIBLES

Most submersibles for civilian use are operated by tourist companies to go down and look at coral reefs and undersea life or transport guests to some of the deep-water habitats and hotels the megacorporations, especially Evo, have developed. I include things like seasleds in this category, but again, they're still typically tourist toys to make scuba diving easier, or hard-core diver tech to get them through or around dangerous areas faster, allowing more time in the places they actually want to explore.

In the shadowy depths, the submersible and seasled are the covert approach vehicles of choice—when they're available. The military, mercenary companies, corporate black ops, and shadowrunners all favor the underwater approach on a seafaring target to the surface route. Visibility beneath the surface is far more limited than on it, where waves and the horizon are often the only limiting factors. Seeing down into water is another problem area, as light doesn't penetrate well, reflects off the surface to obscure vision, and refracts to skew the position of everything that isn't directly beneath the observer. A good pilot can remain nearly invisible using the refraction of light almost all the way to the target. Radar is useless below the surface, leaving sonar as the only truly viable detection method, and that requires highly trained and skilled operators for passive sonar. Active sonar, of course, completely gives away the position of a ship, boat, or submersible, along with creating all sorts of unpleasant encounters with Awakened sea life that are not huge fans of aggressive sounding sonar pings. The rarity and lack of speed are the usual limiting factors for runners using a submersible for an operation on water, but when it is an option, it's usually the best option.

AIRPLANES

Up in the sky, it's a jet, it's a prop plane, it's a glider, it's an airplane! There are a wide array of airplanes out there that are used for personal conveyance, commercial conveyance, recreation, air defense, firefighting, surveillance, reconnaissance, supply drops, crop-dusting, and the list goes on and on. The world has been in love with the idea of flight since the Wright Brothers first made is sustainable, and even before that when DaVinci made his plans. Glider planes and hang gliders are two popular recreational forms of flying, even though it's really just falling with grace. They're the slowest overall, but a sealed glider towed up behind another plane and then released can spend a long time slowly working its way back to the ground. Prop planes are the next up in the speed category, as well as in recreational use. Commercial use kicks up here too, with short-distance flights, older models in less affluent nations, and companies that do a lot of math to determine fuel-cost-to-lift ratios to understand that prop planes are slower but don't guzzle jet fuel. The number of props doesn't necessarily determine speed, but they do determine lifting power, so those multi-prop commercial haulers are going to lift more weight than smaller single-engine Cessnas. Jets are actually not all jets, but it's easier to put them all in one category than to try to explain all of the different engine systems. It's more important to look at purpose. This is where the commercial haulers, affluent personal transports, and air-defense craft come in. They put out tons more lift and power than props and a few are really good at going *really* fast!

Now, how do the shadows abuse the invention of flight? There are so many ways. Infiltration with gliders, jumping out of perfectly good planes, surveillance flights, sneaking into other countries, attacking places, moving illicit cargo, etc. The list could go on. Riggers love planes because they offer such a unique feeling—actual flight. It's the closest sensation to being a bird anyone can get until we can create simsense recordings of birds. Airplanes are a great tool in the shadows, even if some teams just use them to get from one sprawl to another.

ROTORCRAFT

The rotorcraft, man's ultimate "frag off" to the laws of physics. Recreational use of rotorcraft is pretty much limited to people being taken on tours, so it's basically commercial. The ability to operate in a one hundred percent vertical direction is the marvel of the modern rotorcraft. Vertical takeoffs and landings and hovering in place are the main virtues of a helicopter compared other aircraft. So much so that one of the biggest innovations in recent aviation history is the V/STOL (vertical/short takeoff and landing) aircraft, epitomized by the Ares TR-55 series most often identified as the DocWagon Osprey. A blending of the features between a helicopter and a prop plane give these craft remark versatility. Commercially rotorcraft are used for heavy-lifting and making deliveries in places a plane with the same payload capacity couldn't utilize. Within dense urban areas and even out to the less developed surrounding vicinity, rotorcraft are used as short-distance transportation.

When it comes to shadowy applications of the modern rotorcraft, it boils down to two key points; tactical insertions/extractions and increased offensive potential. Rotorcraft have the ability to drop off and pick up shadowrunners from just about any location, especially if those runners have some rappelling and harness-use training. This transportation versatility also falls outside of the standard efforts expected by security at most facilities and police forces in most jurisdictions. The same can be said for the offensive capabilities that can be slapped onto a rotorcraft. While helicopter gunships have been around over a century, they aren't what most people expect to see when a rotorcraft shows up. Consider also, options for concealable weapon turrets and retractable missile and rocket launchers that make a rotorcraft look no different from its more mundane counterpart, and you can understand why these hovering slingers of death and destruction are a prize and a terror in the shadows, all depending on which side of the fight you're on.

LAVS

There are no applications for low-altitude vehicles, also known as LAVs or t-birds, in the civilian world. They are too inefficient to be used as standard haulers or personal transportation. These things are strictly military and security corp on the light side of life. But we're mainly here to talk about how they're used in the shadows.

Smuggling, that's how! That's biggest use for t-birds in the shadows. Whether they're carrying valuable cargo or shadowy people, t-birds are the way to go when making border runs all over the world. They fly low (hence "low-altitude vehicle") to avoid radar. They don't need roads, so they can skip standard checkpoints. They can fly at over 1,000 kph, making catching them the purview of other LAVs and fighter aircraft, two difficult things to have at the right place at the right time. Finish up with the ability to take off and land anywhere with a generally flat patch of dirt and you can understand why the LAV is the vehicle of choice for the world's smugglers. For shad-

owrunners, they are how we get smuggled around. It's usually a little pricier than a commercial flight, but your t-bird jammer—that's the common nickname for T-bird pilots—doesn't ask questions about SINs and cyber, and they'll gladly let you haul whatever gear you want. That usually comes with a caveat of stowing the gear away from where you'd have access in case passengers are suddenly feeling piratey. For security corps and the military, the LAV is a scout or fast-attack vehicle. They usually don't have really big guns, but they aren't defenseless. The main use is either getting into an area and getting a lay of the land, as we've seen in the various Desert Wars seasons, or coming in for a quick hit, usually as a softening precursor to the next wave or as a distraction.

LTAVS

Though their acronyms are similar, lighter than air vehicles, or LTAVs, are basically the exact opposite of LAVs. While LAVs are turbofan blasting, fast-moving, screaming speed machines, LTAVs are slow-moving, peaceful sky whales drifting across the sky. The civilian world uses them for leisurely sky cruises, long-distance cargo hauling to remote areas, or aerial living arrangements in hazardous areas.

The LTAV has always hovered at the periphery of the shadows. In recent years it's been working its way into the shadows more and more, but the lack of speed always seems to be the major drawback that keeps it out of most riggers hangars. Shadowrunners tend to operate in a fast-paced world with a perpetual sense of, and need for, urgency that doesn't fit the LTAV style. Combine that with their generally fragile nature, and they usually just can't stand up to the rigors of shadow work. In recent years, however, materials science improvements that allow for self-sealing gas chambers and design improvements that create a multitude of gas chambers to prevent loss of lift through damage to the balloon are making modern LTAVs far more resilient. With this added toughness, the rougher users such as runners, corp sec, and military are finding more and more uses for the tough LTAV. Long-range reconnaissance from a high and safe vantage point, transport and deployment of drones and smaller aircraft with more offensive capabilities, long-range gunships and missile-firing platforms, mobile-command stations that are safely out of reach, secure communications transfer points using laser data transfers, and cargo and troop movement into difficult terrain are just a few of the newest uses. Runners in the rougher parts of town have begun using dirigible dosses that float above the sprawl for security. It's not a regular thing yet, but it seems to be growing especially in the Aurora Warrens of Denver and Redmond Barrens in Seattle.

DRONES

While the earliest work on drones was done by the military, they have moved into every aspect of both mil-

itary and civilian life imaginable. They deliver goods, direct traffic, record news, and perform a million other mundane tasks in our modern world. Just like their manually operated counterparts they come in every type of drive system and power plant. They range in size from a few centimeters to dozens of meters to fill roles once handled by everything from cheap labor to skilled technicians.

In the shadows it's no different. Drones are used to spy, kill, follow, track, build, chase, infiltrate, deactivate, and imitate. If there is something a metahuman can do a drone either exists or is being designed that can do the

same thing. Yes, there is even research on using drones to cast spells. I never said all of the things they are working on have had a lot of success, but they're trying. Regular runners occasionally use drones for reconnaissance, surveillance, or for a little extra firepower and just let the drone's basic programming run most of the show. Riggers take those basic uses and combine them, all while the rigger actually takes direct control of a drone and leads the charge. Riggers become the drones they operate, and the difference is usually night and day between what a basic program can do while operating a drone and what a rigger can do while "being" the drone.

ALL THE ANGLES

A Roto-Drone whirred. A Dragonfly buzzed. A Dalmatian whooshed. JohnBee was jumped into that one because he had upgraded the sensors of it, and he could hear the noise around him. He needed to know how loud it was, because he needed to know if it should be louder.

There was plenty of noise. He was satisfied, for the time being.

He angled toward the sprawl streets below. It was late afternoon, sun peeking through after a spot of rain, and people were out. At least, managers were. Wageslaves stayed tied to their desks until their twelve-hour shift was over, but one of the perks of power was being able to see the sun when it was out. They were talking in small groups, receiving deliveries of coffee and pastries from small drones buzzing just above the streets. Those drones were much closer to them than JohnBee's crafts. But JohnBee's were louder, and that made people look up.

He scanned the entrance to the Champion Financial building. The guards were showing off their Renraku training—they were keeping an eye on the drones in the sky, but they knew that something that loud could very well be a distraction. They didn't let themselves stop scanning every angle of approach just because something was loud in the air.

So when the back doors of a cargo van opened and two Dobermans came rolling out, they were ready. The drones only moved toward the entrance for a few seconds before the guards were pointing at them and sending messages back and forth. Jamming came quick, but JohnBee wasn't jumped into the Dobies and wasn't even monitoring their output, so he didn't really care. The Dobies moved placidly ahead, ignoring what he was sure were continued warnings from the guards, until they were shot to ribbons by automatic weapons fire.

It was okay. They were mainly just shells, hollowed-out bodies on treads. He had stripped the more expensive parts before this mission.

The guards didn't slack off. When the Crawlers came, trying to sneak through the smoke of the Dobies, security remained alert and ready. They squashed them quickly.

That third wave made it clear that this was serious. JohnBee could see the tension in the guards' bodies as they moved briskly around the building's lobby, watching the ground for another wave, then scanning the skies. Up, down, back, forth, constant scanning. One of them would be on the horn trying to persuade Knight Errant to send in drones of their own and chase JohnBee's machines out of the area. They'd probably succeed in a matter of minutes.

He checked the ARO he kept low and to his left. Five meters beneath the guards, his Tunneler was making steady progress, and they were none the wiser. It worked every time—give people things they can see, and they forget to worry about what they can't.

THE CHROME BALLET

POSTED BY: RIGGER X

One of the secrets to good rigging is using multiple tools at once. Look, if you meet someone who calls themself a rigger and has just one vehicle in their stable, don't hire them. They're a driver, not a rigger. But simply having a clutch of devices is also not enough—they need to know how to use them. Here are some tips on how to use drones and vehicles in beautiful concert.

COORDINATING YOUR STRENGTHS

INTELLIGENCE FIRST

We all know that firing guns and making things blow up is the exciting part of shadowrunning, the part we talk about when we're swapping stories. Gathering intelligence, on the other hand, especially when we're doing it with drones, sometimes makes us feel a little shameful, like Peeping Toms slipping cameras into department store dressing rooms. None of us want cameras and microphones placed in our homes or workplaces, and insofar as we can pretend we have privacy, we don't want it invaded. So when we do the invading, it doesn't seem to be something to brag about.

Let me be clear: That shame should stop. None of us want to be shot, either, but we are happy to tell stories about shooting other people. Slipping a surveillance device into a place where it shouldn't be, getting intelligence only a few people know, and collecting the information that makes a job work is something we should be proud of. It's vital, it can make or break a mission, and it also gives us some incredible pieces of gossip that we can use to make a few extra bucks. So do it, and do it with pride.

Another part of intelligence-gathering that makes it seem less suitable for storytelling is that it can be painstaking. You do not just pilot your Fly-Spy into the window of Saeder-Krupp headquarters and eavesdrop on Lofwyr's personal meetings. Gathering intelligence is not about darting straight toward a target, but rather about drawing a series of concentric circles closing in on the heart of what you need to know. You have to know the front, the back, the sides—all the entrances, all the security, and you need to eliminate as much unpredictability as you can. Critically, you need to know what might mess with and what might detect your wireless signals as you move in. If you give yourself away at any point, the game is up. So know when you need to turn wireless off and let the Pilot program do its work. And make sure you have a Pilot program you can trust.

THE LARGER THE DRONE, THE MORE THE MOTION

This is kind of simple, but I'm going to say it anyway. Smaller drones benefit, generally, from staying hidden. Motion attracts attention, so when they move, they need to move carefully, or someone is going to squash 'em. Use darkness, use cover, and use caution. Larger drones, like a Dalmatian or something, aren't going to sneak into a room and eavesdrop on people like a Fly-Spy will, but they're still smaller than most targets coming from the air, meaning they're going to be harder to hit as they move. I know it's fun to find an ideal vantage point and camp out there, but even someone who is only moderately skilled with a pistol can pick a stationary target out of the air. Your job is to make it harder for the opposition to harm you, and that means keeping your forces on the move.

USE MULTIPLE VECTORS

The legend of the Trojan Horse has endured for millennia because it makes a simple point: Misdirection wins wars. Know where your opposition is looking, and then find a way to attack where they're not paying attention. In terms of rigging, this often means making sure your attack comes in from one or more directions so that the opposition overlooks where the real attack is. Of course, if you're going to pull this off, you need things that come at a variety of angles. That can mean different types of aircraft—smaller drones, for example, can come in a lot lower than larger craft, forcing targets to change their sight lines. And rotorcraft or VTOL vehicles can come in from entirely different angles than typical winged craft, which can throw off defenders. Better yet, though, are attacks that involve both ground and air, staged at different times and keeping the targets flustered. It's kind of a win-win—eventually one of the vectors will catch them off-guard and make it through, or they'll spend so much time reacting to one punch after another that they'll begin to wear out, increasing the odds that sooner or later something will get through. And this isn't just about having drones and vehicles coming from different angles—it's great for directing people toward an ambush you've set up, or away from you if you need to redirect the heat.

Keep in mind that while I'm using attack language above, this is not always about firing weapons. Sometimes, if you're gathering intel, it can help to start with something more obvious, then move in with subtler devices. For example, let's say you're crafty enough to have gotten your hands on a Renraku Dove, despite the fact that they're supposed to be used exclusively by GOD. You fly that thing over just about any corporate facility in the world, and it's going to get attention. It's not large, but people have quickly learned to recognize its bird-like profile, and they know what it means when it's in the area: GOD is watching. The Dove's sensor suite is top-notch, especially when it comes to seeing wireless signals, and the official line from GOD is they are just using the Dove to detect the existence of signals so that they can see if any unlicensed things are floating around that they need to know about. No one, of course, believes that the only thing they are doing is looking at signals—

everyone thinks they are tapping into them, so everyone gets wary when they see a Dove nearby. I promise you, the first five minutes after someone spots a Dove nearby will be chaos and scrambling in anyone who has anything to do with monitoring wireless signals in the area. That means you have five minutes to get something small into the area when people aren't paying attention. (Air ducts are great for this, BTW—they may not be built to hold the weight of people, but a small, crawling drone is something entirely else.)

As I mentioned earlier, if you're a good rigger, you've got multiple vehicles and drones at your disposal. And if you've got multiple vehicles, use them.

FAST, CHEAP, AND OUT OF CONTROL

There is virtue and beauty to a precision drone strike, where every move is planned and executed to perfection, but if that's the only way you operate, you're missing part of the strength of drones. When you control all of the drones and vehicles in your arsenal, you have the comfort (usually) of knowing that their dog-brain isn't going to make them do something stupid. But sometimes something stupid is exactly what you need. A weakly armored drone who flies into a head-on assault. A drone armed with a sniper rifle that has a bad habit of striving for a close-in kill. Those are mistakes an experienced rigger would not make, as they tend to result in the loss of whatever drone or vehicle attempts the stupid move. They also, though, tend to throw the opposition a little off their game. It might just be the excitement of getting an easy kill, but when the unexpected happens, people lose their focus, and the results can be wonderful.

The upshot is, sometimes it's good to take a step back and let your drones go in as a chaotic swarm, because they might do the stupid thing you need to throw the opposition off their game. Just don't try to pull that off with your heavily customized baby that cost you six figures—this is what you do with a pile of cheap drones you got on sale at Kennedy's Cheap Electronics.

Of course, a good chaotic assault is about more than allowing your drones the chance to make stupid mistakes. It's about employing a swarm, an attack coming from different directions, moving fast, hitting hard, pulling back, then moving in for another strike. Again, there may be individual losses within the swarm, but the whole point of the effort—and the rigger's skill—is to make the damage inflicted much heavier than the losses.

LOCK IN

But let's say you don't have cheap drones, and you prefer precision to chaos. In that case, if you're serious about being precise, take your time to get it right. Get a target lock. It might take a few extra seconds, but the reduced amount of weapons fire you may need to get

the job done can make it worthwhile.

The problem, of course, is that pretty much everyone out there knows the virtue of getting a target lock, and they've been working hard to detect and break them right after you get them. It can be frustrating when a target jams your lock right after you get it, but remember: Breaking your target lock takes effort. The time they spend breaking your lock is time they spend not doing anything else. You don't get your immediate shot off, but if you're playing the chess game of moving combat right, you can use the time they're spending breaking the lock to get in position to do something truly annoying.

MOUNTING A DEFENSE

If there's one principle the Sixth World is built on, it's that "Money talks." If there's another one, it's that "For every action there is an equal and opposite reaction." It's more than just basic physics—it's how we battle it out with the other side (whoever that may be). They have every weapon that we have, and they're not shy about bring-

ing them. All that stuff I talked about above? There's a good chance you'll see someone use them against you. Here's some pointers on how to counter some of the tactics opposing riggers will use against you.

OBSCURING INTELLIGENCE

A good rigger will prevent you from seeing what you want to see in your intelligence-gathering efforts. A great rigger will make you think you got what you were looking for, while misleading you the whole way.

There's a proud tradition of this in warfare, espionage, and any other form of conflict you can think about. From John Magruder marching the same troops before Union eyes repeatedly, making his force seem much larger than it was during the United States Civil War, to MI5 using their network of double agents to convince Germany that the D-Day invasion would happen at Calais, letting people see the wrong image is a great way to get them to do the wrong thing. So when you detect a Crawler sneaking in to eavesdrop on your planning meetings, feel free to let it stay and hear some juicy details that sound like actionable intelligence pointing in the completely direction completely.

AREA EFFECTS ARE YOUR FRIEND

I mentioned the advantage of a drone's size and the difficulty of hitting something in motion. This is why artillery bombardments and rifle barrages exist to stop infantry advances—because you want a barrage against smaller targets, not pinpoint efforts. Not sure how many small drones are in an area? Worried about hitting all the drones darting around in the sky? Loft a Powerball into the midst of them, or a nice, old-fashioned grenade. You may not have an accurate count of all the targets out there, but you don't need it. You just need the ability to stop whatever is there.

Yeah, you have to worry about collateral damage and drawing too much attention, but if being both effective and subtle were easy, they wouldn't be paying us so much to do what we do.

A DRONE MOVES MOST LIKE A DRONE

A metahuman is not going to squeeze into the same spaces used by a micro drone, get vertical the same way a VTOL drone can, or hover like a Roto-Drone. If you want to match a drone move for move, get your rigger on the game. That's what they're there for. Your mage performs astral overwatch, your hacker is responsible for Matrix security for the team, so the rigger should take responsibility for defeating any drones that come your way. Yeah, she can call on other members of the team for help, as described above, but she should know the drones and their traits better than anyone, so she should know the best ways to take them down.

And it's not just about movement. Keeping drones moving and shooting correctly requires a continual array of wireless commands, and while riggers are not hackers, they have ways of using those signals flying through the air to their advantage. The most basic form of this is reducing (for their own network) or increasing (for other drones) the noise in the area. It may not be as satisfying as shooting a drone out of the sky, but effectively cutting the connection between a drone and its rigger disables it quite well, letting you get your job done. But we'll get to that in the next section.

BREAK THE LOCK

I mentioned earlier that breaking target locks can be a good distraction that you can take advantage of, but that doesn't mean you shouldn't do it. Just be ready for a follow-up attack.

Better yet, avoid the lock in the first place. Quality Pilot and Stealth autosofts can save you a lot of grief with

your drones, and sneaking is an undervalued skill for drivers. Stay elusive, and you won't have to waste time breaking target locks, because the opposition won't be able to make any.

RIGGERS AND THE HACK

As any runner with a wireless-enabled device can tell you, wireless capabilities mean you might get hacked. The power of a rigger is the ability to remotely control a number of devices in several places all at once. The weakness is the thing. When we're talking about riggers and the dangers of the hack, there are dangers from hackers and dangers from other riggers. We'll tackle them separately.

HACKERS VS. RIGGERS

A hacker's goal when it comes to interfering with your work is simple: He wants control of one or more of your vehicles or drones, and he has the tools and skills to take them over. You have to hold him off.

The basic defenses are well known. Your rigger command console is a critical line of defense. Spend those extra few thousand nuyen to boost the firewall; when a good hacker comes after you, you'll be grateful. A truly skilled hacker, of course, is pretty good at blowing past just about any firewall, so you can't count on built-in defenses to do all your heavy lifting for you. I mentioned noise—use it. You should know how to suppress noise between you and your network of vehicles and drones. Move the conflict away from you—and particularly away from any opposing hackers. If you can increase the noise they experience while suppressing your own, you can gain a critical advantage.

Finally, always be ready to reboot a drone when you need to. Again, a destroyed drone is better than one that's turned on you, so if it breaks apart during the reboot process, suck it up and move on. And remember next time to see how many expenses Mr. Johnson will cover.

RIGGERS VS. RIGGERS

All of the options mentioned above for dealing with hackers also apply to riggers, but there is one fun extra twist. Despite their differences in operations and manufacture, drones tend to speak the same "language," especially when it comes to navigational data. Sending some bad navigation info might push a drone or vehicle using an automated pilot in the wrong direction. Even a single wrong turn can be enough to give you a much-needed advantage, and this can be a great way to hurt drones with a bad firewall even if you don't have a full hacker on your team to take advantage of that weakness. But it's not just for bad firewalls—you can surprise a whole range of drones or vehicles with this little trick. Make sure you have it ready.

GAME INFORMATION

REPAIR RULES

Chances are your drones and vehicles will get a bit banged up over the course of a run. Whether it's bullets, spells, or spirits, you can put them back together again with some parts, tools, time, and elbow grease.

This assumes, of course, that your vehicle or drone is merely damaged. If all of the boxes on its Condition Monitor are filled, then sorry chummer, your baby is totaled (but I know a guy on Maynard who can give you a good deal on a refurb).

SPARE PARTS

To repair a vehicle or drone, you need to have the parts on hand. These can be purchased from any shop, hardware store, or junk yard for five percent of the cost of the vehicle or drone per box of damage on the Condition Monitor that needs to be repaired. You can also scavenge parts off of similar vehicles—more about that later on. If you don't have sufficient parts for your repair, you'll take a penalty to the Extended Technical Skill Test, depending on how short you are: Increase the interval to one day, and for every box worth of parts you lack, you take a -4 dice pool penalty.

SCAVENGING PARTS

You can tear parts out of a working vehicle or drone (the target) for use in the repair of a similar vehicle or drone (your gamemaster will tell you if your scavenging victim is similar if you're not sure). First, decide how much damage you're willing to inflict on the target, in Condition Monitor boxes. Then the target takes that damage (with no chance to resist) and you make an appropriate Mechanic skill + Logic [damage inflicted] Test. For every two hits, you scavenge one box worth of parts for your repair job.

TOOLS

You need at least a toolkit appropriate to the skill you need for the repair (usually one of the Mechanic skills starting on p. 143, *SR5*). Your gamemaster may require you to have a shop or a facility (p. 443, *SR5*), depending on the size of the vehicle.

MAKING THE REPAIR

Once you have the parts and tools sorted out, make an Extended appropriate Mechanic + Logic [Mental] Extended Test, with a threshold equal to the number of boxes of damage to repair and an interval of four hours (one day if you don't have enough parts). The modifiers on the Repair Table apply to this test.

REPAIR TABLE

SITUATION	DICE POOL MODIFIER
Working Conditions	
Distracting	−1
Poor	−2
Bad	−3
Terrible	−4
Superior	+1
Tools and/or Parts Are:	
Unavailable	−4 or not allowed
Superior	+1 or more

ELECTRONIC WARFARE

The rigger is unique in that she fights in the Matrix and meatspace at the same time. As a result, signals warfare is way up there on the list of Things That Are Important to Know About. These actions are used by riggers from beginning drone racers to elite thunderbird pilots in the back-and-forth game of electronic warfare.

All of the following actions are Matrix actions. Yes, you can use them if you're not a rigger.

BREAK TARGET LOCK

(SIMPLE ACTION)

Marks required: None
Test: Electronic Warfare + Intuition [Data Processing] v. Logic + Sensors

Passive targeting and active targeting with sensors are described on p. 184 of SR5. If you know that you've been locked (or suspect it), you can to try to break it. Choose an enemy that has (or you think has) a lock on

you, and make the Opposed Test. For every net hit, you reduce the target's lock on you by one hit. Your RCC's Noise Reduction rating is added as a dice pool bonus for this action.

CONFUSE PILOT

(COMPLEX ACTION)

Marks required: None
Test: Electronic Warfare + Logic [Data Processing] v. Pilot + Firewall

You send a stream of code to a device with a pilot (usually a drone, but sometimes an autonomous vehicle or gun emplacement) that resembles valid instructions but is in fact gobbledygook. If you succeed, the pilot becomes confused, and makes an immediate Simple Pilot x 2 Test to figure out what it's going to do next (p. 269, *SR5*)—the threshold for this test is equal to half of your net hits. Your RCC's Noise Reduction Rating is added as a dice pool bonus for this action.

DETECT TARGET LOCK

(FREE ACTION)

Marks required: Owner
Test: Computer + Logic [Data Processing] (2)

Passive targeting and active targeting with sensors are described on p. 184 of SR5. An active target lock sends wireless and other signals that hackers and riggers have learned to detect. The RCC, commlink, or deck that you're using must be wireless-enabled to perform this action. Your RCC's Noise Reduction rating is added as a dice pool bonus for this action.

SUPPRESS NOISE

(COMPLEX ACTION)

Marks required: Owner
Test: Electronic Warfare + Logic [Data Processing]

As described on p. 268, *SR5*, this action allows riggers to use their RCC to reduce noise between themselves and their vehicles or drones. Reduce noise by the hits on this test, cumulative with any other forms of noise reduction. This effect lasts for the remainder of the current Combat Turn. Your RCC's Noise Reduction rating is added as a dice pool bonus for this action.

TARGET DEVICE

(COMPLEX ACTION)

Marks Required: None
Test: Electronic Warfare + Logic [Data Processing] v. Willpower + Firewall

Pick a wireless-enabled device you've spotted on the Matrix. You can target that device and feed targeting data to any pilot program or person with a Sensor rating or smartlink that is slaved to your RCC. For the rest of the Combat Turn, the slaved attackers receive a dice pool bonus equal to your net hits when targeting the device you're tracking for them. Your RCC's Noise Reduction rating is added as a dice pool bonus for this action.

SWARMS

What do you do with a lot of relatively stupid drones? Create one reasonably smart swarm! A drone (or vehicle) swarm is a network of linked drones all slaved (p. 233, *SR5*) to a single RCC running the Swarm program. You can include as many drones in a swarm as your RCC can slave (Device Rating x 3), or split them up among several swarms (again, limited by your RCC's slave limit). To start a swarm, simply run the Swarm program on your RCC, slave your drones, and command them to join the swarm you designate for them.

Each swarm acts as a single drone with multiple, separate "bodies." Its Pilot rating is equal to the highest Pilot rating of its member drones, or the Device Rating of the RCC, whichever is higher. The swarm uses the highest-rated of each autosoft running on any drone or the RCC, and the highest Sensor rating. It uses the lowest of the drones' Handling, Speed, and Acceleration ratings. When performing actions, the swarm gets a dice pool and limit bonus equal to one less than the number of drones in the swarm.

In combat, all drones attack with whatever weapons they have, but for game purposes only use a single weapon's stats (the others are covered by the action bonuses the swarm receives), although roll scatter for explosive weapons separately. Drones in a swarm must be targeted individually by attackers—the loss of drones from a swarm due to damage, hacking, or other mishaps affects the swarm's bonuses and ratings immediately.

SWARMS

RIGGING PROGRAM	COST
Swarm	600¥

OPERATIONAL TIME

While vehicles use a variety of fuel sources besides simple gasoline, they all still use *something*, which means eventually they run out of what is powering them. Vehicles operating normally can function for six hours before needing refueling/recharging/whatever; operating in a low-power mode (such as idling) extends that time, while higher-powered travels (such as moving at top speeds for prolonged periods) shorten it. Keeping minute-by-minute records is not necessary. The point is to make the players occasionally consider their power needs and not allow them unlimited travel without powering/fueling up, not making them track exact fuel expenditures.

TAKEOFF AND LANDING

Planes and helicopters and such go from ground to air at different angles, meaning they have different amounts of horizontal land they need to traverse before they get airborne—and when they get back down to the ground. There are three different aircraft profiles: long, short, and VTOL. Long distances are used for planes that are not specified to have either short landing or VTOL capabilities, or lighter-than-air properties.

TAKEOFF AND LANDING DISTANCE

AIRCRAFT PROFILE	TAKEOFF	LANDING
Long	2,000	1,800
Short	200	300
VTOL	—	—

ON THE
BLEEDING EDGE

Cayman pointed.

"Stay!"

A short man with a dusting of black hair on his chin that was attempting to be a beard threw his hands in the air.

"I can't do any good back here!"

"Maybe," Cayman said, "But you also can't do any harm. Past experience tells me that's a tradeoff worth making."

"So I'm just supposed to stand here?"

Cayman had started walking toward X-Prime, who was waiting patiently at the end of the alley. He didn't turn when he spoke to Looper.

"No, of course not," he said. "You're too obvious. Sit in the car. Be ready." Then he caught up to X-Prime, and the two of them walked toward the NeoNET subsidiary that hopefully didn't know they were coming.

Looper paced a few times in back of the dumpy brown American. He didn't want to give Cayman the satisfaction of following his instructions.

But then he got bored and tired of standing around, so he got in the car.

It was pointed in the direction Cayman and X-Prime had exited, so Looper was free to look at the suits walking back and forth in the blue-grey light that seemed especially bright compared to the charcoal lighting in the alley. The car was not hidden, and he figured they had at most fifteen minutes before some cop noticed it and ordered a tow. With any luck, he wouldn't have to wait that long.

As it turned out, he didn't. After five minutes, a dark sedan pulled forward to block the alley. No doors opened.

Looper didn't like that. He didn't like the clatter of gunfire that followed, or the flash of light followed by a loud boom that was close enough for him to notice but not close enough to directly cause him problems. He was pretty sure problems were on the way, though.

This car was not exactly a hot rod, but it had the virtue of being very customizable. He was already in manual shifting (he hadn't driven getaway before, but he was pretty sure most professionals didn't use automatic), and he turned off traction control. He had seen a pile of loose nuts and bolts when he came in the alley. Time to use them.

More gunfire. It was probably time to move.

He revved the engine, slipped into gear, and the car lunged forward. His hands moved quickly on the gear shift (he was saving up for an RCC but didn't have near enough yet) and put it in reverse while hanging off the clutch for a second. People in the sedan were moving, the window facing him moving down and the barrel of a gun emerging. But then Looper was on the pile of bolts, and he engaged the clutch. The car hated it, grinding and squealing, but the wheels did their job and spun. Small pieces of metal shot forward, flying above the sedan but also hitting it, and the would-be shooter ducked for cover. The car moved, a natural response to being under fire.

Looper shifted his car back into first gear, and there was more grinding but the American lurched, springing for the sedan, which he nailed between the rear wheel well and the trunk. It spun, then the sedan's acceleration took hold at an inopportune time, and it drove up on a sidewalk and into a wall.

Looper squealed around the corner, saw two people running out of the confusion caused by the gunfire and his sudden emergence, and he shot toward them. A quick flip on an ARO opened the rear driver's-side door as he drew near them, and Cayman and X-Prime dove into the car. Then it was time to accelerate again, before any security could stop them.

In five minutes, they had pulled into a garage, dumped the American, and switched to a blue Honda Citizen. Looper peacefully drove along at a legally boring speed.

Cayman looked over at X-Prime.

"I may have underestimated the skill of our driver," he said.

10W40 IN YOUR VEINS

Some people are born riggers, others work tirelessly to build up the skills that could make them highly sought after. There are a lot of different paths to being a great rigger, and there is not just one way to be great. This chapter has qualities and life modules for use with the life module character creation system (p. 65, *Run Faster*). Dive in to make the tire-screeching, wave-riding, drone-shooting, jet-flying rigger of your dreams.

POSITIVE QUALITIES

CHASER

COST: 4 KARMA

Something about reeling in a car, boat, or plane that is trying to get away from you gives you a sense of urgency and intensity that makes you perform at your peak. The same thing happens when someone is after you. Any time you perform any Chase Action (p. 204, SR5), you receive a +2 dice pool bonus.

DEALER CONNECTION

COST: 3 KARMA

At some point in your wide travels and extra-legal activities, you met someone who has access to retail vehicles, and your connection means that you get vehicles at a discount. When selecting this quality, pick a class of vehicle (ground craft, watercraft, aircraft, or drones). Each time you purchase a vehicle of that class, you receive ten percent off the price. The discount is taken after the gamemaster makes adjustment to the price based on Availability. This quality may be taken up to four times, once for each class of vehicle.

GREASE MONKEY

COST: 8 KARMA

When you were young, you would much rather make a trip to the junkyard than the toy store (possibly because kids in the barrens never have enough money to buy anything at the toy store). As you got older, the allure or discarded vehicle and machine parts on the heaps in junkyards was far stronger than the promise of some new toy. You not only loved monkeying around with these items, but you could often get the devices to work. Gain +1 dice on any skill test using skills from the Engineering skill group.

SPEED DEMON

COST: 3 KARMA

Pushing your vehicle to its limits makes the hair on the back of your neck stand up, but in a good way. You feel alive, alert, and ready to do anything. This increased intensity gives you a +1 dice pool bonus to Pilot tests for a vehicle that is moving at a speed attribute of 3 or high-er (4 for aircraft). Note that your character must either be directly in the vehicle he is piloting or jacked in; the bonus does not apply to vehicles that are simply being piloted remotely.

STUNT DRIVER

COST: 4 KARMA

Whether it's because you spent some time working for a trip studio in LA or because you taught yourself some fancy moves while passing time in the barrens driving some junker car, you developed particular skill behind the wheel/helm/control stick of a vehicle and can pull off stunts with a grace and ease that others envy. When making any vehicle Stunt test (see p. 204, SR5), you receive a +2 dice pool bonus.

SUBTLE [VEHICLE] PILOT

COST: 4 KARMA

Other riggers can be flashy or showy, but you know the value of getting your work done while appearing like part of the normal traffic—or like part of the background you're passing. When you are piloting a craft on the ground, in the water, or in the air, anyone trying to spot you gets a -2 dice pool penalty to their Perception Test to find you. This includes drones, as long as you are directly controlling them instead of letting your software for the work. This quality can be selected once for each particular Pilot skill, including the various Pilot Exotic Craft skills. The type of craft it applies to must be selected when it is purchased.

NEGATIVE QUALITIES

ACCIDENT PRONE

BONUS: 4 KARMA

This driving thing—it may not be for you. You have a talent for steering any vehicle you control into whatever wall, tree, or other vehicle may be nearby. You receive a -2 dice pool penalty on any tests involved in directing a vehicle.

MOTION SICKNESS

BONUS: 4 KARMA

Yes, there is a strong benefit from being able to move from place to place, but if your traveling comes with

too much, well, *motion*, your stomach starts doing flip-flops. Any time you are in a vehicle that is effectively accelerating at a rate of 3 or higher (that is, moving across three or more range categories) or moving at a Speed of 4 or higher, you experience Nausea (p. 409, *SR5*) until the vehicle's Speed or Acceleration drops. Once the vehicle movement drops, the Nausea disappears in (12 – Body) minutes.

TOO MUCH DATA

BONUS: 3 KARMA

With a few vehicles under your control, everything is fine. Once you get too many vehicles moving at the same time, sending you information on what they are doing, where they are going, and who is shooting at them, you start to feel overwhelmed and flustered, and your effectiveness drops. Anytime you are directing four or more vehicles and/or drones that are in motion, you receive a –2 dice pool penalty on any Pilot tests related to the movement of those vehicles. This applies even if some of the vehicles and/or drones are on autopilot—the data streaming in from them is distracting.

LIFE MODULES

Some riggers are shaped by the life experiences they had along the way—their hobbies, jobs, and possibly their early criminal efforts. These life modules reflect some of those experiences, and are for use with the Life Module character creation system found in *Run Faster* (p. 65)

FORMATIVE YEARS
MINOR WHEELMAN

Were you supposed to be behind the wheel before you were even in your teens? No. But you were also supposed to be in school, living under an intact roof, and being looked out for by someone who wasn't constantly on novacoke, so your life never really followed any of the patterns the establishment would approve. Whether running errands for adults too stoned to drive or capturing an illicit thrill in a stolen vehicle, you built up driving skills early, along with a certain reckless streak that comes from doing something stupid and getting away with it.

Attributes: Intuition +1, Reaction +1
Qualities: Speed Demon, Stunt Driver
Skills: Automotive Mechanic +1, Navigation +1, Pilot Ground Craft +2, Professional Knowledge: [Vehicle Models] +1, Street Knowledge: [Vehicle Stunts] +1

SHOP KID

Someone close to you—a relative, a friend, or whatever—had a repair shop, and you spent a lot of time there, hanging out. You grew to love the smell of oil and grease, the sound of metal clanking and ratchets ratcheting, and the sight of a battered mess being restored to functional life. And along the way, you picked up some pointers on how machines work.
Attributes: Intuition +1, Logic +1
Qualities: Grease Monkey
Skills: Automotive Mechanic +2, Industrial Mechanic +1, Professional Knowledge: [Vehicle Models] +3, Professional Knowledge: [Vehicle Parts] +1

TEEN YEARS
BOOSTER

Money isn't easy to come by on the streets of the Sixth World—except for the fact that residents of the Sixth World tend to drive vehicles worth several thousand nuyen over those same streets on a daily basis. At some point in your teen years, whether due to boredom or desperate need, you took to stealing cars, and found you were pretty good at it. You learned that the job has two main parts—getting a vehicle you don't own moving, and then staying out of the hands of the rightful owners or police who want you to give it back.
Attributes: Logic +1, Reaction +1
Qualities: Stunt Driver
Skills: Hacking +1, Locksmith +1, Pilot Ground Craft +1, Professional Knowledge: [Vehicle Models] +2, Street Knowledge: [Chop Shops] +2

FURTHER EDUCATION
TRADE SCHOOL SHOP

You didn't go to school to learn philosophy or read poetry; you went to gain some solid skills with use in the real world. Namely, you learned how to fix and repair things. The undersides of your fingernails may be permanently stained black, but you have skills useful to just about everyone in the civilized world.
Note: This counts as part of the Community College group, and so costs 55 Karma.
Attributes: Logic +1
Qualities: Grease Monkey
Skills: Engineering skill group +1, Academic Knowledge [Practical Mechanics] +2, Professional Knowledge [Industrial Manufacturers] +2, Professional Knowledge [Machine Parts] +2

REAL LIFE
DRONE HOBBYIST

First you found out how to fly a drone in order to get pictures of cityscapes that you could never get otherwise. Then you moved on to smaller drones that could listen and see things where you normally couldn't go. Then you explored drone capabilities beyond just looking and listening. Over a few years and more expenditures than you would care to tabulate, you ended up with some pretty solid skills when it comes to manipulating drones.
Attributes: Logic +1, Reaction +1
Skills: Automotive Mechanic +2, Gunnery +2, Perception +1, Pilot Aircraft +2, Pilot Ground Craft +2, Pilot Walker +2, Pilot Watercraft +2, Sneaking +1, Tracking +1, Professional Knowledge: [Drone Manufacturers] +3, Professional Knowledge: [Drone Software] +2 Pilot Aircraft +2

GETAWAY DRIVER

It started as an insult more than anything else—you ran with a pack of people who, when drek got real, would leave you sitting in the car. "It's for your own good," they said, but what they meant was "We think you might kill us if you came along." That's how it started, but eventually all that time in the car added up to something. You learned quick reflexes, driving savvy, and a calm demeanor—while also learning how to drive really, really fast.
Attributes: Intuition +1, Reaction +1
Qualities: Gearhead, Speed Demon
Skills: Automotive Mechanic +1, Gunnery +1, Pilot Ground Craft +3, Pilot Watercraft +1, Sneaking +1, Tracking +2, Street Knowledge [(Selected Area) Streets] +2, Street Knowledge [Stunt Techniques] +2

TRID STUNT DRIVER

There are a whole lot of bad jobs in the world. The fact that you were able to spend time driving and crashing cars for a living for a short time is no insignificant accomplishment. Yeah, the pay wasn't great, but it kept you fed and sheltered for a time. Until you realized you had developed some skills that might pay off a lot more, if you were willing to be a little loose in your ethics.
Attributes: Intuition +1, Reaction +1
Qualities: Steely Eyed Wheelman (p. 150, *Run Faster*), Stunt Driver
Skills: Automotive Mechanic +1, Demolitions +1, Etiquette (Corporate) +1, Gunnery +1, Navigation +1, Performance +1, Pilot Aircraft +1, Pilot Ground Craft +3, Pilot Walker +1, Pilot Watercraft +2, Professional Knowledge [Stunt Techniques] +3, Professional Knowledge [Trid Studios] +2

THE ORDER OF CHAOS

When an electric sports car is accelerating, it has a few dozen moving parts. Most, of course, are in the wheels, taking the electric current from the battery and turning it into motion. The engine doesn't roar or even purr. The only noise is from the movement of the rotors and the wheels contacting the road. There is a certain purity to it, where the only noise comes from actual movement—the faster you go, the louder it gets. On the occasional trip out of the sprawl, Tucker had driven internal combustion cars, and he had to admit satisfaction in hearing the engine roar when he stomped on the accelerator. The engine dominated internal combustion cars, overwhelming the road noise, sending shudders through the whole body of the vehicle. It had its own thrill, but in the end, Tucker preferred electric. The only rumble came from the road, the only noise from movement. When you got up enough speed on the right stretch of road and managed to jump into the air, the wheels left the ground and their noise briefly vanished, leaving nothing but the wind rushing by, and for the small moment before the frame cracks back to the earth, there is quiet flight. Tucker believed that if more theologians experienced moments like that, they would no longer describe heaven in terms of angels and clouds, but rather talk about suspension, wheels, and motors.

Heaven, though, seemed far distant compared to the hell that well might be waiting for him.

"They're looking for you, Tucker," said Spinnaker over the comm. "I've got you covered so far, but someone's been alerted. They want to find anything that looks suspicious, and they might settle on you."

Tucker eased his low-slung car around a corner, passing a few punks in glowing synthleather who tried not to look like they were ogling his red-striped beauty. But of course they were. The blue light from his hubs briefly shone on the faces of the punks, then passed.

Another nice thing about internal combustion cars was the shifting of gears when you made a turn like this. It gave you a level of control of the vehicle that was not, of course, the same as being jumped in, but made you feel close to the machine, unified with it. With the electric vehicle, you just slid around the corner, all movement controlled by how you massaged the pedal. It was smooth and calm, but a little bloodless.

Tucker thought about jumping in, just to satisfy his vehicle lust, but he didn't think he could afford to be that focused on vehicle movement right now. With a few Fly-Spys providing footage from the downtown area, and footage from

BY JASON M. HARDY

Spinnaker showing the location and movements of the rest of his team, he couldn't get too focused on one thing.

"Motorcycles inbound," Jekyll reported from her mid-air perch. She was currently invisible, being flown around by an air spirit. She'd light up the astral to anyone paying attention, but the heart of the CAS sector of Denver generally had plenty of spirits patrolling the area, so hopefully she wouldn't seem unusual. "Five of them. If they're not Yakuza, I'll eat my familiar."

"They've swallowed the bait," Spinnaker said. "Let's make sure their trip is worthwhile."

"They're heading right to Klub Karma," Jekyll said. "Guns aren't out yet."

Tucker was six blocks away from the club. The car was still smooth and silent. It would not stay that way long. He regretted it. But he was not paid for peace.

"I can't drive straight in," he said. "The Yaks are going to need some time to get chesty first. Then I'll make the run and make sure the chaos takes hold."

"Roger," Spinnaker said.

Four motorcycles roared by Tucker. They weren't electric. The Yaks knew that for this particular mission, noise mattered.

At the next street, Tucker took a left. He needed to take a roundabout route, but he didn't think the Yaks would make him wait long.

The Yaks drove down in front of the club, coming in range of a Fly-Spy Tucker had planted on the marquee. The benefit of the afternoon light was that the marquee was not washing out the cameras of the drone, so he had a good view of the motorcycles revving down the block.

There was an art to what the Yaks were about to do. They had to build tension, but at the right pace. Go too fast, and things would be over too quickly. Any possible spectators wouldn't be aware of what was happening. Go too slow and you'd seem timid, and you might give the opposition too much time to craft some sort of response. They needed to get attention, make some bad things happen, then make them worse, then get out.

They started with the traditional revving of engines and hollering as they drove up and down the block. They swerved from lane to lane, weaving through incoming traffic, certainly drawing the attention of GridGuide authorities. A response would be here soon, but the Yaks were doing an admirable job of snarling up traffic, which would delay the response. Looking out his windshield, Tucker saw some vehicles near him awkwardly jerking to the side of the road, showing that not be long on time.

But they were already escalating. Someone had done a nice bit of programming, so that as the cycles spun around the street, their rear wheels kicked up AROs of color that flew into the air toward the club, spreading virtual stains over the entrance. They were clashing neons, fluorescent colors mixing with browns, making the whole entrance look tacky and ugly—assuming you were able to see AR, and who wasn't? Petty vandalism wasn't going to satisfy the circling Yaks, though. That was just to get attention. The real show was about to start.

It began with a spell, which surprised Tucker. He didn't think they'd send a mage on something like this, but they had, and it was a good choice, because they were able to send up some fire to sear the club doors without having to pull out a weapon. Tucker had to move his Fly-Spy a little to see the results of the spell, and once he did it looked like more light than heat. There were some char marks on the door's brushed metal handles, but nothing more serious. But then the doors open, and two prototypical security mooks in dark suits and sunglasses emerged, large and shiny handguns out. They waved them at the Yaks on cycles and yelled, but this attack was not going to be deterred by words and waves. Another spell from the mage knocked one of the guards on his hoop, which brought an end to the shouting part of the ritual. The non-Awakened Yaks whipped out their guns, while the standing security guard fired three times and dove for cover.

Sadly, the fast move left the other guard as the most obvious target. A barrage of bullets hit his bulletproof vest, which one stray hitting his left arm and another catching his neck. That last one left spurting blood behind it. The guard would not be getting back up.

This wasn't just for show anymore. This was real. And sirens approaching fast indicated it wouldn't be lasting much longer. The Yaks would likely want to make one more big move and then get out before the cops or the mob could mount any credible response.

That meant it was time for Tucker, who was there to make sure the chaos did not end so easily. They were being paid to make this a true incident with plenty of arrests, not a mere skirmish.

GridGuide had ordered him to the side of the road, and he had complied. The twenty seconds of motionlessness had been annoying. Fortunately, they were over.

"Gimme override," he said, and Spinnaker complied. An ARO flashed green, indicating his car was free of any constraints. He hit the accelerator and pushed back in his seat as the car pulled forward.

That was the other difference between electric and internal combustion cars. Internal combustion cars felt like the engine was pushing the car, heaving the inertia forward through sheer power. Electric cars—at least ones as powerful as his Porsche—felt like they were being unleashed, as if without restraint they would accelerate forever until they burst into a

was eager to let it.

Squealing tires was a universal car noise, regardless of the engine, and Tucker laid down rubber turning his way toward Klub Karma. So far, no one had noticed the spell concealing the large tube on the top of his car, but people would be looking soon. They'd notice, assuming they had the skill to see. But that was okay. Tucker wasn't being subtle anymore.

The powers of GridGuide had managed to clear a path for the police that were closing in on the club, and that meant that once he was lined up, Tucker had a clear shot.

He took it. Fire erupted from the gun in his roof, and a large shell hurtled down the street. It hit the street, smoking, then exploded for good measure. A street that was already in chaos got worse.

Tucker came tearing after his shot. If anyone was checking the ID he was broadcasting, he would look all the world like a Mafia car. Whether the Yaks noticed that or not, they knew he was a threat, so they turned on him. Their pistols wouldn't do him much damage, but he was worried about the mage. That's what Jekyll was there for, though.

On cue, lightning sprang from the hands of the Yak mage, but it fizzled just outside the Porsche. Jekyll was doing her job.

Tucker didn't want to go with the big gun again, as he was in closer quarters and didn't have a good path, but he had a handgun and a window just for this purpose. Passers-by had passed by at this point, so he didn't have to worry about hitting the wrong people. He flew through the block, spraying bullets. He wasn't sure if he hit anything, but he damn sure had gotten their attention.

Sadly, after another hundred meters he realized he had gotten more attention than he anticipated. Two more motorcycles were ignoring GridGuide and heading down the street. And two black cars came out from the alley next to Klub Karma, likely the mobile part of club security joining the fight. The Yakuza knew he was firing at them, and if they looked at the registration information he was broadcasting they would think he was Mafia. The Mafia, if they looked at the information he was broadcasting, would know he was lying. And the police wouldn't care what he was right now—they'd just be highly annoyed that he was firing weapons in the heart of the CAS sector.

They would all want to stop him. It would be bad for him if any of them did.

He unleashed the power of his Porsche and let it run. If it became a fireball as he escaped, so be it.

The acceleration was smooth, even, and powerful. The motorcycles ahead of him could not react fast enough. He saw them whipping out handguns as he passed by. They turned and fired, but they were still moving. The shots were awkward. He was not sure where the bullets landed, but it was not near him.

"GridGuide has politely but firmly suggested that you pull over and stop, or the authorities will have to use deadly force," Spinnaker reported.

"Tell them I appreciate the suggestion, but that is not going to work for me at this moment." The street ahead was busy—it was not quite rush hour, but close enough that plenty of cars were out. Most of them seemed to be letting GridGuide do the driving, and they lurched into position as a blockade. Tucker wove between them for a time, but then there was a solid block of cars in front of him that he had no way of avoiding.

He turned sharply toward an alley. He could almost hear his car protesting being reined in. So he let it loose again and sped ahead.

He saw gunfire in the street ahead before he emerged. He didn't know who was firing, but he knew he would not be welcome. The street didn't look as crowded as the one he had left. He hoped that would hold true once he saw more of it.

He came out of the alley and saw a Yak motorcycle no more than fifteen meters away. The driver had his gun out and ready. He fired. Sparks across the hood told Tucker he was losing some of his paint. Dammit.

He had already decided to turn right before he left the alley, which happened to take him away from the cycle. Double dammit. His acceleration was good, but a lightweight motorcycle would be better, especially at slower speeds. He looked back, saw it gaining.

So he slammed on the brakes. The rider was already falling, a bullet scraped Tucker's roof, but the rest of the shots were too high. And the cyclist could not stop as fast as Tucker started. He swerved to avoid hitting Tucker's Porsche and went nearly sideways. It's possible that he might have been able to right himself after the maneuver, but Tucker wanted none of that. He moved in reverse, tapping the motorcycle enough to ensure it went down. He would have run the both driver and machine over, but at this point he couldn't risk damage to his undercarriage. He shifted forward again and sped off.

Ahead of him, dark sedans with bright flashing lights turned the corner. Behind him, two more motorcycles. Above him, there was an unearthly scream of the air ripping in two. Jekyll's air spirit must have taken a hit. He hoped Jekyll would find a safe landing spot before the spirt took too much damage. But he couldn't spare the mage more than that brief thought.

Other things he couldn't worry about: firing his gun, checking a map, watching his gauges. He could only drive. Swerve around the police cars. Spin into an intersection, planning to turn left, see dark Mafia cars coming at him, make the turn into a spin, go a full 270 degrees so that what was going to be a left becomes a right, then move forward again. Let the car run. Use the cars sent to block him as pawns of his own. Give them glancing blows, pushes, send them into spins. Anything to make pursuit difficult. Ignore traffic lights, since now they were all red anyway. Pick a direction, then keep moving to it when you can. He picked east.

Three thuds from above got his attention. Bullets, but not scraping. Thudding. Like they were fired from above. Drones. Dammit.

He swerved right. Bullets hit the pavement next to him. He checked wireless signals quickly, getting a read on what was firing at him. LEBD-2. Law enforcement drone. Unwanted. He waved at a few AROs while spinning around a corner, sending a burst of code to the LEBD-2. If he were lucky, the drone would read it as directions that made no sense, confusing it for a second. He hoped a second would be all he needed.

The drone stopped, turned left with a shudder, traveled a few halting meters. It wasn't pointed at him now. It fired harmlessly into the ground. Then it stopped, turned, and gave chase again.

There was a crowded intersection ahead of him. A fuel truck on the near right corner, pulled over clumsily. A station wagon on the left. Two motorcycles coming at him. An SUV behind. And a drone trying to get a bead on him.

There was no plan. There was only reaction. Switch left, into oncoming traffic. Accelerate. Sedan is directed by Grid-Guide to get in the way. Avoid it. Drone is closing in. A flash warns him of a target lock. His hands move frantically, alternating turns on the wheel while making commands in AROs. Two bursts hit the drone, one breaking the lock, the other sending another set of garbled directions. It works again. The drone turns clumsily. The command to fire had been given. Bullets fly. Into the tanker.

Tucker fires bullets of his own as he goes by. But tankers are not weak. The sides hold.

Fire falls from the sky. Jekyll is up there somewhere, somehow, still. The tanker hadn't been ruptured, but it had been weakened. The fire finishes the job. Flame penetrates the tank, and the whole thing goes up.

The flash and the heat stun the cyclists. Another car comes from the north. The force of the explosion sends the tanker ahead a few meters, catching the newcomer off guard. The tanker hits the car. More chaos. The Porsche is gathering all speed, hurtling through. Past. No one is ahead. Tucker lets his car loose, going up hill.

As he hits the top of the hill, his momentum gives him a brief moment of lift. Behind him, motorcycles swerve, drones fire, and the tanker burns. But the chaos is distant. Tucker's wheels lift off the ground. The only sound is the wind. He is flying clear. The chaos is past. He is at peace.

DEMOLITION DERBY

/5Fargo spun the cylinder on his Colt Frontier and then gave it a quick finger spin before dropping it snugly into the holster on his hip. The western affectation was all part of his look. You had to have a gimmick to make in the shadows of the '70s. Pink mohawks and black trench coats were a dime a dozen. But genuine cowboys were rare.

He checked his other three revolvers for show, threw the leather loop across the single brass button of his duster, and gave a mental command to fire up his mighty steed.

The Nightmare rumbled to life between his legs.

Another command, and the Universe around the corner came to life as well. He was on the way to meet Mr. Johnson and a new team. No way he was rolling up and stepping out of the van so that everyone would instantly label him as just the chauffeur. He'd have wheels nearby in case some of the new guys were too poor or too dumb to own their own ride. Only excuse for not having wheels was being an out-of-towner.

He sent another command for the Universe's autopilot software to follow him and then kicked his iron steed into gear.

"No missiles. What rigger doesn't have missiles?" Cooper asked incredulously. Fargo couldn't help but laugh a little at the fact that Cooper really believed the trids.

"You realize missiles are illegal, right? The possession of them is enough to warrant being shot on sight." Fargo was talking as he turned and didn't see the fist coming when it hit. The blow dropped him to his knees.

"How funny is that! Fuckin' hillbilly." Cooper spat the words as he loomed over Fargo's kneeling form.

"Hilarious," Fargo responded as he hoisted himself up on the tire of his Universe.

"What? You want some more?" Cooper cocked a fist back but never dropped the blow. It was his turn to not see something coming.

Fargo set the series of commands while he was on his knee, but they were a precaution. A just-in-case series of actions that would execute if, and only if, some specific event occurred.

Cooper executed the command with his raised fist. Fargo could have defused the situation with some verbal platitudes and supplicated himself to Cooper, but that wouldn't be very cowboy-like.

The doors opened first. The passenger door hit Cooper in the back and pushed him forward, off-balance. The sliding rear door slid open at the same time, the reason not apparent until the Universe lurched to life. The back end swung around to the sound of screeching tires and clipped Cooper at the knees, tumbling him back into the cab. The doors closed as the van took off. It whipped around the empty parking lot, one hard turn after another.

Everyone standing there could see Cooper being bounced around. Each time he seemed set to break free, the van would jerk and send him off balance.

"I've got different wheels if we want to get on with the job," Fargo said while rubbing his jaw and watching the van.

"No need. We all have vehicles. Shall we meet somewhere more discreet?" Killian spoke for the three other members of the team, who all apparently knew each other, "Cooper was the only one without a ride."

"He's got one now. I'll tell the Universe to bring him once he's calmed down."

"That may be awhile."

"Good thing the battery's full."

WORLD OF WHEELS

POSTED BY: WILMA

- With the positive feedback we got from putting up Armand's catalog, we decided to pull together another similar advert. We went to Armand and he directed us to his sister, Wilma, and her site, Wilma's World of Wheels. A little hello from Wilma, and then on to the World of Wheels.
- Glitch

Hoi, chummers, Wilma here of Wilma's World of Wheels. Thanks for this chance to cobble together a catalog of products every rigger should know and love. Your timing couldn't have been better, since I recently gained access to some serious paydata on the new Dodge and BMW security lines. These things are likely to revolutionize (while at the same time standardize) how corporate police and security operate in and around the shadows. The powers that be said I only have a limited number of slots for descriptions, so I'll make a full list and then narrow it down to my top-tier choices. I'll make the full file available to those who come through me to get their next set of wheels.

- Be wary, folks, Wilma can find something positive in every vehicle on the road. The file might take a week to download. And she loves pictures!
- Turbo Bunny

- Are you saying don't buy from her?
- Hard Exit

- Not at all. She's a great connection for all things vehicular. You just might want to go by her advice instead of trying to read her homage to wheels.
- Turbo Bunny

MOTORCYCLES

Not just the screeching or rumbling conveyance of go-gangers around the world, motorcycles are great for anyone who needs to get around in tight urban environments, outpace pursuit on the open road, or turn a horse trail into an escape route. Some can even be used to just get around town! Something good to point out for those who live under a rock: A lot of the sound we get from motorcycles these days is artificial because electric motors don't make noise, but bikers still want their loud toys.

- Loud pipes are protection, too. Lets the cars know we're sharing the road.
- 2XL

- That's a little bit twentieth-century, but I'll buy it for rural areas. GridGuide pretty much wipes the need for the excessive noise pollution in urban spots.
- Sounder

- First-world runner problems.
- Slamm-0!

DAIHATSU-CATERPILLAR HORSEMAN

A few years back, this radical new concept hit the market and became an overnight sensation ... for about a week. That's an exaggeration, but while the personal mobility vehicle (PMV) market never made a huge boom, they found a niche to fill. PMVs are intended for one person, and as such they are great for transporting employees between work and home. The Horseman has been one of the most successful due to its persistence. A few other models jumped on the bandwagon, but the Horseman jumped out ahead early and used that early success to lock its spot at the top of this small market. The Horseman is a three-wheeled, single-person vehicle powered by an electric motor, and it offers two modes of travel: road and walk. Road mode consists of stretching out flat like a motorcycle, with the driver lying on their back inside the little bubble-canopied pod. In this mode it's barely taller than a motorcycle and is intended to zip through traffic like one. Walk mode moves the wheels closer together and brings the driver into an upright sitting position. When set like this, the Horseman is about the height of an average ork. This mode allows it to move along pedestrian pathways, such as sidewalks and building lobbies, and it can even enter cargo elevators.

Such a small vehicle would often seem of limited use, but the Horseman has several add-on modules to expand its capabilities. These secondary vehicles plug into the rear of the PMV so as to not interfere with its ability to switch modes. The ModPods, as they're called, make the Horseman unwieldy, but it's not the most maneuverable to start. The ModPods include a passenger module that allows one additional passenger, a cargo module that allows extra space for gear and goodies that has about the same volume as a large trunk of a car, an advanced cargo module that has a pair of mechanical arms so the driver can interact with the outside world without leaving the vehicle, a drone module that comes with a small drone rack, and a security module that offers a pop-up turret to chase off would-be attackers.

Riggers dig this vehicle for two big reasons. First off, they're inconspicuous. They don't look at all hostile and are usually associated with corporate wageslaves too scared to step foot in the real world. In the dangerous world we live in, wageslaves have chosen, or been forced by their corporate masters, to travel between their homes and workplaces in a Horseman. To further protect them, the canopies are almost always mirrored to hide whoever is inside—or occasionally *what* is inside, as some corps use these on autopilot to transport goods. Riggers like this because they can roll around in their Horseman looking like your average corporate Joe and run their drone network with less interference. Reason number two is the ability to stick someone or something inside and roll it around, into, or through places without too many second glances.

HORSEMAN (GROUNDCRAFT)									
HANDL	SPEED	ACCEL	BODY	ARM	PILOT	SENS	SEATS	AVAIL	COST
3/1	3	2	4	3	2	2	1	—	12,000¥
Standard Equipment	Enviroseal								
Notes	Pods decrease Handling to 2/1, Speed to 2, Accel to 1; Passenger increase Seats to 2 (6,000¥), Cargo (3,000¥), Advanced Cargo (5,000¥), Drone (4,000¥); Security adds a standard weapon mount (5,500¥)								

ARES-SEGWAY TERRIER

The Terrier is an interesting twist on an old design. It's basically two wheels, a place to stand, and a backrest. It's awkward to drive when you first get on because leaning back makes you feel like you're going to tip over, but once you've got the hang of it, these things are quite fun. The Terrier has no manual controls. Its predecessor, the PT2060, was the last model to still have a control bar in front rather than the backrest. Now it's completely controlled via AR using either the onboard system with control glove and glasses or a datajack.

Riggers, as well as hackers and mages, have been known to use the Terrier to haul them around with their teams when they go shifting their consciousness to other realities, because the gyro-stabilization system keeps the vehicle upright, and the pilot program is decent. With a little modification (i.e., a better sensor package), the Terrier also makes a decent and inconspicuous sensor platform for scoping out areas while looking like an upgraded pedestrian.

- The Terrier is also pretty handy for rolling gunfights once you tweak the motor. It's far more stable than running but just as fast. Run it direct and you're almost as agile too.
- Sticks

TERRIER (GROUNDCRAFT)									
HANDL	SPEED	ACCEL	BODY	ARM	PILOT	SENS	SEATS	AVAIL	COST
5/2	2	1	2	2	2	2	1	—	4,500¥
Standard Equipment	—								

HORIZON-DOBLE REVOLUTION

One of the great things about Horizon getting into the vehicle-building field is the crazy drek they come up with because function just isn't enough. They need form in spades, and that's what the Revolution offers. The Revolution is an enclosed monocycle that puts the driver inside the wheel. They rely totally on AR to see the road because physical view is blocked by the wheel, which is a giant smart tire ring around the rider. It comes with two rider options, Racer and Lounge. Racer seats the rider like a motorcycle, leaning forward, while Lounge has the rider lying back. The Lounge option offers a secondary bit of safety in the form of an optional canopy and seat belt system.

This unique design is not where the rigger love comes from on the Revolution—that's the accessories. As mentioned above, the Lounge seat can have a canopy (though as a note, so can the Racer), but it's not as comfortable, and that canopy is the first of the rigger-friendly upgrades because it closes off the rigger from the outside world and lets her operate the Revolution, or anything else running through her RCC, in full VR while protected from the elements, like raining lead. Optional sidecars are also available that allow for weapons, passengers, additional storage, or small drones. Thanks to the design, a sidecar can be added to each side of the vehicle. That's actually the manufacturer's recommendation, though that might just be to sell more sidecars.

- As one would expect with something so strange-looking, this has been a huge hit with go-gangs, especially thrill gangs that often use the smart tire to drive over other people's vehicles rather than around.
- Stone

- I know a street sam who got a canopy on his racer and then cut slits facing forward and mounted a pair of SMGs. They don't have the ammo capacity of a full mount, but they work for him.
- Sticks

- Beware the canopy and sidecars for maneuverability. They cut the Revolution's ability to lean on turns. And make sure you get two. The balance helps keep the monobike stable and still able to perform all of its cool tricks.
- Sounder

- Surprised Wilma didn't mention the best trick this thing has, the instant 360. The smart tire design allows the Revolution to turn in place. Skilled riders can make the same move going forward at full speed. Traction is usually an issue but the wheel stays spinning and catches pretty quick to send you right back the way you came. Don't try this in half-measures, though. The 180 lays you flat on your side.
- Turbo Bunny

- The 180 is a great trick for going under things, especially since the gyro-stabilization and smart tire can right you on the other side.
- Thorn

REVOLUTION (GROUNDCRAFT)

HANDL	SPEED	ACCEL	BODY	ARM	PILOT	SENS	SEATS	AVAIL	COST
5/3	4	3	6	6	2	2	1	4	8,000¥
Standard Equipment	—								

EVO FALCON-EX

Whenever I see the Falcon, I think it was created by someone who loves snowmobiles but has an issue with skis. The Falcon-EX is a specialized off-road motorcycle intended for the most extreme environments. In place of wheels, the Falcon has a thick, flexible rubber tread that runs the entire length of the vehicle. This tread has a small air compartment inside for a little smoother ride and better traction, but for all intents and purposes it is a tankcycle. The Falcon-EX is the evolution of the Falcon. The original cycle was multi-fuel, but this one is pure electric and offers a fold-out solar panel for recharge on those trips that take you beyond its 800-kilometer range. Yes, 800! The battery is constantly being recharged by static created by the rubber tread. It's an off-road master that can handle anything from snow to sand.

- That "800 kilometer" figure is advertising junk. It's not a lie, but the 800 number comes from operating in the desert where the dry air allows for lots of static. A wet tread from snow or a humid environment cuts the operating distance in half.
- Turbo Bunny

- That's still 400 klicks. I'll accept that for a tankcycle!
- Picador

FALCON-EX (GROUNDCRAFT)

HANDL	SPEED	ACCEL	BODY	ARM	PILOT	SENS	SEATS	AVAIL	COST
3/5	2/3	1/2	7	9	1	1	2	—	10,000¥
Standard Equipment	Tracked Vehicle								

ENTERTAINMENT SYSTEMS CYCLOPS

AR plus gyro stabilization equals no limits on how to design a motorcycle, and in this case we have another monocycle. This one has the wheel under the rider rather than around her, but it is still strange. The rider sits astride a single wheel with the balance aid of the gyro system. Once mass-market production of these became feasible and hipsters latched onto them, it didn't take long for consumers to start snatching them up. The Cyclops was a sporty alternative to the Papoose, and you weren't riding around on something that was named for a baby carrier. It's small enough to be stored easily after the commute, and its electric drive even lets it run indoors for those too lazy to walk to their cubicle. This is not a combat vehicle, but it's small enough to hide between some trashcans, and quick and maneuverable enough to make it handy in a getaway. The presence of the gyro system and a little added rigger kit can also make the Cyclops into an interesting little dronecycle.

- While these things aren't scary, security forces are using them more and more for urban patrols and perimeter security on larger compounds to increase response time. AR or DNI control allows the riders to sit up and shoot, meaning they aren't limited to a pistol or small SMG. They can fire that FN-HAR they've got strapped across their back if need be.
- Sticks

CYCLOPS (GROUNDCRAFT)

HANDL	SPEED	ACCEL	BODY	ARM	PILOT	SENS	SEATS	AVAIL	COST
4/4	4	2	4	4	1	1	1	—	6,500¥
Standard Equipment	Assembly Time Improvement								

YAMAHA KABURAYA

ECHO MOTORS ZIP

The Evo, or should I say Echo Motors, Zip is the most popular personal scooter on five of the seven continents. Designed as part of the Echo Motors meta-friendly line of vehicles, the Zip has an interchangeable component design that keeps costs more manageable. That cost savings is passed on to the metahuman consumer. The Zip has variable seat, pedal plate, and handlebar components for dwarfs, elves, orks, and even trolls!

ZIP (GROUNDCRAFT)									
HANDL	SPEED	ACCEL	BODY	ARM	PILOT	SENS	SEATS	AVAIL	COST
3/2	3	1	6	4	1	2	1	—	3,500¥
Standard Equipment	Metahuman adjustment								

YAMAHA KABURAYA

Yamaha's latest racing bike, the Kaburaya is as sleek and loud as the arrow it's named for. This demon of a bike has more weight in its ultra-lightweight motor than the entire rest of the bike. The low profile and single front fork make this one of the most easy to identify bikes on the streets of '77. Did I also mention that it makes it the fastest? Not since the olden days of internal combustion and the legendary Hayabusa have speeds like this been reached on two wheels.

KABURAYA (GROUNDCRAFT)									
HANDL	SPEED	ACCEL	BODY	ARM	PILOT	SENS	SEATS	AVAIL	COST
5/3	6	3	5	4	1	2	1	—	17,000¥
Standard Equipment	—								

BUELL SPARTAN

This off-road bike offers the kind of power and speed you expect from Buell, delivered to a custom tire and suspension designed for a variety of off-road environments. Even non-gearheads know the Spartan thanks to Vale Runs-as-Deer, the excessively handsome scout for Ares on Desert Wars. He's all over the ads for this bike, Desert Wars, Ares Arms, and the new Predator V. "He

HARLEY-DAVIDSON NIGHTMARE

was born to run as a deer, but now he can hunt like a wolf. Predator V(ale)!" has been on everyone's lips for its flashy flying-through-the-air combat antics and the butchering of the V meaing five into V standing for Vale. Gearheads know the Spartan for its simple design and built-in toolkit, which makes it easier to fix in the field.

SPARTAN (GROUNDCRAFT)									
HANDL	SPEED	ACCEL	BODY	ARM	PILOT	SENS	SEATS	AVAIL	COST
3/4	4	2	7	6	2	2	1	—	11,500¥
Standard Equipment	Off-road suspension								

HARLEY-DAVIDSON NIGHTMARE

Harley isn't likely to give up on their Scorpion line any time in the near future, but if it does, it will be because it was replaced with this beauty. This year's Nightmare is aesthetically similar to last years inaugural design. Rider feedback has led to a few comfort and handling improvements, as well as a whole new AR and security suite available for this sophomore model. Riggers will love the built-in gyro stabilization (marketed for easy parking!), ample storage, extended range, and that aforementioned AR suite. The designers also seem to

have made the bike built for a control rig. Installation of the aftermarket systems on this bike is a breeze.

NIGHTMARE (GROUNDCRAFT)									
HANDL	SPEED	ACCEL	BODY	ARM	PILOT	SENS	SEATS	AVAIL	COST
4/3	5	2	8	8	2	3	2	—	22,000¥
Standard Equipment	—								

YAMAHA NODACHI

While the Rapier still finds occasional use in combat biker arenas, the Yamaha Nodachi is fast becoming the most common bike on the circuit. Corporate brand loyalty is about the only thing that prevents it from being used by just about every player. The Nodachi is a beast of a bike that can plow through a fully armored troll like they were rice paper. Designed with arms and armor integration in mind, the Nodachi reminds car buffs of the early Hummer H1, a combat vehicle made street-legal—barely. Though Yamaha still claims the bike was designed for the street and retrofitted for combat biker, no one buys it. This beast makes my list because it's easier to find one with a control rig than without, the weapon mounts require about six minutes for a bar-

YAMAHA NODACHI

rens-raised troll to install, and it always looks lethal so it rarely draws any more attention than regular bikes.

- This thing has a 360-degree AR field, and Yamaha is developing a *Miracle Shooter*–like game for motorcycles. This bike will likely dominate others and may draw more buyers for the game bonus.
- Slamm-0!

- Those rear cargo boxes seem the perfect size for a mounted SMG to pop out of. Oh wait, they are, since that's what's in them on the combat biker circuit.
- Sounder

NODACHI (GROUNDCRAFT)									
HANDL	SPEED	ACCEL	BODY	ARM	PILOT	SENS	SEATS	AVAIL	COST
4/3	5	2	8	9	2	2	2	12R	28,000¥
Standard Equipment	—								

THUNDERCLOUD MUSTANG

Based on the designs of Thundercloud's cross-country bike, the Pinto, the Mustang is the mixed terrain monster the Pinto should have been. While the Pinto was lauded as capable of traversing nearly any terrain, including water, whenever it hit pavement you realized that those big balloon tires may float on water and get traction like glue, but they also howl like a barghest. To combat this issue, the original off-road tires were replaced with smart tires that widen for traction off-road and narrow for speed on pavement. To keep the Mustang capable of the same limited aquatic operations as the Pinto, Thundercloud hollowed out the rims and frame for buoyancy and added inflatable pontoons that come out from under the frame. All the tech and goodies make this a great workstation for riggers off the grid.

Exports of the Mustang have increased in recent years to replace aging Pintos and increase Thundercloud brand recognition beyond the Contrail and its bad-boy go-gang image. The Pueblo Corporate Council is working with Horizon to get better branding for Thundercloud with some wild Doble versions of the Mustang that will soon come out and get splattered all over the media.

- The Mustang is watertight as well. You can sink it under some water and then remotely activate the pontoons to bring it up.
- Sounder

- Just in case some folks aren't very bright: Remember the water trick only works if you can get a signal through. Water sucks for that. So don't sink it in deep water or where there are currents—you might lose it.
- Turbo Bunny

MUSTANG (GROUNDCRAFT)									
HANDL	SPEED	ACCEL	BODY	ARM	PILOT	SENS	SEATS	AVAIL	COST
4/4	3	2	8	6	1	1	2	3	11,000¥
Standard Equipment	Amphibious Operation								

CARS

The cars of 2077 are a strange lot. The days of "a car in every garage" are long over. Corporate enclaves don't need them, big cities have been pushing them out for over a century, and suburban living is a thing of the past in most sprawls. But that does not keep them from remaining popular symbols of independence and freedom, even if they are only used as a capsule to transport you to the corporate office via GridGuide. Riggers know this and use it to their advantage.

RENAULT-FIAT FUNONE

This tiny two-seater is like a little box on wheels. What makes it so special is the easily adjusted interior. The FunOne has three steering wheel inputs—left, right, and center—for differing countries and differing sizes of drivers. The seats slide forward and back on a rail system and are designed to be completely removable so the cabin can accommodate whatever is necessary. Trolls require a specially designed center seat, but the massive scissor doors open up with plenty of space to climb in and out. Even the rear door opens wide. All this versatility makes this car a dream for the rigger in need of a subcompact.

- Even orks will find a center-set regular seat more comfortable. This setup also allows you to keep your rifle handy.
- Bull

- This thing isn't a speed demon, but it can be a decent tank. Get the model with the sunroof, upgrade the sensor package, then buy about forty sandbags. Build a bunker inside where you can drive from and pop out the sunroof with whatever weapon you have handy.
- Slamm-0!

FUNONE (GROUNDCRAFT)									
HANDL	SPEED	ACCEL	BODY	ARM	PILOT	SENS	SEATS	AVAIL	COST
3/1	3	1	6	4	2	1	2/1	—	8,500¥
Standard Equipment	Metahuman adjustment								

DODGE XENON

The Xenon is a head-turner. As a compact car, it hovers in the world between the ultra-cheap and environmentally friendly subcompact and the family-friendly sedan. This is the car of late teen and twenty-something corporate brats who have decided to strike out on their own. And in that lies the rigger appeal. The Xenon is the leading member of a small class of cars one will frequently see drive out of one megacorporation's property and right into the extraterritorial net of another. The Xenon is also known for its abundant trunk space and vibrant color options.

- The Xenon is great for getting someone to notice the car and not the driver.
- Sounder

- The car has a robust electrical system thanks to the audio system options available. The same wiring that makes the bass go boom, boom, boom, boom can also make the weapon mount go thump, thump, thump.
- Turbo Bunny

- The power system is also good enough to set a charge station for a drone that can pop out and make an easy corpkid snatch a lot more interesting. You get a really good understanding of just how big that trunk is when a Doberman pops out.
- Stone

XENON (GROUNDCRAFT)									
HANDL	SPEED	ACCEL	BODY	ARM	PILOT	SENS	SEATS	AVAIL	COST
3/2	4/3	2	8	6	2	2	4	—	18,000¥
Standard Equipment	—								

ECHO MOTORS METAWAY

Built for the bigger man! This is another one of Evo's new line that looks to be very meta-friendly and not at all bottom-line friendly. This troll-modified compact sports car was designed and built around the average frame of a troll. Great for those troll riggers out there, but I'm not about the single purpose, I'm more about multipurpose or repurpose. The basic design and reputation trades space for comfort but gains an intimidation factor of 10. This is the car that every go-gang will recognize and avoid (exceptions exist for metahatred gangs or nutjobs like the Halloweeners). Roll a quartet of these up to a meet with blacked-out windows, and

ECHO MOTORS METAWAY

thoughts of a double-cross tend to fade. Also, instead of the space for a comfortable troll, a sly rigger can load it with a drone or a smaller metahuman and all their running gear.

⦿ Wilma's got good insight, but she lives in the world of sales, not shadows. This is a small vehicle, literally not much larger than the trolls it is designed for, and for a car, that's small. It doesn't look threatening, and a troll-shaped charge of C-12 makes a big boom. Add in the fact that Echo/Evo has made an enviroseal system standard because trolls rarely live in pleasant places, and, well, let's just say TerraFirst! has bought plenty of these.
⦿ Ecotope

METAWAY (GROUNDCRAFT)									
HANDL	SPEED	ACCEL	BODY	ARM	PILOT	SENS	SEATS	AVAIL	COST
4/2	4	1	10	4	1	2	1	—	24,000¥
Standard Equipment	Metahuman adjustment								

GMC 442 CHAMELEON

The world of tuner cars is a subculture all its own, and creating a popular car isn't about making something to fit the part, it's making something that inspires enhancement. When the GMC 442 hit the market, it was never advertised as something special. It was the first of several brilliant moves that lead to the development of the Chameleon, a stripped-down 442 with a remarkably large array of aftermarket parts—parts that were all made by subsidiaries under the same megacorporate umbrella. For riggers, it's cheap and can be tweaked for any niche or set up as cheap transport for those runners who never seem to have their own wheels.

⦿ Gangs find this car popular. Especially to steal. A few switched-out parts, and it's a whole new ride.
⦿ Sticks

CHAMELEON (GROUNDCRAFT)									
HANDL	SPEED	ACCEL	BODY	ARM	PILOT	SENS	SEATS	AVAIL	COST
4/2	4	1	10	4	1	1	4	—	14,000¥
Standard Equipment	—								

MERCURY COMET

MERCURY COMET

The 2077 model marks the return of the Comet, a sedan for every occasion. Ford/Ares is marketing this as the average car with unlimited potential. This isn't like the Chameleon or the Shin-Hyang with aftermarket tuning—the Comet has been designed with interchangeable body panels to make this a car for everyone. Styles and colors galore fit any taste. Every exterior panel on the Comet can be easily switched out, and changing all the panels takes only about a half hour. Versatility around a rather robust crash cage has put this new offering in plenty of garages.

> * The base Comet is probably the most boring, boxy car I have ever seen. The only curves this car starts with are on the windshield.
> * Slamm-0!

> * The bare box look is really popular, though. The basic metallic paneled box is popping up all over. The price is such a draw.
> * Sounder

> * Surprised Wilma didn't mention the ease of concealing armor in the different panels. The panels are all so lightweight to start and a thin layer of armor polymer goes a long way. The panels and this little trick even let you armor up different sections. Trunk, who needs it; doors, PILE IT ON; hood, depends on what's under there. The options are endless.
> * Turbo Bunny

COMET (GROUNDCRAFT)									
HANDL	SPEED	ACCEL	BODY	ARM	PILOT	SENS	SEATS	AVAIL	COST
4/4	3	2	11	6	2	2	4	—	20,000¥
Standard Equipment	—								

SAAB GLADIUS 998 TI

No one thought the Dynamit would ever be topped ... until the Gladius concept hit the screamsheets, and Dynamit owners started flooding into Saab dealer hosts looking to pre-order this sleek supercar. The secondary market has been flooded with used Dynamits, while the Gladius has become the new hot supercar. That last sentence defines why this car is here. Riggers are

SAAB GLADIUS 998 TI

getting secondhand Dynamits at great prices, while a new state-of-the-art supercar is out there, and every car comes rigger-ready. The Gladius is a 150,000-nuyen BTL habit on wheels.

» Wilma may seem like she drank the Saab kool-aid, but she's not exaggerating. The Gladius is made with rigging in mind, and that includes a feedback package unmatched in a street-legal machine. If you want word straight from the horsepower-junky's mouth, ask Lady Lane over in Bug City. That is, if you can catch her. She got her Gladius and has been making high-speed runs back and forth from Chicago to St. Louis. Her best runtime is about two and a quarter hours. She averaged over 200 kph!
» Sounder

» The Dynamit can get similar speeds, but the electronics suite is out of date. I'd recommend the Dynamit over the Gladius to anyone who isn't wired for it. Manual controls are more responsive in their previous model.
» Thorn

GLADIUS (GROUNDCRAFT)									
HANDL	SPEED	ACCEL	BODY	ARM	PILOT	SENS	SEATS	AVAIL	COST
7/3	9	4	10	5	3	5	2	14	154,000¥
Standard Equipment	Rigger adaptation								

DYNAMIT (GROUNDCRAFT)									
HANDL	SPEED	ACCEL	BODY	ARM	PILOT	SENS	SEATS	AVAIL	COST
5/1	9	3	10	3	2	3	2	8	98,000¥
Standard Equipment	—								

GMC PHOENIX

Someone in the GMC design family has been watching too many old flatvids. The 2077 model Phoenix harkens back to the Trans Am of ninety years ago. This thick and powerful-looking American muscle car has taken design cues from past models, melded them with modern materials and technology, and created a stunning piece of functional art. This car has become the runaround

GMC PHOENIX

toy of middle-aged execs with enough clout to get off the corporate reservation and out onto the highways. It also has a low enough price tag to make it affordable to more than just execs. It's a solid sports car with a modest price tag and a lot of enhancement potential, making it popular for riggers.

- The Phoenix is doing well in NorthAm, and several Pacific and Asian corporations have been reaching out to find individuals who might be able to get some design schematics so they can create the Paskunji, Fenghuang, Firebird, or Simorgh.
- Mika

- Why not just buy one and reverse engineer it?
- /dev/grrl

- The reverse engineering process hasn't worked. While they can get a shell that looks like the Phoenix, the mechanics aren't coming apart and going back together correctly.
- Sounder

- Looks like someone at GMC knew they had a hit and designed in some security features to prevent reverse engineering. That engineer might know how to get past this as well.
- Sticks

- Arlesh Singh is listed as the head engineer on the design project.
- Bull

PHOENIX (GROUNDCRAFT)									
HANDL	SPEED	ACCEL	BODY	ARM	PILOT	SENS	SEATS	AVAIL	COST
4/2	6	3	10	6	2	3	4	—	32,000¥
Standard Equipment	—								

HYUNDAI EQUUS

This flagship of the Hyundai brand, this luxury sedan is entering its seventy-ninth consecutive model year. While that longevity is amazing, it is the fact that the external design of the car hasn't changed since the first decade of this century that makes it a rigger favorite. Materials science has changed, and while the Equus doesn't look any different, the body panels are made with modern polymers. The nice thing is the older parts still fit, so riggers can scavenge junk yards for panels to replace ones that might have been somehow damaged. The older metal panels also tend to take a beating better, and they can be repaired. Rust is an issue for some, but most of the pre-'29 Crash models were made from a non-rusting alloy.

- ◉ Parts from those models can make you some money, but they're hard to find. Add in that all of these cars have looked alike for almost eight decades and it's a big haystack to sift through.
- ◉ Sounder

- ◉ Funny thing is, you won't find a Hyundai logo anywhere but the owners manual. They have an EQUUS tag on the rear and a special hood ornament, but no company name. Early on it was a branding thing to avoid having their lower-end models erode the Equus' reputation, but it stuck and is now just one of the quirks of the car.
- ◉ Turbo Bunny

EQUUS (GROUNDCRAFT)									
HANDL	SPEED	ACCEL	BODY	ARM	PILOT	SENS	SEATS	AVAIL	COST
3/3	4/3	2	12	10	2	3	4	—	40,000¥
Standard Equipment	Amenities (low)								

CHEVROLET LONGBOARD

A blast from the past, this wagon-style car has the look of the '70s—the 1970s—down pat. Wood-paneled sides are standard for the classic wagon sedan. I liked the line from the ads, so I added it. This car really does look like something out of an old flatvid, but it's made with all the modern amenities. Sold for young suburban families who want the space to fit everything but don't like the feel of driving a big van or SUV, this thing is repurposed quite often by riggers who want something with a little extra room but not the hassles of a bigger vehicle. The retro design isn't just on the outside, either. The Longboard features two forward-facing bench seats that both fold down and an open cargo area with a flip up rear facing seat. With all the seats folded down, the inside is big enough to sleep a troll, and VR operation systems are standard like most modern vehicles, so it can still be driven with the seats down.

- ◉ Nice to not mention the other reason riggers end up with these to retrofit. The purchase of a Longboard is like a signal to your employer you have too many kids and too much money if you're an average wageslave. These things get sold off to secondhand dealers all the time when wageslaves get shipped to the local arcology or corp town.
- ◉ Icarus

LONGBOARD (GROUNDCRAFT)									
HANDL	SPEED	ACCEL	BODY	ARM	PILOT	SENS	SEATS	AVAIL	COST
4/3	3	2	12	6	1	2	6	—	31,000¥
Standard Equipment	—								

ROLLS-ROYCE PHAETON

The Rolls-Royce Phaeton was once the premier limousine, but years of competitors copying their style and Rolls-Royce refusing to change made the Phaeton nothing more than another long car like all the rest. When the line ended in '69, many thought they were done, collapsed from being stubborn. Their revelation of a new model for this year will change all that. That is, if Rolls-Royce can keep their new tech in house long enough to get their initial run out the door before their competitors steal their ideas and undercut them again. As a new model, in fact one that hasn't even hit the streets, you have to be wondering how it made a list of rigger's favorites. It's because of the rumors. The new tech in the Phaeton is a SOTA rigger interface that allows a fully jumped-in rigger to slide between the Phaeton and other drones connected to its PAN.

- ◉ If the tech's as good as it sounds, the first Phaetons on the street are going to be extraction targets. People out there are going to want access to what's under the hood.
- ◉ Sounder

- ◉ The entire first run is already sold. They must have something.
- ◉ Thorn

PHAETON (GROUNDCRAFT)									
HANDL	SPEED	ACCEL	BODY	ARM	PILOT	SENS	SEATS	AVAIL	COST
5/3	5/3	2	16	12	3	4	2/8	18	350,000¥
Std. Equipment	Amenities (luxury), anti-theft 2, concealed armor 3, rigger adaptation								

THUNDERCLOUD MORGAN

The PCC has lots of good reasons to keep producing off-road vehicles from Thundercloud. In the case of this auto, one of those reasons is not to make riggers happy. The Morgan is intended for operations in the rugged wilderness that fills much of the PCC. From border patrol operations to chasing off Juggernauts, the Morgan does it all. But it also does all of that without any modern conveniences that a rigger can take advantage of. It's here because this is a vehicle riggers hate to run across—unless they need parts for their own off-roader.

The Morgan is a four-wheel all-terrain vehicle with all manual controls. It's an amazing off-road vehicle that can outrun or run down just about anything on the dirt. If it can't run them down, it also has a second option. The Morgan carries two people: a driver and a gunner. The

ROLLS-ROYCE PHAETON

gunner stands up behind the driver to use the mounted weapon, usually a machine gun of some form.

MORGAN (GROUNDCRAFT)									
HANDL	SPEED	ACCEL	BODY	ARM	PILOT	SENS	SEATS	AVAIL	COST
3/5	4	3	14	6	—	—	2	8	7,500¥
Standard Equipment	Off-Road Suspension, Weapon Mount (external, flexible, manual), Manual Operation								

TATA HOTSPUR

Knowing this was up next is why I said the Morgan can outrun "just about anything on the dirt." Even on the worst terrain, the Hotspur will leave the Morgan in its dust. Hell, the Hotspur can run off-road faster than most cars run on it. It was designed and developed for off-road racing and has evolved to handle the worst conditions the Awakened world can toss its way. Running on wheels with heavy-duty shocks on independent sponsons that allow over a meter of travel, the Hotspur has little reason to slow over any type of terrain.

Unlike the Morgan, the Hotspur is built with riggers in mind, including an option for a built-in rigger cocoon. The navigator still has a normal seat, but the rigger op-

erates the truck from the safety of his own little life pod. Due to the dangers of the Awakened deserts that the Hotspur usually races across, the vehicle is sometimes equipped with weapon mounts. The trucks are usually fitted with a safety system to prevent using the weapons on each other.

- ◎ That's what the non-mounted rifle is for.
- ◎ Stone

- ◎ Actually, the Hotspur is the main design for the off-road version of FX racing. FX is Formula 1 with weapons. FX Truck Wars is gaining popularity, but it's a brutal game. Last season they lost as many trucks to paracritters as they did to each other.
- ◎ Slamm-0!

HOTSPUR (GROUNDCRAFT)									
HANDL	SPEED	ACCEL	BODY	ARM	PILOT	SENS	SEATS	AVAIL	COST
4/5	6	3	16	12	2	2	2	8	60,000¥
Standard Equipment	Off-Road Suspension								

GMC ARMADILLO

Just your everyday average pickup, except that this one comes with an easy-to-swap rear end. You can have a traditional cargo bed in the morning to help haul some dirt for a local gardening project and then swap it out for a sleeper with a few quick latch pops or the flip of a virtual switch. The Armadillo isn't intended as a commuter and comes standard with solid off-road suspension and tires. The interchangeable beds are great for riggers who want to use this as a variable support vehicle. A sleeper command cabin, a workshop, a drone rack, armory, food truck, rigger cocoon, etc.—you name it, the back of the Armadillo can have a bed for it.

- Riggers, watch how you purchase these. Too many picked up on the same SIN is gonna get some attention.
- Fianchetto

- I know a coyote in Denver that uses these to make border hops. A few are painted the same, and she runs them back and forth, filled and empty boxes.
- Turbo Bunny

- Third-world corp sec love these things. Quick and easy switchouts for the back end, and they armor the frag out of the cab.
- Picador

- Some do the same for the rear for personnel transport. I even saw one that came in hot, dropped a big armored box, and let it roll right off the back. Locals lit the box up with everything they had, and when their mags ran dry the box popped open and out came the assault team, guns blazing.
- Balladeer

ARMADILLO (GROUNDCRAFT)									
HANDL	SPEED	ACCEL	BODY	ARM	PILOT	SENS	SEATS	AVAIL	COST
3/4	4	2	13	10	1	2	2/4	—	22,000¥
Standard Equipment	Armory, cargo pod, drone rack, rigger cocoon, off-road transportation, sleeper command cabin, transport, workshop								

FORD PERCHERON

Big trucks for big jobs. The Percheron is designed to haul just about anything with the right setup. It's built for hard work, and that's why riggers love it. Ford built it with power and hauling in mind, and they made sure to install a little extra dogbrain power in these beasts in case of emergency. Smart riggers have found that this means the Percheron can handle tricky situations better than any of its competitors when left to its own devices. The extra-large cab on this truck not only allows for more passengers but also can double as a sleeping space for those long hauls, or that time out in the wilderness waiting for a pickup, if you know what I mean.

- Speaking of tricky situations, Ford is having a slitch of a time trying to use their upgraded dogbrain software in anything but the Percheron. The software isn't taking with any of their other vehicles, and the results have been nothing short of disastrous. I'd guess shadow ops were involved, but I don't have anything solid to back that up.
- Sounder

- The sleeper space is great if you're a dwarf or an average human, but orks and elves can't stretch out and trolls will feel like they're back in the womb it's so tight.
- 2XL

PERCHERON (GROUNDCRAFT)									
HANDL	SPEED	ACCEL	BODY	ARM	PILOT	SENS	SEATS	AVAIL	COST
3/3	3	2	15	6	4	3	6	—	39,000¥
Standard Equipment	—								

JEEP TRAILBLAZER

For decades, the word "Jeep" conjured a specific image in the minds of the masses. When that name was uttered, images of exposed roll bars, four wheeling, soft-top-down cruising in the sun, doors off and foot on the empty hinges, or even associations from the olden days of the military before the humvee, jilter, or empuv would drift in. This is the great, great, great, grandchild of that image, and it makes you question whether cloning was involved. This is the descendant of the model known as the Wrangler, and the Trailblazer name is emblazoned on every one of the iconic Jeep vehicles. It still offers serious off-road capability (with the right package), while keeping in mind that most buyers will never turn off the GridGuide. The great thing about the Trailblazer is that they kept that versatility in mind, and riggers with a gearhead mentality will love the fact that this ride can be stripped down to bare bones and accessorized to the point where no one will know it isn't some custom ride unless they find a Trailblazer RFID tag you missed.

- Even after more than a century of production, the one totally unique feature of this model is the ability for the windshield to lie down against the hood. Custom kits even offer options for splitting the flat windshield and being able to lay down either part of it.
- Picador

- Versions of this vehicle can be found in all countries of the world. It's popular anywhere the roads aren't paved and even more so in places where tourists needed something familiar to convince them to take the back

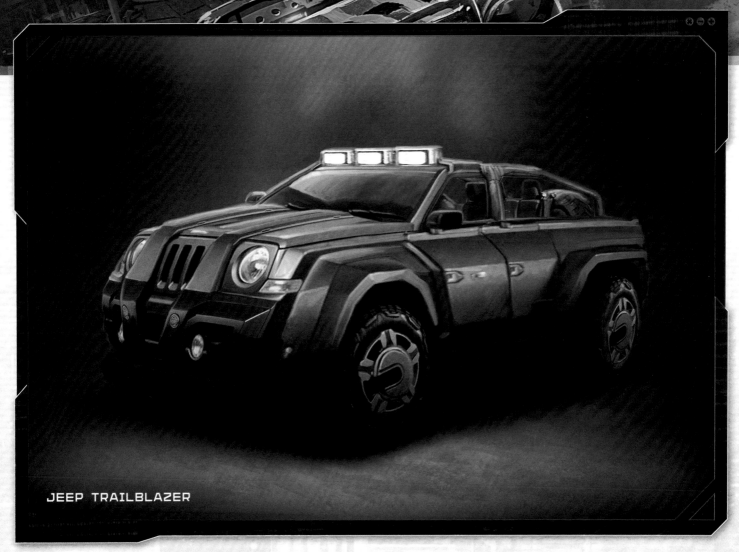
JEEP TRAILBLAZER

roads. The durability of this line shows in the number of countries that still have operational models after decades of use, with some vehicles in African and South American countries approaching the century-old mark.

> ● Traveler Jones

TRAILBLAZER (GROUNDCRAFT)									
HANDL	SPEED	ACCEL	BODY	ARM	PILOT	SENS	SEATS	AVAIL	COST
3/4	3	2	12	6	1	2	4	—	32,000¥
Standard Equipment	Multifuel engine, off-road suspension								

TOYOTA TALON

The Talon is an inexpensive and rather boring little SUV. The designers' image of sharp styling was pretty much standard fare for SUVs, but this is what makes it ideal for riggers and wheelmen. It's boring and blends in with a crowd of other vehicles. It's a little bigger than most sedans, but with a low-slung roof to look very sedan-like. Smaller than the big SUVs, it is still thick-bodied and has enough similar features to other craft in the market that it can be mistaken for them. The taillights match up well with the Ford Tauren; the front quarter panels are like smaller versions of the Jeep Charon; the headlights could be a Dodge; the rear window and trunk a Eurocar.

Underneath is a generally underpowered motor system that makes Talons that have been "sharpened," as their tuners say, true sleepers. They look mundane but have the heart of a racecar hidden beneath. The problem is that the back-end work tends to be a little pricier, since not many people want to tune their Talon. Skilled mechanics are a necessity, and the best work is done with a rigger jumped in and giving feedback on the changes and feel as they're made. Work on a Talon feels almost more like surgery than tuning, with the patient telling you when the implant feels just right.

> ● This process leads to something very interesting: custom rigger adaptations. The rigging module and feedback sensors in the car are for one specific rigger, and when another climbs in it almost feels like putting on skin that doesn't quite fit right.
> ● Turbo Bunny

> ● I'm now picturing Turbo Bunny trying on different skins. It's very creepy but in a rather amusing way.
> ● Slamm-0!

- Some people add a lot of aftermarket chrome and glitz to their Talons to make them stand out. These ones are usually not tuned up, but sometimes they like to pretend. This can also be a great look for a Talon to use to suddenly stick out if you have a properly prepared mage around.
- Sounder

- Ah yes, the old hide-by-being-the-most-obnoxious-thing-around-so-no-one-thinks-it-could-possibly-be-you trick. A classic.
- Winterhawk

TALON (GROUNDCRAFT)									
HANDL	SPEED	ACCEL	BODY	ARM	PILOT	SENS	SEATS	AVAIL	COST
4/3	4	2	12	6	2	2	5	—	30,000¥
Standard Equipment	—								

NISSAN HAULER

While the SUV may have started as a way to haul a little extra cargo, it didn't stay that way for long. Most people think of SUVs as family (albeit *rich* family) vehicles or protective transport for executives. The cargo SUV is rarer in this day and age, but it does a nice job of fitting right in between the too-big-for-a car and too-small-for-a-van slot, and keeping this niche of the hauling market well filled is the Nissan Hauler.

- Nissan keeps their market niche well filled by using runners to sabotage other companies' designs and factories. It seems a bit outlandish, but the market isn't very big, so as long as they keep producing and cut any competition off at the knees, the Hauler is *the* hauler.
- Turbo Bunny

The Hauler is relatively boxy and not exactly a stylish design, but it was never intended to be. It's a utilitarian vehicle used for mostly utilitarian purposes. Want to impersonate a flower delivery company? Don't use a panel van, use the Hauler. Because they do, and people are far less suspicious of the SUV that has been parked on the corner for a while than the van. Vans scream three things to the subconscious of the average wageslave: pedophile, shadowrunner, or corporate hit team about to fire them. Blame it on the media. The Hauler helps you blend in a little better and keeps you off the local wageslave's radar.

- Using it as a team transport is rough but doable. The seating is really designed for just two, but there are fold-up "seats" from the rear door that double as tables for package staging, and the rest of the rear is just open. Fun to roll around in if you're a kid; tough to find a comfortable spot in if you're a grown-up runner in your work kit.
- 2XL

- These are relatively easy to find with a good pilot program and are even adapted for riggers. So many companies use them in automated fleets in conjunction with other delivery drones that the setup is standard fare.
- Sounder

HAULER (GROUNDCRAFT)									
HANDL	SPEED	ACCEL	BODY	ARM	PILOT	SENS	SEATS	AVAIL	COST
3/3	4/3	1	16	8	2	2	4/4	—	30,000¥
Standard Equipment	—								

EUROCAR NORTHSTAR

What the Westwind is to the car market, the Northstar is to the field of SUVs. Referred to as a luxury sport SUV, the Northstar does not skimp on either aspect. Knowing that the largest piece of cargo that was likely to ever go inside would be a set of golf clubs, the designers laid out the interior with luxury space for four, rather than two, with a tiny rear seating area so that it could call itself a four-seater. The Northstar offers basic leather as the standard interior, with options for more exotic skins including behemoth, afanc, and basilisk for a healthy premium. Other than fancy paracritter seats, the Northstar offers a top-of-the-line electronics suite with a premium AR layout and options for installed or ancillary systems coming with the initial purchase. The basic install package is just an image link, but a full suite of eyes is a small step up.

- The Northstar is quickly becoming the power symbol for Herr Brackhaus around Europe and North America. Expensive enough to show they've got cash (or access to powerful friends with cash), and yet roomy enough for their security force.
- Traveler Jones

- Those security force members hate it. The body is made of "tissue paper," as they put it, and no matter how fast they can make it go it doesn't outrun bullets.
- Stone

- That initially purchased cyber system keeps its access to the original system even after the car is sold. It's like keeping a copy of the keys. While the Herr Brackhauses of the world may be trying to keep up a show, their ride can easily be second-hand, especially with how often these are bought by the ultra-rich to drive for a few months and then move to the newer model. Just a reminder, not all the ultra-rich are ultra-secure. Take that how you will.
- Mika

In the area of speed, the Northstar can hold its own versus everything shy of a supercar. This is all thanks to lightweight materials utilization, alongside a top-of-the-line drive system that is Eurocar's latest innovation. The next place this system is likely to end up is inside the Westwind in an even smaller and lighter frame. That is, if someone else doesn't snag the systems first and plug them into their latest ride.

This makes many riggers' wish list for obvious reasons. It's fast, spacious, luxurious, a dream to drive with some corporate executive in the back, and the kind of machine you can pull the guts from, stuff them in your American, and be outrunning the Star in no time flat. The Northstar is great for the hour or two you might be running after you snag an executive, but you need to know about it for the aftermarket value or when you might have a few minutes of driving this dream.

- There is a modified version of the Northstar that has been rolling around the Middle East. Everyone in the region is thinking S-K, since they own the Eurocar brand, but most of the vehicles have been carrying Global Sandstorm executives. I have a feeling that if some digging on the ownership of the Northstars is done, you'll find them stolen. GS is doing a little antagonizing.
- Goatfoot

- That seems like a really bad idea considering the corporate merger that Global Sandstorm was working their way into in order to gain some strength against S-K is a complete drekstorm. Proteus has gone totally turtle. AG Chemie is working the pry bar on that turtle, and FBA is looking elsewhere for a new place to build an alliance for the megacorporate audit (a.k.a., screwing the little big guys).
- Cosmo

- And giving money to runners in the process.
- Picador

NORTHSTAR (GROUNDCRAFT)									
HANDL	SPEED	ACCEL	BODY	ARM	PILOT	SENS	SEATS	AVAIL	COST
5/3	6	2	12	8	3	5	4	12	115,000¥
Standard Equipment	Amenities (middle)								

GMC ESCALADE

Big luxury at its best. That's GMC's tagline for the Escalade, their high-end luxury SUV. The adverts work, since this is the ride that all the newest trid stars and music sensations drop a little piece of their first big payday to own. Rarely do they ever actually drive it, but they certainly like to show that they can afford it. It's after this first big payday that a lot of those stars have second thoughts, and this is the ride they take to run for the hills. And thus, the ride that a lot of riggers working the shadows need to snag control of in order

to get them back where they belong. Or at least back where the runners will get some nuyen on their sticks.

- Wilma seems to be showing her true colors. Anyone got the story?
- /dev/grrl

- She's a former CAS Army rigger. That's according to her, since she's been around long enough to clear any traces of her former life from databases around the world. I've met others who claim to know her from those days, but it's hit-and-miss on the details and accuracy. What we need to know is that she's worked for every Big Ten mega as well as the majority of the world's governments and smaller megacorporations. She's a pro with a reputation for maintaining her reputation.
- Sounder

The Escalade also finds its way onto the secondary market (a.k.a. stolen) quite often. This means they're available for those of us who might not have the SIN required to make a purchase at the GMC dealership. Due to the types of people who often own them in the first place, the Escalade comes with extra baggage frequently enough for me to feel it necessary to mention here. Mob brats, wannabe gangsters, and thugs with image issues don't like having their things stolen. Most folks reading this travel in a far more dangerous crowd, but stupidity and ego can be a deadly combination when one of these disaffected punks comes to get their "ride" back.

Also, thanks to the aforementioned types who often purchase this vehicle, extra protection is a common addition. In order to keep the Escalade as luxurious as owners expect, the extra protection is well-hidden. This means you can't tell if it's been upgraded without taking it apart. While I'm sure we all trust our grey-market dealers, it's just something to look out for if you're buying from someone new.

- I've seen several Escalades that skimped on the armor for the rear end. They put the extra protection on the doors but save nuyen by leaving it out of the rear gate and side panels.
- Mihoshi Oni

- For the long guns in the crowd, get a high vantage if you're firing on one of these. Even the extra armored ones don't have it in the roof unless they have a modified top which is rare and expensive.
- Balladeer

With a rich target audience, the Escalade packs in the features even when they won't be used by most. The standard rigger adaptation is great for security companies with wired drivers, but for most casual buyers, it's something to brag to their golf buddies about. Runners like the option since this thing can dance in the hands of a rigged driver.

- While Horizon isn't known for their vehicle-manufacture or arms division, they have a subsidiary called Ride Rockers, Inc. The company specializes in custom vehicle modifications that it designs, implements, and then offers to other customers. It's a small operation, but their best-selling mod was designed for a certain ork rapper who shall remain nameless to go in his Escalade. The mod added a dozen compartments that blended right into the original interior. Six of the spots could easily fit an SMG, two were pistol sized, three seemed to have been designed for an AK-97, and the last had almost the same dimensions as the Krime Kannon. Ride Rockers even offered customized foam inserts in case you knew what you would always store in there.
- Clockwork

ESCALADE (GROUNDCRAFT)

HANDL	SPEED	ACCEL	BODY	ARM	PILOT	SENS	SEATS	AVAIL	COST
3/3	4	2	16	10	3	4	6	10	125,000¥
Standard Equipment	Amenities (high), anti-theft 2, rigger adaptation								

FORD ECONOVAN

This long passenger van may not seem like something every rigger should know about, but it's ideal for carting a shadowrunner team around, and it happens to be a very common shuttle vehicle. While most riggers tend to go with the Bulldog or Governor, the Econovan has something important that they do not: seats. As a passenger van, it has several rows of seats and can even be purchased or quickly modified to fit a troll-sized seat or two. It can fit more, but too many trolls inside reek havoc on the suspension. The point is, those inside can sit on seats, not just sprawl around the rear, making it safer and a whole lot more mundane looking.

- It's also legal. I've heard so many stories of runners who were just headed to the meet in a Bulldog when the local police force pulled them over because it scanned more than two PANs in a stepvan. Nothing like having to send your wheelman off to ditch your ride while the meet is going on because you left a dead cop behind.
- Balladeer

As a popular shuttle, the Econovan is a regular target for extractions when trying to snag a target on the move. It's also a great ride to use to sneak into somewhere that shuttles employees from off-site housing to the office. Gate security usually lets it pass right in, or out, as long as it looks legit.

As one would suspect, the Econovan comes with practically no added features, but Ford offers a list of up-grades in both comfort and security. EnviroSeal is common along with upgraded onboard systems. Variations on seating arrangement are often installed on vehicles carting executives who don't do bench seating. Ford even offers a wetbar and small fridge option. Secondary companies—usually related subsidiaries—offer custom packages that turn the van into a mini RV.

ECONOVAN (GROUNDCRAFT)

HANDL	SPEED	ACCEL	BODY	ARM	PILOT	SENS	SEATS	AVAIL	COST
3/2	4	1	14	8	2	2	10	—	30,000¥
Standard Equipment	Amenities (low)								

DODGE CARAVANER

Since I'm covering a bunch of other vans, I figured I might as well drop in my favorite minivan. The Caravaner is meant to be a family van for suburbanites. The modern world doesn't have a whole lot of the required suburbs to create suburbanites, but that doesn't keep middle income families from having one of these in the arcology garage for those times they want to drive somewhere (assuming the megacorp will let them go).

The sales volume going to pseudo-suburbanites is not enough to keep a car line afloat, so the Caravaner had to find another market as well: the cargo taxi market. The Caravaner is that boring little bean-shaped van with the ob-noxious adverts spamming the airwaves around it while it drives from place to place dropping off cargo and people. It's spacious enough for trolls, and since it's intended to haul cargo, and sometimes cargo (and trolls) can weigh a lot, it is seriously overpowered for such a small vehicle.

- Half the time you can't even see the vehicle inside its armor of AROs. All the spam made these things the frequent target of hackers early on and later models all got upgraded systems with premium firewall software.
- Bull

- They're also rumored to be high priority on GOD's monitoring system. Helps them smack the daylights out of punk hackers who should know better than to hack a spam-mobile.
- Glitch

That extra power could allow for some additional ar-moring, but no one makes armor kits for the Caravaner that are subtle. There are armored delivery versions of the Caravaner, but they don't look much like the basic model. The armored model replaces the round bubbly shape with a boxy, angular design and the ability to shrug off anything short of an anti-material rifle.

- Banks are known to use the armored Caravaner for the occasional run. We also see this thing carting for science companies, because that back box can be bought with a full EnviroSeal system.

o Ma'fan

o Great for having conversations with less-than-willing participants.
o Kane

CARAVANER (GROUNDCRAFT)									
HANDL	SPEED	ACCEL	BODY	ARM	PILOT	SENS	SEATS	AVAIL	COST
3/2	4	1	12	8	2	2	7	—	28,000¥
Standard Equipment	—								

GMC UNIVERSE

While the Bulldog is considered GMC's armored work-horse, the Universe is GMC's real all-purpose work-horse. Runners dig the Bulldog because it comes standard with some serious protection, but the Universe is far more common in the world's sprawls. Again, I bring out the Universe instead of the Bulldog because you can armor up a Universe for just a little extra nuyen, but what you gain in inconspicuousness is priceless. The Universe also offers the MultiPaint system, a relatively inexpensive way to change the vehicle's colors or advertisement patterns as a simple add-on accessory. While the companies that buy this appreciate the extra money from advertising or the chance to change up the purpose of the van quickly, we all know why runners would like it.

UNIVERSE (GROUNDCRAFT)									
HANDL	SPEED	ACCEL	BODY	ARM	PILOT	SENS	SEATS	AVAIL	COST
3/3	4/3	1	14	8	3	2	2/14	—	30,000¥
Standard Equipment	—								

ARES CHUCK WAGON

A rigger's got to eat, right? One way to have food where you need it is to make it look like you're there to serve food while you're actually spying on local corporate traffic. This mobile food-service truck, usually referred to as a food truck or, much less politely, a roach coach, provides facilities for a variety of food-related activities. Trucks come in three varieties: prepared food, unprepared food, and frozen treats. Prepared food trucks offer things like ice cream, chips, sodas, and prepackaged sandwiches. Inside they're set up with a large storage unit that can be specialized as a freezer and/or refrigerator, along with some heating element for food served warm. Unprepared food trucks offer a limited menu of items usually centered around a certain theme. Inside they have a slightly smaller cold storage area and heating element, along with a sink, sanitation facility, and prep area. Frozen treats trucks serve the standard frozen pops of every kind, with spe-

cialized ones offering scooped ice cream. The back is nothing but freezer space.

The Ares Chuck Wagon is the premier roach coach because it has windows on both sides to increase service speed. Since seating isn't a high priority, the front area includes the driver's seat and one fold-down jump seat. The Chuck Wagon is not a race truck by any means, but at least the ride is smooth and the food is plentiful. If you stock it, of course.

o My favorite surveillance vehicle. Inconspicuous, people to talk to, and plenty of food.
o 2XL

CHUCK WAGON (GROUNDCRAFT)									
HANDL	SPEED	ACCEL	BODY	ARM	PILOT	SENS	SEATS	AVAIL	COST
2/2	3	1	16	5	2	2	2	—	40,000¥
Standard Equipment	—								

HAULERS

AIRSTREAM TRAVELER LINE MOTORHOMES

(CHINOOK, PRESERVE, OUTBACK)

Airstream is a legendary name in the world of travel trailers and RVs. That legendary brand name is now wholly owned by NeoNET. While not well known for their vehicle production, they invested heavily in Airstream over the last decade in order to solidify their American connection. The primary production facility is located in Reading, Massachusetts, just outside the Boston quarantine zone, and it's been operating with limited staff since the lockdown. All of that has nothing to do with why riggers love the Traveler line, but everything to do with why runners may love Airstream in the future. NeoNET has been paying very little attention to the subsidiary since their troubles and Airstream execs are looking for a way to get back in business.

As for the Traveler line itself, the value comes in variability. Airstream produces three primary models for the Traveler line: the Chinook, the Preserve, and the Outback. While built off the same cabin frame, the accessories and amenities make all the difference to set up each model for a different market climate (literally).

The Chinook is a cold excursion model with additional insulation, heat-absorbing paint with internal heat storage technology, a quick-change propulsion system involving a tracked drive and ski system, a radar system for determining ice-thickness, and a satellite communication system.

o Chinooks are most abundant in the AMC and northern Asia. Several run with Karavan, and quite a few of the Yakut tribes have these around.
o Red Anya

The Preserve is the most common model with the fewest extraordinary features. It runs on a six-wheel bus chassis and is designed for the roads and trails of the modern world. This is truly the successor of the iconic silver bullet that roamed the highways of America. Intended for use in those corners of the world where civilization is never far, the Preserve is simply a home away from home.

> * The Preserve is mundane enough to be modified by coyotes. The storage and sleeping areas are set up to tightly pack in those who need discreet transport. It isn't comfortable, but it also isn't intended for long distance transport, just over borders.
> * Sounder

The Outback is the Chinook's hot-weather cousin. Heat storage systems are optional for areas with highly variable day and night temperatures. The Outback runs on a six-wheel system similar to the Preserve but built on a larger and more rugged suspension and wheels. Most of the time. For some of the truly treacherous places the Outback can go (not that many people take it to those places), the Outback has an eight-legged drive system capable of scaling surfaces to the point of complete inversion. A satellite uplink is standard to help overcome the connectivity issues present in the middle of nowhere, where the Outback is most often found. Airstream has a proprietary system on the latest Outback models that gathers and stores water directly from the moisture in the air—even from the arid air of the desert.

> * The Outback is rarely found in cities, but it's not unheard of. Among those standard features that Wilma didn't mention are the airlift hooks designed right into the frame. The Outback can be dropped or picked up using just those. The Chinook offers it as an added feature, but it rarely got picked up. The oversized tires are sometimes switched out for urban areas as well, but they don't need to be.
> * Turbo Bunny

CHINOOK (GROUNDCRAFT)									
HANDL	SPEED	ACCEL	BODY	ARM	PILOT	SENS	SEATS	AVAIL	COST
3/2	4/3	1	14	12	2	2	10	-	145,000¥
Standard Equipment	Amenities (squatter), extreme environment modification (cold), satellite uplink, suncell								

PRESERVE (GROUNDCRAFT)									
HANDL	SPEED	ACCEL	BODY	ARM	PILOT	SENS	SEATS	AVAIL	COST
3/3	4/4	1	16	12	2	3	10	-	134,000¥
Standard Equipment	Amenities (squatter), gridlink, satellite uplink, suncell								

OUTBACK (GROUNDCRAFT)									
HANDL	SPEED	ACCEL	BODY	ARM	PILOT	SENS	SEATS	AVAIL	COST
3/4	3/4	1	14	12	2	4	8	-	158,000¥
Standard Equipment	Amenities (squatter), Extreme environment mod (hot), off-road suspension, satellite uplink, suncell								

MACK HELLHOUND

Transporting goods across long overland routes can be dangerous, so Mack developed the Hellhound. I was going to say something about it being like a real hellhound only without flaming breath, but one of the most common close-defense systems installed on the Hellhound is flamethrowers. This road warrior would make a great post-apocalyptic war rig like the ones in *Mad Max: Furios Child* if it weren't so damn pretty. Though it's meant to deter go-gangs and road-jackers, Mack certainly didn't intend to do that with looks. The Hellhound looks like it's asking you to pet it—so that it can joyfully burn your face off.

> * No joke. Mack started with the guts of their top-of-the-line Boxer and then built a combat Mastiff on top. While protecting the haul was the goal, they wanted a pretty hauler. With doors closed and drones tucked, the Hellhound looks like a show-truck cruising the streets.
> * Turbo Bunny

The Hellhound offers a lot of options for its defensive systems with the use of Ares' track-mounted Sentinel drone series. The Sentinel system rings the top of the rig, and the drones tuck back behind the sleeper cabin when not in use. The rig can mount up to three Sentinel drones in this spot, with three sidetrack rails that are also used by the drones to move around one another or to duck back on for cover. The top ring has two forward facing rails that lead to a ring of rails around the front of the Hellhound. These rings have two Sentinel drones with protective casings that only open up when there's trouble.

> * And guess what, they're wired! They have a port on the inside of the rig to plug the RCC into directly, though many riggers either run wireless or leave the system under the command of the pilot program.
> * Sounder
>
> * Wow! Old school. I've been waiting for a rehash of the Sentinel system. I was surprised it hadn't become more popular when wireless hacking could be done from a MetaLink, but now that wireless access is back under the thumb of the megacorps, I guess they need to protect themselves from each other.
> * Slamm-0!

The Sentinel system is also used on an optional (though everyone gets it unless their trailer doesn't fit) rail kit that fits around any standard trailer. The rail kit is an like an ex-

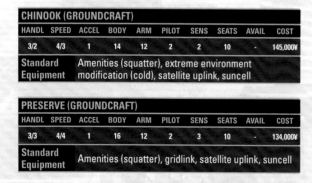

MACK HELLHOUND

ternal cage that folds up over the trailer box. It runs the top rim, bottom rim, and side edges, has four ribs that go all the way around the trailer, including across the belly, and two more rib rails that ring it long ways. The basic system has a power supply for up to four drones, but optional packages include eight, sixteen, and even twenty-four drone battery packs. The added weight of the batteries and drones pulls the range down, but SolarCell systems are available to supplement and recharge the system.

- The 24-drone model is a gunship. Karavan recently got their hands on one of these and they use it for central defense of their governmental rigs. Basically it's just a way for those in charge of Karavan to stay in charge, but the thing is a sight to behold.
- Red Anya

- I've actually seen a Hellhound chilling out at the center of a four-pack of quad Bergens. That's four Bergen mega haulers, each with four trailers. The Hellhound had nothing on the capacity of the Bergens, but its drone loadout was guaranteeing the big boys were getting where they were headed. If they got into a tussle I'm not sure anyone would be able to use the road afterwards, as the majority of the

drones were packing something that made a big boom.
- Turbo Bunny

Back to the main rig. The back of the rig not only has space for the Sentinels but also has a pair of pneumatic launchers. The launch tubes usually contain a pair of Roto-Drones but can be loaded with fifty-gallon drums filled with whatever. That latter option is usually seen in poorer places that have somehow gotten their hands on one of these but can't afford to replace the Roto-Drones that they had to shoot down getting the Hellhound in the first place. The passenger side of the Hellhound is what really tells you this is a rigger's ride. The section where another person might normally sit is replaced with a rack for Microskimmer drones. When the door is closed, it just looks like that side has a big door with no windows. Once opened, it reveals what look like garbage-can lids stacked sideways. This section launches the eight drones like skeet and is capable of launching two at a time. Because of the minimum time needed for the Microskimmers to fire up and fly, the launcher had to be higher, and this left space below for a wheeled drone that can burst from its berth even when the Hellhound is at full speed. Riggers usually launch the drone at the first sign of trouble and then tuck it under the belly of the trailer to come out as needed.

Inside the regular cab is a manual drive system set low, with a rigger cocoon set behind it where the seat can slide back into the cocoon or the rigger can climb straight in. The sleeper area is good sized and allows every standard metatype smaller than a troll to lie out comfortably, and even trolls find it roomier than most troll-sized coffin motels. A secondary rigger cocoon is part of the sleeper area, as this thing usually requires more than one rigger to handle all the drones. It's got a full Matrix hookup and wall screen run through a high-end commterminal with a road warrior theme.

Being assigned to work in this truck is the dream job of wageslave riggers around the world.

- It only seems like a dream job. Because when something happens that you get to play with all these toys, your life is at risk. Honestly, I think Mack made this rig just so they could sell them to Ares Media division for cool trid shows.
- Sticks

HELLHOUND (GROUNDCRAFT)									
HANDL	SPEED	ACCEL	BODY	ARM	PILOT	SENS	SEATS	AVAIL	COST
3/2	4/3	1	20	15	3	3	2	16R	150,000¥
Standard Equipment	Amenities (low), landing drone rack (medium), landing drone rack (micro), landing drone rack (medium), landing drone rack (small), 2 x rigger cocoon, rigger modification, special equipment (drone rail), standard drone rack (small)								

MUNICIPAL/ CONSTRUCTION

OMNI MOTORS OMNIBUS

The Omnibus is not just the local public transportation you see hauling disparate wageslaves from their bleak neighborhoods to their bleak workplaces. Omni Motors markets versions of the Omnibus for urban mass transit, high-capacity urban mass transit, long-distance mass transit, rural mass transit, personal luxury transit, cargo hauling, livestock hauling, and an off-road version of any of those with their patented Oct-O-Gone drive system.

The OOG is an eight-wheel-drive system with independent motors for each oversized wheel and a massive suspension system. The OOG is not street legal in any major metroplex, but when you have the OOG you don't need streets. Part of the OOG package is a SolarCell system to keep it charged in the wilds. Okay, that last bit is a little copy-paste from the catalog, but I liked it.

- This thing is a beast! All-wheel drive, all-wheel steering, and eight wheels with a suspension system that can climb mountains. Okay, maybe not mountains, because it also happens to be huge. A few of these OOG systems, at least the drives, have made it into Chicago. They're great for the CZ.
- Crush

- If they aren't street legal, how'd they get there?
- Netcat

- In pieces, usually. Hence, Crush mentioning the drives. Without the SolarCell systems the range isn't great, but the batteries don't take long to recharge because they're so small. Folks in the zone make do like they have for years by rigging up gas generators or other solar systems.
- Turbo Bunny

- The drive system on these things can be run through a virtual control. The system is meant for use during the box switching, but it can be driven without a box or with anything else on the frame. Some very creative folks can do a lot with this. I even know a Dreamland explorer who has two OOG systems welded together to increase the range and operate as spare parts if he needs any. He's also got extra batteries and a pair of rotating compartments built into the frames. It's quite the Frankenstein creation.
- Kane

The great thing about the Omnibus is its versatility and changeability. The drive system and box are two independent pieces, and changes can be made by a single individual in about an hour, faster if you really know what you're doing and you have a team to help out. Omni did this so mass-transit companies could quickly change out boxes during rush hour times when comfort was sacrificed for the bottom line. It was also marketed for metroplexes and countries that have urban and off-road areas butted up against one another for the OOG switch-out on the edge of civilization.

- Forget about comfort. Worry about the bottom line. How corporate! Why didn't they just leave the high-capacity ones on there all the time? Why worry about comfort at all?
- /dev/grrl

- High-capacity ones are heavier and drain the batteries quicker. It's still always about the bottom line.
- Sounder

OMNIBUS (GROUNDCRAFT)									
HANDL	SPEED	ACCEL	BODY	ARM	PILOT	SENS	SEATS	AVAIL	COST
2/2	3	1	18	10	2	2	53	12	296,000¥
Standard Equipment	Gridlink, gridlink override								

GMC COMMERCIAL G-SERIES

We've all gotten stuck behind a garbage truck or stolen one for cover. Okay, maybe not all of us have done the latter, but we at least all know how huge these beasts are compared to our tiny little urban autos. Most have wondered how many of our little cars this thing would go through before it was stopped or how awesome it would be to hide a team in the rear and infiltrate them into a facility through the garbage shaft. Yep, that was an awesome episode, though a real garbage truck would require a full-face alternate air supply breather because they are that nasty, but it wouldn't look as cool. Back to the point. The Commercial line is a base front cab with alternate carriage packages. The G-series is the garbage truck line, and it comes with a variety of loading, crushing, and capacity variations. It can have forks for grabbing dumpsters, trashcans, cars, or trolls; a funneled front-end loader for the scoop and dump; or drone docks for loader drones. The loaders are usually operated on autopilot, but they can be rigged remotely. Noise keeps riggers from getting fancy with them from home base, but up close they can be quite handy.

- She watches Run Bunnies. I think I'm in love.
- Turbo Bunny

In commercial areas, these things usually operate without a driver and just let the pilot program handle the route and pickups. In residential areas there is usually a driver to keep the image up. They don't have to do anything, but sometimes they'll get out and walk around while the drone systems are working and make it look like they're checking things out on the rig or doing some work. These events usually occur when some attractive suburbanite mom is out watering the lawn or out for a walk. The rough life of a garbageman.

- More often they are sleeping in the cab or drinking in a nearby bar and waiting for the truck to finish the route.
- Sounder

- Or banging those suburban mommies. I know a garbageman out in Snohomish who operates as a gigolo. While the truck does its thing, he does too.
- Cheshire

COMMERCIAL G-SERIES (GROUNDCRAFT)									
HANDL	SPEED	ACCEL	BODY	ARM	PILOT	SENS	SEATS	AVAIL	COST
2/2	3	1	18	12	2	3	2	14	287,000¥
Standard Equipment	Gridlink, gridlink override, maneuver autosoft (2), special equipment								

GMC COMMERCIAL D-SERIES

Next is the dump truck. D-series, G-series, get it? That's the whole line. Not very original, but they are selling a line of commercial vehicles, not trying to market to rich corporate brats. This one has the same drone options, but they are usually mini-front loaders or backhoes and the occasional anthroform. The other thing is that these have a cab, but they are rarely manually operated. The

pilot program usually handles the driving while the drones are programmed with whatever the job is. Meat people are sometimes present to make sure everything is right, but more often than not the only people around are security.

- Not only is this true, but the guys working security on these things are often remarkably good shots. Since they have no other responsibility, they spend a lot of time practicing. Sometimes they even practice on the drones. The little construction drones are hardy, and a light pistol or small-caliber rifle won't do squat to hurt it, but the bored operator gets the chance to practice on moving targets.
- Sticks

- And I thought Dozer was kidding.
- Slamm-0!

The D-series also comes with different options for the dump bed. The most common is the simple lift bed, where the front end raises and everything dumps out the back, but there are side dump models, multi dump models, spreaders that have a conveyer system linked to the drive, filler boxes that are meant to be filled and then dumped off whole, liquid dumpers, concrete mixers, and front pours that lift and dump the load in front of the cab. The D-series has three size lines; D Compact, D, and DD. The compact are comparable to everyday pickup trucks, the D is what you'd expect for basic construction, and the DD are site trucks that don't drive on the roads but aren't quite as big as the humongous things they use in mines.

- The D-Compact models are often commandeered by local militias to act as troop transports or gun trucks.
- Picador

COMMERCIAL D-COMPACT (GROUNDCRAFT)									
HANDL	SPEED	ACCEL	BODY	ARM	PILOT	SENS	SEATS	AVAIL	COST
2/2	3	1	12	8	2	2	2	12	196,000¥
Standard Equipment	Special equipment								

COMMERCIAL D-SERIES (GROUNDCRAFT)									
HANDL	SPEED	ACCEL	BODY	ARM	PILOT	SENS	SEATS	AVAIL	COST
2/2	3	1	16	10	2	2	2	12	248,000¥
Standard Equipment	Special equipment								

COMMERCIAL DD (GROUNDCRAFT)									
HANDL	SPEED	ACCEL	BODY	ARM	PILOT	SENS	SEATS	AVAIL	COST
2/2	3	1	20	12	2	2	2	12	312,000¥
Standard Equipment	Special equipment								

SAEDER-KRUPP KONSTRUCTORS

I know someone is going to laugh at this or wonder why it's in here, but I have my reasons. The first is *Mine Wars*, the new series S-K is running. These massive hauler vehicles are being used to battle in the deepest pit mines. Usually rigged, they've become a popular topic of conversation in rigger bars around the world. The Konstructor series is the most popular line by far, mostly for their awesome aesthetics. Designed with Lofwyr in mind, the vehicles have swept-back exhausts that look like horns, and jagged cabs that look like spikes. The dump truck's bed resembles wings. All these designs are easily painted to look fierce, and that's drawn plenty of *Mine Wars* teams to these models.

- The fact that S-K leaves a crap ton of them and their spare parts behind after mining operations is another reason. I'm not surprised, since they often can't get them out without airlifting them or building new roads into the pit mines. Oh yeah, and S-K is the main sponsor of *Mine Wars*.
- Turbo Bunny

The second big reason is action in Africa. All the mining that has occurred in Africa over the past century has left plenty of these monsters behind. Warlords jump all over these, as there are plenty of structures in Africa one of these can drive right through without slowing. Not that they use them for that. Most of the time these things are turned into mobile bunkers, filled with AK-97–armed locals, and sent out to terrorize in the name of the warlord. Runners contracting with corps that are trying to tame certain parts of Africa are getting jammed up when one of these enters the picture.

Now you know why I mentioned it.

- Those African tribal tanks usually have one really big weakness: a cloth roof. The bunker is made with a canvas top rather than something sturdier to let it breathe and prevent the back from becoming a hot box. A tossed-up grenade may not land inside, but the next one will after the first shreds the top. Though the second is usually not necessary.
- Picador

- Careful of that trick. The locals are wise to it and really good at slapping the canvas top to knock a grenade from pretty much anywhere it rolls to.
- Red Anya

KONSTRUCTORS (GROUNDCRAFT)									
HANDL	SPEED	ACCEL	BODY	ARM	PILOT	SENS	SEATS	AVAIL	COST
2/2	3	1	24	18	4	3	2	16	365,000¥
Standard Equipment	Off-road equipment, special equipment								

MOSTRANS KVP-28

Mostrans introduced the KVP-27T back in the 2050s. Its unique offering of wheels when you can use them and hover when you can't made it an overnight success (by hover vehicle standards). The design had its issues, most coming from the fact that it was a retrofit, rather than a pure design. The KVP-28 is the result of feedback from owners of the 27T and a design done from the ground up. The only feedback they didn't take into account was the size issue. Many users pointed out that the KVP-27T was too big. The 28 is actually larger by a tenth of a meter in every dimension, almost like they were spiting that feedback, but the truth is they were just making this one even bigger so they could market the Mostrans Minsk, which is a smaller version of the KVP-28. The KVP-28 is quite large but still falls within most street legal limits. The upper section of the rear compartment, above the storage area, is commonly a small sleeper not much larger than a coffin motel.

The KVP-28 is marketed to backwater areas with minimal road access or abundant small bodies of water and is primarily a delivery vehicle, mobile store, or RV setup. The mobile store is quite popular in Asia and Northern North America as well as Australia. Then again, that's where all the models are popular. The versatility of the KVP-28 is the key to its success. Tons of modifications have been made to this model already, and many of the modification plans for the 27T that can be found on the Matrix work for the 28 with some minor alterations.

- The Minsk isn't as versatile, but it's much easier to drive in a city. That one is only about the size of a Bulldog Step-Van, and we all know how easy those are to move around town.
- Sounder

- It sticks out more and is easier to remember but if you aren't doing anything memorable it's got better storage and handling than a Bulldog. The Minsk, that is. The KVP-28 is pretty maneuverable for its size but it still isn't parallel parking in the city.
- Turbo Bunny

- It could park on top of another vehicle!
- Slamm-0!

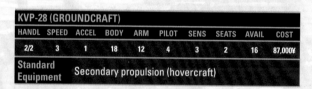

KVP-28 (GROUNDCRAFT)									
HANDL	SPEED	ACCEL	BODY	ARM	PILOT	SENS	SEATS	AVAIL	COST
2/2	3	1	18	12	4	3	2	16	87,000¥
Standard Equipment	Secondary propulsion (hovercraft)								

MINSK (GROUNDCRAFT)									
HANDL	SPEED	ACCEL	BODY	ARM	PILOT	SENS	SEATS	AVAIL	COST
2/2	3	1	16	10	4	3	2	16	77,000¥
Standard Equipment	—								

UNIVERSAL HOVERCRAFT MINNESOTA

All smugglers need one of these in their garage of tricks. Driving on the classic cushion of air, the Minnesota handles any terrain with relative ease. The versatility of a hovercraft to go from solid ground to water is there, but the Minnesota was designed with even more adaptability in mind. The dense and reinforced rubber cushion can flatten foliage and small trees, while cages protect the fan blades beneath so even thin forested land can't stop the Minnesota. The Minnesota has another unique feature that was recently added to this civilian model from the UH-406 Drake military transport and lander. It can "jump" by adding additional thrust under the cushion that will push the hovercraft over obstacles or up on landing spots up to three meters in height. This thrust can also allow a "hover" feature that can lift and hold the Minnesota up at a height of up to two meters in the air over a distance. Maneuverability is poor due to a lack of stabilization, but it opens a lot of eyes when that rabbit comes out of the hat.

The Minnesota is designed as a cargo craft with a cabin for two, with the normal amenities raised up at the center of the craft. The additional height allows great visibility and puts it over both the front and rear cargo spaces. The area beneath the cabin comes with two options: empty to allow for oversized cargo pods or extra cargo space, or as a small cabin with a pair of pullout sleeper spots and a living space with a kitchen. Smugglers usually go for the latter in case they need to make an extended rural layover. The cargo space is split between front and rear, and the base model comes with two custom pods that can be reused or traded out with shippers who use a lot of UH vehicles. While that isn't the norm for smugglers or runners, it means there are spare pods out there.

- Most smugglers I know bring a tent and some rations and use the extra space for more goods. Works just as well and increases the profit on all their runs.
- Turbo Bunny

- Just so it's out there and folks know, there is a UH Manitoba that is based on the same frame as the Minnesota, but it's a huge luxury RV.
- Sounder

One final feature that makes the Minnesota so unique is the airboat option. UH has a contract with American Airboat to add two specialized airboats to the rear of the craft. These boats are intended to be an optional unloading method but also offer a fourth and fifth fan to increase power output. This added power results in additional top-end speed if the load stays standard or allows for more load with no loss of speed. The added fans also make the Minnesota even more maneuverable.

- American Airboat and Universal Hovercraft both trace their ownership to Ares. It's really not a contract between American and Universal, it's just Ares working their assets together.
- Mr. Bonds

- Ares has several other brands of airboat under their umbrella. The American/Universal connection is always renegotiable if another subsidiary comes in with a better deal. Ares only worries about the bottom line when it can be felt on a megacorporate level. Infighting between subsidiaries makes them just hungrier for success.
- Sticks

- So, I get the smuggler thing for why this is here, but why have hovercraft even been kept in production?
- Cheshire

- The hovercraft is not a first-world vehicle. It's primary specialization is that it allows access to areas without roads or separated by bodies of water with no bridges. While these things are rarely seen near the big cities of North America, the more rural areas understand their value. This is especially true of parts of the UCAS and NAN lands where government support for the roadways is a thing of the distant past. They're huge all over Africa, Asia, and Australia as well as the island nations of southeast Asia.
- Red Anya

- The northwestern seaboard of North America has seen a huge leap in the hovercraft market, and the innovations on the Minnesota are a direct result of the needs in that area.
- Mika

MINNESOTA (GROUNDCRAFT)									
HANDL	SPEED	ACCEL	BODY	ARM	PILOT	SENS	SEATS	AVAIL	COST
4/4	4	2	14	9	3	3	2/12	12R	130,000¥
Standard Equipment	—								

VODYANOY ASSAULT HOVERCRAFT

Since I mentioned other friendlier options, I might as well mention a not-so-friendly one too. The Vodianoi (yes, spelled different, read on) was originally designed by Ya-matetsu's Naval Technologies division as a support vehicle for their amphibious operations. After the first dozen floated off the line, their production facility was sabotaged, and design specifications were lost. A month later, Ares introduced the Vodyanoy, which quickly became a worldwide hit. I'm sure something came down from up the well to square these two, but Evo never put together another production plant. The Vodyanoy features some serious armor protection that hammers its maneuverability, but it usually doesn't have to avoid much.

VODYANOY (GROUNDCRAFT)									
HANDL	SPEED	ACCEL	BODY	ARM	PILOT	SENS	SEATS	AVAIL	COST
3/3	4	3	16	16	1	2	3(10)	12F	84,000¥
Standard Equipment	Amenities (Squatter), Hovercraft (built), Weapon Mount (external, turret, manual)								

CORPSEC/ POLICE/MILITARY

Ares, via their Dodge brand, and Saeder-Krupp via BMW are moving into a security vehicle war that is likely to reshape the industry. Ares is hedging their efforts with extra support from Ares Arms and an instant list of buyers in their security divisions, but even Lone Star is on the fence for which to start ordering from since S-K has Onotari tweaking weapon designs to fit better in their models. Both megacorporations are selling every model in their new lines all over the world, including the backyard of their primary competitors.

Someone is going to ask or make a point of mentioning it, so I'll do it here first. There is at least some collusion going on between the megacorps because no, they don't have design overlaps to create competition. Dodge doesn't have a high-speed pursuit model, and BMW doesn't have a command center rig and so on and so forth. Other megacorporations with interests in keeping these two from taking over the entire market are going to be all over stealing their designs or finding and exploiting any weaknesses they can.

- Megacorporations are scary. Megacorporations cooperating on a level like this are absolutely terrifying.
- Balladeer

- They do things like this all the time. We just live in the shadows and experience far more of the backstabbing and corporate espionage.
- Glitch

- At least it's just two of them, and the rest are still going after them. The day to fear is when they come together and separate the world markets like a giant pie, with each getting their share to exploit.
- Plan 9

- Their nature is to always be looking enviously at everyone else's pie.
- Aufheben

BMW BLITZKRIEG

This German legend in the making is a combat bike on steroids. Loosely based on the venerable Blitzen, the Blitzkrieg is all anger and edges with weapon systems designed in, instead of being added on. Both the front and rear have space built right in for specific arms. The front offers an Onotari Arms minigun to shred anything in its path, while the rear mounts anOnotari Arms assault rifle to push back any unwanted advances. The advertising crossover for Onotari Arms and BMW has been quite fruitful. The absolute top reason to choose the Blitzkrieg over any other bike on the market is the pullover canopy. The canopy is really a pullover carapace designed to allow the rider to lie down, or "get small" as riders say, and the canopy can extend over them, protecting them from most small arms. Operating this way requires AR access but also allows for full VR control with an onboard gyro stabilization system compensating for the unconscious form of the rider, who is safely tucked into the carapace. Even without the carapace, Blitzkrieg riders are more protected than average riders with the bike's leg, arm, and torso rails, which help to ward off stray bullets. Even though its adverts describe the Blitzkrieg as being based on the Blitzen, a rather round bike, the Blitzkrieg is all hard angles and sharp edges to match the latest BMW design trend.

- This thing is hell on wheels. That front minigun can lay out a stream of lead that will cut a car in half. The rear gun isn't as potent, but it doesn't have to be, especially when it carries the X Factor IV complete with "underbarrel" grenade launcher. Two weapons on one mount, thanks to the efficiency of German engineering.
- Red Anya

- Get in front, it cuts you in half. Come from behind, and it blows you to pieces. Best approach from the sides. Oh wait, Wilma didn't mention the additional mounts available that ride like saddlebags and provide lateral firepower.
- Kane

- Those side mounts aren't standard for the combat biker model—they're secondary-market items offered by Onotari for the security market. They usually offer them with an Onotari SMG, but I've seen models with shotguns, grenade launchers, and even lasers.
- Sticks

- Don't forget the rockets!
- Slamm-0!

BMW BLITZKRIEG

- I've never seen one with rockets. I'm not convinced the footage flying around the Matrix isn't doctored, and I only speak on bikes I have physically seen in action.
- Sticks

BLITZKRIEG (GROUNDCRAFT)									
HANDL	SPEED	ACCEL	BODY	ARM	PILOT	SENS	SEATS	AVAIL	COST
4/3	4	2	10	8	3	4	2	14R	46,000¥
Standard Equipment	Two heavy weapon mounts (external, fixed, remote; weapons not included with the vehicle)								

DODGE CHARGER

With the multi-market popularity of the Knight-Ares Charger when it was introduced back in the early '70s, it was a no-brainer to use the popular moniker for the "redesigned" model. Truth is, this Charger probably has only two shared components, the Stallion and Ram logos. The Charger EV is the base design and is intended as an escort vehicle, while the base Charger is being marketed as a patrol car. This is one of those rare cases where they designed a vehicle for more arms and armor and then trimmed back. I'd expect some of the patrol cars to be stripped down and end up on the

civilian market in a few years after they've got some mileage on them. There might even be a civilian model by then if they redesign the interior for less cannons and more comfort, but what's the fun in that? As an escort they chose the four-door sedan style but tried to keep some sleek two-door looks. The Dodge tear drop, the signature shape of their new line, comes from the front of the hood and over the top, giving the Charger a heavy-looking front end for more intimidation, while the rear window comes to a sharp point for some slick style. Don't forget that this car was designed to be badass, not just pretty, and that rear point folds open to give the "tail-gunner" (as the buyers are calling that seat) a great view of (and shot at) anything creeping up from the rear. The EV is armed with a pair of front-firing mounts on opposing sides of the hood and the same in the rear, though most of the time these mounts are retracted and kept hidden until they're needed.

- These things are great working in tandem, front and rear. No matter which way you come from, they can open fire on you, and when you swerve to avoid, you drive right into a stream of bullets from the other car.
- Sticks

DODGE CHARGER

- There's rumors of an Ares backdoor on the Matrix. I'm not convinced it's real, but we'd be the people to hunt it down if it was out there.
- /dev/grrl

- Might be my natural disposition, but I figure Ares would just blast the drek out of any Chargers used against them in order to get parts and replacement sales.
- Bull

- Funny you mention that. A rookie I know got a call for a job that involved taking out some escorts on a transport. Just take out the escorts. He figured it was a message being sent or just one part of a bigger play. His Johnson even supplied him with some serious ordnance. The escorts were Chargers and the arms were Ares. Nothing more than a conspiracy theory, but something to be on the lookout for.
- Stone

CHARGER (GROUNDCRAFT)									
HANDL	SPEED	ACCEL	BODY	ARM	PILOT	SENS	SEATS	AVAIL	COST
4/3	5	2	12	12	4	4	5	16R	65,000¥
Standard Equipment	Two standard weapon mounts (external, fixed, remote) front; two standard weapon mounts (External, fixed, remote) rear								

BMW I8 INTERCEPTOR

Security and police firms rarely engage in high-speed pursuits. Once they have a few of these in their arsenal, they're going to have a hard time resisting, and with a much higher success rate. The initial specs on this put it right up there with the latest hypercars, but minus any of the comfort and luxury you might have expected in a BMW. The inside is more like a racecar than a luxury car, and though it's sized like a mid-size, it only seats two; driver and gunner, both usually strapped in and operating completely in VR. The driver handles making this mean machine dance while rocketing after a perp using the i8's SOTA rigger interface, while the gunner controls all of the vehicle's onboard offensive and defensive systems from an almost game-like

BMW I8 INTERCEPTOR

captain's chair interface. Offensive systems include multiple weapon mounts to provide superior firepower. The standard artillery load out is a forward-mounted mini-gun and two rear-mounted assault shotguns. Ammunition load usually depends on jurisdiction, but BMW is offering special rates on APDS through Krupp Arms. The i8 also offers smoke dispensers, an anti-vehicular spike dispenser, and an oil sprayer straight out of James Bond. BMW also integrated the same light defense system as their Stürmwagon assault truck that can be used to seriously disorient an opposing driver from any angle. Combine this thing's speed with the tricks up its sleeves, and we can all see how tough life will be on the other side of the law.

- The dog-brain does a solid enough job with the onboard weapons systems on this thing that the gunner seat will often be taken by a combat decker who is doing his damnedest to break into your rig while you run. If you see one of these things holding back in pursuit, check the 'trix.
- Glitch

- They also hold back because they know they can catch you, but they have no support whatsoever once they do. A crashed van may injure some of the runners inside, but none of them are going to just roll over and surrender.

The i8 has some decent offensive hardware but can't take much of a pounding.
- Bull

- Krupp has been working on a light pattern that induces physical effects. Nausea, headaches, and disorientation are already in the testing phase, but Krupp is trying to discover the pattern that will induce a seizure in anyone.
- Butch

- BMW is testing out another variant of this as an off-road pursuit buggy. Same general style but a big lift and serious suspension. Data on the test results would be worth a premium to competitors with similar desires for an all-terrain pursuit vehicle.
- Red Anya

I8 INTERCEPTOR (GROUNDCRAFT)									
HANDL	SPEED	ACCEL	BODY	ARM	PILOT	SENS	SEATS	AVAIL	COST
5/3	8	4	12	8	4	4	3	20F	114,000¥
Standard Equipment	Heavy weapon mount (external, flexible, remote) front, two standard weapon mounts (external, fixed, remote) rear, oil slick sprayer, smoke projector, road strip ejector, rigger adaptation								

DODGE GOLIATH

DODGE GOLIATH

I wouldn't bet naming yourself David is going to help you bring down the Goliath. Taking lessons learned from the Master series, integrating the upgrades and modifications right into the design, and using marketing that doesn't say Ares anywhere on it are combining to get the Goliath clients no one would expect, including Lone Star. The Dodge teardrop design is integrated into one of the most attractive features of the Goliath: the extended roof. Wondering what's so special about an extended roof? There are two answers. First, it allows those inside to stand prior to deploying out the doors. This means deployment can start at a run, saving seconds and lives in the process. Second, the panels all around the teardrop open to create a 360-degree field of fire. Sensors and Matrix tech, linked wirelessly to the weapons of the individuals, control opening, closing, and sliding panels in order to keep the firer as secure as possible while using the TopFire system. Deployment security was among the top issues in the design of the Goliath. The side-sliding doors are set toward the rear and provide rear exit security on the sides once opened. Combined with the rear drop and lift gate, this provides a secure exit from the rear. To cover the side

doors, every Goliath has four Ares FlaShields as standard equipment that can be used by personnel to cover the doors or locked into mounts on the floor. Once locked in, they operate off the Goliath's network and can be activated remotely.

- The firing panels up top can be used manually, but it takes time and leaves you exposed. The TopFire system also integrates sensor data and other inputs to highlight targets or potential threats.
- Sticks

- Even with the FlaShields in place, the side doors are still accessible to a good shot. A decent compensation system is a must just in case they fire up the shields.
- Stone

GOLIATH (GROUNDCRAFT)									
HANDL	SPEED	ACCEL	BODY	ARM	PILOT	SENS	SEATS	AVAIL	COST
3/2	4	2	16	16	3	3	8	20R	120,000¥
Standard Equipment	Special equipment (extended roof), six gun ports, extra entry/exit point (assault ramp to the rear), ram plate								

BMW TEUFELKATZE

BMW TEUFELKATZE

This SUV, the devil cat, is really more of a MPUV, as it is intended for the triple role of escort, transport, and assault vehicle. Featuring the same sharp look as the i8, this is the Interceptor's bigger, meaner, nastier brother. This hellish predator can run every job a security corp needs with only a few changes—to the personnel. Paired front seats, a trio in the center so the client can get space, and another set of paired rear seats facing toward any potential trouble running up from the back make sure that this cat has more than nine lives. It sounds a lot more angsty in the original German. Then again, everything does. Being designed for a purpose ensures there is plenty of space for stowed gear and additional munitions in handy spots rather than being tucked away wherever they could fit. Security features and counter-measures are also designed right into the vehicle with FlashTech lighting in the front and rear lights, electronic signature dampening in the frame, and the namesake TeufelKatze automated defense system.

- I don't know the TeufelKatze system. Enlighten me?
- Netcat

- Instead of a shock system to prevent theft, this vehicle sets you on fire.
- Slamm-0!

- Do you two ever talk in person?
- Glitch

- Big ears around. Especially for words like "fire."
- Slamm-0!

TEUFELKATZE (GROUNDCRAFT)									
HANDL	SPEED	ACCEL	BODY	ARM	PILOT	SENS	SEATS	AVAIL	COST
5/4	5	3	16	16	3	3	7	16F	76,000¥
Standard Equipment	FlashTech, signature dampening, TeufelKatze flamer								

DODGE STALLION

Every security and police force needs a workhorse. To fill that role, Dodge designed the Stallion. It came as no surprise to the security companies looking to buy the Stallion that this workhorse makes one hell of a war-horse too. The Stallion is a pickup-style truck with an open bed that is accessible from the cab. Since this is a

DODGE STALLION

new Dodge design the expected teardrop is there, and it's going to bring tears to many eyes after it fills many bodies with holes. The weapon mount on the Stallion is integrated into the teardrop, centering on the bulb end and allowing the barrel of whatever weapon is installed to tuck down into the narrow rear. This makes accessing the rear a little tougher when the gun is stored, but how often does that happen? The folks who drive this truck want people to know it's got a cannon mounted on top to remind them to get out of the way in traffic. Speaking of traffic, the rear-facing mounts built over the back wells keep tailgaters from straying too close for too long. Heavy-duty suspension and oversized tires make the Stallion a little unwieldy on pavement, but if you hit dirt, sand, mud, gravel, or even grass, this pony grabs hold and won't let go. The single greatest feature unique to this truck is the prototype Ares Testudo system. The system turns the truck into a heavily armored gun emplacement by shifting body panels around. Mobility is gone, but this feature combines nicely with the General to create a well-protected command HQ.

- The Testudo system is neat, but it creates several other requirements for the Stallion, like the need for solid Matrix defenses, because engaging this system while the Stallion is in motion does not turn out well.
- Netcat

- Brutal!
- Slamm-0!

- The Stallion is one of the most likely models in the new catalog to get a civilian version. It looks cool and has tons of horsepower and awesome off-road potential.
- Sounder

- Check out the Ares Minotaur. It has quite the familiar teardrop.
- Picador

BMW LUXUS LIMO

STALLION (GROUNDCRAFT)									
HANDL	SPEED	ACCEL	BODY	ARM	PILOT	SENS	SEATS	AVAIL	COST
3/4	5	3	16	12	3	3	4	16R	78,000¥
Standard Equipment	Heavy weapon mount (external, turret, manual) top, two standard weapon mounts (external, fixed, remote) rear								

MINOTAUR (GROUNDCRAFT)									
HANDL	SPEED	ACCEL	BODY	ARM	PILOT	SENS	SEATS	AVAIL	COST
4/5	5	2	14	8	4	4	4	—	45,000¥
Standard Equipment	Heavy weapon mount (external, turret, manual) top, standard weapon mount (external, fixed, remote) rear								

BMW LUXUS

If they can get the price down, the Luxus may become the only limousine in use for security-conscious clients. This limo has sharp yet elegant features tipped with the angular front end reflective of the BMW i8, which the Luxus is built around. The limo loses a little top end due to the added weight from its thoroughly armored hide, but while it can't dodge a missile, it can take a hit, even several. Its active defense systems may make it tough for any slow-fliers to get close, however. Speaking of its active defense system, the Luxus can deploy anti-missile mini-guns from both the hood and trunk. While the advertisements call it an active *defense* system, they can be turned on softer targets just as easily. The Luxus comes standard with an EnviroSeal system and passenger-restraint safety systems. Field-testing

involved a Luxus sinking to the bottom of the Nile in Cairo. The driver got banged up going off the bridge but managed to get clear quickly. The four passengers in the back were at the bottom of the river for two hours. When the rescue team got them out, the worst injury was a sprained wrist and possible alcohol poisoning.

» Pulling an active defense system onto soft targets makes it extremely ineffective against its intended targets. If you can get the security team to turn the guns on some local gangers, it will open the Luxus up to a hit. Just make sure you're using something like HEAP or Sabot rounds to get through this fancy monster's armor.
» 2XL

» 2XL's evaluation is correct when you take over the system manually, but if you extend the valid target settings while still leaving it under the system's control, the defenses works fine.
» Turbo Bunny

LUXUS (GROUNDCRAFT)									
HANDL	SPEED	ACCEL	BODY	ARM	PILOT	SENS	SEATS	AVAIL	COST
5/5	5	3	18	16	5	6	8	14R	398,000¥
Standard Equipment	Amenities (middle), anti-theft system 3, heavy weapon mount (concealed, turret, remote) rear, life support system 2, missile defense system, passenger protection system, Vindicator Minigun w/ 250 standard ammo								

DODGE GENERAL

DODGE GENERAL

I want to go work for Knight Errant just to get to drive around in this thing. The General is a massive two-piece mobile command vehicle designed with both form and function in mind. Sticking to Dodge's new teardrop design principle, the General uses the narrowing rear of the main truck for a quartet of oversized double tires to give it a big-rig look. This command truck is based on mobile home technology, so it expands out once in place, but it can operate without extending and even while still on the move. Doors on both sides allow for ambidextrous deployment, and along with only internal access to the driving compartment, it's easy to keep secure. The only other access is via a hatch up to the roof, which is reinforced to support drones, trolls, or gun turrets and has an available hip-height wall for cover when needed. The command center contains a complete command and communications suite, washroom, two-man sleeping quarters, two lock-up cells, two built-in remote command consoles, and a twenty-gun armory.

The rear vehicle may look like a trailer, but it can be operated separately via a small control station at the top or a virtual interface from the inside. It is primarily de-signed for support items and can house a rigger cocoon with another RCC, up four medium-sized drones on racks, a generator, additional communications gear, a drone workshop, a secondary armory that usually includes several drone mountable weapons, and/or additional lock-up space. Additional trailer-units are usually driven to a command site separately, as the General can only haul one, but it is common to see several.

COMMAND (GROUNDCRAFT)

HANDL	SPEED	ACCEL	BODY	ARM	PILOT	SENS	SEATS	AVAIL	COST
3/3	4	1	20	16	5	7	10	18R	344,000¥
Standard Equipment	Additional entry/exit port (roof hatch), amenities (middle), special equipment (bathroom), special equipment (holding cell x 2), special equipment (sleeping quarters)								

TRAILER (GROUNDCRAFT)

HANDL	SPEED	ACCEL	BODY	ARM	PILOT	SENS	SEATS	AVAIL	COST
3/3	3	1	20	16	3	7	1	18R	54,000¥
Standard Equipment	Drone workshop (aircraft repair), 4 medium drone racks, rigger adaptation, rigger cocoon, special equipment (generator)								

BMW STÜRMWAGON SWAT

BMW STÜRMWAGON

The Stürmwagon was intentionally designed as a special tactics vehicle, rather than being retrofitted from some other model. This means all of its systems are integrated, not just tacked on. While most police and security vehicles have had lights added, this one sports a pair of high-intensity LED bars that ring the entire top and bottom. The bars can be used as normal lights and sirens, but they also double as a flash and flare system. The system can be linked with the electronic vision systems of team members to perfectly time flare compensation and lighting systems for maximum benefit. That means that not only can they ignore all the flashes and blinding light, but they see better thanks to perfect light compensation and sensor integration. The forethought put into design also allows this BMW to double as a secondary assault vehicle for special operations teams. The normal elegance of BMW is buried far below the surface, while the intimidation factor is amped up to eleven. Besides tearing down the road on runflat tires, the Stürmwagon's wheels are protected by bulky wheel wells and covers. The wells are commonly augmented with ablative armor to take a little extra punishment. To make an already-intense vehicle even more frightening, BMW has used

their all-wheel steering system on the Stürmwagon to make it handle like a deadly ballerina. Vehicular egress is often an issue in combat situations as doorways become chokepoints with predictable patterns. Not on the Stürmwagon. The rear and side doors have a multitude of opening options. The rear doors consist of four panels that are connected magnetically and can be "hinged" on any side of each square. The side doors have the same magnetic system, though they are twelve-paneled. This allows them to create firing ports at a variety of heights while also offering variations on cover provided when entering or exiting the vehicle. Even better, they can form ramps or bridges when needed. Since no one has invented dimensional warping technology (yet), space confinements still place a finite limit on the systems that could be integrated into the interior, so the designers created an interchangeable pod system and reinforced the roof. These pods connect directly into the vehicle's power supply and device network. They come with a wide range of options, including drone pods, additional weaponry, communications gear, equipment storage, medical supplies, and more. The roof has four plug-in points and two different sized pods (single and double plug).

DODGE RHINO

- Okay, deckheads, here's something for you. The Stürmwagon is usually the tactical hub of a special operations team. Not saying the wheeled stormcloud (that's the standard icon) is going to be an easy nut to crack, but if you can, you own them.
- Stone

- And they then know exactly where to find your team's Matrix support. There's a manual reboot switch for the system. One flip of a switch and you're dumped.
- Clockwork

- Selling drek for BMW now, are we, Clockwork? The manual killswitch is an urban legend. What you need to worry about are the honey pot and isolation chamber. The Stürmwagon will often run hidden while displaying a secondary icon that is full of Matrix ugliness. That's the

honey pot. Then, once you're in, the device locks you in the isolation chamber. Only way out is to jack out and lose all the work you've done. Have fun with these things, script-sammies.
- Glitch

- I was operating in the Sioux Nation and ended up in a chase situation with a pair of special operations vans I didn't recognize. I know now they were Stürmwagons from their AR icons, but that's not my point. They're hot on my team's tail, and we're pinging rounds off this thing left and right. All of a sudden the two trucks even out, and the side doors open. First, the panels fold down, like Wilma's talking about, but then they extend out, and the two rigs connect at the door. Two nut-job Sioux ops guys walk out of each rig out onto this makeshift bridge. Two of them lay down some suppression on us as the rigs pull up fast and deliver the other two right onto the back of our van. It was crazy. This thing is going to have a lot of tricks.

- Sticks

STÜRMWAGON (GROUNDCRAFT)

HANDL	SPEED	ACCEL	BODY	ARM	PILOT	SENS	SEATS	AVAIL	COST
5/4	4	2	17	18	4	5	10	20R	145,000¥

Std. Equipment	Light system allows those subscribed to use the Sensor rating as their limit for relevant tests; additional entry/exit port (assault ramp, rear) firing ports, special equipment (advanced lightbar)

DODGE RHINO

The Rhino is going to be the new star of shadowrunner's nightmares. Images of this beast crushing through flaming walls are already lined up for the advertising push Ares will be spearheading on this, their latest combat achievement. To maintain the common design theme, this urban assault vehicle reverses the Dodge teardrop to create a battering wedge that looks like an axe at the front of the vehicle. The driver sits high and forward, with a hatch and weapon mount directly behind the seat. Below the driver is an AR cocoon for controlling the remote weapon and defense systems. The rear area, where the teardrop is widest, is designed as the cargo and personnel section. The seating in back is designed for a fully outfitted seven-man squad, but little else. The horrifying wedge shearing through the wall is also not the end of the nightmare. The rear of the Rhino opens up at a seam in the center, with both doors shaped like a wedge. They swing outward with a jump seat on each side, usually containing a well-armored rifleman. The rear compartment also has two side doors that drop open but act as seating while closed.

Standard equipment on the Rhino includes a pair of forward-firing anti-material rifles intended to soften walls, twelve smoke dispensers evenly spread around the truck for visual obscurement, eight genuine Ares FlashPak systems, and the new Ares Shockwave electro-defense system.

RHINO (GROUNDCRAFT)

HANDL	SPEED	ACCEL	BODY	ARM	PILOT	SENS	SEATS	AVAIL	COST
4/4	4	2	24	14	6	7	9	18R	225,000¥

Std. Equipment	Additional entry/exit point (assault ramp, rear), anti-theft system, standard weapon mount (external, flexible, remote) front, 2 standard weapon mounts (external, fixed remote) rear

RUHRMETALL WOLF II

Though this is not directly part of the Dodge/BMW battle, I wanted to include the Wolf II because it's a rigger favorite for versatility, and increasing numbers of them are finding their way to strange places like the Redmond Barrens in Seattle and inside the CZ in Chicago. The Wolf II is a six-wheeled combat vehicle, popular with mercenary groups around the world. Based on a modular design, the Wolf II has five standard configurations: troop transport, air defense vehicle, medical transport, mobile staff command post, and light tank. Due to its sturdy construction, it can be airdropped anywhere in whatever configuration, and other pods can drop in parts for alternate configurations.

WOLF II (GROUNDCRAFT)

HANDL	SPEED	ACCEL	BODY	ARM	PILOT	SENS	SEATS	AVAIL	COST
3/3	3	2	24	12	2	2	6	20F	330,000¥

Std. Equipment	Enviroseal, life support (60 hours), Runflat tires
Options	**Troop Transport:** Seats 6/16 (8,000¥); **Air Defense:** add weapon mount w/ missile launcher (4,000¥); **Medical transport:** add 2 stabilization beds, medkit (Rating 6), Seats 6/6 (4,000¥); **Mobile Staff Command Post:** add tacnet, Seats 6/8 (5,000¥); **Light Tank:** add weapon mount w/ cannon, weapon mount w/ machine gun, Seats 6/6 (4,000¥)

RULING THE WAVES

Teacup hated the water. She couldn't swim and couldn't bring her pride in check enough to wear the flowery child-size life vest with the Cutie Cupies all over it. And that's why she was slowly watching the shimmering light of the surface get further and further away while she flailed uselessly in a vain attempt to swim. It was not the ending such a smart and funny gnome should be dealt. It had been a bad hand all along.

Teacup sat across from the Johnson and swung her dangling feet from the barstool. It looked childish, especially from Teacup. Being under a meter tall made her look like a child, and she played the role when she could. It wasn't her favorite role—that would be wheelman—but right now Dagger wanted her to sit up tall, swing her little legs, and bounce, ever so slightly like a happy child. It kept Mr. Johnson's mind off-step.

"We'll do it, but the cash has to be up front. Once this is done, we're in the wind," Dagger barked. The harsh tone of his voice jarred the Johnson's eyes from Teacup.

"Uh, well. My employer ..." he stammered. Quite unprofessional.

"Up front or no deal," Dagger said again. This time Teacup timed her bounce with a little shoulder stretch and stuck out her namesakes. The move caught the Johnson's eye.

"Of course. Up front. Let me just make the arrangements." Mr. Johnson's eyes seemed to light up as a smirk crossed his lips, "No need for your whole team to be delayed. I'll work it out and transfer the money to Miss Teacup here. I'm sure the team trusts her to spread it around fairly."

Teacup almost laughed. The innuendos in his speech were so blatant they almost couldn't be called innuendo. She held it in and smiled demurely.

"Go ahead guys. The cars already warmed up and rolling up front. I won't be long."

No one argued. They knew she could handle this creep if the need arose. She had already sent commands to the car, the van, and six drones in the area while bouncing childishly on a chair in order to preoccupy the mind of the closet pedophile Johnson. Brushing him off was as easy as pointing out how similar she was to a little girl, despite her more mature accoutrements and Mr. J would clam right up.

Two minutes later the money was being distributed, and Teacup was uploading a rather inappropriate proposition from Mr. Johnson to her private storage in case she found a way to use it against him someday.

Teacup shot Dagger a glance as Mackie and Grunt bounded over the back rail of the Kingfisher. They were distant splashes in the water before the glance could be answered.

"You said it. Eighteen seconds to impact. We've got nothing. We gotta bail!" Dagger yelled as he swung out around the side of the ladder from the pilot deck. Graceful even in a moment of panic.

Teacup swallowed hard and then huffed. She almost stomped her feet but stopped the tantrum short when Dagger disappeared out of sight. Instead she jumped over towards the ladder and looked down. Fear and pleading filled her eyes, "I can't ... I can't swim!"

Dagger smiled briefly. The gleeful look evaporated when he saw the tears forming. "You're not kidding."

"No." Teacup actually gasped as she pushed the word past the lump in her throat.

"Shit. Jump down. We'll go together. I'll help you." Dagger raised his arms up like a father waiting for his child to jump down from a tree they had climbed up but couldn't get back down.

"I will. One second." Teacup turned and grabbed her RCC from where it hung over the captain's chair. She slung it across her back as she jumped down toward Dagger's waiting arms.

From the corner of her eye she saw it. The torpedo that was coming their way had a strike booster and sped up once it got close. The strike booster system was intended to make the torpedo hit with more force and punch through the hull before exploding, but it forced the torpedo straight at the end of targeting. That made it easier for small ships to evade it. She could have dodged it.

Instead, she saw the viciously churning water and watched the ship rock while she fell toward Dagger. His legs wobbled but he stayed on his feet. He even caught her.

Just in time for the torpedo to explode beneath his feet. Dagger shielded Teacup from the shrapnel but the concussive force sent her flying through the air and into the water. Water that quickly pulled her down into its depths.

At least they were paid up front.

WET AND WILD

Welcome to Wilma's Wave Works! This is the place to check out my reviews on some of the smoothest craft on or under the waters. I lean my reviews toward those who live in the shadows but I've been trying to make sure I consider those who don't rig in, and add a little in for the casual shadow user. Okay, seriously I'm interested in continuing to develop reviews that are of use to everyone. I'm opening with the powerboats, then sailcraft, followed by yachts, then the oddballs, and wrapping up with a look at the big kid toys.

One of the things to always remember about watercraft is that they are designed to be compact and efficient. This means that bulkier members of metahumanity like orks and dwarfs are rarely comfortable at sea. When it comes to elves, they tend to end up with back and neck issues from crouching so much. Trolls view most boats like adults view the bicycles of their youth. They can ride them, but it isn't pretty, comfortable, or safe. The mass and size of most trolls seriously throws off the balance of small boats. Once we call them ships, trolls, orks, elves, and dwarfs are all good, but up to that point, boats require serious custom work to accommodate the full breadth of metahumanity.

- I know that sounds totally racist, but it isn't. Boats are already built short and narrow. Elves and orks come out tall, dwarves come out wide, and trolls come out all of the above in spades. Add on how heavy trolls are and what that means to displacement when floating, and you'll understand why even Evo, and their naval giant progenitor Yamatetsu, haven't delved far into the world of metahuman boating.
- Red Anya

POWERBOATS

This is a broad category that includes anything that is primarily driven by a motor. Ranging from small two-meter-long personal watercraft through the relatively massive fifteen-meter-long cigarettes built for nothing but speed up to twenty-meter luxury cruisers, powerboats can be found on waterways all over the world under the control of everyone from suburban families to rich executives to charter captains out to make a living.

EVO WATERKING

The Waterking is my favorite offering from Evo and one of the most reasonable in terms of cost to amenities ratio. It's on the larger side, eighteen meters, and designed with traditional boat mechanics in mind right alongside efforts to make room for comfortable living spaces. The rear deck is long but completely houses the drive systems for the boat, leaving everything fore (that's nautical for front) clear for living space. These spaces are split into two levels. The lower has a large galley (kitchen), two heads (restroom), and four small berths (sleeping areas), as well as a small exterior seating area at the fore. The upper cabin contains an aft sitting area, two sleeping cabins, and a fore sitting area. Above both is the pilot house. Secondary controls are also located in the upper floor fore sitting area, complete with aft VR feeds. Though it's rare for owners to spend this kind of nuyen on a boat and not own a top-of-the-line 'link, they don't need it with this boat, as the electronics suite offers the power for a full VR-control feed. Rigger adaptation is offered but not standard, as this boat kind of hovers at the top edge of poor boaters and the low end of yachters.

- I'll back Wilma on this one. The Waterking is a great option for riggers on a budget with a need for a big boat. This thing can be operated by a single rigger with an Ahab pilot program to run it during the sleepy times. The rest of the boat can be retrofitted for whatever purpose is needed. Smuggling, weapon systems—whatever you need can be stuffed in those extra spaces.
- Sounder

The Waterking is not a corvette, built for speed, nor is it a destroyer, built to take a hit. This is just the classic, average, everyday joe of the oceans, lakes, and rivers of the world. Perfect for runners who know how to fit in.

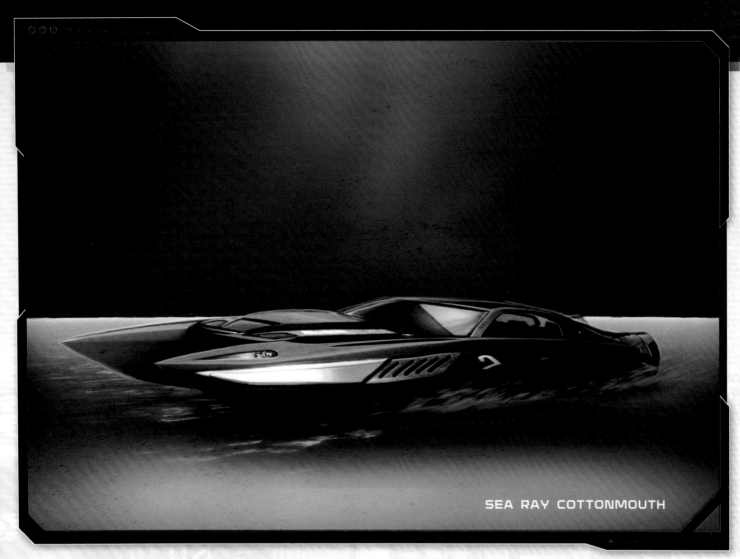

SEA RAY COTTONMOUTH

WATERKING (WATERCRAFT)									
HANDL	SPEED	ACCEL	BODY	ARM	PILOT	SENS	SEATS	AVAIL	COST
3	3	2	14	8	3	2	12	12	74,000¥
Std. Equipment	Amenities (middle), satellite link, secondary manual controls, smuggling compartment								

SEA RAY COTTONMOUTH

The Cottonmouth is truly the viper of the seas. This craft slithers through the waters of the world, ready to open up the throttle and strike at a moments notice. While speed may be the primary weapon of the Cotton-mouth, the creators of this high-speed craft knew the world they lived in. Sea Ray designed a drive system variation that allows for a slight shift in motor and battery position that compensates completely for an additional pair of weapon mounts at the front (the mounts are often referred to as fangs). Another pair are available for the rear, but these don't have the same compensation system and require turret and lift systems to overcome the lift of the front of the boat and prevent over-lift caused by their weight and movement.

The Cottonmouth is a fourteen-meter-long cigarette boat designed with speed in mind. The controls are located in the main cabin near the rear of the boat. The Cottonmouth offers an enclosed cabin option that makes the thing look totally badass but really requires the addition of a full VR control system due to a complete loss of visibility at speed, especially if rear weapons are engaged. Despite these shortcomings there is nothing else on the water with the options for speed and offensive firepower the Cottonmouth possesses. No matter whether the boat possesses the arms or is just running at high speed, it needs a skilled driver because it is not designed to take a hit. It can usually endure hits from small arms enough to stay above the waterline, but anything bigger, especially explosives, will spell a one way trip to Davy Jones' locker.

- To help limit the weak hull issue, the rear weapon mounts can be stocked with miniguns loaded for anti-missile operations. Yup, phalanx-style defense on a cigarette boat. Speed and direction are still limiting factors, as a head-on missile strike cannot be countered by the rear weapon systems, but skilled pilots know when to turn the broadside even if it makes a bigger target.
- Kane

While the Cottonmouth may look like nothing but speed on waves, it has a few amenities. Below you will find a small head (no shower, though), a galley that consists of a small gas burner, a fridge, and a tiny table, and two berths near the fore that would make even a navy lifer cringe at their size. This lower area is not troll friendly, and most dwarfs and orks find it way too tight for their wide shoulders. This water missile is built with fun in mind and lacks the comforts and supply space for much more than an afternoon out on the water. That said, most folks reading my reviews aren't taking this out for cross-Atlantic treks. Maybe some island hopping in the Carib League, but usually just a quick sprint to outrun or outgun pursuit and then into port to lay low.

- The Cottonmouth is popular with several pirate crews in the Carib League. They can run up fast on anything, and while those berths aren't good for a person, they hold quite a bit of booty.
- Kane

- Booty, Kane, seriously?
- /dev/grrl

COTTONMOUTH (WATERCRAFT)									
HANDL	SPEED	ACCEL	BODY	ARM	PILOT	SENS	SEATS	AVAIL	COST
5	7	4	8	4	3	3	4	12	120,000¥
Std. Equipment	Amenities (squatter), rigger interface, speed enhancement 1, 2 x weapon mount (standard, internal, fixed, remote) front, 2 x weapon mount (standard, internal, flexible, remote) rear								

KAWASAKI STINGRAY/ MANTA RAY

The Kawasaki Stingray and Manta Ray are a pair of small one- or two-man jet boats meant for fun and recreation on the water. But what would we care about that? I like them because they're fast, maneuverable, and have a ton of accessories that can be utilized for alternative purposes! For example, they both offer a mount for the bow that can easily be used to strap in an AK or even a Stoner. The top bar offers more places to mount lights, strobes, weapons, or small drones with Kawasaki's clips or a little homemade jerry-rigging. The optional ski holder tube happens to be the same size as the latest LAW single-fire rocket launchers, and you can mount two. Not that I personally ever plan to make use of any of these highly illegal modifications, but I'm sure someone will.

- Check out some of the footage from Amazonia. These things were very popular with river strikers, and that's where most of these modifications were developed. Maybe Wilma had something to do with that?
- Red Anya

- These things get stolen from docks all around the world. They're small enough that no one really notices they're gone until it's time to use them, and most boaters only get to use them on weekends. By then their boat is a new color, has new accessories, or is sunk after its illicit use.
- Sounder

STINGRAY (WATERCRAFT)									
HANDL	SPEED	ACCEL	BODY	ARM	PILOT	SENS	SEATS	AVAIL	COST
5	5	3	8	6	1	1	2	—	13,000¥
Std. Equipment	—								

MANTA RAY (WATERCRAFT)									
HANDL	SPEED	ACCEL	BODY	ARM	PILOT	SENS	SEATS	AVAIL	COST
4	5	3	9	6	1	1	3	—	16,000¥
Std. Equipment	—								

AZTECH NIGHTRUNNER

The Nightrunner has been taking shadowrunners on fishing trips for over three decades despite its complete lack of fishing seats or a fish cooler, and the difficulty of fishing from an enclosed cabin. While that joke has been passed down and remains unchanged, the Nightrunner has managed to upgrade quite a few things since those days. The enclosed cabin was replaced with a slide-open cabin cover, and the Nightrunner gained a new ad campaign back in '73, which led to the addition of scuba storage spaces built into the interior design. The ad made the Nightrunner out to be the ultimate in unobtrusive diving technology to help explain why it had heat-masking paint, an ultra-quiet drive system, and a sonar package rivaling some military craft. We in the shadows know what everyone uses this thing for and can continue the laugh at the dive boat with no access ladder or dive rails.

Even though the craft has been around for a generation, it's still a solid performer. They've done a decent job of keeping it up to date, though retrofits to older models have hit the classic boat snag. Everything is small and designed to fit and function with a purpose. Anything retrofitted has to fit into the same space or displace something else. The Nightrunner is a five-meter-long stealthy speedster, favoring the former over the latter. It's got nothing on the cigarettes, but it will run circles around a cruiser—all the while appearing nowhere on their sensors. Its size has been its biggest limitation. It has a small fore cabin where there is a berth area, a tiny head, and the closets and racks for dive equipment. These spots double nicely for other types of equipment as well.

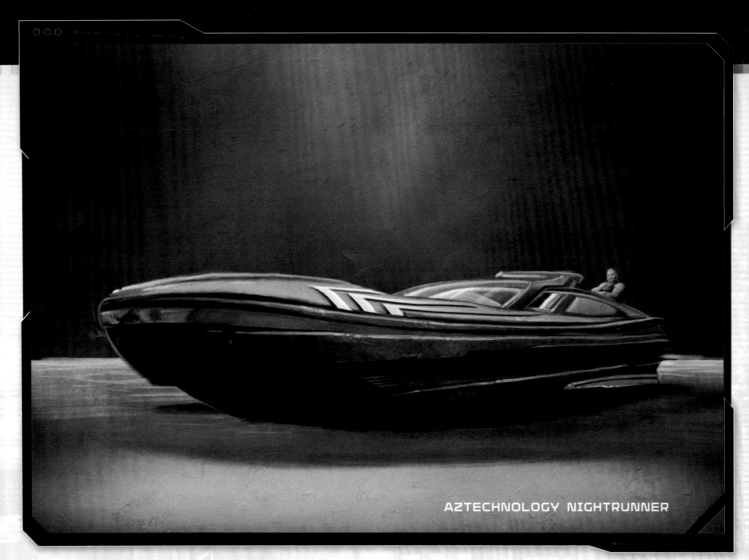

AZTECHNOLOGY NIGHTRUNNER

NIGHTRUNNER (WATERCRAFT)									
HANDL	SPEED	ACCEL	BODY	ARM	PILOT	SENS	SEATS	AVAIL	COST
5	6	3	12	6	3	4	6	10	56,000¥

Std. Equipment	Amenities (squatter), life support 1, rigger interface, satellite link, signature masking 4

ZODIAC SCORPIO

The rigid inflatable boat, or RIB, is rarely referred to as such thanks to Zodiac and a contract with the U.S. military dating back to the last century. Zodiac was the brand, but the name stuck to every other RIB, and right now their Scorpio line is my personal favorite. There are other brands out there, but they all chase after Zodiac for the next innovation in RIB technology.

The Scorpio line is so named for the three mount points—two forward and one rear—usually referred to as claws and stinger by those who use this boat frequently. These aren't traditional mounts, as the Scorpio is designed to be hauled deflated to take up as little space as possible. Instead the mounts are little more than extendable rods that are connected to the craft's onboard sensors and help to compensate for the movement of the boat. Use of the mounts requires a mount clip to be added to any weapon, but the same clip can be quickly fitted for any weapon as it is basically a rubber strap with a mounting pin to connect to the rod. Simple and easily adapted—more reason to love the Scorpio.

The Scorpio is small—only four meters long, and the last half-meter houses its pair of motor mounts. It only has one seat, the pilot's, mounted on the right side behind the small control station. Zodiac was one of the first to offer VR controls and adaptation for riggers, and now they offer AR controls on every new model. The manual controls are usually still there, but those folks who have way more trust in electronics than I can have them removed. The Scorpio offers a bench seat option for behind the pilot, but everyone else will be taking a knee or sitting on the deck.

Weapons and control options are great, but what separates Zodiac from other RIB makers is speed and maneuverability. Motor options for the Scorpio run from mundane to ridiculous, with the latter often causing more problems than it could ever solve, though there is a notable exception. You can lose a motor and still have a backup with serious power. Zodiac crafted their boats with that in mind—you're not supposed to run both of them, as that could create too much lift and flip your boat.

MITSUBISHI WATERBUG

Maneuverability on the Scorpio is managed by an available 360 degrees of rotation for the props rather than a rudder or the standard 180 degrees of rotation. The Scorpio can turn 360 degrees in place, make razor-sharp turns at speed, and even pull some moves that folks usually only see on the trid. These flashy moves usually require the rigger adaptation and a skilled rigger. They're also best performed either in an empty boat or with a fully aware crew, because they frequently toss a rider in the water.

- Zodiac still has the military contract for the UCAS and CAS, but their main money comes from megacorps with offshore or coastal assets. Maersk owns thousands of Zodiac craft that they use to protect their shipping lanes and ships near the coast.
- Kane

ZODIAC SCORPIO (WATERCRAFT)									
HANDL	SPEED	ACCEL	BODY	ARM	PILOT	SENS	SEATS	AVAIL	COST
4	4	2	10	6	1	1	2/6	8	26,000¥
Std. Equipment	2 x weapon mount (standard, external, flexible, manual) front, weapon mount (heavy, external, flexible, manual) rear								

MITSUBISHI WATERBUG

This cute little single seater is the next generation of personal watercraft. The Waterbug is the most maneuverable waterbike on the market, thanks to Mitsubishi's quinjet drive system. The quinjet, as the name implies, is a five-jet propulsion and steering system only available on the Waterbug. Not only does it have the standard rear-facing waterjet system with the standard steering nozzle, but it also has four additional waterjet ports. With two jets on each side, each with their own steering nozzle, the Waterbug can gain extra stability and speed on the straight run, or make turns and maneuvering in tight spots a breeze.

The Waterbug also has a larger model, the Waveskipper, that comes in two and three seater models. The Waveskipper isn't quite as maneuverable as the quinjet technology was added as an afterthought to recent models. A redesigned Waveskipper has been in the works for a few years now but keeps getting bogged down in testing and redesign as they work the bugs out of the system.

- The Waveskipper redesign has been a frequent runner target. Whether caused by corporate sabotage or just

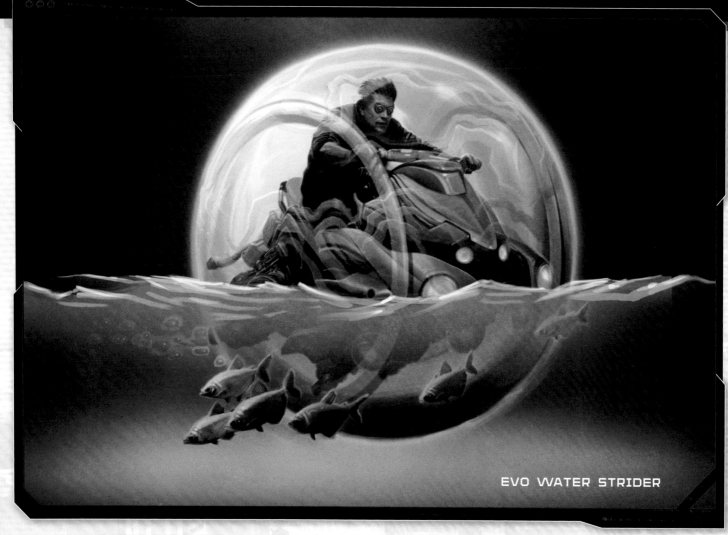

EVO WATER STRIDER

ineptness, this thing keeps suffering from design issues. I've used the Waterbug for some river excursions and while impressed by its nimbleness, I don't know how that can transfer to a larger craft.

◉ Kane

◉ Sepjet. That's the latest redesign effort. Bigger frame, more jets.

◉ Sounder

WATERBUG (WATERCRAFT)									
HANDL	SPEED	ACCEL	BODY	ARM	PILOT	SENS	SEATS	AVAIL	COST
6	3	2	8	4	1	—	1	—	8,000¥
Std. Equipment	—								

WAVESKIPPER (WATERCRAFT)									
HANDL	SPEED	ACCEL	BODY	ARM	PILOT	SENS	SEATS	AVAIL	COST
5	3	2	10	4	1	—	2	—	10,000¥
Std. Equipment	—								

EVO WATER STRIDER

This is a watercraft looking to make it. I called the Waterbug the next generation—this one is a future generation that's being worked through the ends of its paces to make sure it really is ready before it storms the market. At the moment one of the biggest foreseeable problems for the Water Strider is going to be keeping people from driving them over land. They can do it, they are not meant to, and they will break down quickly if it's kept up.

If you're confused by that and have never seen a Water Strider, you aren't alone. The craft looks like a standard waterbike seated inside a clear globe. The globe is made of smart materials, and as it rolls it keeps changing its surface in microscopic ways to create propulsion, whisk away water, and allow air to circulate. While this may sound crazy, the higher maneuverability, insulation in cold environments, complete inability to become submerged without massive damage, and ability to almost instantly reverse direction is getting the Water Strider attention from all quarters. As a recreational craft it has unmatched amusement potential, along with safety and security for all ages. Industries in cold-water environments are looking at the Water Strider as a personal scout or recovery vehicle. Security firms appreciate the maneuverability, sealed environment, and full field of visibility on three axes.

- Add ruthenium to the outer shell and you're invisible.
- Cheshire

- Doesn't work like that. The smart materials aren't really compatible with the ruthenium.
- Sounder

- It does work. I know a guy who did it. He uses his to tool around sunken LA.
- Cheshire

- And I know a guy with oceanfront property in Arizona. Wanna buy it?
- Sounder

- Maybe. Where's Arizona?
- Cheshire

The only major drawbacks I found when I got to test one out was acceleration and speed. In order to accelerate the globe rotates, but the faster it goes, the more it lifts out of the water and the less speed you gain because of the loss of frictional surface. First solution to that is to draw more water into the internal ballast to keep the craft down in the water, but that leads to too much mass and the inability to get up to high speeds. The whole craft is an experiment in advanced tech and materials. Now they just need to add in the math to get the balance right.

- They must have something ready. Pre-orders are open, and the sales guy I talked to said they shipped to their initial investors already.
- Kane

- A real sales guy?
- Slamm-0!

- Could have been a bot. I can't tell the difference most of the time.
- Kane

WATER STRIDER (WATERCRAFT)									
HANDL	SPEED	ACCEL	BODY	ARM	PILOT	SENS	SEATS	AVAIL	COST
3	2	1	8	5	2	2	1	16	11,000¥
Std. Equipment	Life support 1, signature masking 1								

SAILCRAFT ... SORT OF

Normally sailboats are slow as molasses. They usually have a motor but can't get much more speed under power than with the wind. This is such a common conception of everyone who sees a sailboat that Corsair decided to change things up. They wanted to bridge the gap between powerboaters and sailers, and so they created this line of boats. Runners all over the seas have started to see the potential in these craft.

CORSAIR ELYSIUM

The Elysium is the monohull offering by Corsair. Monohulls are the classic boats we all expect to see in the harbor. They have a single body, usually with a cabin amidships and fore, steering and seating in the rear, and several sails but usually a single mast, though some larger boats have more. The Elysium has two sails, a main and jib sail, both of which are furling sails. Furling sails wrap up around themselves rather than fold down, making them easier to handle. That's one reason to love the Elysium.

But not the main reason. The main reason to love the Elysium is the fact that while it can operate as a sailboat and travel on wind power alone, the Elysium has sacrificed its rear berth for a motor cabin and can cruise at speeds normally limited to powerboats. Looks like a sailboat, moves like a powerboat, can sail silent like a sailboat, and can create the illusion of a slow sailboat and catch other craft unaware.

Other features of the Elysium are a small galley, bench, and fold-down table in the main cabin with a head, shower, and twin berth in the fore. The pilot station is located aft with seating around it, but it is easier to handle with VR controls while sitting further fore, though there is no standard seating.

ELYSIUM (WATERCRAFT)									
HANDL	SPEED	ACCEL	BODY	ARM	PILOT	SENS	SEATS	AVAIL	COST
1/3	1/4	1/2	14	10	2	3	6	12	78,000¥
Std. Equipment	Amenities (middle), improved economy, satellite link								

CORSAIR PANTHER

The Panther is a sailing catamaran along the same lines as Corsair's Elysium, except that it removed berthing space at the rear of both hulls so it has twin powerboat motors. The motors are primarily accessed from the rear and on deck rather than through the cabin. The engines give it even more power than the Elysium, but the boat design and positioning cost it some turning radius. When under sail the Panther can unfurl three sails—the main, jib, and spinnaker. The main and jib are the standard sails seen on a sailboat off the main mast and front rigging. The spinnaker is a large parachute-like sail that extends further out in front of the boat.

CORSAIR PANTHER

The access adjustment for the motors preserves the remaining portion of those aft berths to be storage, which allows the Panther extended time at sea. With the repurposed berth space, the Panther sleeps eight rather than ten. The added storage and reduced complement means it can store food and water for all passengers for over two months, its normal sea travel storage max. Mathematically it's 82.5 days, so I could say almost three months.

Below deck the Panther has a large sitting area around the galley with berths in the fore and amidships hull areas on each side. The head and shower are on the port side, with a secondary pilot station and electronics suite starboard. The rear deck of the Panther is like a small covered porch with a pilot station and seating as well as a step down dive deck full aft. The bow has two options, a solid platform that ends a meter before the hulls or a trampoline-like net that runs all the way out. I personally like the trampoline though security conscious folks like the platform.

⊘ Those security folks are just landlubbers. The trampoline is a much better option for prone firing. Only issue is hot

brass from older weapons sometimes collects close to the firer and always seems to find some exposed skin. The trampoline is a flexible kevlar and actually provides some armor and doesn't get burnt by spent shells or muzzle flash.

⊘ Kane

The Panther's biggest limitation is the color options. It only comes in black. While this may seem strange for a vessel that may spend its entire existence in the blazing sun, there is a reason and zero issues. The black paint is a combination thermoelectric and photovoltaic material that constantly feeds juice to the ship's battery system while sapping heat away from the black paint. The power supply isn't enough to run the motors directly, but it allows the secondary batteries to be gaining charge while the main batteries are in use. Main batteries take about twelve hours of sunlight to fully recharge, secondary batteries take eight.

⊘ Story time kids. Gather round. Picture the quiet waters of the western Caribbean Sea with just the slightest sliver of the moon hanging overhead in a cloudless sky full of stars. A well-worn but tenderly loved Beneteau 370 sails on a wisp of wind. It's dashing captain at the helm, his keen eye scanning all horizons for anything that would endanger his precious craft. The swirling green light of his radar screen casting his face in an eerie glow. Peace on the waters.

A sudden flash of red light ignites the air and burns a slash through the captain's sail, causing the perfect wind to begin to whistle through the now-billowing sail. The captain's eyes scan for a source, but the flash was fast and the source still hidden on the dark waters. The captain checks his radar screen and sees nothing.

More red flashes create more gashes in the sail, but this time the captain is ready. He follows the flashes back to their source. And sees nothing but black water. The captain has been a man of the sea for many years and has learned many tricks. He has thermographic goggles handy and quickly pulls them to his face. They reveal the quickly cooling streaks of air and the flashes of intense heat at their source. The empty sea.

Powering the motor up and reeling in the tattered sail, the captain is forced to run from the ghost on the water.
- Kane

- And the ghost was?
- Sounder

- That question took a while to show up. I was thinking people didn't like my story. Anyway, I got some recordings on thermo and did some enhancing. All I got was a vague outline but it was a cat, about the size of a Panther, and it was running a firelance.
- Kane

- Run a laser off the batteries that are recharging constantly on a ship that is always running cold because the heat is being used for energy. Slick. Any idea who was running it?
- Turbo Bunny

- My guess was corpsec, since I'd sailed too close to something valuable.
- Kane

- Accidentally?
- Sounder

- Seriously?
- Kane

PANTHER (WATERCRAFT)									
HANDL	SPEED	ACCEL	BODY	ARM	PILOT	SENS	SEATS	AVAIL	COST
1/3	2/5	1/3	18	10	2	3	8	12	135,000¥
Std. Equipment	Amenities (middle), improved economy, satellite link, secondary manual controls, signature masking 2, SunCell								

CORSAIR TRIDENT

The Trident is a three-hull power-sailer from Corsair, also referred to as a trimaran. These craft have one main hull and two outrigger hulls allowing the boat to sit higher in the water. The Trident has a wide main hull for more living space and plated beams for more deck space. As expected, the Trident also has some tricks up her sleeve.

As with the other two Corsair offerings, the Trident has additional motors over a standard sailing trimaran. While people often expect a trimaran to have more speed than other sailing craft, the Trident can still leave them in shock. Both outrigger hulls have waterjet motors, much like the personal watercraft out their. The main hull has twin motors, giving the Trident four total motors. The waterjets also make a craft that most find unwieldy into something I would call graceful.

The next trick is probably the biggest selling point of the Trident and its pure sail sistercraft, the Triton. The outriggers often make a trimaran unwieldy and difficult to maneuver in tight spots, especially docks. The concept of retractable outriggers isn't new, but retractable deck plated outriggers are. One or both of the outriggers can be retracted in towards the main hull to narrow the Trident.

While similar in length to the monohull Elysium, the Trident is wider and therefore offers a more spacious cabin. It has a full galley, two heads, one shower, a large sitting area, two single aft berths, two double fore berths, and a secondary ladder at the fore as well as one at the aft. The deck area is abundant, and with the extended beams it's downright palatial. The foredeck has a large seating area that can be fitted with a hot tub instead of seating. The aft deck is covered but not enclosed and offers seating and a table. The pilot station is located on a raised platform above the aft deck, with secondary controls linked to a swing-out seat that comes from the aft deck and locks in place.

- When the secondary controls aren't in use, they make a great spot to fish from.
- Sounder

- The Trident and Triton look identical, with the exception of a small hump at the rear of the outrigger hulls and the emblems, which are often removed by the owners in order to put a name on the aft hull of the boat. This is definitely a feature for those who want to own a Trident with its ridiculous speed and make others think they are only dealing with a Triton.
- Turbo Bunny

- Just so it's clear, the Triton can still run down powerboats with a half decent wind and a good captain. It's a straight-line run, but there's something satisfying about gliding past a powerboat at full throttle while you're using nothing but the wind.
- Kane

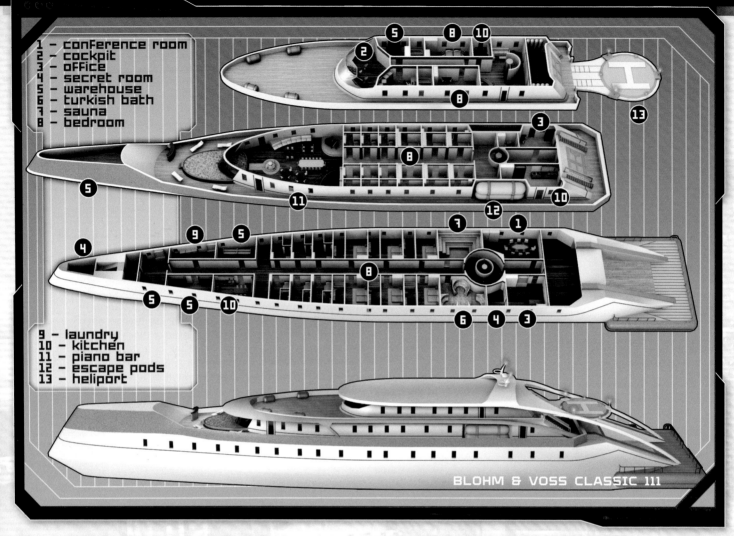

1 – conference room
2 – cockpit
3 – office
4 – secret room
5 – warehouse
6 – turkish bath
7 – sauna
8 – bedroom

9 – laundry
10 – kitchen
11 – piano bar
12 – escape pods
13 – heliport

BLOHM & VOSS CLASSIC 111

- Are we seeing a softer side of Kane? We've got a lot of sailing references.
- Slamm-0!

- Nothing soft about sailing, Slammy. Give it a try and you'll see.
- Kane

TRIDENT (WATERCRAFT)									
HANDL	SPEED	ACCEL	BODY	ARM	PILOT	SENS	SEATS	AVAIL	COST
1/3	4/5	2/3	16	10	2	3	6	12	125,000¥
Std. Equipment	Amenities (middle), improved economy, satellite link, SunCell								

TRITON (WATERCRAFT)									
HANDL	SPEED	ACCEL	BODY	ARM	PILOT	SENS	SEATS	AVAIL	COST
1	6	2	16	10	2	3	6	-	104,000¥
Std. Equipment	Amenities (middle), improved economy, satellite link								

BLOHM & VOSS CLASSIC 111

Blohm & Voss have outdone themselves yet again. This 111-meter luxury yacht features 2070s tech blended seamlessly with turn-of-the-century styling. Harkening back to simpler days when Shiawase was just a corporation, this floating den of opulence will remind every megacorporate executive of where they rose from and where they want to rise to. This is wood, gold trim, crystal faucets, and all the gaudy classic trimmings of the early days of this century.

Designed to sleep twelve guests on the main deck, two on the owner deck, and eight crew on the lower deck, the ship can easily fit ten times that many during a party. The guest sleeping quarters, not berths, six entire rooms, are located in the fore section of the main deck along with attached full bathrooms. The two foremost cabins also have hot rooms between the sleeping quarters and the bathroom. A stairwell is located near the fore that goes up to the social deck. The aft section has a circular stair near amidship followed by a large social/dining room. Beyond that is another large social area built around the glass lower section of the pool on the deck above. A split stairwell near the aft of the ship leads up to the social deck.

The owner deck is the entertainment heart of the Classic 111. The aft section of the deck is also known as the pool deck, because that's where the eight-meter-long pool is, along with its sitting and sunning areas. The pool deck, fore deck, emergency boat berths, and balconies are the only open areas of this deck. The foredeck has seating and sunning chairs along with a bar. It also possesses an access stair to the main deck, along with the anchor rigging and a pair of Zodiac Geminis for porting and emergencies. The enclosed areas of the owner deck contain a large social area near the pool that often doubles as a bar or dance area for parties, a bathroom attached to the club, the central stair with access to the emergency boat decks, and the owners living quarters. The owners quarters consist of an office, conference/ social room, workout room, sauna, bathroom, two walk-in closets, and the master bedroom at the fore. While it may sound like a lot, none of the rooms feel cramped. The conference/social room has floor-to-ceiling windows, as do the workout room and office.

Above the owner deck is the control deck. The fore section of the deck is the control room, where the control room is completely enclosed with access from the lower decks as well as two doors out around the rear sitting area. The rear sitting area is a simple table and seats or a hot tub. This is only accessible through the control room, so it's either for the captain and crew, or it's intended to torture them as bikini-clad elves slither through the control room on the way to the tub.

The lowest deck is all motors, ballasts, and storage. It's all very tight compared to the upper decks, but the owners and guests rarely come down here. If they do, the last thing they are worried about is the cramped space.

The Classic 111 has two other near-identical models, the Neo 111 and Trafalgar 111. The primary difference is style. The Neo is ultra-modern with a lot of chrome and glass, while the Trafalgar resembles the ships of yesteryear complete with AR triple masts and flat sails.

CLASSIC 111 (WATERCRAFT)									
HANDL	SPEED	ACCEL	BODY	ARM	PILOT	SENS	SEATS	AVAIL	COST
3	4	2	24	14	4	4	14	16	14,870,000¥
Std. Equipment	Amenities (high), internal cameras, rigger interface, satellite link								

LURSSEN MOBIUS

Dreaming is allowed. The Mobius is a 140-meter mansion on water. It's an ultra-luxury yacht that gained quite a bit of fame when Johnny Spinrad grounded one on an island in the Caribbean and then bought the island and built the ship into a home. Now everyone is wondering what he's going to do with the second one he bought.

The Mobius is unique in the ultra-luxury realm as it can be fully operated and run by a single person, thanks to its complement of thirty drones. The drones handle everything on the ship, even the piloting. It can be done manually, but manual labor is so out of style. Owners of this class of ship usually hire a real rigger and let them keep everything running smoothly.

The Mobius has five decks; Low, Virtua, Living, Entertainment, and Sun.

The Low deck houses the boats engines, supplies, generators, water supply, and general storage in the aft half of the ship. It's the only cramped deck on the boat and is usually only visited by drones. The fore section houses the internal dock. The dock has slips for one fifteen-meter craft, four five-to-ten-meter craft, and a dozen personal watercraft.

The VirtuaDeck is a Mobius exclusive. It only covers the aft portion of the ship because the dock area is tall, though not the full height of this deck. The slim additional section near the fore houses small motorized wall sections that move out to change the physical character of the VirtuaDeck, while an AR feed creates the rest of the experience in the completely open cabin. The rear five meters of this deck are open around the sides and have a spiral stair at the center that leads up. Seating and a table are usually added, but this craft has a lot of options for this area like a hot tub, fishing setup, and diver deck.

The Living deck has ten basic living quarters, the owners suite, pilot's suite, two galleys, and four dining rooms. Basic living quarters are either queen size or two double beds, a personal bathroom, and a small sitting room. The owner's suite has a king bed, personal bathroom, two walk-in closets, an office, a workout room, a hot tub room, a sauna, a conference room, and an entertainment suite. The pilot's suite is located in the center of the ship. It has a double bed, a bathroom, workroom, and a spiral staircase that reaches every floor.

The Entertainment deck has all the fun stuff. There are four bars, four social rooms, six hot tubs, a pool, a galley, and an open sunning section of the deck near the fore with a ladder up to the helicopter pad.

The Sun deck has two hot tubs, a large social cabin, and a lot of deck space. The pilot house is technically part of this deck but is only accessible via a ladder from the Entertainment deck or the pilot's spiral stairway.

It may look crazy, but it's a beautiful ship.

- The Poseidon's Tear is the name of Spinrad's other Mobius. It's currently docked in Hong Kong but actually spends a lot of time randomly cruising the South Pacific. The guy who runs it is named James Aster, and he has been known to ferry his friends around as long as the boss doesn't need the ship.
- Sounder

LURSSEN MOBIUS

> Wilma mentioned the thirty drones for operating and serving on the ship but left out the ship's twelve defensive drones. It has two mini blimps and ten Roto-Drones, and the onboard contingent contains eight full anthroforms that can be adjusted for security detail if needed.
> Kane

MOBIUS (WATERCRAFT)									
HANDL	SPEED	ACCEL	BODY	ARM	PILOT	SENS	SEATS	AVAIL	COST
3	3	2	36	14	6	5	22	36	84,985,000¥
Std. Equipment	Amenities (luxury), internal cameras, manual control override, rigger cocoon, satellite link, searchlight, SunCell								

SUN TRACKER LAKE KING

The Lake King is a beautiful pontoon boat, designed with slightly longer and larger pontoons than normal to create extra decking on the front and rear of the boat. This also makes it one of the few small watercraft that can handle a troll with ease. The fold-down roof allows for shade or sun and only covers the central section of the boat.

The Lake King is popular with divers thanks to the oversized decks, and some have even been sold for ocean-cruising reef divers, though they stay close to shore and don't sail in rough weather. The little bit of added versatility puts them among my favorites.

LAKE KING (WATERCRAFT)									
HANDL	SPEED	ACCEL	BODY	ARM	PILOT	SENS	SEATS	AVAIL	COST
2	3	2	14	8	1	1	8	—	35,000¥
Std. Equipment	—								

EVO AQUAVIDA

This houseboat is the primary competitor of the Mitsubishi Waterhome. The two companies are constantly trying to one up and out do the other. The Aquavida's latest innovation is an optional subsurface sleeping/ sensory deprivation chamber. The pod is loaded from inside the cabin but then lowers down into the waters below the boat.

The Aquavida comes in one- and two-bedroom versions, with the two-bedroom version losing some of its

EVO AQUAVIDA

outside deckspace. The living area is on the main deck with the quarters, bathroom, galley, and small seating area. The fore has a small external deck space similar to a balcony, and the aft has a larger deck space with seating and a grill. The boat has a second level with the pilot house, along with another open deck area with a table and chairs.

- The Aquavida, and any other houseboat for that matter, makes a great safehouse, especially since they can be moved if you need to. The pod on the Aquavida is a great place to hide out if you're not claustrophobic or a troll.
- Mihoshi Oni

- As folks could easily guess, that pod is getting used for all sorts of things other than sleep or sensory deprivation. It's a nice smuggling tool or a good way to hide things under your boat and then pull them up when you need them.
- Kane

- Speed is a problem, though. The winch needs to be modified to move things up or down quickly, and that's not an easy task. Boats often aren't made with mods in mind.
- Sounder

AQUAVIDA 1 (WATERCRAFT)									
HANDL	SPEED	ACCEL	BODY	ARM	PILOT	SENS	SEATS	AVAIL	COST
2	1	2	20	16	1	3	2/8	10	115,000¥
Std. Equipment	Amenities (middle), winch (basic)								

AQUAVIDA 2 (WATERCRAFT)									
HANDL	SPEED	ACCEL	BODY	ARM	PILOT	SENS	SEATS	AVAIL	COST
2	1	2	20	16	1	3	4/8	12	135,000¥
Std. Equipment	Amenities (middle), winch (basic)								

ULTRAMARINE KINGFISHER

The Kingfisher is basically a cruiser with some added features for fishing. It has berths for four in the bow, a galley with a table that folds down to sleep two more, and a head with an attachment for an on-deck shower. It has less berthing space than a standard cruiser because the pilot cabin is enclosed and pushed to amidship to open up the aft deck for the fishing gear.

Now I could give you a rundown of the great fishing gear this thing has, but the reason I have it on here is not because of the MaxDepth 6200 fish finder. Riggers, and runners in general, have found plenty of alternative uses for the crane that typically is used to hoist caught fish out of the water and onto the boat. This, along with the fish-storage space that can easily be modified to hide other cargo, makes the Kingfisher and other boats like it quite popular.

- The CAS Navy is aware of the Kingfisher's reputation. They don't have the direct procedural means, but they are not above contracting out to find out if a boat is legitimate.
- Sounder

- Don't take that deal if you want to keep working around the water. You'll run across a real chummer and find out why we don't use that term for friends.
- Kane

- Everyone has to make their money somehow. Getting paid by the government or a corp to trim smuggling is perfectly legit. Just because you know the bullseye hits too close to home doesn't mean you have to make threats here.
- Cheshire

- Sorry, kiddo. That was advice. Not a threat. Just making sure you're aware that there are consequences on the water that others might consider personal, but are merely professional.
- Kane

KINGFISHER (WATERCRAFT)									
HANDL	SPEED	ACCEL	BODY	ARM	PILOT	SENS	SEATS	AVAIL	COST
3	3	2	16	12	3	4	6	12	61,000¥
Std. Equipment	Amenities (squatter), satellite link, smuggling compartment, winch (basic)								

AMERICAN AIRBOAT AIRRANGER

I totally dig the AirRanger, not only as a flat-bottom swamp boat, but also as an additional feature available on the UH Minnesota. The AirRanger is driven from a high seat near the center of the boat. It cruises along, pushed by its massive fan, with a draft of less than ten centimeters with a full load. The AirRanger Heavy is a specialized version of the craft that has additional floatation and can hold more massive cargo. This watercraft comes with multiple seating arrangements, though the most common is a two-front, three-back setup for five passengers. As far as swamp boats go, this one is my favorite.

- That heavy load option needs to be used for AirRangers tweaked for trolls. They also adjust the seating to two front and two back, and the pilot's seat isn't as high. The Swamp Ogres, who operate a smuggling and piracy ring in the Louisiana swamps, have a fleet of these. Most with some form of weapon mounted with the front seats.
- Kane

- American Airboat is getting targeted by other boat firms to try to break the contract they have with UH. The contract opens up production so much that American is doing some serious market domination.
- Mr. Bonds

AIRRANGER (WATERCRAFT)									
HANDL	SPEED	ACCEL	BODY	ARM	PILOT	SENS	SEATS	AVAIL	COST
4	4	3	10	6	1	1	6	6	25,500¥
Std. Equipment	—								

AIRRANGER HEAVY (WATERCRAFT)									
HANDL	SPEED	ACCEL	BODY	ARM	PILOT	SENS	SEATS	AVAIL	COST
4	4	3	12	6	1	1	5	8	35,500¥
Std. Equipment	—								

GMC RIVERINE

In 2074, a marine legend returned after a short production hiatus. The Riverine was the bane of smugglers around the world, but its success led to a coordinated effort to disrupt production by those same smugglers. Let it never be said that pirates can't work together. Don't argue that they hired runners, because they still had to communicate to get it started. That would have been one hell of a meeting to get in on.

- It was!
- Kane

The time off and damage to the production equipment gave GMC the perfect excuse to re-engineer a new Riverine. What they came up with is going to be a lesson to criminals around the world that when something's already badass and you decide to trash it, the replacement risks being even more of a hoop-kicking maritime predator, this one with better armor, better arms, better navigation, and an electronics suite that can find a minnow in the Pacific.

New materials technology has armored up the hull as well as the internal compartments and cabins. The Riverine can shrug off most gunfire. Even anti- materiel rifles have a tough time, and the single hole they make isn't going to do much to slow the Riverine.

Anyone trying to get a shot in at the Riverine is going to need some serious cover themselves. The Riverine comes standard with a complement of five mounts. Two rear, one port, one starboard, and one fore. All of them are designed for remote operation, but each can be assigned to a different user station inside the Riverine. Weapon systems vary, but the most common line-up consists of a pair of fully automatics in the rear, anti-materiel cannons at the side, and a multiple missile system up front. Positioning and mounting allows the two rear mounts 360 degrees of rotation and up to 90 degrees up from the horizon. Side mounts only offer 195 degrees of rotation and 65 degrees up from the horizon. The fore mount covers 360 and 90 as well. And remember, that's the basic complement. The Riverine is capable of mounting side batteries consisting of up to six guns on each side and a rear battery of three guns. The rear battery isn't very effective at high speeds, but the entire setup is a rude awakening for anyone who comes creeping up on the boat.

> ❂ The new model can also mount torpedo tubes and depth charges. Despite its small size, this beast thinks it's a destroyer.
> ❂ Kane

The navigation system is fully integrated into the new Matrix and usually links to the Ares Grid, where a special division of GMC monitors all the craft they've produced that are logged on. If there's trouble, they contact the owner while they go check it out. They're usually outmatched due to signal restrictions, but they come en masse and are good at working together as a team.

Finally, the Riverine has been outfitted with an electronics suite to make any rigger drool, including high-end built-in commlink, complete with satellite, premium sensors, full AR and VR control suite, serious targeting and fire solution software, and even some entertainment equipment.

The most impressive thing about the new Riverine is that it looks just like the old Riverine. There are a few subtle changes, but when this beast is buzzing up on you, you aren't going to be looking for subtleties like the direction of the exhaust port or the blade size on the propellers.

> ❂ If the weapons are out it's a dead giveaway, but some of the older models are getting retrofits to mount the new weapon layout. The Riverine is back and ready to take on all comers.
> ❂ Sticks

> ❂ That sounds like a challenge. I'm in.
> ❂ Kane

The Riverine is produced with one of three packages in mind, and they are all built to suit. The Security model is the base and has all the things mentioned above. The Police model adds a light bar, two sets of twin spotlights, front and rear, and a siren. No big surprises there. The Military model has the torpedo and depth charge set up standard, offers the same spotlights as the Police, and sits about a quarter meter lower in the water thanks to the armor increase.

RIVERINE SECURITY (WATERCRAFT)									
HANDL	SPEED	ACCEL	BODY	ARM	PILOT	SENS	SEATS	AVAIL	COST
4	5	3	16	12	4	4	8	15R	100,000¥
Std. Equipment	Amenities (squatter), commlink (DR 7), rigger cocoon, rigger interface, satellite link, searchlight, weapon mount (heavy, internal, flexible, remote) front, 2 x weapon mount (standard, internal, flexible, remote) sides, 2 x weapon mount (standard, external, flexible, remote) rear								

RIVERINE POLICE (WATERCRAFT)									
HANDL	SPEED	ACCEL	BODY	ARM	PILOT	SENS	SEATS	AVAIL	COST
4	5	3	16	14	4	5	8	15R	154,000¥
Std. Equipment	Amenities (squatter), commlink (DR 7), rigger cocoon, rigger interface, satellite link, 4 x searchlight (2 front, 2 rear), weapon mount (heavy, internal, flexible, remote) front, 2 x weapon mount (standard, internal, flexible, remote) sides, 2 x weapon mount (standard, external, flexible, remote) rear								

RIVERINE MILITARY (WATERCRAFT)									
HANDL	SPEED	ACCEL	BODY	ARM	PILOT	SENS	SEATS	AVAIL	COST
5	5	2	20	20	6	6	8	20F	225,000¥
Std. Equipment	Amenities (squatter), commlink (DR 8), rigger cocoon, rigger interface, satellite link, searchlight, signature masking 4, weapon mount (heavy, internal, flexible, remote) front, 2 x weapon mount (standard, internal, flexible, remote) sides, 3 x weapon mount (standard, external, flexible, remote) rear								

AIR SUPERIORITY

Bishop opened his eyes and saw Finch leaning over and yelling at him. It took a few seconds, but the loud ringing slowly gave way to the street samurai's voice.

"... oss! You okay? *Boss*!!!"

Bishop waved his hand, trying to signal he was fine. Taking Finch's arm, he lifted himself upright and immediately regretted the decision as pain shot through his torso and legs from shrapnel.

Propping himself up against an old, rusted heating unit, he looked out over the skyscraper's rooftop but fell back down. On the other side of the heater, he felt heavy rounds impact. Finch rose and let loose with a long burst from his AK, tagging a Northrup Wasp as it flew by. The small security helo trailed smoke but remained airborne. A second Wasp took up the slack, its chin-turret MMG blazing away.

Bishop looked up just as up Finch, defiantly blasting away with his AK, was cut in half by MG rounds. AROs from the team's PI-TAC floated in Bishop's field of vision, fuzzy and distorted. In his ear, Bishop thought he heard someone say something like "ETA, twenty seconds." He tried again to get into the fight but realized his shotgun was gone.

Wracked with pain, Bishop crawled past Finch's body. He saw the rest of his team, all wounded and pinned down by machine gun fire. Moon-Seeker's chest was covered in crimson as Bingo tried to apply trauma patches; the female shaman wasn't moving. Hooper, the other samurai, was army-crawling behind another heater, his right cyberarm hanging on by a few wires. The only one left in the fight was Thunder, but the second Wasp kept the troll pinned down.

The first Wasp formed up with his wingman, both hovering nearby. Under stubby wings hung ripple-fire rocket pods. Bishop knew they were waiting for perfect target locks before they finished his team off. He could see the looks of smug superiority on the pilot's faces. Defiantly, Bishop gave them the middle finger— just as the first Wasp was ripped to shreds by heavy-machine-gun fire.

The second Wasp then banked sharply to the right and accelerated. Another helo, a Hughes WK-4 Stallion, painted to look like a local trid station, pursued. But instead of packing cameras and sensors, it packed its own rocket pod and machine guns. It didn't take long for the Stallion to blast the Wasp out of the sky with its own rockets.

His vision swam, but Bishop felt hands reach under his arms. Bishop looked over his shoulder and saw his team's rigger, Crankshaft, hauling him into the now waiting Stallion. Likewise, Thunder and Bingo were helping Hooper and Moon-Seeker (and the rest of Finch) into the helo as well.

An ork in the Stallion's pilot's seat, wearing a worn flight suit and helmet with the name "Zero" stenciled on it, looked back at Bishop and smiled before mouthing "Need a lift?"

Bishop raised his arm, and instead of a finger he gave Zero a thumbs-up.

FLYING THE UNFRIENDLY SKIES

POSTED BY: KANE

There's an old military saying: he who controls the air controls the battlefield. Well, modern tech and magic may have something to say about that, but there's still something to be said about being able to call in air support, or even better, fly it in yourself, screaming in out of the sun with weapons hot and blowing the ever-loving hell out of some poor unsuspecting bastard. I may be the terror of the seas now, but my first love—other than Kat—is the sky.

- ❂ And yeah, I'm just a tad bit slotted off that the "trinity" went with some second-rate used-boat salesman for the watercraft section. That's like trying to cook a pure Angus steak in a microwave.
- ❂ Kane

- ❂ Wait, what? That doesn't make … oh forget it.
- ❂ Bull

Now, some riggers will argue (and they're wrong) that modern combat drones have rendered manned aerial combat vehicles obsolete. Well, if that's true, then tell me why hasn't it happened yet? Drones are definitely handy in a fight, but they've got their limitations and weakness. One good hack or a jammed signal and you can say bye-bye to your baby birdy. And speaking of that, don't get me started on how fragile most aerial drones are compared to a manned combat vehicle. No, when you need some *real* hot and heavy close air support, accept no substitutes. A manned craft will likely have more weapons, armor, range, and that oh-so-important thing in combat: situational awareness.

Now I know that most of you reading this are already bitching about how superior drones are or that you aren't going to be able to get your hands on or even need something as nova-hot as a sixth- or seventh-generation fighter-bomber. Okay, fair enough. But I'd be willing to bet that a nice helo or LAV may just be the thing to get into (and then out of) some rather

sticky situations. Or maybe you need something for a nice long, extended working vacation. Or maybe you just happen to have an *omae* with a real gunship that can play cavalry for you.

Well, whatever your manned aerial needs are, Uncle Kane has complied a quick list of some of the finest aerial vehicles currently available for some fun shadowy adventures. And instead of just cut-and-pasting some blood-suckin', boot-licking corporate drone's sales pitch from a catalogue, I'll give you the straight scan along with the not-so-humble opinions of some associates of mine, because let's face it—we don't have a lot of true combat pilots hanging around here. So consider these Kane-tested and Kane-approved!

I'll even act professional. For me.

- ❂ Not enough *true* combat pilots? I might actually be offended at that remark if I actually cared about your opinion, Kane.
- ❂ Rigger X

HUGHES STALLION WK-4
(ROTORCRAFT)

Make no mistake; this is one sweet honey of a whirly-bird. The first Stallion flew in 2012 and has been in the air ever since. That should tell you something right there. Sometimes people do realize that if something ain't broke, *don't fix it*! But then, sometimes you can teach old dogs new tricks.

The current Stallion model, the WK-4, started rolling off the Hughes assembly lines in late 2072 and has been a big seller ever since. The first production run sold out within a month, forcing Hughes to expand their production lines. It took almost a year to catch up with the back orders, but now the WK-4 is rolling out at a nice steady pace and is slowly replacing the older WK-2 and WK-3 models (not that they needed replacing, but newer is always better right?). Overall the WK-4 is a slight departure from previous designs. The main rotors on the WK-4 are set farther back and the tail section has been updated. The biggest design changes, however, are the landing skids, which have undergone a major redesign that allows for better landings and reduced drag while in flight.

HUGHES STALLION WK-4

The biggest reason for the Stallion's success is its versatility. She may not be the best at anything, but the base model is really fragging good at doing a *lot* of things and is a true (pun intended) workhorse helo. With a few tweaks, the Stallion can be configured to handle just about every known helo job on the planet in a wide variety of environments. This baby practically *begs* to be hot-rodded! Militaries, corps, governments, and civilians all over the world use the Stallion in one capacity or another, making it one of the most common aircraft in the sky.

Another secret of the Stallion's success is her reliability. Built with ease of maintenance in mind, Stallions feature multiple redundant systems that help keep the bird in the air when dealing with pesky things like, say, incoming fire. Semi-modular parts and convenient access panels allow mechanics to perform maintenance in roughly three-fourths of the time it would take another bird. It also helps that many parts from older Stallion models are compatible with the WK-4.

All this comes in a package that, compared to other birds, won't break the bank.

> My unit got to field-test four enhanced WK-4 prototypes during the war. I can't say enough about these machines. They took, and dished out, more fire that any aircraft their size had any right to and kept on going. And when other helos were grounded by environmental factors, the Stallions kept flying. All of ours looked like patched-up Swiss cheese by the time we pulled out, but they all flew out of South America under their own power.
> Picador

> I'm glad they re-designed the landing skids. The WK-2 and -3 were great birds, but landings were hard on that old mainline body central-strut design. If you didn't perform regular maintenance checks, it wasn't unheard of for it to fail at the most inopportune time. One of the few problems the older designs had.
> Osprey

AZTECHNOLOGY GX-2 AND GX-3AT

- Same about the engine and main rotor placement. The older Stallions flew like a dream, once you learned how to handle them, which was tongue-and-cheekily called "breaking them in" (although if that meant the aircraft or the pilot was up for debate). The WK-4 is a lot more pilot friendly.
- Blackhawk

- I like these things because they're so damn common— they're like the Ford Americar of the skies. Look up in any given city or sprawl and you'll likely see a Stallion or two. With a nice forged IFF or paint job, you could fly around all day and no one would look twice at you. Perfect for shadow work.
- Pistons

HUGHES STALLION WK-4 (ROTORCRAFT)									
HANDL	SPEED	ACCEL	BODY	ARM	PILOT	SENS	SEATS	AVAIL	COST
5	5	4	16	16	4	4	8	12	440,000¥
Std. Equipment	—								

AZTECHNOLOGY AGULAR GX-2 AND GX-3AT

(ROTORCRAFT)

In service for over thirty years, the Agular continues to be the Aztlan military's premier attack helo and the bane of smugglers, coyotes, or anyone operating illegally along the Aztlan border. With a ridiculous mix of speed, armor, and firepower, it's a potent hunter-killer and escort. The Agular often goes to go toe-to-toe with t-birds and even a few fighter-bombers. Popular legend (or Aztlan propaganda) says that border-jumpers would often cut and run based solely on the number of inbound Agulars.

And then, Aztechnology upped the ante.

Just in time for Operations: Marauder and Huntress, Aztechnology rolled out two new designs that quickly made an impression. The first was the GX-2, a modern upgrade on the classic GX chassis. Compared to the original, the GX-2 was even faster and featured SOTA targeting systems and sensors. The second design, -3AT, is basically a flying armored personnel carrier that trades speed for heavier armor and an additional "cabin" in the rear of the aircraft that can carry up to eight average-sized metahuman passengers. Both models feature a traditional two-person cockpit with the pilot seated behind the "gunner". While the aircraft can be controlled by only one person, the control systems are designed to allow both pilot and gunner to jack into the aircraft at the same time for maximum combat efficiency. Although in an emergency one can take over for the other, or they can even switch positions.

Aesthetically, the GX-2 looks the same as the original GX while the GX-3AT has an enlarged "box" area under the raised engine compartment and before tail section; this is the troop/passenger compartment.

After the recent war with Amazonia, Aztlan put several de-weaponized GX-2s and -3ATs on the (semi) open market or sold them to "preferred customers" (read: merc units aligned with Aztlan during the war). While the weapons were removed, the hard points and other systems remained.

* I can attest to the Agular's' efficiency. During the Battle of Bogotá, the GX-2 and -3AT were a nasty combination. Augmented by spotter drones, the GX-2s struck first, deftly maneuvering between buildings and providing close air support with pinpoint accuracy before darting away before they could be engaged. Meanwhile, the -3ATs came straight in, shrugging off all but the heaviest of fire to deploy troops.
* Aufheben

* It's miserable riding in the back of the -3AT. It's extremely cramped (carry eight my hoop), and the engine's vibration rattles everything while the noise deafens everyone. If you're going to ride in this beast, use audio dampeners.
* Hard Exit

* According to my sources, there are some back-room deals in the works for the UCAS to purchase both the GX-2 and -3AT and have them assigned to JTF: Seattle as part of a rumored "Denver Response Unit." And that deal may or may not include a few Aztlan technical advisors to train the new aircrews.
* Kay St. Irregular

AGULAR GX-2 (ROTORCRAFT)

HANDL	SPEED	ACCEL	BODY	ARM	PILOT	SENS	SEATS	AVAIL	COST
5	7	5	20	16	4	5	2	28F	500,000¥
Std. Equipment	Rigger interface								

AGULAR GX-3AT (ROTORCRAFT)

HANDL	SPEED	ACCEL	BODY	ARM	PILOT	SENS	SEATS	AVAIL	COST
4	6	4	22	20	4	4	10	28F	550,000¥
Std. Equipment	Rigger interface								

S-K AEROSPACE SKA-008
(ROTORCRAFT)

In early 2074, S-K Aerospace's newest design burst onto the rotorcraft scene with their out-of-nowhere introduction of the SKA-008. Described as an "executive security aircraft", -008s have been quickly rotated into S-K Prime's aircraft fleet, replacing all other rotorcraft assigned in the executive-protection units.

Nicknamed the "Skate", the -008's design is sleek and the passenger cabin is extremely plush with the normal host of high-priced amenities befitting a VIP. But don't make the mistake of thinking this is just a lumbering, flying limo; the -008 is all business, and that business is keeping VIPs away from or getting them out of trouble. Highly maneuverable and able to turn and land on a dime, the -008 also has a freakishly fast acceleration profile. Combined with some heavy armor, excellent ECM, sensors, and a single hard point in the nose for a single retractable heavy weapon mount, the -008 is just about damn near perfect for getting a corporate big shot out of a danger zone.

While it's very good at its intended role, the -008 isn't without its flaws, and the high performance comes at a price. Like most German-produced products, the -008 is extremely over-engineered. Every part, component, plate, and even the rivets are made to ridiculously high specs, making the craft extremely hard to repair, maintain, or modify. The -008 comes as-is and usually stays that way unless you want to put some *serious* work into it.

* Yeah, to hot-rod this bird, add an extra five to *eight* hours to the job because the internals are fragging tight. And make sure you know what you're doing, because working on this thing is like messing with the innards of a Swiss watch. I've heard of several aero-techs who've fragged up royally repairing Skates, with the pilots and passengers paying the price. Needless to say, their superiors were less than pleased.
* Airman Al

* The design was rushed into service. The airframes and flight systems haven't gotten the normal shakedown period other designs get. Reports are filtering in that during rapid egress maneuvers, the rotor assemblies are being stressed beyond original specs. A lot of the first production run Skates were grounded pending a full maintenance check. If you get one, *quadruple* the diagnostics. Despite this, when Skates are in good shape, they're absolutely wiz!
* Blackhawk

* Huh, you would expect something like this from someone like say, Ares, not S-K. I wonder who got fed to the boss-dragon.
* Cosmo

S-K AEROSPACE SKA-008

* On another note, current S-K protocol dictates that each "Skate" carries no more than three VIPs/principles to allow a minimum six-person security detail and two door gunners. Yeah, this may be hard to modify, but slapping a few slings or gyro-mounts out the side doors is still easy.
* OrkCEO

S-K AEROSPACE SKA-008 (ROTORCRAFT)									
HANDL	SPEED	ACCEL	BODY	ARM	PILOT	SENS	SEATS	AVAIL	COST
6	5	8	16	18	4	4	12	24R	525,000¥
Std. Equipment	Rigger interface								
Note	When modifying/customizing this aircraft, raise the threshold by 2 on all Extended Tests. Any critical glitch during this test results in damage to the aircraft.								

DASSAULT SEA SPRITE

(ROTORCRAFT)

When Dassault first tried to break into the rotorcraft market in late 2052, it was met with a lot of general apathy because none of their early designs stood out. For years that branch of the company floundered and was almost shut down until the introduction of the Sea Sprite in 2060.

An all-weather tilt-rotor search-and-rescue craft primarily used for long-range or maritime operations, the Sea Sprite is more commonly and affectionately known as the Sea Angel. In 2062, it gained worldwide recognition when Sea Sprites were prominently featured during rescue and relief efforts after the Yucatan earthquakes. Because of the exposure (and a massive marketing blitz by Dassault), militaries and rescue agencies from around the world quickly placed orders. By 2064, Sea Sprites were a common sight over oceans and other waterways.

Known for being an extremely stable platform, the Sprite's most distinguishing features are the inverted gull-wings that can raise the wingtip engines high above the airframe during hovering or low-level flight. This allows for greater rotor clearance, the advanced turbo-prop engines, and overall aircraft stability during rescue operations. In certain weather conditions (read: calm), the Sea Sprite is able to land directly on the water. In horizontal flight, the wings assume a more traditional flight profile, allowing the Sea Sprite to rapidly respond to emergencies. Also featured are two rescue winches, one aft just above the rear retracting boarding ramp and a second one at the starboard waist door.

DASSAULT SEA SPRITE

- The Sea Angel is good at what she does; "all weather" is an understatement. I've personally seen one of these things brave category four hurricanes. The cabin was nice and warm when they pulled me out. Last time I take a boat ride through the Carib League.
- Traveler Jones.

- Not just for search-and-rescue, the CAS especially likes to arm them for interdiction duty. Designated "Archangels," these birds operate with drone support, but the biggest threat are the aerial gunners who use assault cannons or anti-material rifles to tag the engines of suspicious watercraft. Then they deploy an inflatable craft for a nice "safety inspection." Of course, they've never tagged me. *grin*.
- Kane

- A lot of Aztlan and Carib smugglers are buying Sprites through back channels and are putting CAS Navy/Coast Guard markings on them. If you try this, make sure your forged IFF codes are good or have a good hacker.
- Marcos

- Sea Sprites operate best in open areas. Those lovely wings are very large and could cause problems in more cramped, urban environments. Plan accordingly.
- Al Dhibi

DASSAULT SEA SPRITE (ROTORCRAFT)									
HANDL	SPEED	ACCEL	BODY	ARM	PILOT	SENS	SEATS	AVAIL	COST
5	4	3	18	12	3	5	14	18R	400,000¥
Std. Equipment	Rescue winches (x2)								

FEDERATED-BOEING PBY-70 "CATALINA II"

(AMPHIBIOUS FIXED-WING AIRCRAFT)

At first glance, the PBY-70 looks like a throwback that belongs in a museum rather than flying in the Sixth World. But this bird, to paraphrase an older flat-vid movie, has "got it where it counts."

In 2050, the Catalina II began as a personal restoration project of F-B's top aeronautics engineer. Using the latest technologies of the time, he completely restored an old WWII Catalina PBY like a classic car, but

FEDERATED-BOEING PBY-70A

with a few upgrades. In 2059, F-B's then-owner/CEO found out about the project and asked for a demonstration. Impressed, he decided to give rival Fiat-Fokker (with their classic Cloud-9) a run for their money in the amphibious aircraft market and authorized the PBY-70 project.

The first new aircraft took to the skies in 2065 and went into limited production in 2070, with full production beginning in 2075.

Outwardly, the Catalina II looks almost exactly like its predecessor, except that it boasts modern turbo-prop engines and is approximately twenty percent larger. While the prop engines make it markedly slower than similar jet-powered aircraft, the Catalina II makes up for it in range. The large wings enables the Catalina to glide and cruise at mid-to-high altitude on only one engine, drastically reducing fuel consumption. Other features include a small but comfortable cabin with modular cots to accommodate a variety of metahuman sizes (three humans is standard) and a sizable cargo compartment that can double as a passenger area (six average metahumans). Just the thing for long working vacations.

For defense, the Catalina has three "gunner" positions at the nose and two at the waist, along with two hard points on each wing. And because she won't break

any speed records, she also boasts a powerful ECM/ECCM unit to help deal with pesky things like missiles.

- They also copied the interior of the old PBY closely enough that the old radio operator/navigator position is there. A couple of chummers of mine who started flying Catalina IIs use them as decker or secondary drone rigger positions.
- Blackhawk

- Or gunner. Even though it's relatively new, the rigger/smuggler communities are taking to the Catalina like flies on drek. I've already heard of the different ways this bird has been modified, like mounting M/HMGs in all the gun turrets and putting rockets pods on the wings. Another went ECM and drone heavy with a decker and drone rigger tag-teaming. And that's just the tip of the iceberg. Who knows the different ways this bird will be rigged in the next few years?
- Airman Al

- Some prefer to let the crew operate the guns manually in the turrets like it was still 1945. I like my retro-fantasies as much as the next slag, but when it hits the fan, I want the

AIRBUS 'LIFT TICKET' ALS-699

maximum accuracy only an RCC can give. Anything else is just stupid.

- Clockwork

- For those like me who're of a larger stature, moving between compartments can be a bit tight, but no worse than an average building. The compartments themselves aren't too bad, and if you take out the other cots, the bunk area is quite comfortable.

- Beaker

- If you're going to get one, do it soon. Sales are slowly increasing, and the first production runs are almost gone. If popularity and word-of-mouth continues, some corp(s) or government(s) will likely put in a bulk order, creating a massive back-order backlog. Or Fiat-Fokker may decide to try and disrupt the line, because we all know something like that *never* happens.

- Kane

FED-BOEING PBY-70 CATALINA II (ROTORCRAFT)									
HANDL	SPEED	ACCEL	BODY	ARM	PILOT	SENS	SEATS	AVAIL	COST
4	3	3	22	14	3	4	16	12	250,000¥
Std. Equipment	Heavy weapon mounts (nose, right/left waist)								

AIRBUS "LIFT-TICKET" ALS-699

(HEAVY ROTORCRAFT)

The direct competitor to the Ares Dragon, the ALS-699 is the latest model of a very successful dual-rotor heavy lift utility helo design. Despite being considered inferior (although it's debatable) to the Dragon in terms of lifting capacity, the aircraft still had (and continues to have) a significant production run in Europe, where it nearly out-sold the Dragon.

The original model, the ALS-690 and its successor the ALS-694, saw extensive action during the Euro Wars, transporting heavy equipment, supplies, artillery, and vehicles directly to the front lines throughout the European Theater. European commanders loved the aircraft for its ability to travel long distances and stability while crossing pesky obstacles such as mountain ranges. It was also easy to maintain and modify for various other jobs such as search and rescue and vehicle recovery.

The newest version, the -699, has the same heavy lifting capabilities as its predecessors but comes with fully modern systems. In terms of lifting, the advanced turbo-shaft engines allow for a maximum load of 16,000 kg. This can be accomplished through the four auto-deployable, high-tensile magnetic grapple cables (or standard cable/hooks) that come standard, or on a modular cargo pod similar to the one on the Dragon.

Despite its outstanding performance and capabilities, the Lift-Ticket has never been able to fully shake the stigma of being inferior to the Ares Dragon. This is in large part because no other aircraft, including the Lift-Ticket, has been able to break the Dragon's aerial lifting record, which Ares marketing likes to remind the world of every chance it gets. To help combat this, Airbus often undercuts Ares by selling the Lift-Ticket at a lower price, even if it means taking a hit in overall profits.

- Yes, but they make their money back with upgrade packages and parts. Still a very good deal.
- Al Dhibi

- Okay, so why's it called the Lift-Ticket? Seems like a goofy name for an aircraft.
- Chainmaker

- The original designer was a Swiss national who loved skiing. No big mystery here.
- Glitch

- The Lift-Ticket is a common sight among mercenary groups who purchased surplus aircraft after the Euro Wars. With a quick upgrade package offered by Airbus, older -694s were quickly brought up to -699 specs. Unless a tech checks the production ID numbers, you can't tell the difference.
- Picador

- With Ares' recent quality control problems, Dragon sales have also begun to slip. It didn't help when three Dragons crashed in Morocco six months ago during humanitarian mission to the Western Sahara region and the cause was ruled "faulty rotor assemblies." Airbus, among others, was quick to jump on that little tidbit.
- Mr. Bonds

- I've flown the Lift-Ticket for years and this talk of it being inferior to the Dragon is pure bulldrek. Yeah, the Dragon out-lifted the Ticket in *competitions*, but have you ever seen a max-loaded Dragon move? It's like a pig in slop! The -699 can carry up to eighty-five percent of its max payload weight, with minimal loss in performance. Put the same load on a Dragon and watch it do nothing more than limp along. That little fact Ares doesn't like to advertise. Real-world performance trumps marketing every time.
- Airman Al

- What world do *you* live in?
- Aufheben

- Not too long ago, during a job in LA, my team and I attempted an exfiltration through the sunken remnants of Downtown via speedboat. Well things didn't go as planned, and the local law was hot on our heels. After nine-hours of playing cat and mouse, my rigger calls a local buddy of his. She saved our collective hoops by swooping in with her Lift-Ticket, using small drones to attach the magnetic cables directly to the boat, and then carries us away while under heavy fire. Damn, what a wild ride.
- DangerSensei

AIRBUS "LIFT-TICKET" ALS-669 (ROTORCRAFT)									
HANDL	SPEED	ACCEL	BODY	ARM	PILOT	SENS	SEATS	AVAIL	COST
5	3	3	16	12	3	4	5	14	325,000¥
Std. Equipment	Retractable magnetic grapple lines (x4), standard grapple lines (x4)								

GMC GRYPHON

(V/STOL)

To make them more viable in the cutthroat markets, engineers often try to design aircraft, especially LAVs/t-birds, with at least some versatility in mind. But the designers of the Gryphon went in the opposite direction, which resulted in one of the most lethal purpose-built combat aircraft in recent years.

Simply put, the Gryphon is a pure gunship.

The Gryphon's design lineage is one of GMC's most closely guarded secrets, but a few details have leaked out over the years. At first glance, many think of it as nothing more than an amped-up Harpy Scout, but the opposite is true. During initial testing, the Gryphon's airframe seemed to be too unstable and the flight control systems inadequate. Out of ten testbeds, seven crashed or suffered massive system failures on the ground. With the project going way over budget, GMC scrapped it. However, the frame was re-tooled and the internal systems re-designed, resulting in the Harpy Scout.

Approximately five years later, the Gryphon's chief project manager was uncovered as an Aztechnology mole and saboteur. With the mole gone, engineers revisited the project and discovered that all the initial difficulties were the result of sabotage and false data, not design flaws. So the project was reinstated.

Not much more needs to be said about the Gryphon. It's fast, maneuverable, rugged, armored, packs the latest in sensor/ECM suites, and it has more weapon hard

GMC GRYPHON

points that any other combat aircraft in its class. Other than a pilot and gunner, it doesn't carry any passengers or drones. Because of its massive engines, any room left in the fuselage is usually taken up by fuel tanks and ammunition bins. In combat, Gryphons usually just overwhelm their targets with sheer firepower.

This is one t-bird you do *not* want to have coming after you.

- The Gryphon is a terror in the skies, but it's expensive and a gas-hog. This is not a t-bird you'll see on any long-distance strikes or escort missions unless it has a refueling aircraft or drones accompanying it. Drop tanks are often used to help offset this, but they take up valuable weapon space.
- Osprey

- In military operations, Gryphons are often used defensively as interceptors tasked with taking out the close air support of their enemies or defending staging areas/bases. Their tactics are simple: move in fast, take out the target, and get out.
- Blackhawk

- That's great for *military* operations, but a lot of corporate security forces make use of them, too. MCT for example, likes to keep a few near their more valuable facilities. In this situation, the range problem is rendered moot.
- Rigger X

- This is one of those craft that is dubious for use by shadowrunners (Kane notwithstanding)—more likely will be used against us. Sure, you'd have a metric ton of firepower at your disposal, but I doubt this thing is very subtle, and it will attract a whole lot of unwanted attention. Good to have the paydata on it, but not very practical for running.
- Danger Sensei

- Come on Sensei, you should know better than that. Sometimes a run calls for finesse, but other times it calls for blowing the ever-loving hell out of something. And this would be the t-bird to do it. Sometimes the right tool for the job is a big gun(s).
- Hard Exit

EVO-KRIME 'KRIME WING'

GMC GRYPHON (V/STOL)									
HANDL	SPEED	ACCEL	BODY	ARM	PILOT	SENS	SEATS	AVAIL	COST
5	8	7	24	24	4	5	2	28F	3,200,000¥
Std. Equipment	Heavy Weapon Mount (nose, left wing, right wing) Rigger Interface								

EVO-KRIME "KRIME WING"

(V/STOL)

What do you get when one of the premier aerospace firms in the world teams up with a small-time renegade company famous for making weapons specifically designed for *cough* "larger metahumans"? First, you get a lot of people who say something like: *What the frag possessed them to do something like that?* And then you get something like the Krime Wing.

Apparently the idea for this t-bird came about when a group of drunken Evo junior execs on a bar crawl found themselves in an establishment that just happened to be the local favorite of Krime employees. By some miracle, the patrons (mostly trolls) decided not to stomp the Evo execs into paste. This was most likely because one of the execs deployed the greatest weapon at his disposal to prevent said pasting: his corporate expense account. Thousands of nuyen in drinks later (this was a bar full of trolls after all), the fragile execs were back at their hotel.

When their supervisor invoiced their expenditures, the execs covered their hoops by claiming it was a planned business meeting with Krime. When said supervisor called them on their bulldrek, the execs went back to Krime to try to cover their hoops. But instead of a cover-up, the Evo execs walked out with an idea for a new t-bird design that fit within Krime's line of products.

Basically, Krime "persuaded" the execs into helping them build a t-bird for trolls. Even funnier was the fact that the project actually became a winner!

A niche aircraft in a niche market, the Krime Wing looks like a (slightly) scaled-down cargo plane with the wings removed and massive engines attached. Despite its size, its performance profile and general load-out is on par with other t-birds, such as the GMC Banshee. The big selling point of the Krime Wing is the sheer amount of interior space it has compared other t-birds. This also translates into a lot more cargo and passenger space than most t-birds. While originally designed for trolls, many Krime Wings have been purchased by non-trolls who are looking to take advantage of the craft's size and carrying capacity; although they'll have to downgrade the internal accommodations first.

- Despite what marketing departments say, all Krime did was give some general specs and put their name on the product. Engineers from Evo subsidiary Yamatetsu Naval Technologies did most of the design, R&D, and manufacturing. Still, it works because Evo gets an opening into a new market (and "edgy" demographic) while Krime gets to say they designed a t-bird.
- 2XL

- Last week the Black Forest Troll Kingdom, Evo, and Krime closed a joint manufacturing deal. Various products, including the Krime Wing, will now be produced in the Kingdom.
- Mr. Bonds

- Sorry, but the Krime Wing is a gimmick, nothing more. There're a lot better t-birds out there. So unless you like flying bricks, look somewhere else.
- Rigger X

- Look, the Krime Wing is proof that if you put enough thrust on it, even a brick will fly, but it's able to achieve a t-bird performance profile is still fragging good. I know a lot of smugglers who use that massive cargo capacity for many things, like converting it into a massive drone carrier. Use some imagination.
- Clockwork

- No wonder you like it.
- Bull

- I'll take function over form every time. And yes, I have one converted to a drone carrier—a *massive* drone carrier. This thing as room to spare, it's like a flying RV and semi-truck all rolled into one. And with a few key mods, I dare anyone to take a shot at me.
- Clockwork

- Don't tempt me.
- Netcat

- Still, the Krime Wing is better suited to a flat-out run at full throttle than trying any kind of tight turn. Getting that much mass to pull off a high-g maneuver is like trying to drive a bus in the Monaco Grand Prix. Still, she's a decent craft, if you know now to handle her; she can be a harsh mistress.
- Osprey

EVO-KRIME "KRIME WING" (V/STOL)									
HANDL	SPEED	ACCEL	BODY	ARM	PILOT	SENS	SEATS	AVAIL	COST
4	6	5	22	18	4	5	10 (20)	24F	2,275,000¥
Std. Equipment	Metahuman customization (troll)								
Note	Smaller figure is for trolls, larger figure is for human-sized occupants. For mixed groups, trolls take two human-sized seats								

LUFTSHIFFBAU PERSONAL ZEPPELIN LZP-2070

(LTA VEHICLE)

In an era of super-fast ... everything, zeppelins maintain a relative level of popularity despite their perceived shortcomings. While the majority of these lifting bodies are for commercial use, transporting bulk goods cross-country, there's still a demand for personal LTAs (lighter than air vehicles). And with demand, there's supply. This is the case for the LZP-2070.

Considered a middle-of-the-road design, the LZP gets little fanfare but still manages to achieve decent sales through mostly customer word-of-mouth. Those who've purchased the LZP have given the craft nothing but positive feedback, citing ease of operation, durability, and a price that's relatively easy on the credit balance.

Nothing more than a lifting body (a.k.a. the balloon) and a small control cabin, the LZP-2070 has become a popular aerial transport in both urban and rural areas. As long as you don't need to get somewhere in a hurry, the LZP is for you.

Besides being a personal leisure craft, the LZP has been pressed into service with various security and law-enforcement companies as a mobile observation and airborne control posts, coordinating drone and vehicle patrols in their assigned sectors. In this role, the LZPs are often given upgraded sensor and communication systems. A few are even known to be armed, but the relatively fragile craft usually avoids combat as much as possible.

- Okay, Kane, spill. How in the seven hells did *this* make your list of "finest aerial vehicles"? You got some kind of super-hyped up combat balloon that takes out jet fighters with a laser you boosted or something?
- Bull

LUFTSHIFFBAU PERSONAL ZEPPELIN LZP-2070

- Would you believe that Kat and I simply like to take the LZP on romantic moonlit flights along the beach? I'm actually quite the romantic soul didn't'cha know.
- Kane

- Normally I'd call bulldrek on this, but then you did hire an army and invaded Aztlan to save Kat so there's that. But now that I think about it, I don't know which one is scarier, the pirate or the romantic.
- Bull

- You should read some of my *love poetry*. Let me give you a sample. *ahem* There once was a elf from Nantucket **<.23 mp deleted by SYSOP>**
- Kane

- Sometimes I'm really happy that I have powers I can abuse.
- Slamm-0!

- This actually has a lot of run potential. Yeah, you won't be using it for a hot extraction or fire support, but with its popularity and the fact that you can find it just about everywhere, it makes a great vehicle for covert observation and legwork. You go flying around in this, and no one is going to look twice at you.
- Danger Sensei

- It also comes with a *very* good autopilot system, and combined with the right drones this could make a decent flying command center, allowing the rigger to concentrate on the drones and not flying the aircraft. Sometimes you can't get to the target at ground level and the only way to go is up.
- Rigger X

- You sure? One good shot from anything larger than a heavy pistol is gonna take this thing down. Better think *way* ahead and have a lot of backup in case things go south, because you are *not* getting away in a hurry.
- Stone

- Like any runner's tool, use the right one for the right job. I've seen these used on runs before, both properly and improperly. I know of a team who used it as a mobile sniper's position to great effect, taking out targets from a half-kilometer away. Another time, they used it as a massive area jammer and packed it with explosives. When their pursuit tried to, well, pursue, they got a nasty surprise when the hydrogen tanks went off. But then I've also seen runners try to use this as a getaway vehicle. Glad I opted out of that run. Heard later that team didn't make it. Big surprise.

- 2XL

LUFTSHIFFBAU LZP-2070 (LTA VEHICLE)									
HANDL	SPEED	ACCEL	BODY	ARM	PILOT	SENS	SEATS	AVAIL	COST
4	2	3	12	6	5	4	6	12	85,000¥
Std. Equipment	—								

RENEGADE WORKS "MOTHERSHIP" LAVH

(CUSTOM LTA)

The LAVH is one of those aeronautical oddities that doesn't fit very well into a particular category but rather blurs the lines between a couple. LAVH stands for: Lighter than Air Vehicle *Harness*. That's right; the Mothership isn't a vehicle per se, but an add-on.

The LAVH is the brainchild of an underground group of riggers and techs who call themselves Renegade Works. They first started working on the Mothership concept two years ago when a smuggler associate came to them, looking for a way to extend the range of his t-bird. At first they considered using multiple custom drop tanks, but that concept proved too cumbersome for the aircraft and actually strained the engines and other flight systems. The techs were at a loss until one of them (reportedly after smoking some good deepweed) made the comment, "We've been trying to attach more stuff to the bird—what if we attach the bird to more stuff?"

The rest is history.

Designed specifically to help t-bird pilots extend the range of their craft by attaching an oversimplified zeppelin frame to it, the idea behind the Mothership is a simple one. The LAVH attaches to said t-bird, and both take off like a normal LAV. The t-bird is uses the LAV's power and fuel to carry it over long distances. Once they reach their destination (or once some emergency occurs), the t-bird simply powers up its engines and the two separate. The Mothership can remain in the area to await the t-bird's return or head to another location.

A cross between a stripped-down LAV and a large drone, the Mothership looks like a flying frame with engines, fuel tanks, grappling arms/struts, and other necessary components attached to the lifting body. It also comes with a small one-person command pod with standard rigger controls so that the craft can be piloted directly with those controls. During normal operations, the Mothership is controlled via the carried aircraft through either a standard wireless connection, or a custom direct link through a fiber-optic cable. When the two aircraft separate, the cable simply detaches and remains with the Mothership.

For a more covert transport experience, Renegade Works offers a custom faux cargo container with remote-triggered blast-away panels for quick egress (additional cost: 1,000 nuyen). Getting a hold of a Mothership can be a bit tricky, as Renegade Works isn't exactly a legit business with a manufacturing facility. Currently, they only take orders through word of mouth or reference. You'll need a good point of contact to be able to put in a reference. And even then don't expect a very rapid response; each Mothership LAVH is handmade.

- Interesting concept, I can see how this would be useful, but here's the question: Does it work and how well?
- Orbital DK

- Renegade Works has been producing them slowly but steadily over the past few years, giving them to trusted associates for field tests. They have a solid rep in the black markets, and the Mothership is gaining popularity within t-bird circles. I got mine last year and used it quite frequently. The flight systems and vehicle interfaces are top notch, but the one concern I had were the grappling arms that hold a t-bird in place. The struts were solid and hold firm, but I recommend checking them frequently for fatigue. Flying in calm skies isn't a problem, but don't try flying it in bad weather. Also, if you use the cargo container, make sure you check the explosive bolts. I have heard that if not used, they need to be replaced every six to eight months or so.
- Blackhawk

- Renegade also highly recommends that coupling the two aircraft together be done *on the ground only*. Mid-air coupling is possible, but often tricky. I know a t-bird jock who tried a mid-air link last month and ended up a fireball. If you got the time, do it safely.
- Osprey

- So what do we know about Renegade Works? I've never heard of them before.
- Mika

- Unless you're a rigger or smuggler, that's not surprising. They're a co-op of riggers and like-minded tech-heads who used to go by the collective handle of "the Garage." Until two years ago, they were based out of Detroit until Knight Errant got tired of their shenanigans and field tests up and down Interstate 75 and finally shut down their warehouses and shops. Those who avoided the dragnet set up shop elsewhere. I won't say where because it's a trade secret, and I like my relationship with them. They'll customize just about any vehicle out there, but a few of

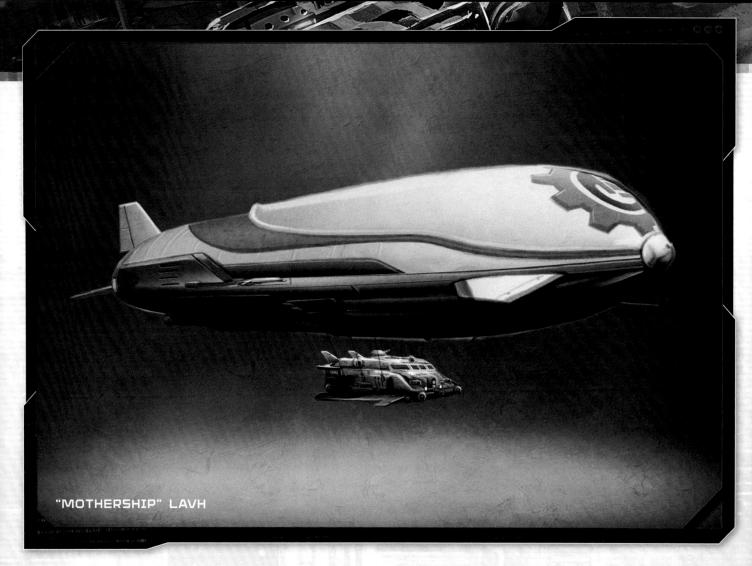

"MOTHERSHIP" LAVH

the techs have been focused on aircraft mods. They're a bit eccentric to say the least, but they do top-notch work. If you ever need a point of contact, let me know. If you want a Mothership or any other of their products, they deliver. But right now there is a massive backlog.
- Turbo Bunny

- Okay, I got an odd question. If the Mothership can handle a t-bird, is it also able to carry other vehicles like, say, a car or van?
- Treadle

- Sure. Just pray the support struts hold out or you don't get intercepted at altitude.
- Airman Al

- Be careful operating Motherships around the Sioux border. The SDF has gotten wind of them and are starting to inspect all incoming LAV traffic a bit more thoroughly. I've heard that a number of t-bird jocks have punched out and left their new toys behind.
- Mika

- Cost of doing business, chummer.
- Blackhawk

"MOTHERSHIP" LAVH									
HANDL	SPEED	ACCEL	BODY	ARM	PILOT	SENS	SEATS	AVAIL	COST
3	3	3	10	5	3	4	1*	24R	50,000¥

Std. Equipment	Metahuman customization (troll) When two aircraft are connected, default to Mothership stats. Can only control Mothership directly from command cabin, otherwise must use remote/direct interface.
Note	To obtain a Mothership, players will need or have access to (through another player for example) a contact with an appropriate contact-type (rigger, smuggler, black marketer, fence, etc.) with a Connection Rating of 4 or higher. *For command cabin only

ONE RIG TO RULE THEM ALL

"I trust the remainder of your team accepts my offer," Mr. Johnson said flatly.

Get smiled. "They wouldn't send me in to negotiate if they didn't."

Mr. Johnson had already questioned why the team's rigger was doing the meet. It wasn't a direct question, Johnsons were rarely direct until it was time to screw you over. Instead he simply asked where Tact was and then accepted Get's answer with a predatory smile. Get wasn't a skilled negotiator, and he knew the Johnson had gotten the better end of the deal for the price of a five-man team. But Get wasn't part of a five-man team today; he was one man, with a wide array of skills and drones to cover any job some other runner might do. Except for negotiating. He hadn't found a good negotiations drone yet. Yet.

The best part wasn't even the money. It was nice that it was all his, and though he'd probably lose a drone or two—he usually did—the pay was plenty to replace those he lost. No, the best part was not having to deal with the drama of a bunch of other runners. Posturing for alpha, divvying the pay unevenly because the mage always thought they deserved more, testing the face to make sure he hadn't skimmed a little extra for himself, dealing with some drama or another caused by the street razor because karma was catching up with their murderous ways. None of it. None of that bullshit. Get was alpha, Get got all the money, and Get knew all his own drama.

"Well then. We are agreed. Your upfront payment is available now. The remainder will be paid upon delivery of the item. Good luck to you and your team."

Get's reply was a quick, "Thanks!" It was all he had time for before Mr. Johnson stepped back out into the dimly lit bar.

Alone in the back room, Get pulled up diagnostics for all of his active drones and lined them up along the right side of his AR window based on altitude. Every one was green across the board despite the local interference. Thanks to his scrubber program, the Vulcan's premium CleanAir technology, and the filtration hardware in the Transys datajack, the signal for even his farthest drone was perfect. At the top of the ARO stack, and over a kilometer overhead, was the center of Get's network, a modified Aerodesign Systems Condor LBSD-41. The mini-blimp was based on the old and sturdy frame, but all of the internals had been updated based on Get's own personal design specs. The systems weren't milspec, but they were better than anything you could buy and he never had issues with compatibility or corpsec backdoors.

Early in his career Get had learned that lesson the hard way. He hadn't earned the grease behind his ears and took a stock MCT-Nissan Roto-Drone on a job inside MCT property.

BY SCOTT SCHLETZ

When the drek hit the fan, the local combat decker slipped a simple shutdown command through the backdoor. Get watched the Roto-Drone autorotate back to the ground right in front of the security force leapfrogging up to push his team out. To rub some salt in the wound, one of the guards even used the drone as cover for a moment and gave the blades a little spin as he moved away.

Get had learned a lot since then.

He issued a command series to the Condor to get it underway. It wasn't fast, and it would take a while for it to get to the target location. He needed his hub in place ASAP—Get wasn't wasting time getting started on this op. The commands would bring the Condor closer to the nearest dronestream, where it would drop the sneaky ninja act and slide into the flow as an advertising mini-blimp. Wing's Asian Take-out would get a little extra advertising tonight.

Once the commands were set, the ARO slid over to the left. As it slipped into virtual place two bars—one green, one blue—popped up next to it. Green was a status bar that warned Get of any issues the drone was having so he could check it out and maybe jump in to get it out of trouble. The blue bar was already getting smaller as it represented the progress of the Condor on its commands. It would flash once it got close to completion.

Next up for commands was the third icon down his right-side AROs. Numbers one and two were custom MCT-Nissan Roto-Drones located inside number three, a GMC Bulldog kitted for drone hauling. The GMC had a half-dozen other drones inside, but none of them were currently active. Get logged commands for the Bulldog to get underway, park on the top floor of a garage a block from the target location, and activate three more of the drones it was carrying: a Doberman, a Crawler, and a Fly-Spy.

After only two minutes, Get had commands out through his rig to a dozen drones as he dropped into the driver's seat of the American he had rented when he first got to the island. The vehicle wasn't rigger friendly, but that was fine, Get enjoyed some manual operation every once in a while. Soon enough he'd leave this car behind and start the job in earnest, but for the next twenty minutes, he focused on the road ahead and drove the old-fashioned way.

The sensation was similar to zero-g, but Get knew gravity was there. He was just lighter than air. Air that held a bit of a chill at his current elevation of 964.25 meters. It was 8.3 degrees cooler up here than at the ground. Temperatures varied all over Get's vision. The land was still warm, even hours after the sun had set. Spots of intense heat showed the locations of lights along the streets that warm blobs glided along. A few bright areas flickered—fires or tiki torches at the resort. The waterfront was a shimmering mix of cool water pulling heat from hot sand with each crashing wave. A line of hot blobs zipped along in the space between Get and the ground, creating a river of warmer air with their exhaust and motor heat.

Get reached up and pulled the overlay back into his view. It was thrilling to take some time to get the full feeling of being the Condor almost a kilometer above San Juan, but work called. The overlay added all of his currently active drones to his field of view. He now had nine icons on the right side of the screen, each with a thin line connected to a matching icon in his field of view. Several were so close together the icons overlapped at this distance. Though distance was irrelevant with his current eyes. He did a flash zoom and made sure things were five by five in the overlaps. Years of experience taught the double-check, and it paid off. Get sent a quick command to move the microskimmer. Its final position only shifted by two meters, but it stayed out of sight by gliding along the wall and around to the other side instead of going over. That little hiccup wouldn't have ruined the op, but it could have started it all off on the wrong foot.

With that one move, everything was in place. It was time for Get to conduct the symphony.

Get's VR persona, a symphony conductor with airman's goggles on his forehead, permanently grease-stained fingers, and vintage Wolverine work boots, sat in the high-backed chair that represented the center of operations for his Vulcan Liegelord. He knew other riggers often customized their captain's chair mode, but Get didn't find it necessary. He spent most of his time jumped in and using the Condor to feed him overall tactical data while he enjoyed the sensations of real rigging. While his persona was that of a conductor, he was more like first chair for every instrument.

Next up was a little piccolo.

Zipping around through the air was exhilarating. His back hummed with the beating of his tiny wings as he dipped and dodged around the various shorts-clad tourists of San Juan's Condado district. He avoided several swatting hands as he buzzed past ears just for the fun of it, and then quickly chastised himself for risking the job. Get was currently in his most fragile drone, an MCT Fly-Spy, and a single lucky swing could end the tiny microdrone.

He flew higher to avoid the crowds and remove the urge to buzz people with his large wasp-like form. It gave him a clear view of his target striding quickly along the sidewalk. The man's movement was too fast for a stealthy approach.

Get kept his altitude, buzzing right along the side of the huge hotel that held his final quarry, and got directly over the quick-stepping target of phase one.

The man's movements were unexpected. Get had considered several options for infiltration, and this was the best, but he never thought a guy delivering flowers would be trying to set land speed records. A string of petals had already been lost along the route from flailing arms. His haste, and damage to the roses—nice, expensive roses—made Get feel a little better that no one would be tipping him for his speedy delivery.

But no tip didn't solve his problem. He didn't have many options this early in the plan. The Roto-Drones weren't in place yet, and while the other drones were, nothing they did right now would slow the world's fastest flower deliverer. It was up to him.

Get buzzed ahead and landed smoothly on the back of a streetlight. As his tiny metallic feet grabbed hold, he could immediately feel them tingle from nearby vibrations in the metal. Quickly rotating in place, he turned to see the long yellow-and-black legs of a spider appearing as it emerged from a rusty hole in the metal only a few centimeters from Get's landing spot.

Once out, the spider raised up four of its front legs in a harrowing threat display. The position gave Get a clear view of the arachnid's fangs, and he understood why other insects might back off. Problem was, he couldn't. He needed this spot. Get was bigger, though only barely, but the spider was clearly defending its territory and not about to let some wasp claim his spot.

While the move might risk the entire operation Get hunkered down to do battle with a banana spider.

Seconds later, and none the worse for wear, Get was once again on mission. He focused on the approaching target while trying not to be distracted by the woman screaming below him who had just received a stunned banana spider in her hair. It was a doubly lucky encounter. Get learned he was pretty good at fighting spiders, and the woman's panic slowed the floral courier enough for Get's next move.

Get launched himself downward toward the courier. Wings folded back and wind zipping over his narrowed form, he made slight adjustments over the short flight. His aim was perfect as he reached the space right next to the deliveryman's ear, opened up to rapidly slow, and then started beating his wings rapidly.

The old bug in the ear trick worked perfectly. While a hand swung up to swat him away, Get landed lightly on the man's lower back. After a few more swings at nothing, the man stopped to look around and Get quickly buzzed over to the flowers, crawled down inside, and jumped over to the next phase.

Skimming along always felt so different from true flight. While he was excited for this next phase, Get made sure to pull the status display up for all the drones. Zooming along within the dronestream that buzzed over Expo Baldorioty de Castro, Get ran down the right side and issued commands to each drone. He ordered the Condor to move south fifty meters to get an angle around the rising smoke. The microskimmer he had just departed was commanded to continue to the rendezvous. The Crawler got orders to dismount the Doberman. The Doberman got commands to tuck in next to the lift and activate its ruthenium systems. The Fly-Spy was ordered to gain visuals but stay hidden. The other Roto-Drone was told to reduce following distance from fifty to twenty-five meters. The second microskimmer got cleared to execute its tagging program. The Nightrunner was released to run its preset pilot sequence. The Artemis received the command to unfurl its wings. And the Bulldog was ordered to move to the lower level of the parking garage.

It was all done in a matter of seconds. No arguments, no suggestions, and no drama. This was the part Get loved.

Still in the dronestream over the highway Get located the smoke rising in the distance and spotted a trio of drones headed in that direction. Two were Roto-Drones, and the third was a Spinmaster, the specialized media drone from Cyberspace Designs. Both Roto-Drones had cameras mounted where most runners see guns, and Get had his window. He broke away from the dronestream and zipped ahead into formation with the other drones as they bee-lined it for the smoke. As Get flew over Avenue Ashford, he received the local policia command to maintain standard media distances. The message had override codes that Get ignored, but he still followed orders. No one was going to notice a failed command if the drone still followed protocol.

Get got himself lined up with a nice view of the hotel's front and back doors, the burning alley of trash, and the garage where the Bulldog was just now slipping into a parking space on the first floor. He unfurled his media ARO for all to see. Then he found himself in a cloud of smoke.

Get drifted in a little closer to the other media drones. He unfurled his media ARO while lining up a great shot of the little Microskimmer as it buzzed off towards the water and away from the cloud of RFID tags it had just spewed into the air.

Get recorded the RFID graffiti for later use and set his position with a clear view of the alley and the derelict, graffiti covered building where this orchestra was really being conducted from. At his current elevation and angle he couldn't see the Artemis unfurled on the balcony or its unconscious cargo, but he knew it was there from the feeds the Condor was offering.

Everything was going as planned.

The view was terrible. Plastic, even the slightly more expensive stuff the ritzy flower shop used, was not easy to look through. Get risked an early discovery and sliced a small slit in the plastic, and then he pressed his little wasp head in close to see out.

He was thankful the deliveryman wasn't walking as quickly and was finally holding the flowers steady. They were nearing the room for delivery; Get could see the numbers on the doors as they passed, so the deliveryman was on his best behavior.

Get played back a little footage from the Fly-Spy's record and discovered the act had started shortly after he stopped at the front desk, and it wasn't because he was a consummate professional. The deliveryman had an escort.

Get couldn't see who was with him, but he could hear the other man's footsteps. They were almost in step, but the escort had a heavier footfall. Knowing the other man was there, Get watched the shadows and figured out the other man's position. Not too far, not too close. Probably hotel security.

Get tucked back in and watched through the plastic, he wasn't going to get this close just to get spotted by some hotel mook.

Get rolled quietly over to the lowered lift. He checked his gun, locked and loaded, and the case he carried. Everything was just as it should be. Some security had been making their way through an industrial-looking back hallway of the hotel, but a few Dragonfly drones at his disposal had given him a look at the situation, and a quick hack took over a cleaning drone that spewed soap on the floor. Following that up with nipping attacks from the drones would keep the mooks confused and occupied. They would stay away while he worked.

"... didn't order any fucking flowers. Now slot off."

Get could hear the anger in the man's voice immediately. Things weren't going well for the flower deliveryman.

"This is the address and room number. This says they go to Mr. Tom Garfield, with love P. Kat. These things are expensive. Really expensive."

Get heard the delivery guy trying to work something for himself and enjoyed a little internal chuckle at the names. There wasn't a damn thing he could do about what happened next.

Get was suddenly crushed inside the plastic prison. His ears rang from the crackling plastic as he was jerked quickly. He thought it was toward the room, but he couldn't be sure. Pain lanced through his arms and legs as they were caught and twisted in what he could only guess was the doorman's grip.

The crushing lessened, replaced by a feeling of weight-lessness and then a crashing of everything around him. More pain hit his back as rose thorns jabbed through his thin wings. He jumped away to escape the pain.

Get hopped over to the door and cut through the glass with a laser on his arm. He caught the falling glass, set it aside, crawled through the opening, and opened the door for the approaching Doberman. He was still a little shaken from the damage to the Fly-Spy. According to the display it was still operational, though he knew several systems, including flight, were not going to be operational. It only had one more task. Hopefully it could manage.

Get led the Doberman to the service elevator and hit the call button after climbing on the larger drones nearly invisible back. The ruthenium was doing a great job of keeping the big perimeter drone out of sight. It helped that they hadn't run into anyone yet either.

When the elevator arrived, that changed.

shots later and both men were writhing on the floor, electricity coursing through their bodies. Get put an extra round into each, just in case, and pushed their twitching bodies out of the way as he rolled into the elevator.

It was always a strange feeling to have pain in a place that didn't normally exist on your body. Get's wings were killing him. One was cracked, the other pierced by rose thorns, and they were both trashed. His legs were in a little better shape, with three and a half still operational. It was enough to crawl, and that was all he needed.

Well, that and the lens.

Get had hindered nearby hacking by filling the air with RFID tags. Physical security could be zapped like the waitstaff, and the bulky cameras on the Roto-Drones shot something other than pictures. Magic was usually the issue. That's where the lens came in.

Get crawled slowly through the wreckage of the flowers and found the slit he had already started. Before slipping through he lowered the small green lens into place in front of his right eyes. As he pushed through the plastic, the room came into clear view.

It was a decent suite, and he could see everywhere but behind the half-wall area that looked like a little kitchen or bar. There were three people in the room, and he could see them talking but couldn't hear them. When Get made the realization that his hearing was gone, he also realized he probably wasn't as stealthy as he thought moving through the flowers.

The lens cast green over everything. Living things came up a slightly lighter green. Awakened things were nearly white. The three men in the room ran the gamut of colors. It was all the info he really needed. He would have loved to have the Fly-Spy in place when the Doberman arrived, but the sudden appearance of a massive cat head sent Get straight into the hallway.

The Crawler wrapped a few times on the door, and Get could hear the people inside coming closer and talking. "Better not be another flower delivery. I'll shoot this one."

There was a long pause when the man arrived at the door, most likely as he peered through the peephole and saw nothing, but it eventually opened a crack.

Get watched the Crawler jam a leg through the space but focused primarily on his efforts to shoot the leery ork eye as he peered through the sliver of open door. Though Stick 'n' Shock rounds are not intended to cause permanent harm, Get was sure the ork would need a new eye once he woke up.

Gunfire followed almost instantly. Get had expected that when he saw one of the other fellows in the room was pretty close to matching the furniture through the Fly-Spy's lens.

Unaware of danger and simply following orders, the Crawler pushed open the door, or at least the remains of the door, and scurried into the room in front of Get. Switching weapons, Get fired a thick stream of greenish-gold liquid into the room.

The coughing began immediately, but that wasn't Get's purpose for hosing the room down with concentrated liquid chlorine. Sure, it slowed the goons down, but the minute the first drop of that stuff hit the air, the real target was on the move.

Get tucked his legs in and prepared to leap into action from his spot behind the half-wall. He issued a quick command to the Doberman and then scrambled out into the path of the cat as it ran for the door. When measuring the gracefulness of things in the Sixth World, riggers can often move their drones far beyond what others would expect. That said, Get had yet to determine how to make a ten-kilo chunk of metal, plastic, and servos match the grace of even the clumsiest of felines. And this was not a clumsy feline.

As the Crawler tumbled from losing the grace-inducing command of the rigger interface, Get tried not to notice that it landed right in front of the doorway to the other room of the suite. If the guards over there weren't totally incapacitated by the chlorine, he was going to be out another drone.

Instead of watching another couple grand get trashed, Get kept his eyes on the prize. Or more specifically, his targeting reticle on the cat. The clumsy strike with the Crawler forced the cat to leap up and off the remains of the door and then out into the hallway.

Get watched and tracked the cat's movement until it cleared the frame where his shot would no longer risk sending the cat back into the room. Then he fired.

At that range, the blast from the barrel peeled away fur and chunks of flesh before the Stick 'n' Shock round even cleared the barrel. When it hit, the cat spun in the air, did a little herky-jerky twitch, and then landed on all fours, moving at a dead run that would make a cheetah proud.

Get swore. He'd expected something like this from a monad cat, but it didn't matter. Even the fastest monad cat in the universe couldn't outrun his targeting software. He finished bringing the barrel around and fired several shots in rapid succession.

Only one missed.

And that was intentional.

Get felt the weight of the Crawler climb onto his back and the chemical chill of the chlorine on his skin. He rolled

quickly down the hallway and opened the case he carried, then stuffed the cat inside.

"I think you can hear me in there, so listen up. If I think you're doing anything funky in my belly, I'll flood your box with the rest of the chlorine in my tank. Not sure that will kill you, but I know it won't feel keen."

Get zoomed along Avenue Ashford toward the hotel where the gunshots had gone off. He was behind the other media drones again, but that was fine. He knew the story already.

Looking down over Condado, Get saw the approaching policia and the buzz of people drawn to the violence like moths to a flame. He monitored his other teammates as he floated further out over the ocean. The Fly-Spy was gone, destroyed by the target cat. The Doberman and Crawler slipped out of the hotel, and once Get sent a remote command to the Americar to speed away and be a distraction, they rolled through alleys and back to the Bulldog. The microskimmers were both zipping along the beach to a rendezvous point where they'd wait for the Bulldog, Roto-Drones, and Condor to arrive before all loading up and heading to the cargo container waiting for them at the airport.

Everyone was doing just what they were told. No double-cross. No "great" ideas. No improvising.

Get watched his limp meat body dangle in the harness of the glider from his place on the water. He kicked and felt the water slide along his belly. He sent a command to the glider to shift its course a few degrees and then turned to glide along the water and line up beneath the descending glider.

When the Artemis reached 25 meters from the Nightrunner it executed its final command. The targeting autosoft lined up a perfect shot and fired at the rear seat of the fast-moving boat. Get timed his mental command perfectly and popped the rear seat up, exposing a metal plate beneath. With a loud thunk, a large magnetic disc slammed into the small metal plate, and the seat immediately dropped closed.

A thin line ran from the disc back to the glider, which now gained lift as the boat's speed increased.

Get focused on the cool water gliding over his smooth skin. He let the overlay go and let himself feel the strange life of a boat. He was not below the surface and not above; he was between, and it was a strange sense unequaled by any other.

Well, except for the feeling of a job well done.

y

w

b

d

f

h

j

n

THE AUTOMATED ARMY

With each small tap on a polyacetylene myomer fiber in the exposed wrist, a finger curled in response to the tiny electric pulse, replicating the contraction of muscle tissue. Satisfied that it was responding correctly, Shui Clark closed the small access port in the cyber-arm, leaned back in her chair, then pushed her goggles to the top of her head as she released a long breath.

"All right, Tater Tot. Time to give your new arm a spin."

With a well-practiced roll of her left shoulder, her current arm clicked and unlocked, allowing her to pull it free with her right, setting the cybernetic one on her workbench beside the shiny new model she'd just finished calibrating. As she always did, she paused for a moment, brushing fingertips over the chrome connector port that divided her flesh even as the car accident had divided her life. She hated that it existed, but the wreck was a decade ago, and the one-armed life was all she could truly remember. She felt a small shudder of revulsion and longing for what could never be as she fetched her new arm. The connector whirred to life as she held the arm to it, hearing it dock smoothly, then a pop indicating completion. Now whole once again, or as whole as she could ever be, she ran through a familiar set of mental commands, turning the limb this way and that, wiggling each finger individually, then closing her eyes to try to touch her nose, ears, and right shoulder for a spatial-recognition test. With all tests passed, she opened her eyes and said, "Now, let's try the new feature."

It was odd learning the secrets of a new limb. Each command was like a creating shadow puppet, learning a new combination of muscles and bends that would activate it, always tricky and clumsy at first until your brain could learn exactly how to make the shape. Retracting her hand was as easy as bunny ears, accessing the tool menu not unlike clenching a fist, but rotating the assembly to get the right tool was going to take practice. Luckily, she had a patient ready to go.

Stepping away from her work table, Shui looked across the garage. Numerous drones looked back at her, from the small Kanmushi perched on posts or clinging to walls like house geckos to the Fly-Spy lurking on a spare tire to the delivery drone whirring just inside the window, waiting patiently with cooling food

below it. "Aw frag, totally forgot I'd called in for some Heli-Tacos." She reached for her left forearm, forgetting momentarily that this arm had a tool assembly instead of an onboard commlink, then fumbled for a few minutes until she found her ordinary 'link in a desk drawer. She added a generous tip, then took her bag before dismissing the drone. Glancing inside as it flew away, she found room-temperature and soggy food within. "Just my luck."

Setting the bag aside for now, she pushed her tummy rumble to one side, instead focusing on the beaten van currently on the lift. "Aleksi, status report?"

The Proletarian drone that rolled from beneath the lift had once been a lovely red, but after many accidents with grease and oil was now a mishmash of red, brown, and black. She should really clean him up, but he always looked adorable mucked up. With a chirp, he stated, "Preliminary repairs are completed as instructed. Damage was primarily cosmetic and easily patched over the indicated portions." An AR projection highlighted several locations in separate panels, each showing bullet strikes or, on the front grill, where she'd had to drive through a closed barrier. "The right rear tire was unrepairable and will need replacement. Several engine components have suffered minor damage from shrapnel and, as instructed, unit designate Aleksi did not attempt repairs. If mistress is ready to begin, unit designate Aleksi is prepared to assist on command."

"In a moment. First, would you please bring me my console?"

"Affirmative."

As the small drone wheeled away, Shui attached a single cable to the van's diagnostic panel, then sat on the floor in the lotus position to await the Proletarian's return. When it arrived, console in claw, it asked, "Will we now begin repairs on unit designate Charlie?"

Attaching the cable to the console, she then ran a second from it through her coveralls, finding the datajack at the base of her spine. "I need to get inside first, see how he feels. Keep an eye out for customers, Aleksi, I'll be right back."

His reply was a distant echo as her consciousness slid from her meat form to the console and, from there, into the Bulldog step-van. Most riggers she knew pre-

ferred wireless commands, and she used them herself, but when time wasn't a factor, there was nothing quite like climbing inside by a direct feed. It was like putting on an old sleepshirt or a raggedy old pair of pants ... everything just felt *right* when connected this way. The connection was more personal and intimate, bonding her mind inside the machine completely until it was her body. She became the van.

The previous bullet holes were well-patched, but she could still feel them like small scabs. The urge to scratch at them was terrible, but there were other issues she had to explore first. Turning her drive train, she felt the flop in her right ankle and knew that it wouldn't hold her weight. The tire was flat, but she could feel the small grind in her ankle that indicated a minor bend in the rim as well. Small enough that you couldn't have seen it with the naked eye, but a rigger's awareness was something else entirely. More troubling was the phlegm in her lungs and the stress in her heart. The engine damage was more widespread than she'd first realized, hardly fatal but enough that she'd be short of breath, unable to reach top speed, keep a good pace, or pull a large load. Her team needed to know that, when things got hot, they could count on her to get them out of there like she did three nights ago. But as it stood now, there was no way she could. If she couldn't breathe, she couldn't run. There was a feeling like flush to her cheeks as she realized that she'd thought of Charlie as her true self again, an impossible response as she didn't currently have cheeks, and she idly wondered if she'd turned on the van's heaters in response. She ran a few more diagnostics, wiggling her fingers and toes, blinking and opening her eyes wide, wriggling her nose to make sure the windshield wipers would work, making mental notes about what needed to be fixed and what was fine.

In time, she realized that she was procrastinating. She'd noted all the damage but hadn't returned to her body. Here, she felt strong; her Bulldog frame was heavy steel and powerful compared to the 1.53-meter flesh frame she normally called home. She swept the room with her sensors, experiencing infrared and standard visuals at once, low-end sonar giving her an approximate location of everything within ten meters, atmospheric sensors bathing her in numerous scents and an awareness that, of course, it would soon be raining in Seattle. She knew her normal five senses were blind, deaf, and dumb compared to this, the sensor arrays showing her what the world was actually like in a way that she could never experience normally. She allowed herself to simply lie there, floating in space, a gentle pressure against her torso where the van's frame was supported by the lift, just enjoying the sensors ... until a rough series of coughs jolted her with pain.

Right. Engine damage.

With a resigned pang of disappointment, she slid back out of the van and into her natural form, groggily disconnecting the cord from her spine. As she did, she felt the familiar pins and needles in her legs as her neural pathways reconnected and blood began flowing properly. She stood on wobbly legs before setting her console to one side. She shivered a bit, vulnerable flesh thinking the room was cooler than her metal skin had, then glanced around at how much darker the room was without the van's eyes.

She held up her left hand, retracting the fist inside the arm cuff of her forearm, then extending a ratchet from the aperture. "All right, Aleksi, let's get that tire off. We're going to need to get that rim straightened out afterwards."

"Affirmative, mistress. Unit designate Aleksi is always ready to serve."

On her workbench, a small bag of soy tacos continued to cool, forgotten as it dangled from the loose grip of her old arm. Just another casualty of a rigger's life.

- So, why are we letting Clockwork do this again?
- Slamm-0!

- We're not "letting" him, we *asked* him.
- Glitch

- After Rigger X told us no. Full disclosure.
- Bull

- What was it he said again? "Who cares about toys and glorified vacuum cleaners?"
- Glitch

- I get that, but ... Clockwork? Come on.
- Slamm-0!

- I know that you two have history, Fred, but remember, FastJack recruited him for a reason, same as the rest of us. You at least owe it a look-over for that if nothing else.
- Bull

- ... Frag. All right, put it up.
- Slamm-0!

- Already on it.
- Glitch

DRONING ON AND ON AND ON AND ON AND ...

POSTED BY: CLOCKWORK

It never ceases to amaze me, how few people really get drones. I mean, they're everywhere, right? It should be a no-brainer, but no, they're too common now. They're like AR spam or pollution, the background noise of life that everyone looks over, through, or past. I'm here to tell you that you shouldn't, and further to show you what you're missing. But first, it's a tradition around here to talk about the distant past, and I'm not one to skip steps. As such ...

IGNITION

The history of civilization is filled with machines, from the Simple Machines of Archimedes in antiquity to the Five Mechanisms of Heron of Alexandria near the year 1, to Leonardo da Vinci's Renaissance inventions, to the electric masterpieces of today—each one given purpose simply by existing, serving humanity by definition. While the first machines were simple things of wood and rope, as time marched on, we adapted them to new materials, new applications, but always as a force multiplier. If one man couldn't lift a rock by himself, he could use a

pulley to do the work of five, making every action more efficient. If it took a man a week to travel a distance, we could put wheels under him and have a horse pull him in half the time. Later, we replaced the horse with an engine and got even faster. Faster, stronger, better—we made machines work for us.

The first time drones were weaponized is debatable. Old Chinese stories of clockwork soldiers and magical automatons of Europe should be disregarded in the name of science, leaving us the first verified use in 1849 when, on August 22, the Austrians released firebombs via balloon into Venice, lighting the way for the future with fire. Balloons, manned this time, were further developed over the next few decades, leading to aerial observation and reconnaissance more than bombing work, as the strength of eyes-in-the-sky became realized. Over the next few decades, an unwillingness to sacrifice pilots combined with a need for more aircraft resulted in a race for drones, either remote-operated, or self-guided, weapons that could get the job done bloodlessly.

- Bloodless for one side, that is. As bloody as possible for the other!
- Aufheben

- So dismissive of the magic of the past. Do you think it has never bubbled up before?
- Man-of-Many-Names

The dawn of the space race brought even more work into the field as robots—a word invented by a Czech named Karel Capec and *not* a Japanese word for "servant," as so many people seem to think—became a cultural fascination. Elektro shocked the world at the 1939 World's Fair by speaking, smoking, and moving about, while Robbie the Robot from *Forbidden Planet* and Rosie the Robot from *The Jetsons* captured the minds of youths who would bring about the robot revolution half a century later. General Motors' Unimate showed that robots could accomplish tasks too dangerous for humans, a task they did so well at that whole factories were soon given over to automation.

- And with the invention of the automated loom came the Saboteurs, those who threw their shoes into the works to destroy the machines that took away their livelihood. Workers have protested the replacement of man by machine ever since!
- Chainmaker

- Now now, let us not throw stones (or shoes) at this point. Some of my best friends are machines.
- Icarus

WARMING UP THE ENGINE

Automation had progressed so much by the turn of the century that robots were able to do many jobs humans were once chained to, with industrial work the most obvious target sector, but agricultural right behind. During the Food Riots of '99, some took to raiding the fields even as auto-pickers were in use, resulting in several avoidable injuries and a few deaths. As would so often happen over the next few decades, public opinion of robots soured, shelving much of the progress that would have followed. This was made even worse by the Crash, which eradicated so many records of the past. You didn't see drones of any real ability for decades after that.

> Not entirely true. Certain anthromorphic robots were active in the 2030s, after all.
> Turbo Bunny

> There are several incidental cases like that out there, where someone retained knowledge of technology past a collapse and wouldn't share it with anyone afterwards. Technology of 2077 isn't terribly more advanced than what they had in 2000 in many ways due to that.
> Snopes

> Like the Nightwraiths, which were all remote-operated planes controlled by David Gavilan!
> Plan 9

RETICULATING SPLINES

It was 2060 when everything really changed. We always think of the human and financial cost that came from the Seattle Arcology shutdown, but the work Deus did in there advanced drone technology by leaps and bounds. Nanomachine advances, bee-sized drones, vicious combat robots, all designed and produced in-facility by a mad AI. Each development was eventually captured and examined by top men in corporate and government circles. With that head start, years of research was completed in months, even weeks. Renraku had been surging ahead in a dozen engineering fields before this, but even their accomplishments paled before the creations of Deus.

> "You have to break a few eggs to make an omelet" is the vibe I'm getting here, and I don't much care for it.
> Pistons

> He knows nothing of Deus. *Nothing.*
> Puck

ALL SYSTEMS ARE GO!

Today, drones are everywhere, from delivery of foodstuff by roto-drone to advertising blimps to construction robots to security work to remote tele-medical research, drones are at the cutting edge of science, exploration, and industry. Most people don't even drive these days, preferring to let their cars do the work while they relax, giving control to devices that are autos in every sense of the word. Today's drones do our taxes, polish our boots, and mow our lawns. They pick our fruit, monitor the weather, and compose music for our amusements. In another fifty years, metahumanity itself could find itself retired to a life of leisure while machines do all the work. Truly, a utopia.

> He clearly hasn't read the book, *Utopia.* What a horrible place to live! How it became a go-to word for perfect society, I'll never know.
> Butch

> Come now! A place where the wise rule, children mind their manners, and slaves know their place? Sounds like paradise! Well, other than the gold bit. Sir Thomas More could have used a course on economics.
> OrkCEO

> He is biased, but that does not make him wrong. Even as drones explode as a hobby, they are slipping into the workforce, displacing thousands of low-skill workers who are left unemployed and, worse, unemployable. That delivery from Heavenly Noodle used to involve a pimply teenager's first job. That teenager would then go on to join the workforce with some level of skill. His drone replacement never gets a promotion, and now that kid is left both jobless and bored, soon to stir up trouble. For the right price, I could direct you toward any number of societal studies on this.
> Icarus

> It's important to remember how overlooked drones are by most workers today. They forget that each one's full of electronic eyes and ears, treating them as they would the furniture while chatting about any number of topics. A wise runner should take advantage of that.
> Balladeer

> Drone defenders are also seeing more use. They aren't affected by bribes, fatigue, or mind-magic, never call in sick, and won't be flirted away from their station. They generally aren't as skilled at the job as metahumans, but they're far more reliable.
> Hard Exit

> I love it when people forget how easy it is to hack into most commercially used drones.
> Netcat

> Don't forget the military side of things! Ares has been trying to field an all-drone team in Desert Wars for years but hasn't yet gotten permission to do so. Civilian casualties are still horrible news leads for any war, so most world governments are looking to replace as many flesh-and-blood soldiers with machines as possible.
> Sticks

- The '60s were a terrible time for drones, no matter how good the science had gotten. Rogue Als, technomancers, and commlink scriptkiddies were making a mockery of most security protocols, taking drones on joyrides, strafing neighbors, and more. Political pushes drove lethal-armed drones almost to extinction and, even today, people just flat-out don't trust a robot with a gun. (Nobody ever thinks about the two-thousand-kilo machine that they take to work each day as a weapon, of course. Remember what I said about not seeing drones? It goes double for cars.)
- Hard Exit

- Danielle de la Mar hasn't forgotten, and her next project is to try and deal with "massacre machines," to drive out grenades, automatic weapons, and, yes, weaponized drones from polite society.
- Nephrine

- I don't think she knows how much money the corps make from those things. They might have backed her before, but I'd lay good odds that she'll be blocked on this.
- Slamm-0!

- Good odds you say? How good? <leer>
- /dev/grrl

- Girl's got a problem …
- Turbo Bunny

I know you guys are hot for the catalogue, but before you see the product, you really need to meet the salesmen. Drones are an industry that runs like, well, clockwork, and if you just start poking around the machine, it's gonna grind you up and spit you out.

THE MAINSPRING: MITSUHAMA

While it isn't fair to say that nothing happens in the drone industry without Mitsuhama Computer Technologies deciding to make it happen, it's not terribly far from the truth. For the most part, other manufacturers are defined by finding niches that MCT hasn't filled or having their own spin on an existing area of operation. MCT casts an enormous shadow on the rest of the industry and keeps a constant level of pressure that forces the others to keep pace or break down. Industrial robots, hazardous environment machines, security drones, mining, production, even the automated service industry after some horse trading with Renraku, they keep a finger in every market you can imagine and a few that you don't know exist. The only area where they were weak was in the consumer side of things, and even there they bring in more income in the field than their nearest rival.

- MCT innovated the Zero Zone (zero penetration, zero survivors) but found that, no matter how well-trained, some security teams were squeamish about the level of brutality required for that level of security. Turns out that robotic guns and toxin gas panels don't care whose hoop they dismantle.
- Hard Exit

Mitsuhama's strength is in the physical design of drones, but their software has always lagged behind some of the major players. As part of the Yamato Damashi spirit surging through the Japanacorps, Renraku has been helping their chief rival in this regard, upgrading their pilot technology and sharing autosoft research, even selling them some of their older, successful designs as they reposition themselves in the service market. I'm not sure what Renraku's getting in return, other than nuyen.

- Isn't that enough?
- Riot

- Not at the level they play at. Megacorps are frenemies, helping one another one day, then undercutting each other the next. Renraku doesn't need the mechanical or industrial strength of MCT, and while they've been snapping up subcontracting work in the larger corp's wake, like a remora with a shark's detritus, there's not enough there to justify losing their software advantage.
- Butch

- You're all looking at the wrong side of the corp. Renraku's giving up technology, but they're getting magical knowledge in return. Renraku's always been weak in the magical area, while MCT's second only to Aztechnology, and may actually be in front. More about this soon. Gotta see if a hunch pays off.
- Haze

THE GRINDING GEARS

While these are all top-level drone manufacturers, none of them have ever knocked Mitsuhama from that top spot. Renraku's been the closest, and arguably did so during the Golden Year of 2059, but the Seattle Arcology Shutdown cut them off at the knees before they could really take advantage.

RENRAKU

Traditionally MCT's primary rival, Renraku makes superior software and operating systems (pilots, autosofts, and so forth), while MCT makes the better hardware. With Renraku's new tilt to a metahuman-and-service focus, they've been quietly pulling back from the intense R&D required to stay at the top of the scrap pile. This shouldn't be read as them leaving the industry, far from it, but it's just that their focus has changed for some strange reason.

- <cough> Deus <cough>
- /dev/grrl

With the strength of both GridGuide™ and now HarborGuide™ in their pocket, Renraku's new angle is SkyGuide™, a program intended to control flying drones but not airplanes. Turns out that those who went through both the second crash and the outbreak of technomancers afterward are a tad nervous about removing control from pilots. SkyGuide is intended to control drone traffic in an urban environment, automatically redirecting them from air traffic and turning them from restricted airspace, also providing information to law enforcement should one be brought down through vandalism (or, of course, used in a crime). By casting a wide wireless net over a 'plex, they can ensure a reduction in accidents, destruction, and collisions.

- Huh. A net in the sky? Wonder why they didn't go with the obvious name?
- Turbo Bunny

ARES MACROTECHNOLOGY

Ares is actually the tops in one subset of the industry: military drones. Flying drones that silently unleash targeted mini-missiles, self-guided missiles, and support weapon platforms are obvious, but also noncombat support, like the Mule equipment transport drone or a law-enforcement drone for the bomb disposal team. It used to be called the military-industrial complex, but these days, it's just "Ares."

- You're selling them short, Clockwork. Ares is known for firepower, but they made their name in aerospace. They're the leading producers of all manner of aero and space assets, from atmospheric sensor drones to spy sats to deep-space repair robots. Not really covered in your report, but it should be remembered.
- Orbital Bandit

SONY

The only AA-rated corporation that can play at this level is Sony. For over a century, they've been at the cutting edge of robots, keeping a high level of technological expertise even if they don't match the raw industrial production of the bigger boys. Every year, they roll out an astounding breakthrough in artificial intelligence, only for Renraku to top them the next year. Mitsuhama's "glass jaw" in terms of consumer robotics is due to Sony and Renraku dominating the market, and no one can rival them in the field of medical robotics.

- The advanced R&D Sony does is later sold to the other players (MCT, Ares, and so on) a couple of years after they've invented it, in a sense operating as a subsidized research lab for the other robot masters. Doesn't keep the other megas from blocking them from triple-A status, mind you, but it keeps them from being preyed on quite so much.
- Glitch

- Huh. That's pretty wily of 'em!
- Slamm-0!

THE WORTHY COGS

Technically second-tier corps in the market (but don't say that to any of their executives' faces!), the Cogs have all found a place to make a profit while looking to advance one step higher. Each has their own specialized niche or a broad diversity that can't match sales with the big guns, but they're always hungry for more.

AZTECHNOLOGY

While the Azzies have, as always, been happy to steal technology, file off the serial numbers, then re-market it as their own at a lower cost (and much lower quality), the past few years have seen a turnaround that makes them an actual consideration. They've always had knockoff Ares drones on hand, but the war with Sirrurg resulted in some bottomless R&D budgets and risk-taking of the sort that tends to bear fruit. With "Dragon-Slaying" miltech having gone nova-hot, they're seeing a market hungry for their weaponized drones. Beyond this, they've long had a significant presence in the field of consumer drones, and the marketing push for "Juan" is creating record sales. If they can keep this up for a decade, or if Ares keeps falling, they could move up.

- While the Azzies are selling a lot of combat drones, they don't use them anywhere north of Monterrey; flying death machines are all well and good for blowing away Awakened critters and conscripted peasants, but they're not high-quality enough to face CAS electronic-warfare specialists, let alone Pueblo.
- Kane

EVO

Traditionally third in the military side, behind Ares and MCT, Evo continues to invest in both military and security drones, as well as large-scale industrial technology. The one area that they continue to lead is submersible drones, focusing on the industrial and exploratory rather than the artistic like Sony. Of particular note is that Evo drones are notorious for being clunky but borderline indestructible, reflecting the Russian technological heritage that they now stamp on so many of their goods.

- And, again, they have a huge space focus via CosMos. Honestly, Clockwork, the world doesn't end with the atmosphere.
- Orbital Bandit

- You don't see them in North America often, but Yamatetsu makes slick drones for the Asian market.
- Sunshine

SAEDER-KRUPP

An odd duck, S-K should be scrapping hand-to-hand (or, well, claw) with MCT in this field, but they've never seemed too interested. They have the technology, the computer expertise, and the industrial demand—hell, they already have ludicrously large machines like the Bagger 318, and when they decide to create a high-end pilot program, it's a thing of perfection. But Lofwyr just never seems to care, so the drones are rare, if excellent.

- I asked a source about this. Their thought is that "Playing with dolls is for children. Golden Snout was born too old for that." As always, take with a grain of salt.
- Frosty

SHIAWASE

With Mitsuhama, Renraku, Sony, and Evo (formerly Yamatetsu) all operating out of Japan, you wouldn't think that Shiawase would find a niche, and yet here they are. They have an investment in "drone homes," living quarters that network with a central administrator to keep lights, sounds, and supplies at optimal levels, but their real money is sunk into agricultural robots and in medical telepresence. The quiet war between them and Sony in senior-care robotics is vicious, and they recently leveled a shot across the bow of Horizon, letting them know in no uncertain terms that they shouldn't consider the market of selling agricultural support to the NAN to be an open field.

- That was an odd one, as Horizon only recently entered the agricultural market via the Wind River Corporation. They're using Renraku models, with their own drone production being cinematic in focus. Wonder if there's more to this?
- Sunshine

- There's always more. You, of all people, should know that.
- Icarus

DRONE MODIFICATION

While every rigger mods their cars, not many do many mods with their drones other than strap guns onto them. In part this is due to the compact design leaving little space, but surprisingly few riggers even consider that they can make mods in the first place. Vehicles are investments while drones are "toys," and thus, disposable. Time to think again.

These rules provide detailed options for drones and can be used as an optional rules system for adding modifications to them. Players who do not want to use a separate system can use the rules provided in the **Building the Perfect Beast** chapter (p. 150).

THE BASICS

Drones have a much more limited space to work with than ordinary vehicles. Every drone is given a number of Mod Points equal to their Body. These Mod Points work vaguely like Essence, a reserve of points that is gone once they're all used up, meaning no further modifications are possible unless you first rip something out. Some drones have some, or all, of their Mod Points already spent in order to carry advanced equipment. Due to this, a new indicator has been added to the drone attributes that shows how many points are available for a new drone of that make, shown thusly: Body X(Y), where X is the actual Body rating of the drone while (Y) is how many points are available. In many cases, this is the same number, but not always. Drones from other *SR5* supplements have been added to the master chart with this taken into account. Several older drones have had their stats adjusted to fit the rules presented in this book. This new statline replaces the original details for games using *Rigger 5.0,* otherwise the older information remains valid.

ADDING UPGRADES

Adding an upgrade is easy enough: Check to see if you have enough Mod Points available, find someone to do the work (this can be yourself, of course), and pay the fee. Once it's installed, you're good to go. As an added bonus, all drones have a bit of wiggle room for expansion, be it more memory and more advanced software installs for the Pilot program, a better grade of engine component for speed, and so on. This means that any drone may have an attribute increased from the base by 1 (or 3 for Armor) without expending any Mod Points. Increasing an attribute further than that requires at least a partial rebuild, and the expenditure of Mod Points equal to the increase minus 1. This means a +2 Speed increase costs 1 Mod point, while +4 Speed would cost 3, and so on. The only attribute that can never be increased is Body; this is the inherent frame of the drone, and if you want it bigger, you should just buy a larger model. Adding one attribute point requires an appropriate toolkit, while more extensive upgrades require an appropriate shop.

ENDURING DOWNGRADES

Drones may also be given Downgrades, worsening an aspect of the machine by using inferior parts. The advantage to this is that you could trade off a feature that you don't care for as much in order to free up space for what you need. In a car, this would be ripping out seats to make a racing vehicle faster, while in a drone this can be removing sensors, going with a smaller and simpler control computer, and so on. Any single attribute may be worsened by 1 (or 3 for Armor), providing 1 Mod Point. This cannot be used to lower an attribute below 1 except in the case of Speed (which can go to 0), and obviously the attribute must be lowerable (So, no reducing a 1 to a 1 for a free Mod Point!). Furthermore, no matter how many Downgrades you make, you only receive a single extra Mod Point.

ATTRIBUTE MODIFICATIONS

The most basic level of mod, attribute modification lets you change the attribute of your drone. The one thing to remember is that a drone's attributes can never by higher than twice their starting value (so if you had a Handling of 3, it can never be modified higher than 6). When you need to use a 0 for the math, like a micro-drone's Body score, use 0.5 instead. No multiplying by 0 to get infinite free upgrades—nice try, though.

HANDLING

(Availability = Upgraded Rating x 2)

Better gyroscopes, improved shocks, spoilers and airdams, counterbalancing rotors, and more. Of the physical components, only speed is more expensive in the long run! Cost equals the upgraded Handling multipled by the Body, then multiplied by 200. This means that increasing to Handling 5 on a Body 2 drone would cost (5 x 2) x 200, or 10 x 200, or 2,000 nuyen.

SPEED

(Availability = Upgraded Speed x 2)

Everybody loves more speed! Bigger engines, better engines, louder engines! The most expensive upgrade for a drone, so brace for sticker shock! Cost equals the upgraded Speed multiplied by the drone's Body, then doubled, then multiplied by 200. So increasing to a Speed of 5 on a Body 2 drone would cost ((5 x 2) x 2) x 200, or (20) x 200, or 4,000 nuyen.

ACCELERATION

(Availability = Upgraded Rating x 4)

A little nitro never hurt anyone, right? Wait, it can actually suffocate you? Oh. Well. Regardless! Brace for G-forces, it's better Acceleration! Cost equals the upgraded Acceleration multiplied by the drone's Body, then multiplied by 200. Increasing to an Acceleration of 2 on a Body 2 drone would cost (2 x 2) x 200, or (4) x 200, or 800 nuyen.

BODY

(Availability = Mod Points Gained x 3)

While it cannot be upgraded, you can make some tradeoffs on integrity for modification diversity. That is to say, if you get a lighter, more fragile frame, you can do more things with the weight savings—but when things break, they break badly. Reducing the drone's Body by 1 produces 2 Mod Points, resulting in a net gain of 1 Mod Point. A drone's Body may not be reduced lower than half the starting value in this way. Thus, a Body 3 drone may be reduced to 2 Body for 1 Mod Point, but not to 1 as this is lower than half the starting Body, which would be 1.5.)

ARMOR

(Availability = Upgraded Rating, may be R or F)

For some strange reason, people want their drones to survive. Funny, that! Adding armor is frowned upon by polite society, however, so you might have to face a few questions from authorities worried that you're making some kind of aerial assassination robot. Not that you'd do that, of course. Armor greater than 6 is considered Restricted, while Armor greater than 12 is Forbidden. In addition, Armor is heavy. A drone may bear the weight of Armor equal to three times its Body without a decrease in ability, but for every 3 points beyond this, the drone suffers -1 Handling and Speed, while every 6 points also reduces Acceleration by 1. If this results in Handling dropping below 1, or either Speed or Acceleration dropping below 0, then the drone is unable to move at all. Cost equals the upgraded Armor multiplied by the drone's Body, then multiplied by 200. Increasing to an Armor of 15 on a Body 3 drone would cost (15 x 3) x 200, or 45 x 200, or 9,000 nuyen.

SENSOR

(Availability = Upgraded Sensor x 2)

Cameras to see, mics to hear, and short-range radar for parking. Sensors take many shapes and sizes, but fortunately they don't take the size of the drone's frame into account. Upgraded Sensors are thus much easier to calculate. The cost is equal to the upgraded Sensor rating x 1,000 nuyen. A single sensor may be upgraded instead of the entire array for (Rating) x 100 nuyen.

PILOT

More on this under Software Solutions!

OTHER MODIFICATIONS

Each of the following mods is listed with a cost in Mod Points, Availability, and nuyen. Not all mods are appro-

While the speed of many vehicles was listed in SR5 (p. 200), there are advanced rules. Speed for drones is listed with an appropriate letter code indicating its type of travel: G for ground, R for rotor, J for jet, or W for water. When comparing speed across modes, note that in order of relative speed, they line up like this (from slowest to fastest): Water, Ground, Rotor, and Jet. Drones will have trouble catching up to a drone or vehicle traveling in a faster mode. For more information, see chapter nine, **Maximum Pursuit**.

WEAPON MOUNTS

MOUNT	MP	AVAIL	WEAPON
Micro	0	8R	Single-shot bullet or dart.
Mini	1	4R	Hold-out pistol, light pistol, reach 0 melee weapons, single-shot grenade
Small	2	8R	Heavy pistol, machine pistol
Standard	3	10F	Sub-machine gun, under-barrel grenade launcher
Large	4	12F	Shotgun, hunting rifle, assault rifle, grenade launcher
Huge	5	16F	Sniper rifle, light or medium machine gun
Heavy	6	20F	Heavy machine gun, rocket launcher, assault cannon

priate for all drones, of course; the gamemaster is the final arbitrator in what is and isn't allowed.

WEAPON MOUNTS

Probably the most common drone mod is finding a way to strap weapons onto one. Due to the small size of drones, standard vehicle mounts aren't always appropriate, so drones use weapon mounts from the following chart. Each weapon mount added uses up the listed number of Mod Points (listed as MP), allowing a drone to sometimes mount several smaller weapons rather than a single large one. All weapon mounts are at least Restricted, while some are Forbidden outside of military use as shown. In addition, authorities are quite interested in what weapons are mounted in them! In most nations, it's illegal for a drone to mount anything other than non-lethal weaponry. The CAS is a notable exception to this rule.

OPTION: POP-OUT MOUNTS

Ordinarily a weapon mount is quite obvious, as is the weapon mounted therein. Since shadowrunners tend to have quite illegal things mounted on their drones, this can be problematic, as you might imagine. There are two disguises for weapon mounts that can be used on drones. The first are blow-away panels. These are simple coverings that are designed to be ejected just before the weapon is triggered. Once blown away, the weapon is left exposed and obvious, but this method

is both cheap and easy. Blow-away panels may be installed with a simple Kit, and cost 25 nuyen x the MP of the weapon mount. A Perception + Intuition [Mental] (2) Test will reveal that there's something covered, but not what it is. Once the panel is blown away, it cannot be recovered.

The other option is "pop-up" weapons (or pop-out, or pop-under as the case may be). These are weapons stored inside the body of the drone, deployed on command (requiring a Free Action), then retracted again with another command (also a Free Action). Much harder to detect (requiring a Perception (4) Test) and re-usable, the mechanisms are a bit cumbersome and complex, adding 1 to the number of MP consumed by a weapon thus concealed. (For example, a standard mount with pop-up options would cost 4 MP.) Pop-up mounts may be installed with a Shop, and they cost 100 nuyen x the increased MP of the weapon.

OPTION: EXPANDED AMMUNITION BAY

Unlike normal vehicular weapons, the tight constraints of a drone's body offer limited ammunition reserves.

Any weapon mounted on a drone uses the weapon's normal ammunition limits, rather than the expanded version of a vehicle's. There are, however, two optional ammunition bays for drones. The first is simply adding a second bin, which holds the same number of ammunition as the weapon ordinarily holds, and a small switching unit to feed the weapon when one runs dry. This may be installed with a Kit, uses 1 MP, and costs 50 nuyen.

The other option is a full belt-feed system, replacing the weapon's normal ammunition feed mechanism entirely. This requires a shop, makes the weapon belt-fed, and provides enough room for an entire belt of 100 rounds. Additional expanded ammunition bays may then be added, each holding another 100-round belt. A belt-feed system requires a Shop, uses 2 MP, and costs 500 nuyen.

REALISTIC FEATURES

One of the most-requested modifications, realistic features are found on several spy drones, allowing them to blend in with local birds or insects. This type of modification also remains popular with anthropomorphic drones in an effort to humanize them. As the design approaches a more realistic model, the cost, as you might imagine, increases. Realistic features are available in four ratings, each rating serving as the threshold on a Perception test to tell if it's machine or a living being.

Rating 1, Availability 2, Cost (Body x Body) x 100
Rating 2, Availability 4, Cost (Body x Body) x 500
Rating 3, Availability 8, Cost (Body x Body) x 1,000
Rating 4, Availability 12R, Cost (Body x Body) x 5,000

While many drones can be made realistic (receiving Rating 1), allowing them to pass at a casual glance at a distance or at night, wheels, quad fans, and so on are quite difficult to disguise. Most drones cannot be given Realistic Features beyond Rating 1, while some cannot even obtain that level. (The gamemaster is the final arbitrator on what is and isn't appropriate.) Realistic Features 2 can be added with a Shop, but higher than this requires a Facility (most drones this realistic are designed as such before being sold).

AMPHIBIOUS

An amphibious drone comes in two ratings: Rating 1 allows it to float on the surface of a body of water, as long as it's relatively still, and while vulnerable to being submerged, it's waterproof on the underbody. Rating 2 Amphibious makes the entire drone waterproof, allowing it to be submerged without harm. Note that in either case, you'll want a motive system! Rating 1 requires a Shop, 1 Mod Point, and costs (Body x Body) x 100 nuyen. Rating 2 requires a Facility, 2 Mod Points, and costs (Body x Body) x 1,000 nuyen.

ASSEMBLY TIME IMPROVEMENT

Many drones are designed to be partially disassembled to allow for ease of storage and transport, most notably several winged drones whose propulsion method and wings can be removed so that the entire rig can be transported via car, then re-assembled for use. To assemble or disassemble a drone with this modification requires (Body) minutes and an appropriate Mechanics + Logic test with a threshold of 2. This upgrade can be done with a Shop, requires 1 MP, and costs (Body) x 100 nuyen.

CUSTOMIZED

Pure cosmetic differences, including flashing LED lights, snazzy paint, or chrome trim, can make a world of difference in making your drone what you want it to be. There is no game effect from these mods, but they're pretty to look at! Customization can be done with a Kit, uses no MP, and can cost anywhere from 10-10,000 nuyen.

DRONE ARM

Similar to a cyberarm, a drone arm is much cheaper due to the lack of flesh-chrome connections and sensory translation. Unless otherwise noted, use the standard cyberlimb rules, though the limb costs half of the normal price. (Upgrades for the arm are at full price, however.) A drone's cyberlimb starts with a Strength equal to its Body and an Agility equal to its Pilot. If the drone is using the arm for a test that would normally be Agility-based, use the limb's Agility, rather than the drone's Pilot Rating. A drone limb may have the base drone's starting attributes as much as doubled, no matter how many increases that is. The limb attributes may not go higher. (This means a Body 5 drone could have a strength increased from 5 to 10, ignoring the usual cap of +4 to an attribute, but may not go higher.) Drone limb armor does not affect the drone in any way, but having a limb provides +1 to the physical condition monitor as normal. Adding a drone arm requires a Shop and uses 1 MP.

OPTION: PRIMITIVE ARM

While a normal drone arm has a metahuman's level of functionality, some drones save money by using a simpler arm. These arms have brushes, or suction cups, with a more limited range of options. These limbs suffer -2 to any limit on tests requiring fine manipulation or weapon use with that limb, but the limb costs ten percent of the normal price, rather than fifty percent.

DRONE LEG

Walkers have legs, sometimes two, usually more. These operate similar to a cyberleg, but much cheaper as per drone arms. Drone speed is never based on limb Agility, so there is usually little point to upgrading this and, as per drone arms, cyberlimb armor placed on a drone doesn't affect the drone in any way. Drone legs do *not* add extra boxes to the drone's Physical condition monitor.

GECKO GRIPS

By coating the motive systems with gecko-glove-like materials, the drone can cling to virtually any surface. This allows it to climb vertical, or even hang upside down, as long as the surface has a Barrier Rating at least equal to the drone's Body x 3. Gecko grips require a Shop, use 1 MP, and cost (Body x 3) x 50 nuyen. Note that larger drones may have gecko grips, but will have a hard time finding a surface able to hold them!

IMMOBILE

A drone that is immobile can't move under its own power. These drones have a Speed and Acceleration of 0, which cannot be upgraded. On the positive side, they gain +2 Mod Points for not having a drive train. Making a drone immobile requires a Shop but doesn't cost anything other than a day's labor.

SKYGUIDE

By linking with SkyGuide, a drone can use the network's own guidance systems to get where it needs to be. The downside is that the system takes priority over the owner's commands, allowing the drone to be controlled by the Guide, or Riggers employed by SkyGuide, against the owner's wishes. The upside is that SkyGuide provides both a Navigation (6) autosoft and a Maneuver (6) autosoft to any drone while it's logged in to the network. Standard issue on flying drones sold form 2078 forward, it may be added to older drone with a Kit, requires 0 MP, and costs 5 nuyen, plus a 10 nuyen/year user fee.

SPOTLIGHT

Mounted externally, a drone spotlight acts as a flashlight in all ways. It requires a Kit, uses 0 MP, and costs 50 nuyen.

SUSPENSION MOD

Ground drones have an easily modified undercarriage, ultimately allowing the owner to replace the motive systems with some work. The base Handling of these suspensions is as follows; Standard 4/2, Tracked 3, or Off-road 2/4. Changing from one to another requires a Shop, uses no MP, and costs (Body x 3) x 100 nuyen.

TIRE MOD

Wheeled drones may have the wheels replaced in a pinch, serving a role roughly akin to a modified sus-

pension but not quite as good. The wheels increase the lower Handling Rating by 1, while lowering the better Handling by 2, until they are replaced again. (Thus, a 4/2 becomes a 2/3, while a 2/4 becomes a 3/2.) This exchange requires a Kit, uses 0 MP, and costs (Body x 3) x 25 nuyen. (Note that the old tires may be kept and this mod removed at a later time, restoring the normal Handling.)

SOFTWARE SOLUTIONS

What, you thought modern cars were all about mechanical grease monkeys and wrenches? Pfft! If you're working on anything made in the past quarter-century, you need to know computers to get it to run, and if you know computers, you'd know how much you *don't* know about the subject. For the most part, both vehicles and drones are simple things, needing enough brainpower to go from A to B, do something when they arrive, then wait for more orders. Cars that come when you signal or drones that swoop over an area for recon are basic, but most riggers want to take over for anything more complex. I'm here to tell you that that's not always needed. A good Pilot program can handle more than you think, since you're mostly used to dog brains on low-end commercial models, and while you've not been paying attention, the autosoft market got smarter.

PILOTS

It all starts with the Pilot, the main brain of your new machine. For ninety-five percent of the people out there, the pilot of their car or house-cleaning drone is what they're used to. It can play music, keep your car at the right speed, or clean up a spill, but you wouldn't trust it with anything important (he says, knowing full well that most commuters tell their car where to go, then lean back, fire up their commlink, and entertain themselves until the car tells them that they've arrived, never realizing that they have a two-ton bullet under their butt). Security drones have a more advanced Pilot program, with advanced fire/don't fire protocols based on potential targets in the area (or the known value of stored supplies) that can also use predictive algorithms to guess where you'll be next when you get out of sight. "Retail brains" are simple pilots on par with cars, able to do one thing, for instance your taxes or legal research, but nothing else.

Then you get fancy.

Advanced Pilot programs are comparable not to dogs, but to small children or, in some cases, adult metahumans. There aren't many that can make this claim, but led by military research where drones had to account for dozens of factors at once, Pilot programs have gotten smarter. I'm partial to the Djinn-IV Pilot from Saeder-Krupp myself; it's like having a child around the house, curious about everything and capable of some astounding leaps of logic. The top-end programs are restricted to military use, but I've gotten my hands on a few and, each time, they've developed personalities beyond what I ever expected. Like the armored personnel carrier that liked to "dance" to the almighty Troggs.

The Pilot program determines the Rating of the drone as a whole, serves as the primary source of attributes for skill tests, serves as a cap on the highest rating autosoft the drone can run, and more. Is there any reason that it's in such high demand? Civilian Pilot programs are generally Rating 2 (or, rarely, 1), restricted security Pilots are 3 to 4, while military-grade Pilots (5 to 6) are Forbidden for general use. Cost and Availability are shown on the chart below:

PILOTS

RATING	AVAIL	COST
1	4	100¥
2	—	400¥
3	8R	1800¥
4	12R	3200¥
5	16F	10,000¥
6	24F	20,000¥

AUTOSOFTS

It all ends with autosoft programs, the detailed commands that ensure a Pilot does what you want, when you want it. New autosofts are released every year—some expected, some quite the surprise. They don't cover all situations yet, but there's much more a drone can do than spy or shoot. Some of the most common ones are shown below.

A Pilot program may not run an autosoft of a higher Rating than itself (meaning a Rating 3 Pilot may run an Autosoft with a Rating of 1, 2, or 3, but not 4 or higher). When using a rigger command console, the console may run a higher-Rating autosoft and share that with the drone, allowing it to exceed its normal capabilities. So if you have an Aztechnology Crawler Clearsight 6 autosoft slotted into your RCC, each of your Aztechnology Crawlers may use it at the full value of 6.

Some skills are Restricted or Forbidden. Those will be indicated on the individual autosoft profile. Remember also that an autosoft is designed for only a single drone; you cannot slot a Clearsoft autosoft designed for an Aztechnology Crawler into an Evo Proletarian. (Well, you *can*; it just doesn't do anything.)

SMARTSOFT (RESTRICTED)

This is the same smartlink provided in eyeware or video enhancements, integrated into the sensors of a vehicle

AUTOSOFT PRICES

While this is in the official *SR5* Errata, not everyone has access to the Internet and, quite frankly, there's no better place to list them than Rigger 5.0. So here they are!

SOFTWARE	AVAIL	COST
Autosoft (1–6)	(Rating) x 2	(Rating) x 500

or drone. The Smartsoft is considered a Rating 3 autosoft and allows the full use of smart weapons.

GROUP

A shared-signal autosoft that allows each drone equipped with it to answer the same command, rather than requiring you to issue commands to one at a time. The Group autosoft is considered a Rating 2 autosoft.

SKILLSET

The Skillset autosoft gives the listed skill to the drone. The Rating can be from 1 to 6 as normal, but note that some Skillset autosoft are Restricted. The following skills may be taken as an autosoft:

Academic Knowledge (any single knowledge)
Chemistry (Restricted)
Demolitions (Restricted)
Electronic Warfare (Restricted)
First Aid
Hardware
Instruction
Language (any single language)
Lockpicking (Restricted)
Mechanic (any single Mechanic skill)
Medicine (Restricted)
Melee (as Targeting, but for a specific melee combat weapon)
Navigation
Performance (any single perform skill. Song-a-Mat evolves!)
Professional Knowledge (any single knowledge)

SOFTWARE TWEAKS

There are also some minor modifications that can be made to programs that have no real effect on the overall performance but allow for some customization.

PERSONALITY

(Availability 4, Cost 100¥)
Many people treat their drones as pets, and a personality tweak can go a long way to help. A Pilot with a Personality will develop a "flavor" all to itself, evolving

a unique set of features over time depending on how it's treated and what it regularly does. Some are playful, some are territorial, some adorably clumsy, some are calm—the exact personality can be specified when purchased, but most allow their drone to develop naturally.

LINGUISTICS

(Availability 4, Cost 50¥)

When a drone is designed, it comes pre-loaded with two languages: one native to the manufacturer and one native to where it will be sold. In the UCAS, this is usually Japanese and English, but not always. A Pilot may contain as many Linguistics autosofts as its Rating, so few add more than the initial two, but more can be added, or old ones deleted and replaced, as long as room is present. Keep in mind that Linguistics are used for verbal commands and have a very limited vocabulary; you cannot use your motorcycle's German Linguistics to eavesdrop on Hans Brackhaus and expect it to tell you what was said. Come here, go there, shoot that guy, find the nearest McHugh's, and similar commands are about as much as it can handle. (However, there was enough demand that Renraku introduced actual translation software, the Language autosoft, which other corporations quickly picked up on.)

DRONE CATALOG

And now the part you've all been waiting for! I've culled this list from several different sources, picking a few personal favorites, some up-and-coming specials, and some old classics. There's a lot going on down below, so hang on to your command console!

MICRODRONES

HORIZON "NOIZQUITO"

(PILOT AIRCRAFT)

The Aztlan-Amazonian War was ostensibly about two nations fighting over resources, but it was also a proxy war between Aztechnology and Horizon, who were fighting for the hearts and minds of the world. In this fight, Horizon attempted to act primarily through cat's-paws and cut-outs, avoiding a direct confrontation that could lead to bad press. Thus, rather than providing weapons and materiel to the Amazonians, Horizon developed a drone that could do what Horizon does best—harass and annoy.

The NoizQuito was developed as a flying micro drone with a few special tricks. Visually similar to a mosquito, the body of the drone can only house a small number of features. The most prevalent and obvious of these features is the speaker system. The drone can blast sounds as loud as 160 decibels (which is the volume of high-end race cars), which are used to produce distractions and possibly even minor ear damage in

those unfortunate enough to be near the drone when it activates. Additionally, the drone's wings and body are covered in small LEDs that are powerful enough to produce blinding levels of light in a bewildering array of strobe patterns.

> ◉ I hate these things. They hurt friends and foes alike, and a swarm of them is enough to drive someone insane. Whichever Horizon R&D guy designed this thing deserves to be shot.
> ◉ Picador

> ◉ If you'd like, I can put together a package. PM me to make arrangements.
> ◉ Cosmo

> ◉ Horizon didn't get this drone out fast enough to make an impact on the outcome of the war, and they lost out big on the opportunity to advertise this drone to the world as a result. They're making their way through the market now, but progress has been slow.
> ◉ Dr. Spin

Standard Upgrades: Flying, speakers, strobes

Game Information: When activated, the strobes impose a –2 penalty to all actions by those who are currently looking in the direction of the drone. This penalty is reduced to –1 if the target has flare compensation. The speakers impose a –2 penalty to all actions by those within earshot of the drone, which is lessened to –1 for those with a sound damper system. If there are multiple drones acting as a group, the penalties are cumulative for each drone (meaning that if three drones are working as one, the target can take as much as a –12 penalty to all actions).

Note: "Earshot" has the potential to be quite far, but the physics calculations for determining actual earshot are too complicated for a roleplaying game. As always, the gamemaster has the final say in determining who (or what) is affected.

HORIZON "NOIZQUITO" (MICRO DRONE)								
HANDL	SPEED	ACCEL	BODY	ARM	PILOT	SENS	AVAIL	COST
4	3R	2	1	0	3	3	10R	2,000¥

SONY GOLDFISH

(PILOT WATERCRAFT)

Sized to realistic proportions and capable of dives of up to four meters deep, the Renraku Goldfish is a prime example of an entry-level water drone, suitable as a trainer for youths who look toward a future as robotic operators or hobbyists who wish to explore local watering holes below the surface.

Standard Upgrades: Submersible

Similar Models: Mitsuhama Minnow, NeoNET Pinkeens

- You'd be amazed how many executives have fish tanks in their office. Nobody expects a water-based bug. It can be expensive to make them realistic-looking, but the payoff can be worth it.
- Sunshine

- Keep in mind that water does awful things to signal strength. You'll have to get back in to retrieve the data.
- Sounder

SONY GOLDFISH (MICRO DRONE)								
HANDL	SPEED	ACCEL	BODY	ARM	PILOT	SENS	AVAIL	COST
2/4	1W	1	0	0	2	2	6	500¥

MINIDRONES

AERODESIGN SYSTEMS CONDOR LDSD-23

(PILOT AIRCRAFT)

Solar-powered and hydrogen-filled, the Condor is a long-duration observation drone constructed with transparent and radar-invisible materials, allowing it to hover in place for days, even weeks, rather than the hours that a conventional drone can manage. The trade-off, of course, is that the Condor is completely vulnerable if detected and unable to flee. While the Condor's balloon is nearly as large as kitchen table when inflated, when deflated the entire unit is smaller than a bowling pin.

Similar Models: Ares Cloudship, Renraku Buzzard

AERODESIGNS CONDOR (MINI DRONE)								
HANDL	SPEED	ACCEL	BODY	ARM	PILOT	SENS	AVAIL	COST
2	0R	0	1(1)	0	2	4	6R	4,000¥

AZTECHNOLOGY HEDGEHOG

(PILOT GROUND CRAFT)

A specialized sub-design of the Aztechnology Crawler, the Hedgehog is the leading security-sniffing drone on the market today. Intended to find opposition command, control, and communication broadcasts, it can listen in passively while running decrypting software. Parked in a hidden location, it can eavesdrop for up to forty-eight hours on a single charge, gathering data by the gigapulse.

Standard Upgrades: Electronic Warfare (2) Autosoft,
Similar Models: Ares NS-Aardvark, Lone Star Mockingbird

- Age hasn't been terribly kind to the Hedgehog. It's still good, but wireless protocols have advanced since it rolled out.
- Rigger X

AZTECHNOLOGY HEDGEHOG (MINI DRONE)								
HANDL	SPEED	ACCEL	BODY	ARM	PILOT	SENS	AVAIL	COST
3	1G	1	1(0)	0	4	3	8F	8,000¥

CYBERSPACE DESIGNS DRAGONFLY

(PILOT AIRCRAFT)

Perhaps the smallest drone-hunting drone in production today, the Dragonfly is designed to follow surveillance drones anywhere they hide and bring them down. A sleek quad-copter design with in-body rotors that are protected from collisions in tight corners, the Dragonfly comes pre-equipped with a chomping "beak" of blades, allowing it to shear through the wings or body of other mini-or-micro-drones, ripping them from the sky. Against larger drones, the Dragonfly can swarm, nipping away in small bites, but it isn't designed to cut through any appreciable levels of armor plating.

Standard Upgrades: Melee Bite (Acc 3, Reach —, Dam 3P, AP -2), Targeting (Melee) Auotsoft
Similar Models: Ares Sparrowhawk, Renraku Yokujin

- The Ares Sparrowhawk is similar but mounts a modified Ares Light Fire 70. Gotta love the CAS.
- Kane

CD DRAGONFLY (MINI DRONE)								
HANDL	SPEED	ACCEL	BODY	ARM	PILOT	SENS	AVAIL	COST
4	2R	1	1(0)	3	3	2	12R	4,000¥

FESTO PIGEON 2.0

(PILOT EXOTIC VEHICLE)

Saeder-Krupp's small Festo subsidiary mastered the art of lifelike simulation for drones, producing the first realistic flying "bird drone" almost fifty years ago. The design has continued to be refined over the decades, and now stands as a work of art. The baseline model is a chrome-plated beauty, but a more lifelike model is available and is commonly used as a surveillance drone.

Similar Models: Sony Nightingale, Renraku Bluebird
Standard Upgrades: Realistic Features (1)

FESTO PIGEON 2.0 (MINI DRONE)								
HANDL	SPEED	ACCEL	BODY	ARM	PILOT	SENS	AVAIL	COST
4	2R	1	1(1)	0	2	2	8	3,000¥

HORIZON CU^3

(PILOT AIRCRAFT)

A simple single-fan vectored thrust drone, the CU is a cheaper version of the professional camera drones used by most major trideo broadcasters. The fan traded off speed for stability and whisper-quiet operation, allowing the camera to focus on the target without overwhelming the sound with the typical whirly-whoosh. Hugely popular with the P2 crowd, where it follows them everywhere and records their day, allowing them to do live updates or edit the footage later. The professional version has an improved camera, Pilot, and software, and usually operates in threes (thus the cubed designation), allowing for three camera angles in any given scene.

Similar Models: MCT Redlight, Evo CultureCapture
Standard Upgrades: Clearsight (2) Autosoft
Optional Upgrades: Professional Upgrade: Pilot increased to (4), Clearsight increased to (4), for +3,000¥

HORIZON CU^3 (MINI DRONE)								
HANDL	SPEED	ACCEL	BODY	ARM	PILOT	SENS	AVAIL	COST
4	1R	1	1(1)	0	2	3	4	3,000¥

RENRAKU GERBIL

(PILOT GROUND CRAFT)

A tiny wheeled drone, the Gerbil's sized to travel through not only any ventilation shaft, but most pipes, allowing it to enter a surprisingly large number of otherwise-secure areas. It's surprisingly quick and nimble, able to evade most pursuit from metahumans long enough to find a hidey-hole,

Similar Models: GM-Nissan Mouse, MCT Zipper

- A touch larger than most spy drones, the Gerbil uses that extra size for a speedy motor. Not a tradeoff for everyone, but certainly interesting.
- Turbo Bunny

RENRAKU GERBIL (MINI DRONE)								
HANDL	SPEED	ACCEL	BODY	ARM	PILOT	SENS	AVAIL	COST
4/2	2G	1	1(1)	0	2	2	4	2,000¥

RENRAKU SCUTTLER REMOTE CYBERHAND

(PILOT WALKER)

A subtle way to sneak a drone into an area, the Renraku Scuttler is a detachable cyberhand that includes remote rigger controls and a computer system to allow for remote operation. The middle digit is further equipped with a sensor suite (if a poor one), while the other four are used for locomotion. The Scuttler has manipulative ability that similarly sized drones lack, but it isn't

CYBERWARE

CYBERWARE	ESS	CAP	AVAIL	COST
Remote Cyberhand	0.25	(5)	8	8,000¥

as quick or nimble due to the shape constraints of the metahuman hand. Due to the size of the drone system, the Scuttler lacks any Capacity for further upgrades.

Similar Models: Evo Hi-Five, Ares Thing

SMALL DRONES

ARES ARMS SENTRY V (AND MERCURY)

(PILOT GROUND CRAFT)

The venerable Sentry rail-drone system has some three decades of experience behind it. Hanging from a railing, the Sentry can traverse an entire facility via small "doggie doors" high on the walls, giving them complete access to areas without compromising security. The Sentry both draws power and accepts commands via the rail system, leaving it impervious to wireless hijacking and, due to being kept on a secondary, dedicated power supply, functional even when the rest of the facility is blacked out. In the mid-'60s, enterprising Ares executives decided to take advantage of the rail system by creating the Mercury, an unarmed courier that would allow messages or packages to be shuttled around the office with greater reliability and safety. As the Sentry was nigh-ubiquitous, the Mercury is now found in over ninety percent of Ares facilities, serving as a mobile mailbox. In the event of an active hostile situation, Mercuries store themselves out of the way, leaving the rails clear for Sentry deployment.

Standard Upgrades: Standard weapon mount, Colt Cobra TZ-120, 30 standard ammo, Targeting autosoft (3), SmartSoft

Similar Models: Shpagina Evo-2, Shiawase Minebea GridSys

ARES SENTRY (SMALL DRONE)								
HANDL	SPEED	ACCEL	BODY	ARM	PILOT	SENS	AVAIL	COST
4/—	1G	1	2(0)	6	3	2	4R	4,000¥

CITRON-BROUILLARD SMOKE GENERATOR

(PILOT GROUND CRAFT)

A simple design, the tracked Smoke Generator is equipped with a single function: creating smoke screens. Capable of generating clouds for up to twelve minutes, and IR-blocking thermal smoke for three more, it can be kept stationary, creating a billowing screen some 150 meters in diameter, or left rolling, in which

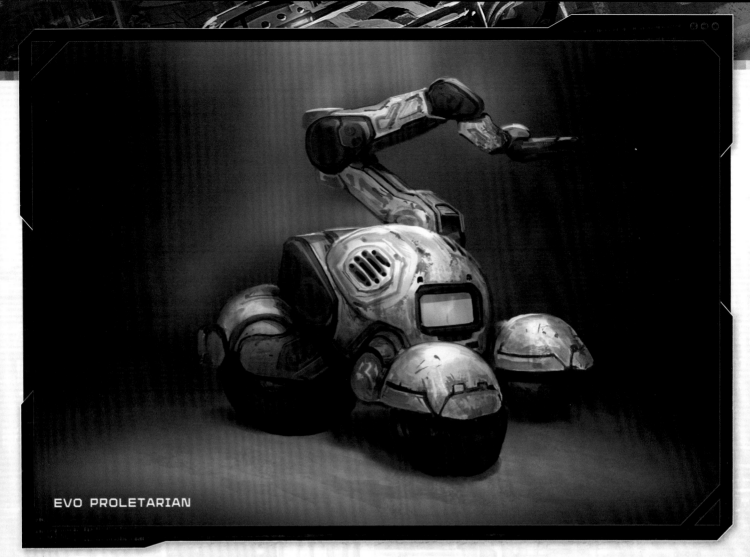

EVO PROLETARIAN

case it creates a smoky trail 100 meters wide by 250 meters long. In either case, the ten-meter-high cloud begins to dissipate one minute after the smoke generator is turned off, at which point it becomes a light cloud. It fully vanishes a minute after that.

Standard Upgrades: Smoke generator (holds twelve one-minute doses of smoke and three one-minute doses of thermal smoke)

- You can fill the tank with other gasses, but don't expect that kind of volume. The Brouillard's proprietary smoke fuel is legendary.
- Rigger X

C-B SMOKE GENERATOR (SMALL DRONE)								
HANDL	SPEED	ACCEL	BODY	ARM	PILOT	SENS	AVAIL	COST
3	1G	1	2(0)	0	2	2	8	4,000¥

CYBERSPACE DESIGNS WOLFHOUND

(PILOT AIRCRAFT)
A basic recon drone that sacrifices durability or armaments for high-send sensors and breakneck speed, the Wolfhound is the only drone of its size that's broken the sound barrier. It usually stays at subsonic speeds, to better conceal its skyward location.

Similar Models: Ares Sergeant, S-K Dawnrider

CD WOLFHOUND (SMALL DRONE)								
HANDL	SPEED	ACCEL	BODY	ARM	PILOT	SENS	AVAIL	COST
3	2J	1	2(1)	0	2	4	12	30,000¥

EVO PROLETARIAN

(PILOT GROUND CRAFT)
The mechanic's best friend. These little guys are amazing. At the core, it's a simple dome-headed, three-wheeled drone with a single functional arm, but they're just about perfect for pitching in around the garage. They're advanced enough to be trusted with simple work, banging out dents, changing tires, checking the oil, and so on, but they are also handy assistants for harder work, presenting you with tools when you need them, keeping vehicle schematics displayed on their chest screen, and keeping an eye on things when you're beneath an undercarriage. They even have good speakers for use as a mobile stereo system. Evo hired

Renraku to create a wide array of autosofts for them, giving them an option for repairing anything, handling electrical or construction work, even serving as butlers as parties.

Standard Upgrades: Drone arm (Strength 4, Agility 2), Automotive Mechanic Toolkit, Automotive Mechanic (2) autosoft

- Like you've ever been to a party.
- Netcat

- They serve as cheap labor in some areas, taking entry-level jobs from metahumans. I can't tell if the name is ironic or tragic.
- Chainmaker

EVO PROLETARIAN (SMALL DRONE)								
HANDL	SPEED	ACCEL	BODY	ARM	PILOT	SENS	AVAIL	COST
4/2	2G	1	2(1)	0	2	2	6	4,000¥

FERRET RPD-1X WHEELED PERIMETER DRONE

(PILOT GROUND CRAFT)

One of the oldest security drones still in production, the Ferret is a small patrol drone used as a cheap alternative to security guards. Armed with a flashlight and a taser, it's perfectly able to handle drunk college students and would-be trespassers, but shadowrunners are a different breed. That said, they see wide use in college campuses, shopping malls, and many homes, serving as basic light security. It should be noted that they're awful off-road, and so they need to stay on established paths.

Standard Upgrades: Mini weapon mount, Defiance Shocker, 4 taser darts, flashlight

Similar Models: Aztechnology IDS, NeoNET Janus

- Since they're so common, it's a good idea to keep one or two around the house where you can mod the exterior to match the ones protecting a site, allowing you to have a Trojan Horse that can blend in for pre-scouting.
- Hard Exit

- You can laugh off one easily enough, but when a dozen of them pile on, that voltage *hurts*!
- 2XL

FERRET RPD-5X (SMALL DRONE)								
HANDL	SPEED	ACCEL	BODY	ARM	PILOT	SENS	AVAIL	COST
4/2	1G	1	2(1)	3	3	3	8R	4,000¥

FESTO SEWER SNAKE

(PILOT EXOTIC VEHICLE)

Able to both slither and swim, the Sewer Snake's long, narrow design allows it to access areas that differently shaped drones cannot and handle whatever environmental conditions it faces. The Snake's surface is coated with several small gecko grip points, allowing it to climb vertically when pressed, and it can handle the pressure of a ten-meter dive. There's little room for further modification, but in terms of eyes that can go anywhere, you're hard-pressed to beat the Snake.

Standard Upgrades: Submersible, gecko grips

- I hate this thing. I hate snakes, and this moves so realistically that it triggers my phobia.
- Sounder

- Rumor has it that Saeder-Krupp has a larger version that's weaponized for assassination.
- Plan 9

FESTO SEWER SNAKE (SMALL DRONE)								
HANDL	SPEED	ACCEL	BODY	ARM	PILOT	SENS	AVAIL	COST
3	1G/1W	1/1	2(1)	0	2	2	10	6,000¥

HORIZON MINI-ZEP

(PILOT AIRCRAFT)

A simple lighter-than-air drone, the Mini-Zep's only notable due to the electrochromatic coating along the airbag's surface. This allows the Mini-Zep to be programmed with ads for virtually anything and they can either be scrolled through or changed completely with a simple wireless signal from the home office. They also have a small radio transmitter inside, allowing them to spam AR ads to any nearby commlink. Due to being a LtA drone pushed gently with fans, they can easily loiter for eight hours, giving maximum eyeball time to their ads. In emergency situations, they can even do live rebroadcasts of weather alerts, law enforcement APBs, or anything else.

Standard Upgrades: Electrochromatic coating

- You can't go a block in any metroplex's downtown without having one of these things blaring at you. Damned nuisances.
- Bull

- Super-fun to hack, however! You can post all *kinds* of pictures on these things. Hubba hubba!
- Slamm-0!

HORIZON MINI-ZEP (SMALL DRONE)								
HANDL	SPEED	ACCEL	BODY	ARM	PILOT	SENS	AVAIL	COST
2	0R	0	2(4)	0	2	2	4	2,000¥

KNIGHT ERRANT P5 PURSUIT DRONE

(PILOT GROUND CRAFT)

An unusual "limpet" drone stored in some Knight Errant police cruisers, the P5 is a small drone that sacrifices durability for raw speed. When at top speed, the batteries last a whopping ten minutes, but that's more than enough for this little beast. The P5 drops down from beneath the cruiser, races ahead, then magnetically attaches itself to the undercarriage of the pursued vehicle. This allows KE to follow the wireless signal instead of engaging in a high-speed chase. Simple, but effective.

- The drone's broadcast signal is based off a second battery and has a twenty-four hour life; plenty for KE to come find you.
- Turbo Bunny

- There are some sneaky runners out there who fill these things with plastique. Ride go boom!
- Red Anya

KNIGHT ERRANT P5 (SMALL DRONE)								
HANDL	SPEED	ACCEL	BODY	ARM	PILOT	SENS	AVAIL	COST
4/2	6G	2	2(1)	0	3	2	10R	8,000¥

LONE STAR CASTLE GUARD

(PILOT GROUND CRAFT)

"Worried about your loved ones being victims of a late night? Stay at work safely while Lone Star guards your castle!" Notice the subtle dig at their primary law enforcement rivals? Lone Star is unique in the home-security drone market in offering a pistol-armed drone, as opposed to the non-lethal options other security drones carry as standard arms. Much more common in the CAS than the UCAS, the Castle Guard ads push that lethal force is the only true way to keep your family safe while you're grinding away at your job. The Guard comes with four SmartSafety bracelets to ensure that it can't accidentally fire at family members, and additional bracelets, or pet collars, can be purchased for 50 nuyen each. The drone itself is average-sized, four-wheeled, and has enough armor to turn aside small arms or baseball bats, but not so much that one going wild can't be easily stopped by heavier firepower. The marketing on these things is damned impressive, even if the actual drone's average at best.

Standard Upgrades: Light weapon mount, Targeting autosoft (3), Smartsoft, four SmartSafety bracelets

- Keep in mind, drones made in the CAS use different tools than the metric tools that everyone else on the planet uses. You need to buy new kits to work on 'em.
- Kane

- I had to go take a look. 3/16ths of an inch! Who the frag thought these measures were a good idea?!
- Slamm-0!

LS CASTLE GUARD (SMALL DRONE)								
HANDL	SPEED	ACCEL	BODY	ARM	PILOT	SENS	AVAIL	COST
4/2	1G	1	2(0)	6	3	2	8R	10,000

MITSUHAMA GUN TURRET

(NO PILOT REQUIRED)

If you've ever gone into a Zero Zone, you've run into these bad boys. MCT's been selling them to anyone with nuyen to wave around for over fifty years. They're immobile (other than rotating), but they're both cheap and well-armored, allowing them to do the job efficiently. The most common variants are Retractable or Up-Armored, but some choose a larger weapon mount instead.

Standard Upgrades: Standard weapon mount
Standard Downgrades: Immobile

- MCT normally uses these in packs of three. One will be obvious, such as just above the front door of a facility, and well-armored. There's often a handy planter to hide behind and observe it. While you do that, two more guns pop up behind your flanks in a triangle while you're watching forward. Simple but effective.
- Hard Exit

- As runners learned to watch behind them for that, MCT upped the game and put land mines around the planters. Guns pop up, you take cover naturally, and then it turns out that the whole game was to get you behind that cover so that radio-detonated mines could take you out. Zero Zones, chummer. They're not worth it.
- Stone

MCT GUN TURRET (SMALL DRONE)								
HANDL	SPEED	ACCEL	BODY	ARM	PILOT	SENS	AVAIL	COST
—	—	—	2(0)	6	3	2	4R	4,000¥

MITSUHAMA SEVEN

Launched on New Year's Day 2077, the Mitsuhama Seven are intended to capture the North American casual drone market, targeting both drone beginners and advanced modders with the same product. The Seven (a number chosen for marketing reasons) is a bare-bones model with laughable programming. These things are half-blind but dirt cheap. While the "Seven Dwarves" have official numerical designations (77-MPD-01, 02, 03, etc.), they quickly developed nicknames that standardized across the Matrix. The core wheeled model is "Wheelie," treaded is "Treads," off-road suspension is "Dirty," the four-legged "Quad," the surface-aquatic "Swims," the quad-copter "Hovers," and the traditional flyer "Soars." I never claimed that they were *good* nicknames, but they're better than numbers, right?

Standard Upgrades: None

- It's all about the after-market mods on these things. The base models are junk.
- /dev/grrl

- I know that they're designed fragile to bring customers back for replacements often, but Goddamn, I think the last batch I bought were made out of tissue paper. They just fell the hell apart.
- Kane

- After an Aztlan patrol boat shot them.
- /dev/grrl

- I know, right? Too fragile.
- Kane

MCT SEVEN (WHEELIE) (SMALL DRONE)								
HANDL	SPEED	ACCEL	BODY	ARM	PILOT	SENS	AVAIL	COST
4/2	2G	1	1(3)	0	1	1	—	2,000¥

MCT SEVEN (TREADS) (SMALL DRONE)								
HANDL	SPEED	ACCEL	BODY	ARM	PILOT	SENS	AVAIL	COST
3	2G	1	1(3)	0	1	1	2	2,000¥

MCT SEVEN (DIRTY) (SMALL DRONE)								
HANDL	SPEED	ACCEL	BODY	ARM	PILOT	SENS	AVAIL	COST
2/4	2G	1	1(3)	0	1	1	2	2,000¥

MCT SEVEN (QUAD) (SMALL DRONE)								
HANDL	SPEED	ACCEL	BODY	ARM	PILOT	SENS	AVAIL	COST
4	1G	1	1(3)	0	1	1	4	2,000¥

MCT SEVEN (SWIMS) (SMALL DRONE)								
HANDL	SPEED	ACCEL	BODY	ARM	PILOT	SENS	AVAIL	COST
3	2W	1	1(3)	0	1	1	4	1,000¥

MCT SEVEN (HOVERS) (SMALL DRONE)								
HANDL	SPEED	ACCEL	BODY	ARM	PILOT	SENS	AVAIL	COST
4	1R	1	1(3)	0	1	1	6	4,000¥

MCT SEVEN (SOARS) (SMALL DRONE)								
HANDL	SPEED	ACCEL	BODY	ARM	PILOT	SENS	AVAIL	COST
3	2J	1	1(3)	0	1	1	8	4,000¥

NEONET PRAIRIE DOG
(PILOT GROUND CRAFT)

Recently decommissioned by the PCC military, the Prairie Dog was the Pueblo military's standard jamming/ECM drone for infantry platoons. The large off-road wheels and shocks allow it to handle the worst terrain with ease, with plenty of speed to keep pace with dismounted infantry. The Prairie Dog's distinctive antennae are no less impressive, even with the reduction in capabilities given this de-militarized version.

Standard Upgrades: Electronic Warfare (3) autosoft, directional jammer (4), area jammer (6)

NN PRAIRIE DOG (SMALL DRONE)								
HANDL	SPEED	ACCEL	BODY	ARM	PILOT	SENS	AVAIL	COST
2/4	2G	1	2(0)	3	3	4	12F	8,000¥

PRATT & WHITNEY SUNDOWNER
(PILOT AIRCRAFT)

A simple, low-speed aircraft used in agriculture to spray fields, or more rarely for skywriting for those looking for some retro communication. The Sundowner isn't great but has little competition in this niche.

Standard Upgrades: Aerial chemical sprayer (holds ten doses of a chemical, each able to cover a line 125 meters long, twenty-five meters wide, and ten meters high; these large spray doses cost ten times the normal cost of a dose)

Similar Models: Shiawase Hyakusho, Aztechnology Roundup

- If they look familiar, it's because they were used to saturate Bug City with Strain III.
- Puck

- That didn't exactly go as planned.
- Bull

- Especially for the ghouls.
- Hanibelle

P&W SUNDOWNER (SMALL DRONE)								
HANDL	SPEED	ACCEL	BODY	ARM	PILOT	SENS	AVAIL	COST
3	4R	1	2(0)	0	2	2	8	10,000¥

PROTEUS A.G. "KRAKE"
(PILOT WATERCRAFT)

Proteus A.G. is well known for its arkoblocks, and the corp had a well-publicized spat with Ares in 2063. Since the Corporate Court's ruling against Proteus, they have attempted to submerge themselves into their private research. While shadowrunners typically have had

PROTEUS KRAKE

difficulty infiltrating these facilities to perform corporate espionage, one team recently managed to surface with plans for a very unique drone.

- This drone is simply fintastic!
- Slamm-0!

- Water you talking about?
- /dev/grrl/

- Make these puns stop!
- Netcat

- Why are you so crabby?
- Slamm-0!

- Oh whale. I sea what you did there. You shore did all that on porpoise. You're all washed up.
- /dev/grrl/

- Winner!
- The Smiling Bandit

Since the best drone designs are based on natural evolutionary perfection, Proteus decided to model the design of the Krake drone on a squid. The six tentacles are used to propel the Krake through the water and can flex to provide a full range of motion options, making this drone incredibly agile in the water. Additionally, one of the tentacles is equipped with a plasma torch and multitool, which are presumably used for underwater welding and cutting tasks. Due to the small size of the Krake, it can reach areas that are normally inaccessible to metahumans.

The seas are dangerous though, and Proteus has repeatedly shown that they are willing to fight it out with the merfolk and even the Sea Dragon. So the Krake are occasionally retrofitted for security detail, adding a small cluster of micro-torpedoes and a sort of "ink pouch" feature. From the blueprints that were recovered, the micro-torpedoes have a limited payload, but when used in a cluster they are more than devastating. The "ink" that can be released by the Krake is designed to scramble electronic sensors, as well as prevent visual targeting.

- A word of warning: the payloads for these torpedoes can be devastating. Instead of their typical explosive warheads, some of them have been outfitted with a chemical that eats through hulls.
- Sounder

- Word is that Evo NavTech is trying to find a way to utilize this design for patrolling the waters of Kowloon Bay. If they can figure out how to correct the effect of water refraction on radio waves, they could have a fully autonomous drone force that is nearly undetectable. Scary thought.
- 2XL

Standard Upgrades: Plasma torch, specialized weapon (ink pouch), tool kit (Nautical Mechanic), weapon mount

Game Information: The plasma torch can only be used in immediate touch range, and therefore is useless in combat scenarios.

The ink pouch can release a cloud of manufactured ink into the water along with a chafe of metal flakes. The ink obscures vision (even electronic) in a five-meter radius, applying a penalty equal to Heavy Smoke for any attacks made through the cloud.

The micro-torpedoes can be outfitted with either a chemical or an explosive warhead. The explosive warheads are treated as anti-vehicle rockets, providing –4 armor penetration to non-vehicle targets and providing a –10 armor penetration to vehicular targets. The chemical warheads apply an acidic adhesive to the target, providing continuous damage to the target each Combat Turn until the adhesive is removed with a simple solvent (glue solvent, p. 448, *SR5*).

PROTEUS 'KRAKE' (SMALL DRONE)								
HANDL	SPEED	ACCEL	BODY	ARM	PILOT	SENS	AVAIL	COST
5	3W	4	2(0)	2	4	3	18F	10,000¥

MICRO-TORPEDO					
TYPE	DAMAGE	AP	BLAST	AVAIL	COST
Chemical	6P	–4	1m radius	18F	3,000¥
Explosive	18P	–4/–10	–6/m	18F	2,500¥

SAAB-THYSSEN BLOODHOUND
(PILOT GROUND CRAFT)

A hazardous-area exploration drone with advanced sensors, the Bloodhound is used to investigate areas that might be contaminated by biological agents, chemicals, or radiation before sending in organics. Not only can the Bloodhound identify these materials, it also marks them with small color-coded flags (equipped with RFID of course). It also has a small scoop and storage compartment where it can collect and hold soil samples.

Standard Upgrades: Geiger counter (6), olfactory scanner (8)

S-T BLOODHOUND (SMALL DRONE)								
HANDL	SPEED	ACCEL	BODY	ARM	PILOT	SENS	AVAIL	COST
3	1G	1	2(0)	0	2	4	8	10,000¥

RENRAKU DOVE
(PILOT AIRCRAFT)

A Renraku product, the Dove is licensed exclusively to GOD. It flits quietly around major sprawls, searching for illegal wireless signals. While the Dove is, in general, an unimpressive design, the radio-snooping technology is top-notch, while the software can alert GOD operatives to activity, drawing attention from support operators who then call in larger, more combative drones to deal with the lawbreaker.

Standard Upgrades: Radio signal scanner (6)

RENRAKU DOVE-4 (SMALL DRONE)								
HANDL	SPEED	ACCEL	BODY	ARM	PILOT	SENS	AVAIL	COST
4	2R	1	2(1)	0	2	2	4	5,000¥

RENRAKU JARDINERO
(PILOT GROUND CRAFT)

Renraku has numerous lines all based on the same chassis (which is why the Jardinero has the wrong suspension for the work it's doing), but the Jardinero is the top-selling, so gets the nod. The basic model is simply an automated lawn mower, handling all of the upkeep of suburban grass with silent electrical motors and whisper-quiet blades, then returning to a solar recharge station until told to mow again. Other versions handle vacuum duties, floor polishing, repainting parking lots, and similarly menial jobs.

Similar models: Dozens

- There was, briefly, a version with an extendable arm and hedge clippers for landscaping, but after a rather hair-raising incident involving four of them, a crazed Technomancer, and a Renraku exec, that line was, uh, pruned.
- Baka Dabora

- While middle-class suburbanites love these things, wealthier landowners hire metahuman landscapers as a show of decadence. Renraku, of course, is the primary source of those jobs. Gotta love Renraku's cons; they'll get your money one way or the other.
- Haze

RENRAKU JARDINERO (SMALL DRONE)								
HANDL	SPEED	ACCEL	BODY	ARM	PILOT	SENS	AVAIL	COST
2/4	1G	1	2(1)	0	2	2	4	2,000¥

RENRAKU JOB-A-MAT

(NO PILOT REQUIRED)

It all started with the Song-a-Mat, a simple desktop unit that allowed consumers to put together music to their own taste, allowing everyone to become a musician of sorts. This revolutionized the entire music industry, giving us today's model where live performances are the sign that you've made it, while struggling young bands have to put out singles for wageslave pay. Since then, Renraku's found that the basic chassis was ideal for loading other software modules into and a new market was born. Keep in mind that Renraku never plasters their name on these things and that each of the two dozen or so models is marketed in a different way. The BarristaBot is marketed to small business owners that want to add a small drink area, while the Intern line fills up legal offices and insurance firms, grinding out paperwork.

Standard Upgrades: Profession or Knowledge (2) Autosoft
Standard Downgrade: Immobile

- Renraku's new focus on the service industry competes directly with their Job-a-Mat line of drones, but each brings in profit, so they push whichever one seems more likely to break open a market.
- Haze

- Abominable things. It wasn't enough to drive out the blue-collar workers?
- Chainmaker

- Keep in mind, these things only handle the basic functions. When faced with an odd request, they call in rigger backup to deal with the situation. There's a big difference between metahuman ability and Pilots.
- Glitch

- For now.
- Icarus

RENRAKU JOB-A-MAT (SMALL DRONE)								
HANDL	SPEED	ACCEL	BODY	ARM	PILOT	SENS	AVAIL	COST
—	—	—	2(2)	0	2	2	4	3,000¥

RENRAKU PELICAN

(PILOT AIRCRAFT)

You've seen these quad-copters around for years, but I bet none of you knew what the actual name was. Renraku keeps the marketing for these things aimed at wholesale, not retail. The Pelican is a simple flying drone with a modular storage compartment underhung. Heated or cooled, they come in sizes for pizza, noodle boxes, and more, and are used by everyone from Pizza Hop to Heli-Taco to Heavenly Noodles, to make sure you get your food in thirty minutes or less anywhere in the sprawl.

Standard Upgrades: Storage compartment
Similar Models: MCT Transporter-3, Evo Kourier

- The booming drone-livery market is what led to Renraku developing the SkyGuide software. Nice to invent a disease that you just happen to have a cure for, eh?
- Glitch

- You hush your mouth! Those emergency deliveries of SkyScoop ice cream save my bacon on a regular basis.
- Slamm-0!

- Goes without saying, but if you dress your drone in the right paint, you can deliver more than food to an open window without raising suspicion.
- Hard Exit

RENRAKU PELICAN (SMALL DRONE)								
HANDL	SPEED	ACCEL	BODY	ARM	PILOT	SENS	AVAIL	COST
4	2R	1	2(1)	0	2	2	2	4,000¥

TELESTRIAN INDUSTRIES SHAMUS

(PILOT GROUND CRAFT)

A rare entry from the secretive Telestrian Industries, the Shamus is basically a forensic analysis laboratory rolled into one compact drone. The drone's design appears to be partly canine, partly arachnid. Four legs with multiple joints support the body, while a cluster of sensors in front suggest compound eyes below a more conventional head. The sensor suite built into the Shamus is extremely impressive, boasting a full range of visual sensors, X-ray scanners, ultrasound sensors, and even a biomatter sampler for checking biological samples. Additionally, the Shamus is capable of projecting a trideo display into open space, connecting to an investigator's PAN to easily allow the investigator to re-create a crime scene in real time.

However, the feature that sets the Shamus apart from all other drones in this space is the quicksilver camera. Normally a quicksilver camera requires a magician to operate, but the Shamus has been outfitted with a unique (and proprietary) blend of reagents that can operate the camera in lieu of a magician. Mana plates are still required for operation, and they are available for purchase through Telestrian Industries-affiliated vendors.

- I call bullshit. There's no way that Telestrian managed to mix magic and tech without the whole world hearing about it.
- Snopes

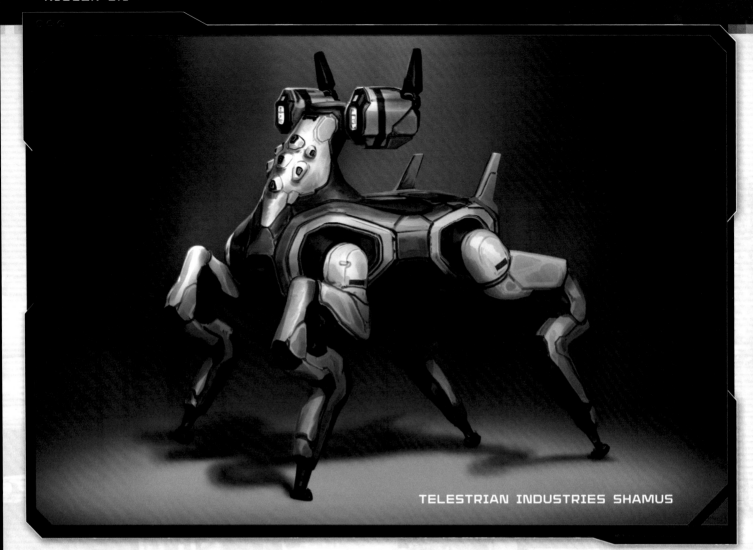

TELESTRIAN INDUSTRIES SHAMUS

- Normally I'd agree with you, but I've actually seen one of these in use. The final product of their camera isn't as high-quality as that used by a magician, and it takes more than twice as long to develop, but it works.
- Sunshine

- One could argue that all alchemy is a merger of mana and technology. If I can use a gun or a cyberdeck as an alchemical lynchpin, then why would this be much different?
- Lyran

- Hagersburg's police force has a Shamus. I heard that they outfitted it with a personality chip that tells bad jokes and responds to "Horatio."
- Kay St. Irregular

Standard Upgrades: Quicksilver camera, sensor array [Rating 8, w/ atmosphere sensor, camera (low-light, normal, thermographic), Geiger counter, MAD scanner,

olfactory sensor, radio signal scanner, ultrasound, X-ray]

Game Information: The quicksilver camera requires a mana-sensitive film plate (p. 214, *Street Grimoire*) for each use. Standard rules for the quicksilver camera apply, with the following changes: development time takes five minutes instead of two, and the threshold for tests made with developed images are increased by 1.

TELESTRIAN SHAMUS (SMALL DRONE)								
HANDL	SPEED	ACCEL	BODY	ARM	PILOT	SENS	AVAIL	COST
3	3G	1	4(0)	4	3	8	10	30,000¥

MEDIUM DRONES
ARES CHEETAH
(PILOT WALKER)

Originally more of a technological "Can we make this?" from the early days of drone research than anything, the Cheetah is the world's fastest quad mech, matching

FEDERATED-BOEING KULL

speed with any living animal and many of today's cars. This quad is based off of the African cheetah (obviously) and trades maneuverability for raw speed. The claws are just for traction, but the Cheetah comes with working jaws that are quite able to chomp down on metahumans if needed. Rarely, buyers replace the jaws with a taser-equipped head whose teeth are just for show.

Standard Upgrades: Fragile (1), Jaws (Acc 3, Reach —, DV 5P, AP –3)

- Metahumans have never lost their primal fear of being chased. The Cheetah takes full advantage of that.
- Icarus

- It's true. Hearing copters buzz overhead or watching wheeled drones roll around looking for you? All part of the job. Seeing one of these chrome cats run someone down and worry them with bites? Utterly terrifying.
- 2XL

ARES CHEETAH (MEDIUM DRONE)								
HANDL	SPEED	ACCEL	BODY	ARM	PILOT	SENS	AVAIL	COST
4	6G	2	2(0)	6	3	2	12R	14,000¥

EVO KROKODIL

(PILOT GROUND CRAFT/ PILOT WATERCRAFT)

A fine example of Russian design, the Krokodil looks to be made entirely out of solid iron, welded at right angles, with Soviet-era tractor-treads and a clunky design that's ugly as sin but takes a beating and keeps on chugging. The Krok is a rare amphibious design, able to roll into a river and pop out on the far side, never needing to slow down. Beyond that, it's a simple medium-sized drone, easy to modify due to the basic design, but you have to be careful that you reseal it properly or it'll sink, and while amphibious, it's not submersible; the Krok dies if you dunk it in more than a meter of water.

Standard upgrades: Amphibious

- The Krok *does* float, with only a tiny bit poking out of the surface, allowing it to easily enter "loiter and record" mode for hours. While many people would suggest flying drones, since they're more able to escape if detected, most people these days know to glance around in the air for spotters. Nobody ever looks down.
- Sounder

EVO KROKODIL (MEDIUM DRONE)

HANDL	SPEED	ACCEL	BODY	ARM	PILOT	SENS	AVAIL	COST
3	2G/3W	1	3(1)	6	2	2	8R	12,000¥

FEDERATED-BOEING KULL

(PILOT AIRCRAFT)

A mid-sized aerial drone with a small internal cargo component, the Kull is best known for the underwing "bomb racks" that allow it to attach a pair of disposable, parachute-equipped supply crates. By flying over a target zone, the Kull can quietly drop off supplies to a forward scout team, emergency medical supplies, and so on. The Kull requires a much shorter landing strip than a full-sized plane as well, making it an ideal smuggler.

Standard Upgrades: Two single-use "bomb racks"

Similar Models: Espirit Industries Recon-TF1, Saeder-Krupp Bussard

- The Kull's small enough to confuse radar, fast enough to escape most drones, and dirt cheap.
- Kia

- Thing's unarmed and unarmored, useless in a fight, and the sensors are average at best.
- Rigger X

F-B KULL (MEDIUM DRONE)

HANDL	SPEED	ACCEL	BODY	ARM	PILOT	SENS	AVAIL	COST
3	4P	2	3(3)	0	3	2	4	10,000¥

MCT TUNNELER

(PILOT GROUND CRAFT)

Standard safety equipment at any mine and most other resource-removing sites, the Tunneler is a basic crawler drone fronted by a drilling mechanism, allowing it to create a tunnel large enough for most metahumans to uncomfortably shimmy through. Orks and trolls have to wait for larger rescue machinery, but in the event of a collapse, humans, dwarfs, and elves have an escape option. As you can imagine, runners have been happy to use them for our own nefarious ends, but the drilling is as loud as it is slow, so don't expect to get away with rapid silent intrusions.

Standard Upgrades: Drill mechanism (can dig through a barrier with Armor 12 or less at a rate of 1 meter an hour.)

- These tunnels are usually unstable. More than one person's been killed when they collapse.
- Traveller Jones

MCT TUNNELER (MEDIUM DRONE)

HANDL	SPEED	ACCEL	BODY	ARM	PILOT	SENS	AVAIL	COST
3	0G	0	3(2)	6	2	2	8R	10,000¥

RENRAKU LEBD-2 LAW ENFORCEMENT BACKUP DRONE

(PILOT AIRCRAFT)

The LEBD-1 was a Ford-built police drone that never found a market with KE, Lone Star, or Eagle Security. It was quietly discontinued after dismal sales. Renraku picked up the plans for virtually nothing and redesigned it somewhat for use with their Neo-PD subsidiary. The new LEBD-2 builds on the reliable roto-drone's ability to be slotted into a charging mount on the back of a patrol car to create one-officer, one-drone teams, combining a human's gut instincts and friendliness with a drone's expendability and perfect recording of events. The drone can be sent to flank a home, provide fire support via the included taser, and even help with paperwork. Most officers are as loyal to their drone partner as a K-9 officer to their dog, and assaulting an LEBD-2 is treated as an attack on an officer in most Neo-PD subsidiaries.

Standard Upgrades: Mini weapon mount, Yamaha Pulsar, 4 taser darts, Smartsoft, Targeting (4) autosoft, Clearsight (4) autosoft, Knowledge: Legal Codes (4) autosoft

- The LEBD's strongest weapon is the camera. It can scan a crowd, run facial-recognition software, cross-reference with Renraku's staggeringly large databases, and produce warrants and criminal histories in record time. If you've been seen in a Renraku facility in the past year, avoid these at all cost.
- Sunshine

- They have trouble with goblin faces. The work Renraku's doing in the Underground is dramatically improving this.
- Bull

RENRAKU LEBD-2 (MEDIUM DRONE)

HANDL	SPEED	ACCEL	BODY	ARM	PILOT	SENS	AVAIL	COST
4	2R	1	3(0)	9	4	4	12R	20,000¥

TRANSYS STEED

(PILOT GROUND CRAFT)

There are a few people in this world who can't manage cybernetics. Some are mages, some have unique nerve designs, while others believe that chrome "eats your soul" and refuse it. Some of these people can't walk, due to either disability or infirmity. Enter the Steed, a

ARES MULE

motorized chair with wheels that can be controlled by a simple trode-based DNI. Street-legal in the city, it can also move around inside a building with ease.

Similar Models: Evo Freedom, DocWagon Chariot

TRANSYS STEED (MEDIUM DRONE)								
HANDL	SPEED	ACCEL	BODY	ARM	PILOT	SENS	AVAIL	COST
4/2	1G	1	3(1)	0	2	2	2	4,000¥

LARGE DRONES
AEROQUIP DUSTOFF

The full details on this one are in *Bullets and Bandages*, but I should point out that a few enterprising runners had started modifying these things as personal transports. For the cost of a motorcycle, you got an admittedly cramped personal helicopter. Prices shot up once the hack got popularized online. Fraggin' Invisible Hand!

ARES MATILDA
(PILOT GROUND CRAFT)

If you pushed over a refrigerator and gave it tank treads, you'd have a Matilda. Blocky design, clumsy, and slow, the

Matilda's main claims to fame are the two blast doors—essentially riot shields—that fold out from its side, allowing officers to use it as mobile cover while advancing on reinforced positions. The Matilda comes standard with a small minigrenade launcher that can lob gas grenades ahead for disruption, leaving the officers protected. Knight Errant credits the Matilda with saving the lives of over two dozen officers this past year, absorbing fire so that they don't have to. She ain't pretty, but she works.

Standard Upgrades: Two riot shields, standard weapon mount, underbarrel grenade launcher, Targeting (3) autosoft

(if a shot hits the Matilda from a rear flank while the shields are deployed, armor is halved.)

ARES MATILDA (LARGE DRONE)								
HANDL	SPEED	ACCEL	BODY	ARM	PILOT	SENS	AVAIL	COST
1	2G	1	8	8	3	1	12R	18,000¥

ARES MULE
(PILOT WALKER)

Another ancient design that dates back to DARPA research in the old United States, the Mule is a simple four-legged drone designed to haul cargo around for soldiers in the field, leaving them well-supplied but lightly equipped enough to hustle when shit goes down. With four legs and an excellent sense of balance, the Mule can go anywhere a soldier can, but it can carry an entire squad's worth of supplies without slowing down—a good thing, considering it's as slow as a marching soldier. Nearing fifty years old, the Mule predates the idea of arming a drone, but the head can issue a surprisingly strong grip when called on.

Standard Upgrades: Drone arm (Strength 6, Agility 2)

- It doesn't come with guns, but you can damn sure strap 'em on these days.
- Stone

- The head and neck are as flexible and functional as a primitive cyberarm. You'd be surprised at how often this is overlooked.
- Kia

ARES MULE (LARGE DRONE)								
HANDL	SPEED	ACCEL	BODY	ARM	PILOT	SENS	AVAIL	COST
4	1G	1	4(3)	6	2	2	4	8,000¥

ARES PALADIN

(PILOT GROUND CRAFT)

After the debacle that was the Excalibur project, Ares has been working hard to re-establish the trust they lost among their most important customers: militaries and law enforcement. In order to help rebuild that trust, Ares decided to take a chip shot and release a simple, effective, and affordable drone that could not possibly go wrong. They call it the Paladin.

The design of the Paladin is as straightforward and utilitarian as they come. A simple tracked platform houses the primary components of the drone, which is outfitted with a pair of hydraulic arms that lift a sheet of plasteel and Kevlar on command. The drone is designed to be integrated with a sensor network to allow it access to cameras, microphones, and other devices. A simple version of the old Ares TacNet software is used to analyze data from these various sources and determine if a shot has been fired. If a shot has been fired, the arms swing up very quickly and attempt to intercept the round in mid-flight.

Once the plate is engaged, the drone's dog brain transitions to an escape plan. These plans can be pre-loaded, or the pilot can be relied upon to utilize the network's data to create an escape route on the fly. The Paladin has already seen several successes, most notably in foiling a recent assassination attempt upon the president of Kenya in Nairobi.

- Knight Errant is supposed to be working on using the Paladin to protect their HTR units during breaches.

Instead of having a metahuman holding a riot shield, they're going to use the drone. The biggest problem they've been running into is getting the drone to run *toward* the gunfire.
- Turbo Bunny

- That's not the only obstacle they're facing. The drone isn't exactly quick. HTR teams often have to operate at least as fast as a street samurai, so they're jacked up on all sorts of combat drugs. The drone just can't keep up with that level of reaction. Ares is a long way from phasing out metahuman bodyguards.
- Mihoshi Oni

Standard Upgrades: Tracked platform
Game Information: The Paladin has limited functionality without a network. When operating in a network, the drone makes a Perception test as soon as a shot is fired anywhere within detection range of any device on the network. The number of hits that are achieved on the test are treated as extra armor for the protected VIP for that Initiative Pass. Afterward, the plate acts as Good Cover for the VIP (p. 190, *SR5*) as long as the VIP is using the Take Cover action. If the Paladin is operating by itself, it cannot provide the Armor bonus when a shot is fired. Instead, it can only be used as Good Cover for the VIP.

ARES PALADIN (LARGE DRONE)								
HANDL	SPEED	ACCEL	BODY	ARM	PILOT	SENS	AVAIL	COST
5	4G	1	5(0)	18	3	2	8R	5,000¥

CRASHCART "MEDICART"

(PILOT GROUND CRAFT)

Long seen as the little brother of DocWagon, Crash-Cart has recently gained a step on their competition. The MediCart was unveiled at DroneCon at the end of last year, and it has quickly gained a coveted position in almost all disaster-recovery units around the world. The tracked platform allows the MediCart to haul tremendous amounts of weight, and traverse almost any terrain conditions that might be in the way of its destination. Within the large frame resides a set of hydraulic rescue tools (commonly referred to as the "Jaws of Life"), a pair of extendable arms that can lift up to 200 kilograms, and medical tools.

The drone's dog brain prioritizes targets that it can detect first and attempts to get to those people who are nearest to its location. During the Boston Lockdown, a number of MediCarts were deployed to areas that had seen the worst rioting. The rescue tools can cut through most materials, and the arms can be used to lift debris or patients. The medical tools are often deployed and operated remotely, but the built-in software allows the drone to perform basic life-support functions.

Since its release, the MediCart has been credited with saving over a dozen corporate lives, and sales have been through the roof. Not to be outdone, DocWagon has recently announced plans for a drone similar to the MediCart, but with a built-in Valkyrie module and the ability to lift up to 300 kilograms.

Standard Upgrades: Tracked, specialized tools (hydraulic rescue tools, medkit)

Game Information: The hydraulic rescue tools on the MediCart are capable of tearing through metal that has been seared together, and it comes with the necessary appendages to puncture even plascrete. When attempting to perform an act that would normally require Strength + Body (such as lifting, forcing something open, or tearing), use triple the MediCart's Body Rating for all tests. This means that the MediCart can easily carry 270 kilograms without requiring a test. The MediCart is capable of deploying a medkit to anyone within two meters of the drone. The drone's Pilot rating replaces the medkit's rating for tests. The medkit comes with twenty uses but cannot be used without the drone. Normal replacement components are sufficient to refill the medkit.

CC 'MEDICART' (LARGE DRONE)								
HANDL	SPEED	ACCEL	BODY	ARM	PILOT	SENS	AVAIL	COST
5	5G	1	6(2)	5	4	4	6	10,000¥

GTS TOWER
(PILOT AIRCRAFT)
A fairly standard lighter-than-air drone, slow, unarmored, and unarmed, the Tower pulls double-duty as a retransmission drone, extending a rigger's own wireless signal, as well as serving as an "airbase" for up to four minidrones or eight microdrones. These passengers can be used for protection, but mostly are used to scatter and scan a large area swiftly. Several police corporations park Towers over events with large crowds in order to keep a wide-eye on the surroundings.

Standard Upgrades: Drone rack (4), retrans unit

Similar Models: Cyberspace Designs Nexus, GN-Nissan Beehive

GTS TOWER (LARGE DRONE)								
HANDL	SPEED	ACCEL	BODY	ARM	PILOT	SENS	AVAIL	COST
2	1R	1	4(0)	6	2	2	8	10,000¥

SAEDER-KRUPP MK-17D NEPTUNE
(PILOT WATERCRAFT)
Designed to fit into a standard torpedo tube, the Neptune can either be launched from a submarine as originally designed or, far more common these days, be deployed in a more traditional manner. Fully submersible to depths of a kilometer, the Neptune has become the industry-standard exploration and underwater survey drone. The Neptune has a more-advanced Pilot than most drones due to the difficulty, if not impossibility, of radio communication once it dives, leaving it to operate in a fully autonomous state, surfacing in designated locations at designated times, allowing it to be gathered up and data transferred.

Standard Upgrades: Submersible, Searchlight
Similar Models: Proteus Tiefaucher, Shiawase Suredo

- Too expensive for most runners, priceless to coastal smugglers.
- 2XL

- Needs more boom.
- Kane

- You can tether a drone via cable to get around the wireless transmission issues faced by water, but your dive is limited by the length of the cord. Cut the cord and the drone's pilot has to take over as best it can.
- Sounder

S-K NEPTUNE (LARGE DRONE)								
HANDL	SPEED	ACCEL	BODY	ARM	PILOT	SENS	AVAIL	COST
2	3W	1	5(0)	3	4	3	10R	17,500¥

MITSUHAMA MALAKIM
(PILOT AIRCRAFT)
The standard response drones for GOD, the Malakim are quad-copter drones that pack non-lethal weaponry and high-level jammers, released in support of agents on foot. The Malakim's job is to block off communication, keep updated via reports from Doves that are scattered around watching potential escape routes, and serve as a last line of offense should a takedown be needed. While well-armed and armored, the Malakim's larger size prevents it from entering some areas, so if you're being pursued, move from building to building and never get caught out in the open; if you do, it'll drop you.

Standard Upgrades: Standard weapon mount, area jammer (6), directional jammer (6), Targeting autosoft (4)

MITSUHAMA MALAKIM (LARGE DRONE)								
HANDL	SPEED	ACCEL	BODY	ARM	PILOT	SENS	AVAIL	COST
3	6R	2	4(0)	9	4	4	20F	40,000¥

HUGE DRONES
ARES KN-Y0
(PILOT GROUND CRAFT)
Designated as an unmanned micro-tank, the KN-Y0 series of combat drones shows that Ares isn't sitting idle

MESAMETRIC KODIAK

in the wake of the damage it's taken over the past few years. Unfortunately, the UCAS government has been cool to new designs, so Ares is currently testing other markets with the KN-Y0, to see if there are any takers for a full production run. There are three sub-designs: the Y1, Y2, and Y4, better known as Phobos, Deimos, and Eris. While all three share the same tread-based firing platform and stout armor, the turret of each has a different weapon design and the model is thus given a different tactical consideration. The Phobos sports an RPK heavy machine gun with two hundred rounds of on-board ammunition, putting it into an anti-infantry role. The Deimos mounts a Panther XXL assault cannon and fifteen rounds of ammo for anti-armor work. The Eris has an Antioch MGL-12 grenade launcher and a clip-switching mechanism that allows it to select from any of the two dozen grenades it carries as well as a directional jammer for inhibiting opposition C&C. Intended to be deployed together, the three offset one another's weaknesses, or may be attached as heavy support for patrols.

Standard Upgrades: (all) Targeting (5) autosoft, Smartsoft, (Phobos and Deimos), heavy weapon mount, (Eris) large weapon mount, area jammer (6), directional jammer (6), Electronic Warfare (5) autosoft

- ⊙ I happen to have one full set available for purchase.
- ⊙ Red Anya

- ⊙ Huh. The Eris is the Y4 model. Wonder what happened to Y3?
- ⊙ Bull

ARES KN—Y2 (DEIMOS) (HUGE DRONE)

HANDL	SPEED	ACCEL	BODY	ARM	PILOT	SENS	AVAIL	COST
3	2G	1	6(0)	18	5	3	20F	220,000¥

ARES KN—Y4 (ERIS) (HUGE DRONE)

HANDL	SPEED	ACCEL	BODY	ARM	PILOT	SENS	AVAIL	COST
3	2G	1	6(0)	18	5	3	24F	270,000¥

ARES KN—Y1 (PHOBOS) (HUGE DRONE)

HANDL	SPEED	ACCEL	BODY	ARM	PILOT	SENS	AVAIL	COST
3	2G	1	6 (0)	18	5	3	16F	250,000¥

MESAMETRIC KODIAK
(PILOT GROUND CRAFT)

If a bulldozer, a backhoe, and steamroller had a freaky three-way, the Kodiak would be their collective baby. A massive drone designed for road work, be it clearing, constructing, or destroying, the Kodiak is a common sight in the NAN, taking care of long stretches of roads that the smaller population can't maintain. A quarter-century ago, it was designed to handle these needs for the Sioux military, but sales to civilian governments quickly showed where the real need was. There are several industrial variants now, for tree cutting and planting, powerline repairs, and more, but the core Kodiak is fraggin' everywhere.

Standard Upgrades: Drone arm (Strength 12, Agility 2), bulldozer blade, Road Engineering (2) autosoft

- They've ripped up most of the roads from the old U.S. of A. out in NAN territories. Damn shame. I'd give my left arm to have driven on some of those things. The historicals are so romantic!
- Turbo Bunny

- Ugh. Trapped in a hot car for days, driving through cornfields and small towns? Glad they're gone.
- /dev/grrl

MESAMETRIC KODIAK (HUGE DRONE)								
HANDL	SPEED	ACCEL	BODY	ARM	PILOT	SENS	AVAIL	COST
2/4	2G	1	6(2)	12	2	2	12R	40,000¥

NEONET AVENGING ANGEL
(PILOT AIRCRAFT)

The last of the GOD-specific designs, the Avenging Angel is the Thor Strike of drones. No muss, no fuss, the Avenging Angel is a multi-MACH milspec drone that carries a single fuel-air bomb, capable of leveling an entire city block, for when you absolutely, positively, have to make sure that decker nest is rooted out. Officially, none have ever been used. Officially.

Standard Upgrades: Heavy weapon mount

- For all intents and purposes, it's a jet fighter without a pilot.
- Kane

- NeoNET and not Ares? That is unexpected.
- Balladeer

- Notice that the three core members of the Wireless Matrix Initiative make the three GOD drones? Saeder-Krupp and Aztechnology have a seat at the table, but at the end of the day, GOD and the corporate court know who the strongest Matrix corps are.
- /dev/grrl

NEONET AVENGING ANGEL (HUGE DRONE)								
HANDL	SPEED	ACCEL	BODY	ARM	PILOT	SENS	AVAIL	COST
3	6J	2	6(0)	12	6	6	40F	1,000,000¥

ANTHROPOMORPHIC DRONES

Anthromorphic drones operate somewhat differently than most walker drones. For starters, they come with a full set of two drone arms and two drone legs, which are usually Obvious but may be Synthetic instead. In addition, they have a Physical condition monitor of 8 + (Body/2), being more durable than most drones. Being able to go anywhere a metahuman can, with similar limbs and build, they can even use some metahuman equipment, such as clothing, weapons, or tools. This makes them far more versatile than most drones, but the price point reflects that.

AZTECHNOLOGY CRIADO JUAN

"I want Juan! I need Juan! I gotta gotta HAVE Juan!" The ad campaign that will haunt my fraggin' dreams. The Juan started off as simply "The Criado," a cheap Azzie knock-off of the Renraku Manservant that was used around the houses of pureblooded Azlan aristocrats in place of mestizo half-bloods. A PR fluff piece on "Ding" Ramos happened to catch one on camera. When asked what it was, Ding laughed and said, "Oh, that's just Juan. Don't you have Juan yourself?" Calls started coming in from middle-class types who wanted to know where to get "Juan," and Aztechnology PR flacks jumped on the chance. The next thing you know, "I gotta gotta HAVE Juan!" was plastered on every AR feed they could find, with guest spots on dozens of trid programs and pop-up Matrix ads. The drone itself is an average house-bot at best, with a comical tubular body and spindly limbs, but like the Manservant it reflects, it's generally seen as harmless and non-threatening due to these structural weaknesses.

Similar Models: Renraku Manservant, Telestrian Industries Jeeves

- The onboard pilot's about as good as you'd expect from a budget Aztechnology crapstack as well. Until you start loading up on the overpriced autosofts (seriously, a thousand nuyen for cooking?!), it's not able to handle much more complex than domestic cleaning. Then again, that's kind of the point.
- Glitch

- It comes with the benefit of not being a mixed-blood peasant, of course. Aztlan racism is weird.
- Butch

On the plus side, it's domestic help that the head of the household can't sleep with. On the negative side ... it's domestic help that the head of the household can't sleep with.
- Slamm-0!

Amazing how a punk runner can still absorb cultural sexism and class exploitation.
- Aufheben

On a related note, since the Juan's introduction this past year, unemployment in Aztlan has gone up by one percent. Work is also getting harder to find for quite a few simple services as Juans take over mowing the yard, janitorial work, and similar duties.
- Icarus

Am I the only one who noticed how much Ding's personal version looked like Juan Atzcapotzalco?
- Plan 9

CRIADO JUAN (ANTHRO DRONE)

HANDL	SPEED	ACCEL	BODY	ARM	PILOT	SENS	AVAIL	COST
2	2G	1	2	0	2	2	2	8,000¥

HORIZON LITTLE BUDDY

About as large as the average five-year-old human, the Little Buddy is designed for working parents with a single child to serve as a nanny, teacher, babysitter, and playmate. The Little Buddy teaches as it entertains and is equipped with a variety of age-appropriate lessons on shapes, colors, letters, words, and numbers, as well as a selection of bedtime stories and lullabies. The Little Buddy is designed to contact the parents whenever faced with a situation it's not pre-programed to face, or when certain conditions are met, such as a wounded or missing child. Never leave your child alone... get them a Little Buddy™!

Similar Models: Hasbro Playsalot, Sony Headstart
Standard Upgrades: Instruction (2) autosoft

A more modern version of the classic Bust-a-Move toy, pushing the Horizon edu-tainment model down your throat. It's designed to make little Jimmy into a model corporate citizen and serve as psychological support for the parents who work too much to raise their own kid. It's too expensive for most people to raise a second child, so it's like having a brother or sister. Ish.
- /dev/grrl

Early versions were somewhat more lifelike, but there were problems in beta testing with childless adults adopting them as if they were real. Little Buddy was stripped down from there to the current non-threatening

plastic look. It's available in a variety of colors, and the voice selector can be set for boy or girl. There's no other difference between models I know of.
- Netcat

These things aren't very bright out of the box. A clever kid can trick them without too much trouble, at which point they freak out and start calling mommy and daddy. As is the case with most of the drones here, the manufacturers break even on the physical frame but make a killing in the software department. That said, the "Play Doctor" first aid autosoft option might be intended for skinned knees and swallowed pennies, but it can set a broken arm, help with asthma attacks, or even apply a trauma patch if needed. Good stuff.
- Stone

HORIZON LITTLE BUDDY (ANTHRO DRONE)

HANDL	SPEED	ACCEL	BODY	ARM	PILOT	SENS	AVAIL	COST
2	1G	1	1	0	2	2	4	2,000¥

MITSUHAMA COMPUTER TECHNOLOGIES KENCHIKU-KIKAI

The oldest model anthromorphic drone still in service today, the K-K has been working at MCT construction sites for over three decades now. Roughly the size and strength of an Ork, but without that pesky non-human repulsiveness that MCT hates so much, the Kikai is a tireless construction machine, able to use metahuman construction gear, such as jackhammers, welders, or rivet guns, but it also has enough raw strength to carry heavy loads or even bend rebar with its core hand actuators. They're slow, a little clumsy, and not terribly bright, but as long as they have metahuman oversight for when tasks get complicated, they can get the job done like a proper crew, only cheaper. Until modern nano-construction techniques largely left them obsolete, the K-K dominated the construction industry, putting tens of thousands of laborers out of work. With the recent nano-pocalypse, the K-K has been salvaged form the dustbin of history and put back into service.

Similar Models: S-K Colossus, Ares JHI-65
Standard Upgrades: Industrial Mechanic (2) autosoft, limbs enhanced to Strength 8

Security protocols on these used to be laughable, since the software was seven generations behind, but they predate wireless so you either had to get in there and insert a datacord manually (always a dicey prospect) or hack the central command core that they access each night for recharging and downloading the next day's work program.
- Pistons

- While new machines are out that include a wireless feed, Renraku's been slotting in more anti-technomancer protections, just in case. Over ninety percent of the units are still throwbacks from pre-wireless days, however, so hack carefully.
- Clockwork

- The raw strength that they have makes them dangerous in terms of collateral damage, but they're so slow and clumsy that they're not really a big risk to living people. Well, unless you're in your car when they flip it over. That'd hurt.
- Beaker

- As a reminder, while these things are intended for construction use, you can slot any sort of autosoft into them with a bit of work. Quite a few can be found as one-off units in small warehouses, for instance, to serve as a walking stacker, moving pallets about or barrels too heavy for metahumans, or simple first-aid programs at hospitals to serve as orderlies for thrashing patients far stronger than the nurses can handle. Keep in mind the limitations of the simple processor's power.
- Nephrine

MCT KENCHIKU-KIKAI (ANTHRO DRONE)								
HANDL	SPEED	ACCEL	BODY	ARM	PILOT	SENS	AVAIL	COST
2	2G	1	5	3	2	2	8R	20,000¥

NEONET JUGGERNAUGHT

Tired of your officers being out-gunned, out-armored, and out-muscled? Need some heavy artillery to put street scum back in their place? Then try the NeoNET Juggernaught! Pushing the very limits of modern anthromorphic design, the Juggernaught is the largest two-legged mecha on the market today, standing fully a head taller than the average troll and armored from head to toe. Specially designed with multiple weapon mounts (weapons sold separately) for lethal, or less-lethal, armaments, anti-riot grenade dispensers, and emergency point-blank gas dispensers, the Juggernaught also possesses fully articulated hand actuators that are capable of picking up and using additional resources as required or applying physical restraint when called upon. The NeoNET Juggernaught—operators are standing by to take your order now!

Standard Upgrades: One standard weapon mount in each arm, two one-use grenade drops.

- What a joke. These things have been the biggest boondoggle in NeoNET's history. They were originally conceived back in the late '40s as a military drone, a pet project of Villers' side of Fuchi, but internal stresses kept it from going anywhere. Nuyen bled into the project with

nothing to show for it for decades, and when it finally got rolled out in '69 after thirty-plus years of development hell, it failed almost every test the UCAS Army threw at it. It's been cleaned up, reprogrammed, and repackaged for civilian security use now, but at the core it's a failed military design, and it shows. It has too many systems for such a limited processor and sometimes uses the wrong one, it's too big to fit easily into urban environments but too small to just smash its way through. Metahuman stairs sometimes give way under it, and floors are never pretty after it goes stomping through. It's just this big, clumsy oaf of a machine that's prone to Frankenstein-like flailing when it gets confused.
- Clockwork

- I was *wondering* about those big ugly chicken feet! Being intended for off-road use in the field of battle or through an occupied urban warzone (where you don't really care about the décor) makes much more sense than police work.
- /dev/grrl

- They make for drekky cops and drekky soldiers, but they're intimidating enough to be used for anti-riot patrol. Kind of a niche product, but hey, whatever makes some of your nuyen back, I guess.
- Puck

- You can sometimes find them parked in larger garages and warehouses in corporate facilities (or organized crime storage locations), used as intimidating security. That usually lasts until a break-in occurs and the things spray heavy weapons fire everywhere without consideration for collateral damage. Dealing with three teenage corpses is easy enough, but when ten grand of merchandise is filled with bullet holes, well, then there's some 'splaining to do.
- Kat o' Nine Tales

- The single best use I've found for those overgrown paperweights is as the centerpiece in some TactiCool's basement. Oh, and if you think the official NeoNET models are bad, you should see the Russian knockoffs. Go visit your local Vory weapons dealer, and he'll likely have one leashed around back somewhere. They keep the weapons unloaded for a reason. *ClickClickClickClickClick* "Halt and produce your identification!" *ClickClickClickClickClick* "Identification approved!"
- Kane

NEONET JUGGERNAUGHT (ANTHRO DRONE)								
HANDL	SPEED	ACCEL	BODY	ARM	PILOT	SENS	AVAIL	COST
3	4G	1	6	12	3	3	14R	100,000¥

SAEDER-KRUPP DIREKTIONSSEKRETAR

The name's a mouthful, but the Executive Secretary from Saeder-Krupp is a true marvel of modern engineering. The core piloting program is a semi-autonomous know-bot for all intents and purposes, learning the mannerisms and schedule of its owner and factoring those in on responses and in trying to maximize workflow. They handle standard datapushing tasks, manage finances, keep books up to date, clean, file, take notes, and, oh yes, they can also be pressed into service as additional security when needed, with a subtle armored core around the most vital internal parts, fully articulated hands that can handle a wide array of weaponry, topped off with enough speed and power to deliver mortal blows even unarmed. Absolutely amazing.

Similar Models: Sony Orderly-4, Ares Pygmalion

- The Secretary has the single most advanced processing unit of any of the drones being detailed here. You can slot all manner of autosoft in there, from pistols to driving to Swedish massage. Just brilliant work.
- Slamm-0!

- The baseline drone isn't going to be mistaken for human, but, like the i-Doll, layers of customization are present, should the owner want a more fully functional, and anatomically correct, assistant.
- Glitch

- I wonder how well it fits data in the yar?
- Bull

- … Pretending to be Kane today, Bull?
- Slamm-0!

- Just making a joke that's way too old. Nevermind.
- Bull

- I'm told that there are dozens of these models in place with fully customized appearances, blended in at important institutions all over the world such as banks, megacorporate offices, the Intercontinental Climate Data Center, and so on. These dopplegangers blend in with society but send regular reports back to their dragon master or, if the need is great enough, they can be remotely activated to sabotage a facility, direct finances his way, or any number of other acts of espionage.
- Plan 9

- What, not going to claim that Hans Brackhaus is secretly two dozen of these robots?
- Snopes

- Don't be ridiculous. Everyone knows that Brackhaus is a disguise that Alamais used to keep tabs on Lofwyr's activities.
- Plan 9

S-K DIREKTIONSSEKRETAR (ANTHRO DRONE)								
HANDL	SPEED	ACCEL	BODY	ARM	PILOT	SENS	AVAIL	COST
4	4G	2	4	3	4	4	12R	40,000¥

SHIAWASE I-DOLL

The latest in a long line of humanoid robots from Japan, the i-Doll is perhaps the most customizable one yet. The core model is designed to be a domestic servant, doing the cleaning and the cooking as expected, but the big selling point is the "Build your own!" section of the Shiawase i-Doll website, where you can make it more lifelike, select personality traits, hair color, and so on as you see fit. Sometimes derided as "robo-girlfriends," only the most expensive i-Doll models can even try to pass for human. The rest make good listeners, and sometimes it's just nice to have a pet in the house to talk to, but it's the high-nuyen realism market that really makes Shiawase profit.

Similar Models: Renraku Nadeshiko, Spinrad OoLaLa
Standard Upgrades: Realistic Features (1), Cooking (3) Autosoft

- Class 2 is the most popular model, despite the cost. Able to pass for human but with enough robotic features that it doesn't trigger the uncanny valley, it's a nice bridge between cost and aesthetics. Everybody loves the eartennae look.
- Clockwork

- Class 3 Dolls are as lifelike as synthetic cyberlimbs, but the usual problems, such as cold skin and eyes that aren't quite right, really makes some people uncomfortable. Then again, they sell a ton of these, so what do I know?
- Sticks

- The Class 4 models are where Shiawase's talent shows. Body temperature, replicated breathing, subtle facial expressions and body motion … they're more real than real.
- Turbo Bunny

- Some of the more human-centric AIs have been trying them out as bodies, to interact more with the metahuman world. The limited processing power is crippling, however, and most don't stay for long.
- Netcat

SHIAWASE I-DOLL (ANTHRO DRONE)								
HANDL	SPEED	ACCEL	BODY	ARM	PILOT	SENS	AVAIL	COST
3	3G	1	3	0	3	3	4	20,000¥

DRONE MISSILE
ARES "GARUDA"
(PILOT AIRCRAFT)

Several years ago, Ares was first-to-market with a rigged missile system. The main drawback was that it required a rigger who was tremendously skilled to operate sufficiently. Additionally, when the missile exploded, the rigger could suffer dumpshock as a result. Since then, Ares has been hard at work on the next iteration: the Garuda.

Like the mythical Indian god, the Garuda is the sort of missile you launch to blot out the sun. Rather than a single missile that causes the rigger to suffer dumpshock upon detonation, the Garuda is a cluster munition, allowing the rigger to operate the core of the drone, fire off the cluster rounds, and continue moving to prevent dumpshock.

Another major upgrade is the addition of a secondary launch mechanism that allows the drone to operate slowly at first, but then activate a booster module to gain speed tremendously fast. This allows less-skilled riggers to operate the Garuda in a fashion similar to most drones, but be able to "turn on the jets," so to speak, in order to catch up with a fast-moving target.

The booster module and the cluster munition mechanism give the Garuda a dual purpose—it can operate similarly to a normal airborne drone, but can also be utilized as a missile. The Garuda can be outfitted with anti-vehicle, fragmentation, or high explosive warheads. Additionally, the Garuda is small enough to be shoulder-launched, or it can be fired from a mounted missile launcher. The Garuda is, however, incapable of underwater operation, as the engines require oxygen.

Standard Upgrades: Launched, cluster munitions, laser guidance

Game Information: The cluster munitions act like multiple small explosives. The statistics for each warhead type are described on the table "Grenades/Rockets/Missiles" on page 435 of *SR5*. Note that the costs of these explosives are not included in the cost of the drone missile and must be purchased separately.

ARES 'GARUDA' (DRONE MISSILE)								
HANDL	SPEED	ACCEL	BODY	ARM	PILOT	SENS	AVAIL	COST
6	3J/6J	2/4	2	2	4	3	20F	8,500¥

BUILDING THE PERFECT BEAST

Turbo Bunny winced as the bullets spattered off of the Bulldog's armor. She winced because she felt them, felt them just like sharp needles pricking her own skin. She also felt the wind whistling against her skin, the glare of the city lights, the roar of the engines in her ears, and the ache in her calves from the strain of running. As far as her brain was concerned she *was* the van and could move it just as nimbly as being able to move her own body. She slipped between the cars in traffic, keeping as many of them as she could between her and her pursuers. An ache in her calves let her know that the van couldn't keep up this speed much longer, and a splitting pain in her side let her know that the vehicle had taken some serious damage. She had the munchies too, which also meant that the Bulldog was running low on fuel.

Safely enclosed in her rigger cocoon, Turbo Bunny brought up the visual feed from the aerial drone that she had shadowing them. Then she saw a new problem. Just a couple of kilometers ahead, Knight Errant had set up a roadblock. A big one. Frag. She checked the road map: there were no exits off the highway before the road block. Pursuit cars were closing in from behind. She flipped back to the aerial view from the surveillance drone. Then she saw it, another way off of this road. She suddenly wrenched the Bulldog hard to the left, sending the passengers in the back tumbling, sprawling, and cursing. With a flip of a mental switch, twin panels in the front bumper slid back to reveal rockets behind them.

With the front of the vehicle aiming straight for the concrete wall that bordered the highway she fired rockets, smoke trails streaking straight for the wall. She pinned the accelerator as twin explosions sent chunks of concrete flying in all directions and the van sped toward the freshly made hole.

"Hang on," she blasted through the van's internal speakers. It was time to try out that new modification she had just installed. Sparks flew from the flanks of the vehicle, and she felt like multi-bladed razors rake her ribs as the vehicle ripped its way through the hole and plummeted into the empty space beyond. As the nose tipped and rushed toward the waters Puget Sound below, Turbo Bunny activated the brand-new modification. Her head rocked and her vision swam when the van hit the water.

Once she came to her senses, Bunny checked over the new systems.

Water Seals: Engaged.

Internal Air Supply: Active.

Water Jets: Ready.

"Don't be alarmed. Please return to your seats," she piped over the van's internal speakers. "We will now resume travel to our previous destination by way of lovely, murky, and heavily polluted Puget Sound. Enjoy the ride."

Turbo Bunny switched on the high-beam headlights, engaged the underwater propulsion system, and smiled to herself as the Bulldog slipped on toward the opposite shoreline.

MODIFICATION RULES

Runners who use their vehicles day in and day out to pull their jobs rarely want to keep them as they are off the shelf. In the highly competitive world of shadowrunning, runners need to get every edge they can to avoid winding up dead. This means riggers and others who use vehicles for their jobs will modify them in a variety of ways to suit whatever needs they have. That may be making them faster and more maneuverable to avoid pursuit, giving extra armor and weapons to turn them into a mobile firebase, or packing them with surprise tricks to give themselves an ace up their sleeve for the right situation.

There are three aspects or factors in getting a modification installed in a vehicle: parts and plan, tools, and skill.

PARTS AND PLAN

The first thing a runner needs for a modification is the parts and the plan, or procedures for installing the modification. The Modification List (p. 154) shows the base threshold for acquiring the parts for a modification, which is based on its obscured and complexity. The gamemaster is free to modify these values if there are special circumstances that would make the parts easier or more difficult to acquire. Depending on the source, these parts may be provided "as is" or will have the plans or instructions on how to install them on the vehicle in question. If the parts were not provided with a plan, the character can attempt to find one with contacts and legwork, or by doing a Matrix Search (p. 241, SR5) with threshold and modifiers set as appropriate by the gamemaster. A plan is not required to attempt the modification, but if available the plan provides a bonus to the Build/Repair Test (as per p. 146, SR5).

TOOLS

The complexity of installing a modification varies widely, but in general they all require some sort of tools. This can be a set of simple hand tools, ranging all the way up to a building full of complicated and sophisticated equipment. Each modification lists the required level of tools for the job: Kit, Shop, or Facility. If the required tools are not available, the modification can still be attempted but will suffer the Inadequate (if not the right level) or Unavailable (for none at all) modifier (as per p. 146, SR5).

SKILL

With the plan, parts, and tools all (hopefully) in place, the character can attempt to install the modification in the vehicle. Installing a modification always uses the Mechanic skill relevant to the vehicle (Automotive, Nautical, etc.). The installer makes a (Mechanic Skill) + Logic [Logic] (threshold, 1 hour) Extended Test, applying all appropriate modifiers from the Build/Repair Table (p. 146, SR5). The process can be interrupted and resumed at a later time, but the gamemaster can determine if some or all of the vehicle's systems cannot be used until the modification is complete. Only one modification can be applied at a time. If a critical glitch is rolled, the modification automatically fails and the parts are ruined; the character must start over. Once the required hits have been accumulated, the modification is complete and ready for use.

If the modification list a **Special Skill** then one additional die roll needs to be made before the modification is complete. The character must succeed at a (Special Skill) + Logic [Logic] (4) Test to complete the modification.

MODIFICATION SLOTS

Every vehicle has a certain number of *Modification Slots* that determines how much extra stuff can be packed into the vehicle. Each vehicle modification has a number of Modification Slots equal to its Body in **each Modification Category**. There are six Modification Categories: Power Train, Protection, Weapons, Body, Electromagnetic, and Cosmetic. So a GMC Bulldog with a Body of 16 has 16 Modification Slots in each of the six categories. Modifications only take up the slots for their category. Once a vehicle has used up the Modification Slots for a category, no more modifications may be installed from the category. A vehicle *cannot* exceed its Modification Slots in any category. Not even a little.

REMOVING MODIFICATIONS

A modification can be removed to free up the slots that it originally took up. This will allow further modifications in that category to be installed. Removing a modification takes the same tools and skill(s) that the original modification took, but the threshold is halved. Removed modification parts are assumed to be not be reusable in any other vehicle, but they may be kept for re-installation in the original vehicle, at the gamemaster's discretion.

EXAMPLE

ADDING A MODIFICATION

Rigger X wants to add a weapon mount to his GMC Bulldog to provide some fire support for the team. He wants heavy firepower while remaining able to drive around downtown, so he chooses a heavy internal turret weapon mount. That modification has a Slot cost of 8 (4 + 2 + 2 = 8), a threshold of 28 (10 + 6 + 12 = 28), an Availability 20 (12 + 2 + 6 = 20), and a cost of 10,500¥. Installing it requires a Vehicle Facility. The Bulldog has the modification slots available, and Rigger X has the nuyen from his last job. He has a chummer with a Vehicle Facility he can use, and his Fixer owes him a favor and got him the parts. Now all that is left is to install the gear.

Rigger X will be making the modifications in his chummer's Facility, which is in a renovated old gas station garage in the Barrens. Not ideal, but it'll do the job. He managed to score AR-guided plans for the modification, giving him a +2 bonus. With his Logic of 5 and Automotive Mechanic skill of 5, he has a total of 12 dice for the test. Time to get to work.

On the first test, Rigger X rolls 5 hits, a good start. He drops down to 11 dice and keeps rolling, getting 4 more hits and then drops down to to 10 dice. Continuing like that, Rigger X rolls hits of: 3, 3, 4, 3, 2, 2, 1, and 1 for the necessary 28 hits. In total, installing the weapon mount took Rigger X 10 hours (probably with a break for sleep in the middle). It was a lot of work, but the LMG that the Bulldog is now sporting will come in handy for his team!

VEHICLE EQUIPMENT

The following are not considered modifications to the vehicle since they do not integrate into the systems of the vehicle in a significant way. They are standard pieces of equipment that can be purchased and easily installed or used.

MORPHING LICENSE PLATE

While most modern governments primarily use electronic identification for vehicles, they still require some sort of physical identification plate to uniquely identify a vehicle. Since being positively identified is something that an average shadowrunner wants to avoid, most install a special morphing license plate. Made from smart materials, a morphing license plate can reshape itself with a Complex Action and mimic any of the forms used in governments around the world today. Runners will typically also purchase a spoof chip (see below) to keep their vehicle from being identified.

SPOOF CHIP

All governments in the civilized world require that a vehicle be uniquely tagged and broadcast that identification on demand. This allows law enforcement and any authorized government agency (and some unauthorized) to quickly identify and track a vehicle. All of that may sound great to the common wageslave, but those are all things that a shadowrunner wants to avoid like a VITAS plague. Consequently, installing a spoof chip has become a common practice for anyone wanted to use a vehicle for their shadow activities. The spoof chip mimics a standard vehicle identifier chip but can be commanded with a Complex Action to change its identifier to a different random value that is arithmetically generated to appear authentic. Installing a spoof chip requires a Hardware + Logic [Mental] (2) Test.

ROAD STRIPS

Road strips use a myomeric rope to stretch out over a length of about fifteen meters (approximately four lanes of traffic) in order to cause some effect on the vehicle(s) that drive over it.

Spike Strip: This strip consists of sharp, penetrating spikes that damage the tires of any vehicle that drives over it. The vehicle's tires immediately blow out unless they are run flat tires (see below), forcing the driver to make an immediate Vehicle Test to avoid crashing. Even if the crash is avoided, flat tires give a –2 dice pool penalty on Vehicle Tests.

Zapper Strip: The zapper strip is equipped with hundreds of tiny "feelers" that extend upward to brush against the chassis of a vehicle that passes over. When a

vehicle drives over it, the strip sounds a powerful electromagnetic pulse into the chassis of the vehicle, attempting to damage its electronics. A vehicle that drives over a zapper strip suffers 10(e) DV damage. A zapper strip has enough power for 10 discharges before needing to be recharged.

Tracking Strip: The tracking strip is a subtle way to gather information about vehicles that pass by. Once deployed, whenever a vehicle passes over a tracking strip, it "fires" a stealth tag (p. 440, *SR5*) that attaches itself to the vehicle. A tracking strip contains fifty stealth tags.

SPECIAL TIRES

Tires are one of the easiest ways to customize a vehicle. The following tires are available for all wheeled ground craft. Changing tires requires a Automotive Mechanic + Logic [Mental] (4, 5 minutes) Extended Test; or you can get your brother-in-law to do it for a case of beer, though that tends to take longer.

Off-Road Tires: Designed specifically for rough terrain, these tires are not as effective as standard tires on standard roads. When equipped, the vehicle's off-road Handling is increased by +1, and on-road Handling is reduce by –1. Off-road tires are also considered run flat tires (see below).

Racing Tires: The flip-side of off-road tires, racing tires are designed to maximize vehicle performance in urban conditions. When equipped, the vehicle's on-road Handling is increased by +1 and off-road Handling is reduced by –1.

Run Flat Tires: A common upgrade for shadowrunners, run flat tires are filled with a dense but flexible foam instead of air. They continue to operate even when the tire has been punctured but will quickly deteriorate if the tire suffers significant structure damage.

TOOL KIT

It never hurts to be prepared! A smart vehicle owner will purchase at least an Automotive Mechanic Kit in their vehicle to affect emergency repairs, and possibly others if the vehicle has more exotic equipment (see p. 443, *SR5*).

VEHICLE EQUIPMENT

NAME	AVAIL	COST
Morphing license plate	8F	1,000¥
Spoof chip	8F	500¥
Spike strip	8R	200¥
Zapper strip	12R	2,500¥
Tracking strip	8R	600¥
Off-road tires	6	400¥/tire
Racing tires	6	250¥/tire
Run flat tires	4	250¥/tire

MODIFICATION LIST

Unless otherwise stated, a modification may only be taken once for a vehicle. When a vehicle stat such as Speed or Acceleration is listed as part of a modification attribute (like cost), use the vehicle's base or *unmodified* value in the calculation. In the case of Handling, which has two values, always use the *higher* value in any calculations.

POWER TRAIN

Power train modifications all deal with how a vehicle is controlled and how the vehicle moves.

ACCELERATION ENHANCEMENT

Using a variety of techniques, like adding fuel accelerants (such as nitrous oxide), turbochargers, optimized air intakes, afterburners, or hydrofoil drives, the acceleration of a vehicle is increased. Due to inherent limitations in a vehicle's design, its acceleration performance can only be increased so far. In the end, though, there's nothing like going from zero to gone before you get shot. Acceleration enhancement can be taken at Rating 1 or 2, with the Rating of the modification being added to the vehicle's Acceleration value.

GECKO TIPS

Using cutting-edge technology, the portion of any vehicle that contacts a surface can be made to strongly adhere to that surface. With the gecko tips modification, small vehicles can be made to literally climb walls or adhere to surfaces at an extremely sharp angle. The larger and heavier a vehicle is, the more extensive the modifications that are necessary to make the gecko tips system work. There are definite limits to the technolo-gy however, as it can only practically be installed on small mass vehicles and still allow them to move. If the gecko technology was applied to larger vehicles, they would literally rip away chunks of the surface they were adhered to if they tried to move. A vehicle installed with gecko tips can move on surfaces with angles that would otherwise be impossible, including vertically.

GLIDING SYSTEM

For those rare but frightening times when you find your (non-flying) vehicle plummeting to the ground, you'll thank the Great Ghost you installed a gliding system. The gliding system deploys a large-scale parachute and uses a series of small thrusters installed on the hull of the vehicle to provide limited maneuverability while descending. For vehicles with an exceptionally large mass, there is an upgraded system that uses other methods, including multiple parachutes and retro-thrusters, to slow the descent. While the system allows a vehicle to fall and not be utterly destroyed, the landing is far from graceful. When it lands, the vehicle takes (Body / 2) damage just as if it had crashed (p. 201, SR5). Owners planning on using the gliding system on a regular basis will often install a Passenger Protection System (see p. 159). After it has been deployed, the parachute(s) in the gliding system can be released with a wireless or manual command. Repacking the parachute(s) for reuse is a manual process requiring about one hour.

HANDLING ENHANCEMENT

By adjusting the suspension and/or adjusting the workings of control systems, a vehicle can be made more responsive to manual or electronic controls. This can range from optimizing control system response times, to more dramatic changes like gyroscopic stabilizers, or destabilizing the structural integrity of the hull. Handling enhancement can be taken with a Rating of 1 to 3, with the Rating added to the Handling (both on-road and off-road) of the vehicle.

IMPROVED ECONOMY

With this modification, the fuel consumption of the vehicle has been optimized to use the minimum amount necessary for standard operation. Additionally, the vehicle is fitted with a variety of different means to gather operational power from the environment around it including sunlight, static electricity, and wind. A vehicle with improved economy doubles its operational time as long as it is operating within normal parameters—no high speed chases.

MANUAL CONTROL OVERRIDE

For runners that are extra paranoid about the Matrix security on their vehicle (or just unwilling to pay for

CORE VEHICLE MODIFICATIONS

Vehicles from the *Shadowrun* core rulebook (starting on p. 461) have the following Standard Upgrades.

Dodge Scoot: Improved economy
Harley-Davidson Scorpion: Metahuman adjustment (troll)
Yamaha Growler: Off-road suspension
Hyundai Shin-Hyung: Four extra Body Modification Slots
Eurocar Westwind 3000: Passenger protections aystem (Rating 6), anti-theft system (Rating 2)
Mitsubishi Nightsky: Amenities (Luxury), life support (Level 1)
Toyota Gopher: Off-road suspension, special equipment (open box storage)
GMC Bulldog: Four extra Body Modification Slots

Yongkang Gala Trinity: Assembly/disassembly, smuggling compartment
Morgan Cutlass: Two heavy weapon mounts (external, turret, armored manual)
Proteus Lamprey: Standard drone rack (medium)

Artemis Nightwing: Signature masking (Rating 4)
R-F Fokker Tundra-9: Alternate propulsion: amphibious (surface)
Nissan Hound: Two standard weapon mounts (external, flexible, remote)
Northrup Wasp: Heavy weapon mount (external, flexible, remote)
GMC Banshee: Rigger cocoon, ECM 4

Shiawase Kanmushi: Gecko tips
MCT Fly-Spy: Realistic features (Rating 2)
Lockheed Optic-X2: Signature masking (Rating 3) *This explains the penalty listed on p. 466, SR5; it does not increase that penalty.
Ares Duelist: Two light weapon mounts (external, flexible, remote), realistic features (Rating 1)
GM-Nissan Doberman: Standard weapon mount (external, flexible, remote)
MCT-Nissan Roto-Drone: Three extra Weapon Modification Slots
Steel Lynx: Heavy weapon mount (external, turret, remote)

it), they can install a manual control override system. Nearly every modern vehicle made in the 2070s has the ability to be piloted remotely or purely through its electronic controls as well as its manual/mechanical controls. If a rigger is really nervous about those electronic controls being taken over, they can install a switch so that the manual controls will always take priority over the electronic ones. In order to prevent the switch from being remotely deactivated, it is always mechanical in nature with the physical pressing of the button making or breaking connections to ensure the precedence of the manual controls. In game terms, when manual control override is activated, piloting a vehicle via AR or VR is not possible. The system can only be activated by someone physically in the vehicle, within reach of the switch (usually the driver's seat), and by using a Free Action.

MULTIFUEL ENGINE

For teams that frequently find themselves needing to travel far away from the comforts of modern civilization, modifying a vehicle with a multifuel engine has provide invaluable. First, a portable plasma furnace is installed on the vehicle that can render small quantities of matter down to its constituent parts. Then, the vehicle's engine is modified to be able to consume the raw material output of the plasma torch. This allows nearly any matter to be fed into the vehicle as fuel. A vehicle with a multifuel engine can always be refueled as long as there Is raw material around to be processed.

OFF-ROAD SUSPENSION

For those that like to make their own roads rather than follow them, there is the off-road suspension. Most modern vehicles are designed to operate on a smoothly prepared road and do not respond well out of that environment. With an off-road suspension, a vehicle's suspension system has been replaced with one designed to operate in more rugged environments. The downside, however, is that the vehicle loses some of it responsiveness when operating in regular on-road environments. A vehicle with an off-road suspension has +1 Handling when driving off-road, but –1 Handling on-road. This stacks with bonuses from off-road tires (see p. 153).

REMOVED MANUAL CONTROLS

Riggers who are completely confident in their Matrix skills and security but worried about their lack of physical security will often add a removed manual controls modification. Almost all vehicles in the 2070s are capable of being piloted by either electronic or manual controls. With this modification, the owner simply removes the option for manual controls, relying entirely on the electronic ones. Anyone wishing to pilot the vehicle who is not the owner must succeed on a Control Device Matrix action (p. 238, *SR5*).

RIGGER COCOON

For riggers, there is no safer place where they would leave their body than a rigger cocoon. Generally built into the driver's seat of a vehicle, the cocoon is designed solely for the safety and comfort of someone who's consciousness is going to be somewhere other than their body. The cocoon has ballistic cloth and hard armored plating for physical protection, is fire resistant, has its own oxygen supply, and carries a host of biomed sensors to monitor the occupant's condition. Additionally, the cocoon has a variety of safety systems to keep the occupant safe through the most extreme vehicle maneuvers and even crashes. Getting into a rigger cocoon takes about a minute, but it can be exited with a Complex Action using a quick-release system.

Treat the rigger cocoon as a barrier with an Armor of 12 and Structure of 8 (p. 197, *SR5*). The occupant of the rigger cocoon receives +6 dice to resist damage from crashes or other vehicle maneuvers.

ROCKET BOOSTER

Vehicle operators who are truly daring (or have a death wish) cannot resist installing a rocket booster. This extreme modification installs a high-powered rocket propulsion system to allow the vehicle to make short jumps over intervening terrain or obstacles. That could be a gap in an unfinished road for a ground vehicle, or a dyke or dam that a boat might attempt to leap over. For aircraft, this allows them to take off with half the normal required distance. The rocket is angled to generate an upward lift of about 5 meters, similar to a jump ramp, allowing the vehicle to clear an object or gap about the size of a semi trailer or train car. The gamemaster should have the driver make a Vehicle Test with a difficulty they feel appropriate for the jump. Activating the rocket system takes a Complex Action and is in no way subtle, but it is spectacular. When landing the vehicle must resist (Body) DV damage, following all of the rules for Crash damage (p. 201, *SR5*). Additionally, the driver must make an immediate Vehicle Test to maintain control. If successful, the vehicle can continue driving as normal, but if it is failed the vehicle crashes.

SECONDARY MANUAL CONTROLS

Does your team have a backseat driver who's always wanting to take control? Or maybe your always sitting in the vehicle of teammate and wishing you had your own gas control so they would just *get moving*? Both of those problems can be solved with the secondary manual controls modification. This modification literally provides a second set of manual controls that can be used to pilot the vehicle, just like the primary set. Either set can control the vehicle, but the primary set always has priority. If the vehicle also has manual control override, the system can be set to switch only when a manual switch is activated. Secondary manual controls are useful for teams that may need a secondary person to control a vehicle while the driver is otherwise occupied or particularly vulnerable.

SECONDARY PROPULSION: HOVERCRAFT

A well-traveled rigger knows that lots of areas in the world have demanding terrain. Plus, the work of a runner means that they often need to take the path less traveled. For a truly versatile vehicle, there is the hovercraft upgrade. As with all secondary propulsion systems, this is an extensive upgrade that adds an entire alternate means of motion to the vehicle. A large rubber skirt is added all around the vehicle that can be inflated on demand. Steering and control mechanisms are added so that the vehicle can be directed while hovering, which usually involve using compressed air or expanding gas. While hovering, the vehicle only lifts a few centimeters off of the ground, but it can travel across water. Maneuvering is sluggish compared to most standard modes.

SECONDARY PROPULSION: AMPHIBIOUS

There are times when only the most dramatic action will break off a pursuer, and having your vehicle ditch into the water and *keep going* is definitely a dramatic action. An amphibious operation package is a dramatic modification that allows the vehicle to travel on water (if it didn't already have the means to do so). The modification comes in two versions, surface and submersible, depending on how far the owner wants to take the modifications and what the needs are for water travel.

With the **surface** version, the vehicle is able to float on top of the water. This could involve a variety of systems including a secondary hull shaped to displace an appropriate amount of water, inflatable skirts or ballasts that expand to create flotation, or pontoons attached to the hull of the vehicle. Regardless of the exact form, the modification is fairly extensive, and it is immediately obvious to any observer that something dramatic has been done to the vehicle. When operating on water, the vehicle can use its normal means of propulsion or a low-powered propeller. If the latter is used, speed and maneuverability are fairly limited, but the vehicle at least functions. It probably wouldn't do well crossing an ocean or large lake, but it can easily get across a river, sound, or bay.

With the **submersible** version, the vehicle has been modified to operate under the water. This modification is much more extensive but also more subtle than the surface version. Seals are put in to make sure the vehicle and its essential components are watertight. A secondary propulsion system is then installed to allow it to move while submerged. Classically, this means a propeller powered by the vehicle's drive train, but it can also be a ducted waterjet system for those that like later technology. Finally, internal or external ballast tanks/balloons are added so that the vehicle can control its depth. While the vehicle is capable of moving underwater, it does not handle extreme conditions well and can only handle depths of about 100 meters.

SECONDARY PROPULSION: ROTOR

For many years, experimental riggers had been trying to make a rotor secondary propulsion system work, and in 2074 they finally did it. The plans broke on the shadow grids and instantly blew up in popularity. Like other secondary propulsion systems, the modifications are extensive and costly, but they can be life-saving when you *really* need your vehicle to just *take off and fly*. A rotary secondary propulsion system includes installing the rotors on the top of the vehicle that can fold and partially retract themselves. Additionally, a tail fin with stabilizing rotor is constructed to also retract either into the body, beside, or underneath the vehicle. Although the system is functional—the vehicle does fly when it didn't before—it handles like a barn with rotors. Don't expect to be winning any dogfights, but the vehicle just might get you out of a jam in a way nothing else could.

SECONDARY PROPULSION: TRACKED

Another in the line of secondary propulsion modes, the tracked mode is the ultimate in conquering off-road terrain. This ingenious modification features a system where jacks are deployed to lift the vehicle off the ground, then the tires (or other regular propulsion) are retracted partially into the body, and the tracks are deployed. Finally, the jacks are retracted, and the tracks become the means of propulsion. Smugglers that use a watercraft as their primary vehicle have found this system extremely helpful in allowing their boat to make short excursions into the typically rugged terrain frequented by smugglers. Others who have installed them in ground craft do so because they find other methods of off-road travel not good enough, or they want the versatility of being able to switch from a primary on-road system to the tracked system without making a sacrifice to either.

When moving in tracked mode, a vehicle can move through extremely rough terrain without issue, including crossing trenches and climbing steep angles. Gamemasters should reduce driving difficulty as appropriate. Though the vehicle's speed is limited, it can pivot on the spot since both tracks can move forward or backward independently.

SECONDARY PROPULSION: WALKER

For truly exceptional or demanding terrain, some riggers install a walker system of secondary propulsion on their vehicles. Using a variable number (four to eight, as needed) of retractable mechanical legs, the vehicle can deploy the system to give the vehicle the versatil-

SECONDARY PROPULSION ADJUSTMENTS

Whenever a vehicle switches to a secondary propulsion mode, it uses the Handling, Speed, and Acceleration values of the secondary mode, shown below, instead of the regular values. Attributes of secondary propulsion modes cannot be improved.

SECONDARY PROPULSION MODES

NAME	HANDLING	SPEED	ACCEL
Amphibious (Surface)	2	2	1
Amphibious (Submersible)	2	2	2
Hovercraft	2/2	3	2
Rotor	2	3	2
Tracked	2/4	2	1
Walker	5	1	1

ity and mobility of a walker. When deployed, the body of the vehicle is lifted about a meter off of the ground to provide clearance from the terrain, with each leg able to move backwards or forwards independently to provide a walking motion. When in walker mode, a vehicle is able to traverse far more rugged terrain than any other propulsion and still be highly maneuverability, though its speed is severely limited. When using the walker mode of secondary propulsion, the vehicle uses those stats for Handling, Speed, and Acceleration. Additionally, while in walker mode, the vehicle has the basic maneuverability of a metahuman meaning it can stop instantly and pivot on the spot.

SPEED ENHANCEMENT

Using a variety of techniques and equipment (depending on the vehicle), including things such as superchargers, fuel distribution optimization, and parts replacement, the top speed of the vehicle is increased. More dramatic increases in top end speed require more extensive modifications to the vehicle as it is pushed far beyond its original design and limitations. Some designs can only be pushed so far. In the end, though, having that raw top-end speed can save your hoop. Speed Enhancement modification can be taken with a Rating of 1 to 3, with the Rating adding to the Speed attribute of the vehicle.

POWER TRAIN MODIFICATIONS

MODIFICATION	SLOTS	THRESHOLD	TOOLS	SKILL	AVAIL	COST
Acceleration Enhancement						
Rating 1	4	12	Shop	—	6	Accel x 10,000¥
Rating 2	8	24	Facility	—	6	Accel x 25,000¥
Gecko Tips						
Body 1–3	1	8	Shop	—	6	1,000¥
Body 4–6	4	16	Shop	—	6	5,000¥
Body 7+—Not Possible						
Gliding System						
Body <= 12	5	16	Facility	—	12R	Body x 3,000¥
Body > 12	10	24	Facility	—	16R	Body x 4,000¥
Handling Enhancement						
Rating 1	4	8	Shop	—	6	Handl x 2,000¥
Rating 2	10	16	Facility	—	8	Handl x 5,000¥
Rating 3	18	24	Facility	—	10	Handl x 12,000¥
Improved Economy	2	12	Facility	—	4	7,500¥
Manual Control Override	1	4	Shop	—	6	500¥
Multifuel Engine	4	20	Shop	—	10	Body x 1,000¥
Off-Road Suspension	2	8	Shop	—	4	Vehicle cost x 25%
Rigger Cocoon	2	6	Kit	—	8	1,500¥
Removed Manual Controls	1	4	Shop	—	2	200¥
Rocket Booster	10	36	Facility	—	16F	Body x 5,000¥
Secondary Manual Controls	2	10	Shop	—	4	1,000¥
Secondary Propulsion:						
Amphibious, Surface	4	10	Shop	—	6	Body x 200¥
Amphibious, Submersible	8	20	Shop	—	12R	Body x 2,000¥
Hovercraft	8	16	Shop	—	12	Body x 1,000¥
Rotor	10	24	Facility	—	12R	Body x 3,000¥
Tracked	6	14	Shop	—	10	Body x 1,000¥
Walker	8	16	Shop	—	12	Body x 2,000¥
Speed Enhancement						
Rating 1	5	8	Shop	—	6	Speed x 2,000¥
Rating 2	14	16	Facility	—	8	Speed x 5,000¥
Rating 3	20	24	Facility	—	12	Speed x 12,000¥

PROTECTION

Protection modifications are all based around providing various defensive measures for the vehicle or its occupants.

ANTI-THEFT SYSTEM

No self-respecting rigger wants to let their precious vehicle be stolen by some gutter punk with a screwdriver. The anti-theft system modification provides a variety of protection options, depending on the level rating.

Rating 1 simply installs sensors that detect an unauthorized intrusion and alerts the owner with physical lights and sounds, or sends an electronic message, or both.

Rating 2 includes the sensors from the previous level and adds the ability for the owner to remotely lockdown the vehicle, making it physically impossible to drive until the release code is sent by the owner. This system can be circumvented by decking the vehicle, or mechanically disabling the fail safe with a Hardware + Logic [Logic] (4) Test.

If all of that is just for soft-ass corporate drones, then **Rating 3** may be for you. This level includes all of the previous features, with the addition of an electro-shock system inflicting 9S(e), or a gas release system equipped with the toxin of your choice (see p. 409, SR5).

Rating 4 is the final word in vehicle protection; it includes all of the previous level's features and adds a remote triggered self-destruct option. The modified vehicle is reduced to medium-to-small component parts. The explosion has a base damage of 12P and –2 AP, with damage from the blast –2/m.

ARMOR

Need to protect your vehicle? Then give it some armor! Vehicle armor comes in two varieties: standard and concealed. **Standard** vehicle armor is additional plating bolted or welded to the exterior—crude but incredibly effective. However, it is immediately obvious to any observer that the vehicle has a bunch of extra plating slapped on to it. While that will win a runner some points in the barrens, it may not sit too well with security forces in downtown. **Concealed** armor is installed in such a way as to be noticeable only to a trained observer (Perception (4) Test), but does not allow nearly as much protection to be installed. A vehicle must choose the standard or concealed option for all additional armor taken—there cannot be some armor of one type along with some of the other. Regardless of type, each point taken for this modification adds a point to the vehicle's Armor value for Damage Resistance Tests. The most armor any vehicle can add is equal to vehicle Body (meaning maximum armor = Body + existing armor Rating). This is true even if there are remaining modification slots on the vehicle.

PASSENGER PROTECTION SYSTEM (PPS)

The passenger protection system (PPS) is a well known and trusted series of systems and modifications made to a vehicle to keep its passengers safe in the case of a collision or other "adverse vehicular situations." PPS components include four-point harnesses, padded surfaces, quick-deploying air bags, and in some cases fast-drying foam. A PPS has a Rating of 1 to 6, with the Rating added as dice pool bonus to any Damage Resistance Tests by passengers from damage due to crashes or any other vehicular activity (including ramming) that is not an attack by a weapon.

PERSONAL ARMOR

Shadowrunning in a vehicle can be dangerous for the occupants. Besides just faithful (or mercenary) teammates, there may be precious cargo or passengers that need protecting. Personal armor is a modification that adds additional ballistic protection to the occupants of a vehicle in the form of protective lining, ballistic cloth, and ricochet-reducing materials. The modification has a Rating of 1 to 10, with each Rating point adding to the armor used in Damage Resistance Tests for damage to passengers from attacks originating outside the vehicle.

SPECIAL ARMOR MODIFICATION

With this modification a vehicle's armor can be made more resistant to a specific type of damage. Special armor modification works in the same was as modifications for personal armor (p. 437-438, SR5), with vehicles able to take only Chemical Protection, Fire Resistance, Insulation, Nonconductivity, Radiation Shielding, and Universal Mirror Material. Each modification can be taken with a maximum Rating of the armor value of the vehicle. Special armor modification may be taken multiple times, each time with a different armor modification.

WEAPONS
AMMO BINS

Are you one of those runners that feel that any problem can be solved with enough bullets? Is "spray and pray" your personal street proverb? Then you probably want the ammo bin modification. Each ammo bin modification provides an extra 250 rounds of ammunition for one of the vehicle's weapon mounts. The modification may be taken multiple times, providing more rounds for different weapons or even multiple times for the same weapon (if you really need a *lot* of bullets).

PROTECTION MODIFICATIONS

MODIFICATION	SLOTS	THRESHOLD	TOOLS	SKILL	AVAIL	COST
Anti-Theft System						
Rating 1	1	4	Kit	—	4	500¥
Rating 2	2	8	Kit	—	6	1,000¥
Rating 3	4	12	Shop	—	8R	2,500¥
Rating 4	6	16	Shop	Demolitions 12F	5,000¥	
Armor						
Standard	Rating x 2	Rating x 2	Shop	Armorer	6R	Rating x 500¥
Concealed	Rating x 3	Rating x 3	Shop	Armorer	12R	Rating x 3,000¥
PPS (Rating 1-6)	2	Rating x 4	Shop	—	6	Rating x 2,000¥
Personal Armor (Rating 1-10)	2	Rating x 2	Shop	Armorer	(Rating)R	Rating x 500¥
Special Armor Modification	2	12	Shop	Armorer	(As Mod)	(As Mod) x 2

DRONE RACK

A drone rack is an indispensable tool for a rigger who relies on drones to accomplish critical tasks for their team. Drone racks consist of a metal framework or harness designed to allow for quick and easy deployment of a drone in an instant, turning a vehicle equipped with several of them into a powerful, multipurpose drone carrier. Any drone carried in any kind of drone rack can be deployed by spending a Complex Action, or Simple Action if it is wireless enabled. Each drone rack can carry a single drone of a maximum size depending on the size of the rack. Additionally, each drone rack can be standard or landing type.

All **standard** drone racks deploy drones as above but require a manual process to re-embark the drone. This involves physically putting the drone back into the rack, a process that takes about one minute per drone.

Landing drone racks have a mechanic or electro-magnetic grapple system that can automatically re-embark a drone that is directly beneath or adjacent to them with a Complex Action. This can even be done while the the vehicle is in motion, as long as the target drone can match the vehicle's speed.

Micro drone racks can hold up to ten micro drones, **mini** drone racks can carry a drone of up to Mini size, **small** drone racks can carry up to a Small drone, **medium** drone racks can carry up to a Medium drone, and **large** drone racks can carry (you guessed it) up to a Large drone.

GUN PORT

For those times when you want your vehicle to be less "car" and more "armored personnel carrier," there is the gun port mod. A gun port is a small flap or slot installed strategically in the hull of the vehicle that allows a single passenger (or the driver, if you can multitask) to shoot a hand-held weapon at a target outside the vehicle, while still staying completely protected by the vehicle's armor. The port provides a ninety-degree cone of visibility, and a small stability harness that provides 4 points of Recoil Compensation. The gun port mod can be taken as many times as possible for the vehicle, though provides no benefit beyond the amount of passengers that a vehicle can reasonably carry.

MISSILE DEFENSE SYSTEM

While this item normally reserved for military use, a resourceful and properly connected shadowrunner has been known to get their hands on a missile defense system (MDS). Using a highly complicated and specialized set of software, the system ties in control of one or more on-board weapon systems to shoot down incoming missiles and rockets while in flight. The system requires the vehicle to have a Sensor rating of 5 (minimum) and at least one weapon capable of Full-Auto fire, or a laser weapon, to be attached via remote control turret weapon mount. When an incoming projectile is detected, the system takes control of all weapons tied into it in order to intercept in the incoming projectile. This supersedes any other current controller of the weapon(s). Ballistics weapons use 20 rounds of ammunition each time the system activates. In game terms, each ballistic weapon tied into the system gives the defender +2 on Defense Tests made against missiles and rockets. Each laser weapon provides +4 dice.

OIL SLICK SPRAYER

Some runners say that old tricks are the best tricks, and they're the ones who most love the simple but effective oil slick sprayer. Using a few nozzles and a reservoir of slick fluid, the ground immediately behind the vehicle can be made extremely hazardous to pursuing ground-based vehicles. Activating the oil slick sprayer is a Free Action; following activation, any ground vehicles in pursuit at Short Range must make a Reaction + Vehicle Skill [Handling] (2) Test to avoid crashing. The oil slick sprayer has 6 charges and can be completely refilled for 50 nuyen.

RAM PLATE

While ramming might be a last resort for some, it is a first resort for others, and the ram plate is the perfect modification for those people. Ram plates come in a huge variety of shapes and sizes, from wickedly engineered sharpened bifurcating blades to a motley collection of extra car parts that the gangers welded to the front. All are equally effective. When making a Ramming attack (see p. 203, *SR5*) the damage done by the ramming vehicle is increased by one level, as if it were going one speed category higher. Damage taken to the ramming vehicle is unchanged.

ROAD STRIP EJECTOR

The road strip ejector is another classic but effective countermeasure from the good old days. Using a simple powered release mechanism, a belt that is extremely hazardous to ground vehicles is deployed with a Free Action. A road strip ejector can be equipped with any one type of road strip (see **Vehicle Equipment**, p. 152). The strip ejector can carry six individual strips. Refills cost the price of six of whatever road strip is desired.

SMOKE PROJECTOR

Another oldie but a goodie, the smoke projector continues to prove that simple never goes out of style. One or two canisters with aerosol nozzles are attached to the

WEAPON MODIFICATIONS

MODIFICATION	SLOTS	THRESHOLD	TOOLS	SKILL	AVAIL	COST
Ammo Bin	1	4	Shop	Armorer	6R	200¥
Standard Drone Rack						
Mini	1	8	Kit	—	4	500¥
Small	2	10	Shop	—	4	1,000¥
Medium	3	12	Shop	—	6	2,000¥
Large	4	16	Shop	—	8	4,000¥
Landing Drone Rack						
Mini	2	10	Shop	—	6	1,000¥
Small	3	12	Shop	—	6	4,000¥
Medium	4	14	Facility	—	8	10,000¥
Large	5	20	Facility	—	12	20,000¥
Gun Port	1	4	Kit	—	6R	500¥
Missile Defense System	3	16	Facility	Software	12R	15,000¥
Oil Slick Sprayer	2	8	Shop	—	8F	500¥
Ram Plate	1	8	Shop	—	6R	Body x 250¥
Smoke Projector	2	8	Shop	—	6R	750¥
Thermal Smoke						+100¥
Road Strip Ejector	2	10	Shop	—	10F	800¥ + strips
Weapon Mount						
Light Size	1	4	Kit	Armorer	6F	750¥
Standard Size	2	6	Shop	Armorer	8F	1,500¥
Heavy Size	4	10	Shop	Armorer	12F	4,000¥
External Visibility	—	—	—	—	—	–
Internal Visibility	+2	+6	Shop	—	+2	+1,500¥
Concealed Visibility	+4	+10	Shop	—	+4	+4,000¥
Fixed Flexibility	–	—	—	—	—	–
Flexible Flexibility	+1	+4	Shop	—	+2	+2,000¥
Turret Flexibility	+2	+12	Facility	—	+6	+5,000¥
Remote Control	–	—	—	—	—	–
Manual Control	+1	+4	Shop	—	+1	+500¥
Armored Manual Control	+2	+6	Shop	—	+4	+1,500¥

vehicle, releasing a huge cloud of dense smoke on command with a Free Action. Once deployed, all actions of vehicles up to one hundred meters behind the vehicle are affected by the Moderate Smoke Visibility Modifier (p. 175, *SR5*). For a little bit more nuyen, the system can be installed with thermal smoke (p. 435, *SR5*).

WEAPON MOUNT

Shadowrunning is not a business where one wants to be defenseless (or offense-less, for that matter), so riggers often awant to put weapons on their vehicle. While a small number of security or military-class vehicles are designed to mount weapon systems, the vast majority of vehicles are designed and built for civilian use, so installing a weapon system is strictly an after-market affair. Just like the weapons that they support, weapon mounts come in a large variety of shapes and sizes to suit the needs of the weapon as well as the owner. All weapon mounts have four attributes: Size, Visibility, Flexibility, and Control.

Size defines what kind of weapons can be attached to the weapon mount. *Light* weapon mounts can hold weapons in the following categories: Melee, Tasers, Hold-Out Pistols Light Pistols, Heavy Pistols, Machine Pistols, and Submachine Guns. *Standard* weapon mounts can hold Tasers, Hold-Outs, Light Pistols, Heavy Pistols, Assault Rifles, Sniper Rifles, Shotguns, Exotic Ranged Weapons, Flamethrowers, and Special Weapons. *Heavy* weapon mounts can hold any of the previous, as well as weapons from the following categories: Machine Guns, Cannons, Launchers, and Lasers.

Visibility defines where a weapon is mounted on a vehicle and how noticeable it is. An *external* mount places the weapon on the outside of the vehicle, on its hull somewhere, which is plainly obvious to any observer. An *internal* mount has the weapon inside the vehicle until it's deployed using a Simple Action. Once deployed the weapon is externally visible and easily seen, but while internal the weapon cannot be seen from outside observation. A *concealed* mount is an internal mount but further conceals the weapon behind false paneling and other vehicle features such that it is not obvious even when searching the inside, requiring a Perception + Intuition [Intuition] (4) Test to find.

Flexibility defines how movable a weapon is on its mount. A *fixed* mount cannot turn independently from the vehicle it is attached to and so relies on the driver of the vehicle to aim the weapon; it cannot change its direction of fire unless the vehicle direction also changes. A *flexible* mount has a limited range of motion, able to move ninety degrees horizontally and vertically. A *turret* mount allows for a full 360-degree of movement but can be constrained depending on where on the hull of the vehicle the weapon is placed. Most smart riggers will put a turret mount on the roof of the vehicle to fully utilize its range of motion.

Control determines how the weapon attached to the mount can be fired. These days the default is *remote*, meaning the weapon can be fired by making a Control Device Matrix Action (the owner of such a device automatically succeeds). For the security paranoid, or those that just like the hands-on approach, *manual* control can be applied to a weapon. This option removes the possibility of remote, electronic control in favor of direct mechanical operation of the weapon, meaning a metahuman must physically operate the weapon, which tends to put them at bodily risk. *Armored manual* control is an option where the operator of the weapon is protected by armored panels and shields while operating the weapon. This gives the firer +6 armor against ranged attacks while operating the weapon.

To calculate the final cost of the weapon mount modification, start with the Size. The apply the modifiers to Slot, Threshold, Availability, and Cost when choosing the other options. Use the highest requirement for Tools from the options chosen

BODY

Body modifications modify the hull or structure of the vehicle in some form.

ASSEMBLY/DISASSEMBLY

No rigger likes to see their vehicle "baby" in pieces, but at least with the assembly/disassembly modification they know it can be put back together. For times when a rigger or their team needs to get a vehicle to (or into) a location but can't get it there whole, they put in an assembly modification. While this can be used on larger vehicles to give more flexibility in how they can be transported, it is far more common for smaller vehicles like drones. Secure facilities will commonly search and scan for illegal or banned drones, such as small surveillance "bugs," but detection can be circumvented by breaking the drone down into innocuous parts and smuggling those in separately.

The assembly/disassembly modification allows a vehicle to be broken down into several smaller pieces and then reassembled for operation. Disassembling or reassembling a vehicle takes a (Vehicle Mechanic Skill) + Logic [Logic] (Body, 30 minutes) Extended Test. When broken down, the parts are extremely difficult to identify, requiring a Perception + Intuition [Intuition] (4) Test as well as having an appropriate Knowledge Skill to even recognize that the parts could be a vehicle component.

CHAMELEON COATING

Not just for the flighty owner who can't settle on a paint color for their vehicle, chameleon coating is an essential tool for keeping a vehicle used for shadow activities inconspicuous. A vehicle with the coating has its exterior hull covered in a specialized kind of polymer that allows it to display any kind of image sent to the system with an electronic signal. This can be as simple as changing the color of the vehicle, or as complex as covering it in moving advertisements and video. Changing the output of the coating is a Free Action. Particularly clever riggers have linked the video feed from their external sensors into the system so that the exterior of the vehicle mimics the environment around it, resulting in a crude (but effective) "cloaking" or blending system. When running in this mode, as long as it is not moving faster than its Walking rate, Perception Tests made to find the vehicle suffer a –3 dice pool penalty.

EXTRA ENTRY/EXIT POINTS

There are plenty of situations when a runner may need to get in or out of their vehicle in an unusual way, for an unusual situation. A vehicle equipped with extra entry/exit points has a variety of extra points on the vehicle that can be used to get in or out of the vehicle. These could be an ork-sized sunroof, or a special trap door in the floor of the vehicle. In game terms, any occupant of the vehicle is assumed to have a convenient entry or exit point accessible to them, no matter what state the vehicle it is in (including upside down), or from what position they are attempting to access the vehicle (such as from the roof).

EJECTION SEATS

Remember that time when there was an annoying person in the back and you wished you could just push a button and fire him out of the vehicle? Well, with ejection seats you can! Using a simple expanding gas propulsion system, activated remotely with a Free Action, any seat in the vehicle can become a means to eject the occupant of that seat. Seats can be equipped with parachutes if the system is being used for safe egress of someone that you want to be whole when they land, or without if not. Traditionally, ejection seats launch vertically upward, but they can be configured to launch horizontally, or even straight down (particularly vicious in aircraft or watercraft).

EXTREME ENVIRONMENT MODIFICATION

Most vehicles are manufactured with the anticipation and intention that they will be used in common or banal environments—basically, those found in the day-to-day life of most of the population. There are plenty of times, however, when a rigger will need his vehicle to operate smoothly in environments outside of those normal conditions. Since most vehicles were never designed to handle such conditions, several special modifications are needed on a variety of systems, depending on the environment. This could include additives and micro-heaters to ensure the vehicle's liquid

systems do not freeze in extreme cold, or super-coolers to keep it running in extreme heat. Each time this modification is taken, the vehicle can operate normally in a specific selected environment (desert, arctic, etc.). If the environment itself will be damaging to the vehicle, it needs a special armor modification (see p. 159) to maintain protection. Note that this modification only allows the vehicle itself to continue to operate; keeping occupants of the vehicle alive would be handled by a life support system (below).

INCREASED SEATING

While no riggers likes to be the "team mom" or the "runner taxi," there are plenty of times that they will need to carry more people than their vehicle originally allowed, especially if they're driving some super-slick European sports car that could only carry two to begin with. With increased seating, a vehicle can comfortably carry more passengers than its original design. This is far more than just jamming a couple of extra think people in the trunk—the modification includes all features for carrying people including comfortable (enough) seating, incorporating the vehicle's safety systems (including PPS if installed, see p. 159), and other personal comfort features such as ventilation and lighting. This can mean rearranging the internal layout of the vehicle, extending it slightly, or even adding "external" seating, such as a sidecar on a motorcycle. When this modification is taken, the passenger capacity of the vehicle is increased up to a fifty percent increase of its base value, though the gamemaster has final say on exactly how many passengers the vehicle can reasonably carry.

LIFE SUPPORT

The world outside of a vehicle is often dangerous or outright hostile to shadowrunners and their targets. In order to keep their occupants secure, many vehicles install a Life Support system. This system comes in two levels, depending on the need. In a *Level 1* system, all normal "leak points" in a vehicle—such as door and window frames—have been made air and water tight; air only circulates through the vehicle's ventilation system. The system also includes a variety of detection systems and filters to help prevent airborne toxins and diseases from harming those inside a vehicle. All occupants of the vehicle gain +4 dice for any resistance test to an airborne drug, toxin, or disease that comes from outside the vehicle. A *Level 2* system includes everything from the Level 1 system while also allowing all external air intakes to be shut off, making the vehicle completely air and water tight. Additionally, the vehicle is equipped with its own independent air supply, allowing passengers to survive where there is no air, such as under water or in space. Level 2 also counts as a Chemical Seal (p. 437, *SR5*) for any game situations where that applies.

MECHANICAL ARM

Did a teammate ever ask you to give a hand? Well, with the mechanical arm modification your vehicle actually can! This modification essentially gives your vehicle an (extra) appendage, and comes in two different forms. Arms in both forms have a length roughly equal to Body x 10 centimeters, and five centimeters for a Body 0 vehicle. The arm has a Strength equal to the vehicle's Body / 2 (rounded up). A *basic* mechanical arm is a simple system with a limited range of motion that is very useful for basic grasping and carrying operations. These are generally used to load and unload cargo from the vehicle or something near it and can be used for any operations reasonably similar to that, such as putting a drone back into a drone rack (see p. 160). An *articulated* mechanical arm is a mechanical reproduction of a metahuman arm mounted on a vehicle. It has fine motor abilities and can grasp and use tools. A rigger jumped into a vehicle with an articulated mechanical arm can use any of their Technical Skills with the arm, though the gamemaster can impose a penalty if the vehicle is only equipped with one and the task regularly requires two arms. Most surprisingly (for those that don't expect it), an articulated mechanical arm can make a melee attack against any target within range. To make a melee attack, roll Melee Skill + Agility [Accuracy]—if a rigger is jumped into the vehicle, the test uses their appropriate melee skill. If the vehicle is attacking autonomously use (autosoft) + Pilot.

NANOMAINTENANCE SYSTEM

While many people have (understandably) gotten skittish about injecting nanites into their head, most of the population still considers it safe to have them operate on something inorganic like their vehicle. The nanomaintenance system installs a series of specialized nanobot hives around the body of the vehicle and in key sections designed to repair and maintain the vehicle's body and systems. This includes reshaping body panels and filling holes, cleaning critical systems, and even rebuilding/reshaping parts on a small scale. Nanomaintenance systems come in Ratings 1 to 4. When repairing damage done to a vehicle, an owner can let the nanomaintenance system attempt its job autonomously, or make repairs in conjunction with the system. If repairing autonomously, roll the Rating of the nanomaintenance system. Each hit repairs one box of vehicle damage, with the whole process taking one hour. Alternatively, the owner can repair the damage with the assistance of the system. In this case, the owner makes a standard Repair Test, with the nanomaintence system giving a bonus equal to its Rating (see p. 146, *SR5*). Either one option or the other must be chosen for each instance of damage to be repaired—the two cannot be combined on the same damages.

REALISTIC FEATURES

When undertaking surreptitious surveillance, making a drone look like *not* a drone is an essential asset. For this reason, many riggers will wrap smaller drones, or anything up to humanoid size, in a synthetic skin material. The intricacy of the disguise can vary depending on how much time and resources are put into it. This can range from a simple coating of realistic-looking skin made from a synthetic material, to a full covering of living tissue fed by an artificial circulation system with devices to simulate organs. The realistic features mod has a Rating of 1 to 4. The Rating sets the threshold of the Perception Test to recognize the machine as artificial. When the modification is made, the installer chooses a single living being that the modification is trying to replicate. This modification is designed to be made on vehicles no bigger than the size of a large animal. The gamemaster can decide whether the modification is even possible, given the size and design of the vehicle, but nearly all drones should be able to accept the modification. The true nature of the vehicle is instantly recognizable by Assensing.

SMUGGLING COMPARTMENT

You don't need to run very long before you encounter a situation where you need to keep something (or someone) hidden from authorities that are trying to find it. In these situations, the smuggling compartment is what you need. This modification adds a storage compartment to the vehicle, one that is designed to not easily be found. In general, a smuggling compartment cannot be seen unless a person is specifically looking for hidden compartments or doing a thorough search of the vehicle, and even in that case the Perception Test to notice the compartment is made with a –6 penalty. Smuggling compartments are hidden by purely visual means, so if the contents of the compartment make it detectable by other means—chemical, radioactive, thermographic—these do not suffer a penalty. Compartments can have *shielding* installed on them to make the compartment difficult to detect by a particular non-visual sense. If this is done, then the –6 penalty applies to that sense as well. Shielding on a smuggling compartment may be taken multiple times, each time specifying a different sensory type (auditory, chemical, radioactive, astral, etc.). The gamemaster determines if an object can fit in a smuggling compartment, based on the size of the vehicle. In general, smuggling compartments are about ten to twenty percent of the overall size of the vehicle itself.

SPECIAL EQUIPMENT

Depending upon its intended role, a vehicle may have a variety of specialized equipment. This modification is a "catch-all" category for any specific piece of equipment that a rigger may want installed on their vehicle. This could include such things as a dozer blade, snowaremoval device, asphalt dispenser, road-paint applicator, or temperature controlled storage. No fixed costs are provided, as the gamemaster has final say on what can be installed on the vehicle and what effect it may have.

VALKYRIE MODULE

If you have teammates that just can't seem to stop from getting themselves critically injured, then they are going to thank you for installing a Valkyrie module. Named after the mythical maidens that carry a Viking warrior to the afterlife, the Valkyrie module is a small-scale, portable, automated emergency room. The module includes a bed with a transparent, enclosed lid and a host of sophisticated medical equipment with built-in software that can quickly analyze and treat almost any injury.

Any person placed in the Valkyrie module is automatically stabilized (p. 209, SR5). The systems on the Valkyrie module are equivalent to a Rating 6 Medkit (p. 450, SR5), with all of the same functionality. Additionally, the Valkyrie module operates as an autodoc, and so can be operated remotely (p. 208, SR5).

WINCH

For those times when a runner needs to pull or tow something and they don't want to call an underpaid and overweight member of the auto club, there is the winch modification. The *basic* winch hasn't changed its design much in about a hundred years. It has a heavy gauge steel cable ending with a hook or latch and wraps around a powered drum. A winch can be mounted on the front or rear of the vehicle, and comes with about one hundred meters of cable and can support a load of up to ten tons, provided the vehicle itself is heavy enough to support this. If wireless enabled, the winch hook can be released remotely with a Free Action. An *enhanced* winch is generally found in heavy industrial or rescue vehicles but can be useful to a runner. Its winch replaces the hook with an advanced system using a combination of gecko-grip technology and magnetism that can attach to any surface on its target without the need to manually place a hook on an appropriate part. The system can be activated or deactivated remotely with a wireless command (if enabled). The enhanced system can support a load of up to one hundred tons and includes additional stabilizers deployed from the vehicle and onto/into the ground to double the towing vehicle's weight for lifting purposes.

WORKSHOP

For the true tinkerers who can never be apart from their tools, a vehicle with ample enough space can be made into a mobile workshop. Niceties and comfort items are removed to make room for shelving, work spaces, and

equipment. A vehicle modified in this way counts as being a Shop for the purposes of tool availability (p. 443, SR5). The type of shop (Automotive Mechanic, Armorer) must be chosen at the time of the modification and cannot be changed.

ELECTROMAGNETIC

Electromagnetic modifications are connected to or modify a vehicle's electronic systems.

ELECTROMAGNETIC SHIELDING

When a rigger wants absolute control over the signals that come in and out of their vehicle, there isn't a better option than the electromagnetic shielding modification. This system builds a system of conductive metal bands into the exterior body of the vehicle, designed to conduct away and dissipate all wireless signals that attempt to penetrate the body of the vehicle, going in or out. This modification only works on vehicles that create an enclosed space—it is useless for vehicles that are open, such as a motorcycle. In game terms, the body of the vehicle acts as a Faraday cage for Noise purposes (p. 231, SR5) meaning that no communication is possible through the barrier. When the system is installed, the owner can choose to have certain systems or features be able to move through the barrier by running a physical wire through the cage. Any device that can connect to the body of the vehicle with a wired connection can bypass the Faraday cage.

ELECTRONIC COUNTERMEASURES (ECM)

Savvy riggers and deckers know that it is often easier to attack the signals controlling a device than to attack the device itself. To that end, a vehicle can be equipped with an electronic countermeasures (ECM) suite. This modification allows the vehicle to function exactly like an area jammer (p. 441, SR5), with all of the same rules. Just like a jammer, the modification comes with a Rating of 1 to 6.

GRIDLINK

Gridlink is a fairly ubiquitous feature for modern vehicles in the Sixth World, at least in the areas where the sun of corporate control continually shines. Using a system of embedded power lines in the road system, any vehicle equipped with gridlink can use these lines to draw operational power and thus have an unlimited running time as long as it is connected. As with everything in the Sixth World, there's a downside. In exchange for the free power, vehicles running on gridlink essentially give up control to the owner of the local GridGuidesystem. A vehicle is identified and tracked every second it is attached to the system, is limited to

BODY MODIFICATIONS

MODIFICATION	SLOTS	THRESHOLD	TOOLS	SKILL	AVAIL	COST
Assembly/Disassembly	2	Body x 4 (Min. 1)	Facility	—	6	1,000¥
Chameleon Coating	2	10	Facility	—	12F	Body x 1,000¥
Extra Entry/Exit Points	1	8	Shop	—	8	2,500¥
Extreme Environment Modification	2	12	Shop	—	6	2,000¥
Increased Seating	2	6	Shop	—	4	2,000¥
Life Support						
Level 1	2	10	Shop	—	8	Body x 500¥
Level 2	4	20	Shop	—	12	Body x 2,000¥
Mechanical Arm						
Basic	2	8	Shop	—	4	1,000¥
Articulated	3	16	Facility	—	6	5,000¥
Nanomaintenance System (Rating 1-4)	Rating	Rating x 4	Shop	—	(R x 5)R	Rating x 5,000¥
Realistic Features (Rating 1-4)	Rating	Rating x 4	Shop	Medicine	(R x 3)R	Rating x Body x 1,000¥
Smuggling Compartment	3	16	Facility	—	8F	1,500¥
Shielding	n/a	12	Facility	—	12F	3,000¥
Special Equipment	variable	variable	variable	variable	variable	variable
Valkyrie Module	4	6	Shop	Hardware	8	2,000¥
Winch						
Basic	1	8	Shop	—	4	750¥
Enhanced	2	12	Facility	—	8	4,000¥
Workshop	6	20	Facility	—	8	10,000¥

the legal speed limit set for the area, and can be remotely shut down by the owner of the system. Most vehicles constructed come with a gridlink system as standard, but the system can be installed afterward with a vehicle modification.

In game terms, the host that controls the gridlink system is automatically assumed to have 3 marks (or be the owner) of any vehicle connected. Needless to say, runners consider the GridGuide system to be a major liability to their work and will always (if they're smart) remove the system or install a gridlink override (see below).

GRIDLINK OVERRIDE

Using a combination of hardware and software modifications, a vehicle can be equipped to override its gridlink system, and retain independent control. When

activated, the vehicle appears to be a interacting with the system normally but cannot be shut down, can exceed the posted speed limit, and randomly rotates its identifier so it cannot be tracked for an extended period. Since even runners are pragmatic, the vehicle still draws its operational power from the gridlink system, as long as it is available, because who doesn't love stealing from the corps?

PILOT ENHANCEMENT

More than just another program, vehicle Pilot programs are some of the most sophisticated software programs in use today. Enhancing a drone's Pilot program takes more than just loading a new program: select chips on the hardware set are replaced and upgraded, new communication channels are installed to enhance information gathering, and control systems are upgraded to provide improved sensitivity and additional maneuvering options. Unlike other modifications, the Pilot enhancement replaces the Pilot Rating of the vehicle, rather than adding to its existing Rating. A Pilot program can have a Rating of 1 to 6.

RETRANS UNIT

For riggers that want to cast a wide net of drones, or those wanting precision in a high-noise zone, the retrans unit is essential. Using a specialized system of signal capture and algorithmic reconstruction, the retrans unit rebuilds and rebroadcasts a specific signal, eliminating all the noise that accumulated on the signal up to that point. Thus the signal behaves as if it had originated at the point of the retrans unit. A vehicle equipped with a retrans unit that is part of a network of other devices can be used to rebroadcast all signal communications on the network. In game terms, when calculating the effect of Noise due to physical distance (see p. 231, SR5), the distance from the source or the destination to the retrans unit (whichever is greater) can be used instead of the total distance from source to destination. In other words, the Noise level is calculated as if the signal was originating or arriving at the retrans unit, picking the higher of the two. Note that this only works for communications across the network of drones, not beyond it; that is to say, a retrans unit cannot be used as a sort of bridge to eliminate noise for a decker attempting to hack into devices beyond the drone.

Although multiple retrans units in a single vehicle provide no benefit, multiple vehicles equipped with retrans units can be used to form a "chain" such that only the single highest noise value of all devices is used. A retrans unit can provide its functionality for all devices on a PAN.

EXAMPLE

Rigger X is trying to communicate with a long-range aerial-surveillance drone that is on the other side of the city, 15 kilometers away. Normally, this would result in a Noise level of 5. However, Rigger X has placed a drone equipped with a retrans unit at a point nine kilometers away from him and one kilometer from the surveillance drone. The distance from Rigger X to the retrans unit has a Noise level of 3, and the distance from the retrans unit to the target drone has a Noise of 1, so Rigger X uses the higher value of 3.

SATELLITE LINK

Want to have a drone keep tabs on your doss while you sit on a beach halfway across the world? You need a satellite link. Any vehicle equipped with this modification communicates exactly like it is equipped with the satellite link accessory (see p. 439, SR5).

SENSOR UPGRADE

Just like the Pilot program, a vehicle's sensors are a complicated and highly integrated part of the vehicle's electromagnetic systems. Vehicles that are massed produced for civilian use aren't designed with accessibility and enhancement of their sensor systems in mind, so improving a vehicle's sensor suite is no easy task. Sensory devices themselves generally need to be replaced to be improved, as well as the processing hardware and software that controls them. As such, the sensor upgrade modification replaces the vehicle's Sensor rating rather than adding to its existing rating. Sensor Enhancement come with a Rating of 1 to 6.

SIGNATURE MASKING

When you're pulling a run, going undetected is more than half the battle. With the proliferation of sensor suites in the Sixth World, this is far easier said than done, but signature masking will go a long way to making a vehicle harder to detect. With this modification, a vehicle's EM profile is reduced using a complicated (and expensive) set of techniques including: coating the vehicle in radar-absorbing materials, changing the angle on body panels, and thermal and aural dampening materials and systems. Signature masking comes with a Rating of 1 to 6, where the Rating determining the amount and extensiveness of the modifications done to hide the vehicle. Whenever an attacker attempts to either find the vehicle with a Sensor Test, or attack the vehicle using Active or Passive Targeting, the Rating of the signature masking is applied as a negative dice pool modifier, along with any other Signature Modifiers (p. 184, SR5).

SUNCELL

For runners that are economically or environmentally minded, the SunCell modification provides a great option. Using powerful solar-energy collectors and a battery system, a vehicle can be powered by collecting solar energy. If operating exclusively during sunny daylight hours, a vehicle has unlimited operational time and needs no other fuel source. In any other conditions (where sunlight isn't readily available), the vehicle will use up all power stored in the battery and then switch to its standard means of power production (likely a fossil-fuel engine). If operating in a mix of conditions, the SunCell system roughly doubles the operational time of the vehicle between refueling stops.

ELECTROMAGNETIC MODIFICATIONS

MODIFICATION	SLOTS	THRESHOLD	TOOLS	SKILL	AVAIL	COST
Electromagnetic Shielding	2	20	Facility	—	6R	Body x 500¥
ECM	2	20	Shop	Hardware	(R x 3)F	Rating x 500¥
Gridlink	2	4	Shop	Hardware	4	750¥
Gridlink Override	1	8	Kit	Hardware	8F	1,000¥
Pilot Enhancement						
Rating 1–3	[Rating]	Rating x 3	Kit	Hardware	R x 2	Rating x 2,000¥
Rating 4–6	[Rating]	Rating x 4	Shop	Hardware	R x 3	Rating x 5,000¥
Retrans Unit	2	4	Kit	Hardware	8	4,000¥
Satellite Link	1	6	Kit	Hardware	6	500¥
Sensor Enhancement						
Rating 1–3	[Rating]	Rating x 3	Shop	Hardware	R x 2	Rating x 2,000¥
Rating 4–6	[Rating]	Rating x 4	Shop	Hardware	R x 3	Rating x 5,000¥
Signature Masking (Rating 1–6)	[Rating]	Rating x 6	Facility	—	14F	Rating x 2,000¥
SunCell	2	16	Shop	Hardware 6	6	Body x 500¥
Touch Sensors	3	16	Shop	Hardware 8	8	Body x 500¥

TOUCH SENSORS

When a rigger jumps into a vehicle, they experience the world around them as if they were the vehicle, with the hull of the vehicle feeling like their skin. With touch sensors, that experience becomes even more realistic, but it comes with a danger. When touch sensors are installed, the hull of the vehicle is suffused with thousands of micro sensors that relay a variety of sensory information. Consequently, when a rigger is jumped into a vehicle equipped with touch sensors ,they are able to feel and experience the world around them as if the hull of the vehicle was their own skin, possibly even better. In game terms, a rigger jumped in to a vehicle equipped with touch sensors gains +2 dice pool modifier to any Perception or Sensor Tests, and the vehicle's Handling has a +1 modifier. However, the hyper-sensitivity increases the rigger's vulnerability. Whenever the vehicle takes damage, the rigger receives a -2 penalty to resist the Biofeedback Damage (see p. 229, SR5).

COSMETIC

Cosmetic modifications exist in the realm between vehicle modification and vehicle equipment (like tires). They are more permanent and integrated into the vehicle itself than removable equipment, yet nowhere near as invasive as any modification. As such, they are listed as a modification, but do not take up any modification slots.

AMENITIES

Sometimes it's not enough to just get from place to place—you want to travel in comfort and style. With the amenities modification, the "living conditions" of a vehicle are upgraded to provide a more pleasant experience. A standard vehicle provides accommodations equivalent to Low lifestyle, by default, but amenities can be improved to middle, high, or luxury. With *middle*, the vehicle is equipped with comfortable fabric seats, pleasant ergonomics and decorating, and basic AR entertainment options. *High* has the seating made from fine materials, and temperature controlled refreshment options available. There is also a full suite of Matrix and non-electronic entertainment options to keep anyone entertained for hours. With *luxury* amenities, every aspect of the vehicle maximizes comfort: the seats keep you warm and massage you according to a scan of your muscle tension, and they are made of a non-synthetic material (possibly some kind of dead animal hide). The refreshment unit contains

exotic alcohol and real food, along with access to every Matrix entertainment channel or game available. Alternatively, the vehicle can have its amenities downgraded to *squatter* (equivalent to most public transit), in which case it automatically gains the effects of the increased seating modification (see p. 164).

Skill tests (such as Social Skills or Healing Checks) that happen in a vehicle with an amenities modification are considered to be happening in the equivalent lifestyle of the amenities. Gamemasters can apply bonuses to Social Tests for situations where a display of wealth or comfort would be advantageous. A character can choose to live in their vehicle, but must still pay the full cost for the chosen lifestyle.

ENHANCED IMAGE SCREENS

While every vehicle in the 2070s features some degree of imaging screens to communicate important vehicle information, many riggers and vehicle owners want to enhance that image displaying capability. With enhanced image screens, every sufficiently flat surface on a vehicle (including windows) can display an electronic image or video. Theses images are hyper realistic and can be used to project a false image of the outside world in an attempt to deceive passengers. A Perception Test with a -4 penalty is required to notice that the images are false. Enhanced image screens can be used to display any visual feed on a PAN, perfect for team members unable or unwilling to use their AR, or tie their commlink or deck into the same PAN. They can also be used for plain-old entertainment. A vehicle with enhanced image screens can display any and all Matrix AROs that they can see/access on the inside of their vehicle, making them visible to characters who do not have AR equipped.

METAHUMAN ADJUSTMENT

As time marches on in the Sixth World, death, greed, and racism seem to be constant. Despite the best efforts of many metahuman activist groups over the last few decades, most vehicles are still designed and built with human (or human-equivalent) size in mind. As a result, any metahuman who wants to comfortably use a vehicle must have it adjusted to their body. For trolls and dwarfs, this means adjusting the position of vehicle controls to fit their size. For orks and elves, this means more minor adjustments that take advantage of their distinct physiology. Orks and elves attempting to pilot a vehicle that has not been adjusted suffer a -1 penalty to any Pilot Tests, and dwarfs and trolls suffer a -2 penalty. Pixies and centaurs shouldn't even try.

COSMETIC MODIFICATIONS

MODIFICATION	SLOTS	THRESHOLD	TOOLS	SKILL	AVAIL	COST
Amenities						
Squatter	—	6	Shop	—	—	100¥
Middle	—	6	Shop	—	2	500¥
High	—	10	Shop	—	8	1,000¥
Luxury	—	20	Shop	—	16	10,000¥
Enhanced Image Screens	—	12	Shop	—	8	5,000¥
Metahuman Adjustment	—	4	Kit	—	4	500¥/seat
Rigger Interface	—	8	Kit	—	4	1,000¥
Interior Cameras	—	6	Kit	Hardware	6	2,000¥
Searchlight	—	4	Kit	—	4	800¥
Vehicle Tag Eraser	—	8	Shop	Hardware	6R	750¥
Yerzed Out (Rating 1–4)	—	Rating x 4	Shop	—	(R x2)	(Rating x 1,000¥)

RIGGER INTERFACE

By the 2070s rigger control of vehicles have become so common that even if a rigger adaption isn't installed as standard for a vehicle, it can easily be added after-market. This modification allows a rigger to jump in to a vehicle and control it with a full sensory experience. This includes installation of the "black box" that processes the sensory impressions for human consumption, along with a suite of sensors and relays connected to various parts of the vehicle. All drones come equipped with a rigger interface by default.

INTERIOR CAMERAS

In the course of jumping through multiple vehicles and taking in multiple streams of information from different sources, a rigger can easily lose contact with their immediate surroundings—namely, the interior of their own vehicle. As a result, many riggers install interior cameras into their vehicle so they can easily keep track of their own meat body and any passengers in the vehicle by routing the feed from the interior cameras into their PAN. Interior cameras allow a rigger to make a standard Perception Test to notice anyone or anything inside of their vehicle, even while they are in full VR mode.

SEARCHLIGHT

Hey, sometimes your needs are as simple as having a light to shine on things when it gets dark. The searchlight modification installs a high-powered light mounted somewhere on the exterior of the vehicle, capable of all-around movement for wherever it happens to be mounted. It can be operated remotely or manually, as long as it is physically accessible. When activated and pointed in the appropriate direction, the searchlight reduces the penalties due to darkness by one step (p. 173, SR5).

VEHICLE TAG ERASER

All of the RFID tags installed on things makes them convenient to find and track, which is exactly what a runner *doesn't* want. With a few simple steps, a tag eraser (p. 441, SR5) is installed on the interior or exterior of the vehicle. Drawing power from the vehicle itself, the tag eraser can activate once every ten minutes.

YERZED OUT

Do you have a style all your own and want to show that to the world? Then you probably have a yerzed out vehicle. Drawing from the increasingly popular movement of incorporating slang from the ork language of Or'zet, the term is a modification of the Or'zet word "yerzon," meaning "wealthy" or "rich." Despised by most ork rights advocates, the term has nonetheless caught on. Popular trid programs show how to creatively "yerz out" a vehicle in a variety of different ways. Note that a person who drives such a vehicle is often called a "yerzer." While highly individual, in general a yerzed-out vehicle will be aesthetically customized to the owner's unique style and tastes. This includes the color of the vehicle (inside and out), as well as cosmetic additions and modifications such as custom AR, additional (and superfluous) lights, sounds, and maybe even a custom sensations broadcast for the simsense-equipped.

The yerzed out modification can range in Rating from 1 to 4. The Rating provides a dice pool bonus on Social Tests of the owner in situations where the people would be impressed by yerzing. Conversely, the Rating provides a dice pool penalty to Social Tests of the owner where the customization is frowned upon. Additionally, because it is intentionally unique and memorable, any attempts to gather information about the owner with people or groups that known (or know of) him have a dice pool bonus equal to the Rating, since the vehicle is quite distinctive and memorable.

MAXIMUM PURSUIT

A cold rain impacts Reylen's visor in a suicidal staccato. His high-speed race through Seattle on a dark and rainy night is practically a cliché. His job is just as typical. "A simple milk run," Mr. Johnson said. Does he really believe what he's saying, or is it scripted? As the streets get more cracked and faded, he knows he's getting closer to Oorting. He jumps into his cycle as the pavement ends to get a feel for the terrain. His sensors/ eyes pick up the thermal signature from a few shacks as he approaches the coordinates. He pulls up to the first shack and flashes his headlight.

A man with a shotgun exits the building. Reylen waits for the password before even going for the package. The man smiles, amused by the cloak and dagger.

"Nice night eh? Should be a harvest moon with Orion in its zenith."

Reylen recognizes the password and replies, "It's summer on Venus, so it should be just as bright." Reylen pulls out the package and hands it to him.

The man turns his back and takes a quick peek at the contents, out of Reylen's view. He goes back into the shack. Reylen quells a momentary panic attack and checks the sensors. Thermals show the man bringing out another box, this one a little taller and rounded. "Keep it cool," he says with a smile and heads over to the other shack.

Reylen drives off to finish the delivery. Jumping back in, he looks around. He was about to put the bike on autopilot when he hears the sound of drone rotors shredding dry leaves in the trees behind him. He immediately swerves off the road and into the trees, weaving between trunks for cover. Silenced gunfire snaps as it tears bark from trees and rocks from the ground. Going deeper into the foliage, Reylen sees a drone fast approaching and slams on his brakes, raising his rear tire, which the drone bounces into before veering off into the branches of the trees.

Dodging more gunfire, Reylen swerves around a large tree and nearly collides with a second drone on the other side. Without thinking, he ducks under it and drags his bike around ina a spray of dirt and dead leaves. Snatching up a fallen branch, he swings it into the drone's rotor and brings it crashing down. Coming around, Reylen accelerates back into the foliage. He feels the impact of metal on metal as a third drone gets a lucky shot on his bike. Reylen runs deeper into the woods. He takes a beating riding through a briar patch, but the pursuing rotodrone doesn't fare any better and gets tangled up, unable to give chase.

For another klick, Reylen moves through the woods, hoping no one is keeping track of him. As he gets close to the scattered illumination of Puyallup barrens, he checks on the cargo. The package is mostly intact, but there's a wetness; white fluid stains the saddle bag. He opens up the container and finds three vials in a nitrogen refrigeration unit; one vial is mostly empty. The label on each shows a smiling cow and the words "2% fat."

Stunned, Reylen can't help but smile. "Huh, it really was a milk run ..."

ADVANCED DRIVING RULES

Advanced Driving Rules are new optional rules for expanding the use of vehicles and vehicle combat in a *Shadowrun* campaign. They further enhance the rigger's role with more functionality and risk/reward options, as well as adding some distinction between vehicle types. Several of these actions can be used even when not everyone is in a vehicle. Advanced driving rules revolve around five components in combat: Speed, Terrain, Control, Range, and Actions.

Vehicle chase/combat can end in four ways:

1. A vehicle escapes by getting beyond Extreme range in a chase.
2. A vehicle's handling is reduced to 0 in a Combat Turn. This means that the vehicle has been pinned and has no room to escape.
3. A vehicle's Acceleration and Speed are reduced to 0 in a Combat Turn. This again means that the vehicle is stuck and cannot get any momentum to escape.
4. Vehicle's condition monitor is filled, meaning the vehicle is destroyed.

SPEED

Speed is controlled by the pilot of the vehicle as he accelerates or decelerates in chase/combat. The vehicle still has a maximum Speed and an Acceleration limit to how quickly a pilot can change speeds in a Combat Turn (p. 199, *SR5*). Speed is defined as a general value rather than a rate of meters per turn (p. 199, *SR5*) allowing the use of Speed as a modifier in some vehicle actions. Some actions can also temporarily reduce another vehicle's Speed or Acceleration. Note that the Speed value is relative only to the vehicle classification. Later in this chapter are additional modifiers to add when mixing vehicle combat with different vehicle types and against pedestrians.

TERRAIN

Terrain is the situational combat modifier where the vehicle combat is taking place. It consists of all the environmental and situational obstacles that the pilot faces when performing actions. When a player is using a vehicle or drone, the gamemaster sets this modifier. All vehicle actions have a threshold that includes this modifier, though basic driving does not require the use of this threshold modifier unless the gamemaster requests it. (If you're driving in heavy traffic and want to be on time to a meet, you may have to roll.) There are

TERRAIN MODIFIER EXPANDED (P. 201, *SR5*)

DESCRIPTION	VARIABLE	DETAIL
Open	+0	Highways, flat plains, open sea, clear sky
Light	+1	Main street thoroughfares, rolling hills, dock areas, intracity air traffic
Restricted	+2	Side streets, light woods, rocky mountain slopes, light traffic, shallow waters, heavy air traffic
Obstructed	+3	Low-altitude flying over heavy terrain, high traffic, riptide currents
Tight	+4	Back alleys, heavy woods, steep slopes, driving against traffic, swamp, heavy rapids, flying through winding canyons/cityscape
Impossible	+6	Flying at street level through a city, ten-meter waves and hurricane winds, driving in an office building, situations where you just don't want someone to tell you the odds!

vehicle actions that can change this modifier, but only with the approval of the gamemaster.

CONTROL

Control is keeping the vehicle doing what you want it to do without crashing. Every Combat Turn, a pilot must make a Control Vehicle Complex Action (p. 203, SR5) to keep the vehicle under control. Riggers may opt to spend Edge for Zen Control (p. 177) instead of using a Complex Action. If a Control Vehicle action is not taken in a Combat Turn, then all characters within the vehicle receive a –2 dice pool modifier to all their actions in the following Combat Turn until a Control Vehicle action is taken. The vehicle is considered Out of Control. If a pilot doesn't take a Control Vehicle action in the Combat Turn while the vehicle is considered Out of Control, then the autopilot (Pilot program if it hasn't been disabled or a vehicle running GridGuide) will take over at the end of the Combat Turn. If there is no autopilot to take over, then Newton's first law takes over until the vehicle finds something immobile to meet. The end result should be very unpleasant for all involved.

The factory-installed autopilot will obey traffic laws (slowing down to the speed limit, using turn signals, etc.) and will not take evasive action against attacks. If the vehicle is damaged, the autopilot program will find the nearest location that is safe for passengers and crew to exit from (a plane will land, a ship will find shore, a car exits traffic, and so on).

RANGE

Range is a requirement for many actions and attacks. Range can describe a specific distance measured in meters (mostly for ground vehicles), or simply an approximate degree of separation (especially for aircraft). In either case, it's the range category that matters.

CHASE RANGE

RANGE	ENVIRONMENT APPROX. DISTANCE (M)
Close	0–2
Short	2–10
Medium	11–50
Long	51–150
Extreme	151–300
Spotter (only with aircraft)	301–500

VEHICLE ACTIONS

With the exception of passenger actions, each vehicle action requires a Vehicle Skill + Reaction [Handling] (X) Threshold test. The X in the threshold is based on the terrain plus other modifiers, such as Speed and stunts. Each vehicle action describes the threshold, along with the modifiers added. As always, the VCR rating reduces this threshold (p. 199, SR5). Many actions have an optimum Speed in order to be performed perfectly. Pilots can increase their Speed by an amount up to their Acceleration value (or decrease it by one) in any Combat Turn in order to meet the required Speed to perform the vehicle action. If there is an optimum Speed for the vehicle action, then a Speed modifier value equal to the absolute value difference between the vehicle's current Speed and the action's ideal Speed is added to the threshold of the action.

Vehicle test modifiers (p. 201, SR5) still apply to all vehicle actions. Unless stated otherwise, actions here are Complex Actions.

GENERAL ACTIONS

CHANGE LINKED DEVICE MODE

(P. 202, SR5)

Change Linked Device is a Free Action

CHANGE SPEED

(ANY SPEED)

Change Speed is a Simple Action, allowing the pilot to adjust their Speed value. Speed can be increased by increments up to the Acceleration value in a Combat Turn, but braking or deceleration with this action can only reduce Speed by 1 per Combat Turn.

BOOTLEG TURN

(ANY RANGE, ANY SPEED)

When you find your target vehicle going in the opposite direction and you need to chase it down, the driver makes a Vehicle Skill + Reaction [Handling] (Terrain + Speed) Test. The Speed portion of the threshold is the Speed value of the target vehicle. Net hits put the acting vehicle in a chase position behind the target vehicle. With one net hit, the chasing vehicle is behind the target vehicle at Extreme range; each additional net hit moves the chasing vehicle one category closer, up to Close range (net hits beyond that have no effect).

CATCH UP/BREAK AWAY

(ANY RANGE, ANY SPEED)

A vehicle may wish to close the distance between them and another vehicle, or increase it. Either way, the driver makes an opposed Vehicle Skill + Reaction [Han-

dling] (*) Test. Threshold is terrain + the current Speed difference between acting vehicle and target. If the acting vehicle has the current fastest speed of all vehicles, then the threshold is just terrain. Every hit above the threshold allows the vehicle to shift one range category toward or away from her opponent, up to the vehicle's Acceleration value. If the acting vehicle is the chaser, net hits can shift the acting vehicle to right behind the pursued vehicle, or even in front of the chased vehicle if they get enough hits. If this action results in the acting vehicle moving the range value beyond Extreme range, the pursuing vehicle(s) are each allowed a final Vehicle Skill + Reaction [Handling] (terrain + current Speed difference) Test. Each net hit reduces the chased vehicle's range shift by 1. If the acting car still has enough successes to put them beyond Extreme range, then she has gotten away and the pursuit ends.

If an aircraft is chasing the acting vehicle, then there is the Spotter range that's farther out than Extreme. If the acting vehicle shifts the range further than that, then even the aircraft has lost sight of the acting vehicle.

CONTROL VEHICLE

(P. 203, SR5)

This is a Complex Action that keeps the vehicle under control for the Combat Turn. It's only needed during vehicle combat, not daily operation.

CRAZY IVAN

(ANY RANGE, ANY SPEED)

Crazy Ivan is the nautical term for subs to check if someone is following them. In this, the action is to check if a vehicle/drone is following them. The acting vehicle makes a few unexpected turns (called Crazy Ivans) to see if any vehicles react. The vehicle being chased makes a Vehicle Skill + Reaction [Handling] (terrain) Test. Each net hit reduces the Sensor or Perception Test threshold in finding pursuing vehicles.

CUT OFF

(SHORT RANGE ONLY)

The acting vehicle makes a sudden move to cut off a

target vehicle that is behind it, forcing it to crash. Make a Vehicle Skill + Reaction [Handling] (terrain) Opposed Test. If the acting vehicle achieves more hits, the target vehicle must make an immediate Vehicle Test to avoid crashing, with a threshold equal to the terrain + net hits on the test.

DISCREET PURSUIT

(ANY RANGE, ANY SPEED)

Sometimes you just want to follow a vehicle to see where it goes without being detected; other times you want to slowly sneak up on the target. The closer you are, however, the riskier it is to follow another vehicle. The acting vehicle makes a Vehicle Skill + Reaction [Handling] (Terrain + Range) Test. Range values are (Close 5, Short 3, Medium 2, Long 1, Extreme 0). Net hits from this test increase the threshold value for detecting the acting vehicle, up to 1 + the current terrain modifier. If the terrain rating is 0, the maximum increase is 1.

DRIVEBY/BROADSIDE

(MEDIUM OR SHORT RANGE, OPTIMUM SPEED 2)

This action gives passengers in the acting vehicle a steady, clear field of fire as it speeds past the target vehicle. When passengers are shooting at multiple targets (using burst fire or full auto), the driver makes a Vehicle Skill + Reaction [Handling] (Terrain + Speed) Test. Net hits add to the passenger's dice pool according to the rules for Teamwork Tests (p. 49, SR5). If there are multiple passengers, the pilot can divide the net hits among the passengers shooting, up to their skill in dice.

FIRE A VEHICLE WEAPON

(P. 203, SR5)

A driver or passenger may fire a vehicle-mounted weapon.

END RUN

There is a limit to the paths of vehicle pursuit. If there is difference in size or type of acting and pursuing vehicles, the gamemaster may increase the threshold for the Like a Glove action by 2 for the acting vehicle. If the acting vehicle succeeds, then the pursuit ends as the path the acting vehicle took is impossible for the pursuer to follow. This may be a watercraft submerging when pursued by regular ships, a microdrone down the drain, or even a car crossing the tracks before a train arrives.

HOLD IT TOGETHER BABY

(RIGGER ONLY, ANY RANGE, ANY SPEED)

When the condition monitor of a vehicle is completely filled, it cannot be driven any further. While the rigger is jumped into a vehicle, she may spend a point of Edge with an action in a Combat Turn to continue operating the vehicle. This must be done every Combat Turn—otherwise the vehicle becomes a brick with momentum. This doesn't remove the dice pool penalties when performing an action.

LIKE A GLOVE

(ANY RANGE, ANY SPEED)

Normally the change of terrain modifiers is dependent on the story and how the vehicle is traveling, but with this vehicle action, the character takes charge of the change—basically, the driver/pilot moves in a path that others find challenging, making it more difficult for them to be in the same area. Characters must decide which category they want to be their new modifier, and then make a Vehicle Skill + Reaction [Handling] (terrain) Test, with the terrain modifier being the new value chosen. The new terrain must have a higher modifier than the existing terrain. If the acting vehicle fails, it takes ramming damage based on acting vehicle's Speed + the selected terrain modifier. After resisting damage, the vehicle continues with the old terrain modifiers. If successful, any opposing vehicles must make a Vehicle Test with the new modifier. If they fail, increase the distance between the acting vehicle and opposing vehicles by 2 and subtract 2 dice in any Catch Up/Break Away vehicle action made by opposing vehicles until the terrain modifier changes. This new modifier lasts until the end of combat.

PICKUP

(CLOSE RANGE, OPTIMUM SPEED 2)

This is a tricky vehicle action where the pilot slides his vehicle toward a target and picks him up without stopping. The vehicle must have a vehicle entrance wide enough to pick up the target, most often an open door. If successful, the target is considered inside the vehicle and given the usual benefits (see **Damage and Passengers**, p. 205, SR5). Failure means ... well, see ramming rules (p. 204, SR5). An unwilling target may avoid extraction by this vehicle action by an Opposed Gymnastics Test. The target must get more net hits than the pilot and meet a threshold equal to the speed of the vehicle, otherwise—*splat*.

PIT

(SHORT RANGE ONLY, ANY SPEED)

A PIT vehicle action (precision immobilization technique) is done when an acting vehicle attempts to force a vehicle in front of it to crash. Make a Reaction + Vehicle Skill [Handling] (terrain) Opposed Test. If the acting vehicle achieves more hits, the target vehicle's handling is reduced by the number of net hits. If the target vehicle's handling is reduced to 0, it has become pinned by the acting vehicle. The acting vehicle may also stop and spend a Complex Action to keep the target vehicle pinned. If the acting vehicle fails, reduce its current speed by the deficit in hits.

RAM

(SHORT RANGE ONLY, ANY SPEED)

The acting vehicle attempts to collide with a target vehicle. Make a Vehicle Skill + Reaction [Handling] (terrain) Opposed Test. If the ramming vehicle achieves more hits, the vehicles have collided. The base Damage Value of the attack is determined by the ramming vehicle's Body and Speed, as noted on the Ramming Damage Table, plus any net hits achieved. From behind, the ramming damage is calculated by Speed difference between the vehicles. From the side, use the Speed of the acting vehicle, and from the front, add the Speed of the acting and targeted vehicles. If the acting vehicle hits the target vehicle in any direction other than head on, the acting vehicle resists only half the damage (round up). If the acting vehicle hits the target head on, the acting vehicle takes full damage.

RAMMING DAMAGE TABLE

SPEED	DAMAGE VALUE
1–2	Body / 2
3–4	Body
5–6	Body x 2
7–8	Body x 3
9–10	Body x 5
11+	Body x 10

Note as stated later, Speed is relative. Aircraft damage from a ram is calculated at 3 times the current Speed when calculating damage.

SHAKE THINGS UP A BIT

(ANY RANGE, ANY SPEED)

With this action, the driver brushes against other vehicles or objects as she passes by, causing debris to fall into her wake and making pursuit more dificult. Air and sea vehicles could generate more turbulence or wake behind them. The driver must make a Vehicle Skill + Reaction [Handling] (Terrain) Test. If successful, terrain difficulty increases by 1 for the rest of the

Combat Turn for any vehicle actions made by vehicles following within 100 meters. This can be done once per Combat Turn.

SWITCH THE SIX

(ANY RANGE, ANY SPEED)

For most vehicles, weapon platforms are forward-facing. This means when the vehicle is chased, it can't fight back. A favorite tactic of pilots in aerial dogfights, Switch the Six enables the acting vehicle to trade places with a target vehicle behind him. This is a Vehicle Skill + Reaction [Handling] Opposed Test. For every range category above Close between the two vehicles, the target gets a +1 dice pool modifier to this opposed test. If successful, the acting vehicle is now behind the target vehicle at Extreme range. Each net hit puts the acting vehicle one range category closer to the target.

ZEN CONTROL

(RIGGER ONLY, ANY RANGE, ANY SPEED)

Once rigged into a vehicle, blood and high-octane fuel flows just the same for the character. He is subconsciously aware of his surroundings and involuntary functions keep the vehicle steady. A rigger may spend an Edge point in one action per Combat Turn to keep the vehicle under control instead of making a Piloting Test. This can only be done for the vehicle/drone that a rigger has jumped into.

VEHICLE TEST

(P. 203, SR5)

A forced action to check if the vehicle is still under control.

USE SENSORS

(P. 202, SR5)

This is a Simple Action to use sensors.

USE SIMPLE DEVICE

(P. 202, SR5)

Simple Action to manually activate/deactivate a device.

GROUND VEHICLE ACTIONS

CLEAR EXIT

(ANY RANGE, OPTIMUM SPEED 1)

A challenging stunt where the driver exits the vehicle while it's still in motion and remains poised enough to take a Simple Combat Action (hopefully while on their feet). The vehicle may continue on its journey controlled or uncontrolled. The character must be able to exit on the ground. A character can always exit a vehi-

EXAMPLE VEHICLE CHASE

Sherman has been assigned to follow Mr. X's car to see where he's going and who he's meeting. He's sent Itchee (a Dragonfly drone) and Scratchee (a Wolfhound drone) to follow at a medium range (11 to 50 meters behind the target). Sherman is rigged into Itchee. It's evening with light city traffic (terrain threshold is 2), so hopefully Mr. X doesn't notice the drones. Sherman attempts to bring Itchee up to Medium range. Sherman tries Discreet Pursuit and orders Scratchee to do the same but at Long range (terrain 2 plus Long 1). Mr. X doesn't see anything (perception), but he tells his driver to check. The driver attempts a Crazy Ivan (p. 175) then checks sensors. While he didn't see Sherman's Itchee, Scratchee has been spotted. Mr X's driver tries to Break Away (p. 174), but fails. He then shakes things up a bit, hoping to help get away. Sherman swears as things got public real fast as a Lone Star Roto-Drone drops into a nearby intersection. Sherman decides not to pursue and tells the team to try plan B.

BEHIND VEHICLE SCENE 1

Sherman has a control rig Rating 2. Mr. X's chauffeur has no control rig.

Sherman performs a Discreet Pursuit action and rolls a Pilot Aircraft + Reaction Test with a threshold of 2 (terrain 2 plus Medium range 2, minus 2 for his control rig). Sherman gets 4 hits. This means 2 net hits, which means Perception and Sensor Tests to notice his pursuit have their thresholds increased by 2.

Scratchee also performs the Discreet Pursuit action, Vehicle Skill Test with a threshold of 3 (terrain 2 plus Long range 1). Scratchee has a dice pool of 8 and gets 3 hits, which means no change.

Mr. X's chauffeur performs a Crazy Ivan action. With a threshold of 2, he gets 4 hits, which counters the Discreet Pursuit by 2.

The chauffeur then rolls Perception + Intuition [Sensors] vs. Sherman's Sneaking + Reaction [Handling] and Scratchee's Pilot rating + Stealth autosoft [Handling]

Mr. X's chauffeur loses 3 dice due to the signature size of his pursuers (drone).

The chauffeur rolls 3 hits, Sherman rolls 4 hits, Scratchee rolls 3 hits.

With Discreet Pursuit, Sherman adds 2 hits. With Crazy Ivan, Sherman and Scratchee lose 2 hits.

This means: The chauffeur has 3 hits, Sherman has 4 hits, and Scratchee has 1 hit.

This means that the chauffeur has spotted Scratchee following him. Because the chauffeur pulled a Crazy Ivan, it becomes apparent to everyone that something is going on. The gamemaster determines that a Lone Star Roto-Drone will investigate the erratic traffic behavior.

cle while moving, though they might suffer road rash (see Bailout, p. 179). The character must make a Vehicle Skill + Reaction [Handling] (Speed + Terrain) Test. If successful, the character can make a single Simple Combat Action this Combat Turn. If unsuccessful, see Bailout.

DRIFT

(ANY RANGE, OPTIMUM SPEED 2)

Drift is the intentional oversteering of a vehicle causing loss of traction while maintaining control. In racing, drifting allows for faster vehicle actions through turns as the vehicle slides into the new forward direction. Successful use of this action adds +1 die to any Catch Up/Break Away test made in the same Combat Turn. The character must make a Vehicle Skill + Reaction [Handling] (Speed + Terrain) Test.

MAKE A HOLE

(MEDIUM RANGE, OPTIMUM SPEED 4)

This vehicle is going to plow through the terrain to give following vehicles that are at Medium or Short Range an easier path to follow. The character must make a Vehicle Skill + Reaction [Handling] (Speed + Terrain) Test. Each net hit reduces the terrain modifier by 1 for following vehicles for this Combat Turn. The acting vehicle takes (Body/2) + terrain modifier in damage.

AIRCRAFT VEHICLE ACTIONS

LEAF ON THE WIND

(ANY RANGE, OPTIMUM SPEED 0)

Unlike ground vehicles, when aircraft have been completely damaged or have their Speed reduced to 0, they become gravity-controlled projectiles waiting to crash. The pilot may still come out of this alive; by spending (not burning) a point of Edge, they can make an immediate Vehicle Skill + Reaction [Handling] (terrain + damage penalty) Test, where net hits reduce the damage penalty during their control test to lessen the impact when "landing."

FALLING LEAF

(ANY RANGE, OPTIMUM SPEED 2)

Aircraft don't normally stop in midair. With this action, a fixed-wing aircraft can stall itself without going into a spin. The character must make a Vehicle Skill + Reaction [Handling] (Speed + Terrain) Test. In a chase, the use of the Falling Leaf action drops the acting vehicle out of aerial combat. Net hits add to the distance between acting vehicle and pursuing vehicles as the aircraft drops out of the sky. Speed of the acting vehicle is reduced to 0 after performing this action. A glitch in this test puts the vehicle out of control; players must make a Vehicle Skill + Reaction [Handling] (Handling)

Test. If they meet the threshold, the Handling of the vehicle is unchanged (the particular nature of this test means generating net hits typically will not happen); for each net miss on the test, Handling of their vehicle is reduced by one. On a critical glitch, the pilot takes a –4 dice pool penalty on the test.

STRAFE

(MEDIUM OR SHORT RANGE, OPTIMUM SPEED 2)

With this vehicle action, the driver of the vehicle makes a Vehicle Skill + Reaction [Handling] (Terrain + Speed) Test. Net hits add to subsequent Fire a Vehicle Weapon actions done with this vehicle in the same Combat Turn as this action. The disadvantage is that the vehicle cannot make a Catch Up or Break Away action in that same Combat Turn.

DRONE VEHICLE ACTIONS

SWARM

(CLOSE OR SHORT RANGE, ANY SPEED)

Used with multiple drones, this action allows pilots controlling the drones to coordinate an attack more efficiently, dancing in a deadly ballet. When rigged into one drone, the driver makes a Vehicle Skill + Reaction [Handling] (Terrain + number of drones) Test. If successful, net hits are added to the dice pool for any drone involved in the test for any subsequent attacks during the same Combat Turn per the rules for Teamwork Tests. If unsuccessful, the drones are as coordinated as the Three Stooges, and each receives a penalty to its actions equal to the difference between the threshold and number of hits. This action must be performed with two or more drones.

PASSENGER/PILOT VEHICLE ACTIONS

BAILOUT

Bailout gets the character out of the vehicle as fast as possible. This Simple Action is not the most graceful of exits, but it gets the character clear of the relative danger of the vehicle. The character resists (Speed x 3) Stun damage from exiting a land or watercraft while in motion (if you exit a moving, flying aircraft without a parachute, you're likely facing more damage than you can adequately soak). Characters may take additional physical damage based on terrain, falling, or water depth. This additional damage is up to the gamemaster. If the acting character is attempting to get more than himself out of the vehicle, like rescuing someone, this action becomes a Complex Action.

FIRE WEAPON

(P. 203, SR5)

GRAPPLE/BOARD

(CLOSE RANGE, ANY SPEED)

This isn't your opening-the-door-to-get-in-the-car-parked-in-the-street challenge. This is the thing you do when you are traveling at 80 kph and you want to get in a vehicle you're chasing. Characters must make a Gymnastics + Strength [Physical] (Terrain) Test to move from one vehicle to the next. If there are no openings into the target vehicle, the character is considered to be hanging onto its outside surface. At the end of every Combat Turn while the car is moving, the character must make a Strength check to continue to hang on. If the target car makes a Break Away action (p. 174) while the character is on the outside, the character must make a Strength test with a threshold equal to the net hits from the Break Away test. If the character fails to get on the vehicle or falls off, he must resist (Speed x 3) Physical damage.

MELEE ATTACK

(CLOSE RANGE, ANY SPEED)

Like attacking mailboxes with a baseball bat, this action is the same as any melee attack action a character can do normally. Damage, however, is increased by the Speed of the vehicle. If the Speed of the vehicle is equal to or greater than the strength of the attacker, then the character must make a Strength test with a threshold equal to the Speed of the vehicle or lose the weapon after impact. Melee weapons can be added to vehicles to take on nearby targets. Such weapons use half the vehicle's Body for Strength and then add that to the Speed of the vehicle for damage.

WATERCRAFT VEHICLE ACTIONS

CAPSIZE

(CLOSE OR SHORT RANGE, ANY SPEED)

This action can be done as a ram, but it's more about using the acting vehicle's weight, engine wake, or thrust of water from the propeller/jet to compromise the target vehicle's buoyancy on water. Make a Vehicle Skill + Reaction [Handling] Opposed Test against the target vehicle. If the acting vehicle succeeds, the target vehicle's Speed and Acceleration are reduced by the net hits. If both attributes are reduced to 0, the vehicle has been swamped and is adrift. While Capsize is used for targeted watercraft, it can be attempted against land vehicles or aircraft if they are close to deep water, but add 2 to the target vehicle's dice pool for the Opposed Test. If successful, the target vehicle's engine sucks up water and stalls.

EXAMPLE VEHICLE COMBAT, SCENE 2

The team meets at a pub near the barrens to plan how they will find Mr. X. They don't realize that someone working for Mr. X dropped a Fly-Spy microdrone to keep tabs on them. They're too busy eating soy nachos and drinking synthbeer to notice the Fly-Spy.

The team exits the pub after the decker traces Mr. X to a hotel downtown. Unfortunately for them, Mr. X hired his own team after tracking them down. After a couple of synthbeers, no one notices the ganger, Thrasher, and his team slowing down in a Hyundai. Thrasher performs a Driveby, assisting his team. The gang opens up with autofire. Sherman, Manicore, and Nybbles are hit badly, but Samurai Jacques flees the scene with only a light wound.

After Samurai Jacques escapes, he finds himself in an abandoned building. Four Dragonfly drones follow him inside. They are equipped with blades and plan a death by a thousand paper cuts. In an elegant dance of speed and grace, they Swarm Jacques.

BEHIND VEHICLE SCENE 2

Team members make Perception Tests to see the Fly-Spy. Because of the drone's size, each runner reduces their dice pool by 3 to perceive it.

The Fly-Spy rolls Piloting + Stealth [Handling] vs. Perception + Intuition [Mental] for the runners. The Fly-Spy gets 4 hits, while the runners' best effort is 3 hits. The drone is not seen as it hovers quietly above the table.

Thrasher performs Driveby/Broadside for the pair of team members sitting in the back seat of his car with automatics.

Thasher has a Rating 1 control rig. The terrain is relatively light (+1 modifier), and the vehicle is moving at a Speed of 2. The threshold for the Driveby is 3. Thrasher gets 6 hits, but since he's in the Hyundai Shin-Hyung, the Handling of 5 reduces the hits to 5. Since this functions as a Teamwork Test, he gives 1 die to each ganger.

Both go full auto and split the dice pool between two runners apiece. The targeted characters are left feeling quite perforated.

Samurai Jacques comes face to face with four Dragonflies, one of which has a rigger jumped in. The rigger performs the Swarm action. Terrain modifier is 1, with 3 drones, and control rig Rating 1; all of that combines to make the threshold 3. The rigger gets 5 hits, which becomes 2 net hits. So for the remaining Combat Turn, the three drones get an additional two dice when they attack.

The drones attack using a blade weapon. When they hit successfully, their damage is half Body + Speed. Since they are flying and their Speed is 3, while Body adds nothing, the damage is 3.

When Jacques tries to attack the drones, he takes a –4 dice pool penalty: –2 for Speed and –2 for the drone's size.

DRIVING WITH STYLE

Stunts are what separate the riggers from the Sunday drivers. With advanced driving rules, stunts have added benefits that a pilot can choose from. They can be performed alone or added to other vehicle actions. The rating of the stunt is chosen by the pilot. While there is no upper limit, the gamemaster may dictate the rating of a specific stunt. If done alone, it's a Complex Action using Vehicle Skill + Reaction [Handling] (stunt rating + terrain). If done as part of another action, the stunt rating is added to the threshold. Any action that includes a stunt (or a stunt alone) that fails must make an immediate vehicle test with a dice penalty equal to the stunt rating or crash.

Note only riggers and drivers of vehicles may perform stunts. Pilot programs are just too logical to try actions this crazy.

PEDAL TO THE METAL

Terrain and Speed modifiers work when the vehicles are of the same size and type. When the vehicles are not equivalent in size or type, then the modifiers can increase or decrease. With regard to speed, aircraft are the fastest, otherwise they fall out of the sky. Consider their speed at three times the value when calculating speed modifiers for vehicle actions.

STUNT BENEFITS*

- Add stunt rating as hits to determine range change (this can go beyond the Acceleration limit of the vehicle).
- Add rating as dice to soak vehicle damage from an attack or crash.
- Add rating to reduce another vehicle's Speed or Handling for this Combat Turn.
- Add rating as hits to avoid being struck by an attack.
- Add rating to handling for any action in this Combat Turn.
- Add rating as dice to one Social skill test. Target audience must be able to have seen the stunt or as far as they are concerned, it didn't happen.
- Some crazy stunt for some other benefit.** (For example: Drive a vehicle through the air, rolling it just enough to have a hook from an overhanging crane knock a bomb off the bottom of the vehicle before it explodes.

*These stunts can be done multiple times, but cannot add more than +4 dice to a test or increase a limit (Handling, Acceleration, etc.) to more than twice its value in any given Combat Turn.

** The player must also spend a point of Edge to attempt this stunt, receiving the customary bonus dice for using Edge. Gamemaster should determine difficulty.

Terrain should also scale with the size of the vehicle. While a car driving through heavy traffic is difficult (+3), a drone pursuing the car would be less inhibited by the terrain. The gamemaster should figure out the base terrain modifier value for the most common vehicle type, then reduce or increase the terrain modifiers by the size difference to the common vehicle. In this example, if the Lockheed optidrone (small drone) is pursuing a Honda Spirit through heavy traffic, the drone would only be at a +2 terrain modifier.

Size modifiers also affect other skill tests, such as perception and actions that target vehicles. Target size modifiers in this case add or subtract dice when engaging with target. Shooting and hitting a jumbo jet is quite easy (unless it's moving high in the air).

Speed is relative to hitting a target. It is hard to hit a small drone, it's even harder to hit a small drone that's moving fast. For people, walking and running modifiers already exist. Vehicles can move much faster compared to a person and so need special consideration. When calculating modifiers of a stationary object (turret, etc.) or pedestrian, if a target vehicle or drone is moving (that is, has Speed greater than 0), add the vehicle's Speed as a negative dice pool modifier to hitting said vehicle. For other vehicle actions (Ram, Chase, etc.), adjust the speed by the mode of movement using a multiplier, as follows: 0.8 for Water, 1 for Ground, 3 for Rotor, and 4 for Jet.

TARGET SIZE MODIFIERS

SIZE	MODIFIER	EXAMPLE
Minuscule	–3	Micro drones
Tiny	–2	Mini drones
Small	–1	Small drones
Average	—	Vehicles and drones (Body 8 or less)
Bulky	+1	Vehicles and drones (Body 9 to 14)
Large	+2	Vehicles and drones (Body 15 to 20)*
Huge	+3	Vehicles and drones (Body greater than 20)*

*If the vehicle has 10 or more seats, add +2 to Body when calculating size for every 10 seats.

EXAMPLE

EXAMPLE VEHICLE COMBAT SCENE 3

It's combat biker season. Unfortunately for the team, this means a little amateur hour in the arena. Rigger Daft takes a bike out with the Crimson Crush, a minor-league team. While combat biking is dangerous, someone out there is getting serious in taking out players for higher bets. The odds are 10 to 1 against the Redmond Tiger, so guess who's getting targeted? Daft drove around the bumps and cinderblock walls. The Redmond Tigers are on the offensive. Daft is spotted by two Tigers and chase begins.

Tiger 1 gets up in his face and gets into an ugly punching match. Tiger 2 pulls into the lead. As Tiger 1 pulls away, Tiger 2 tries to cut off Daft. Daft is very skilled and avoids Tiger 2's antics.

Daft takes the lead to a small jump, where he flips into a handstand and swings a leg out, kicking Tiger 1. He uses this stunt to intimidate Tiger 2. As Daft comes up aggressively on Tiger 2, the latter bugs out.

Daft doesn't pursue and continues to drive around the zone, looking for someone out of the ordinary. Daft sees a small structure where a man is perched on a wooden structure with what appears to be a sniper rifle. Daft makes a beeline toward it. He then jumps off, letting his vehicle roll into the structure. The sniper has no chance to react as the motorcycle rams into the structure, collapsing it.

BEHIND VEHICLE SCENE 3

Terrain modifier for this situation is 2. Daft's Speed is currently 2. Daft has a control rig with Rating 2, Tiger 1 and Tiger 2 have no control rig—they're just really good.

Tiger 1 and Tiger 2 dive past Daft and perform a Bootleg Turn to pursue. Each makes a vehicle test with a threshold of 4. Tiger 1 gets 6 hits, Tiger 2 gets 7 hits. This means 2 and 3 net hits. This puts Tiger 1 at Medium and Tiger 2 at Short range.

Daft tries to lose them through a Break Away action, increasing his Speed to 3. Daft isn't jumped in, but he has the highest Speed of the vehicles involved in the chase, so he has a threshold of 2. He gets 2 net hits; if nothing else changes in this initiative pass, Tiger 1 will fall back to Extreme range, while Tiger 2 will drop to Long.

They don't want to lose ground, though, so Tiger 1 and Tiger 2 attempt to Catch Up. They increase their Speed to 3, making the threshold for the test the terrain modifier only, which is 2. They both get 4 net hits. Tiger 1 will finish the pass at Close range, while Tiger 2 will move in front of Daft.

Tiger 1 uses the Close range to make a melee attack against Daft.

Tiger 2 pulls a Cut Off maneuver. The threshold is 2 for both riders, giving them even odds. Tiger 2 gets 2 net hits, while Daft luckily gets 3. He avoids crashing. If the successes were reversed, Daft would have had to make a vehicle test at threshold of 3 or crash his bike.

Daft tries a melee attack against Tiger 1. He spends Edge to get more dice as he's also adding a Rating 2 stunt to the action to boost a subsequent Social test. With a threshold of 4, he manages to get 4 net hits.

Daft's next action is to play chicken with Tiger 2. He makes an Opposed Intimidation test using the additional 2 dice from the stunt, and Daft scares off Tiger 2 from pursuit.

Daft finds his target sitting in a wooden scaffold structure. He heads for the structure at full throttle (Speed 3) and then attempts a Clear Exit to get clear of the motorcycle as he sends it into a collision. His threshold is 4—2 for the terrain and 2 more for being beyond the optimum speed. While he makes the attempt, he fails to get enough hits, so while he exits, it's not graceful. The motorcycle crashes into the wooden structure, taking the motorcycle's Body in damage. Daft also resists 9 boxes of Stun damage from the road rash. Not pretty, but effective.

MOTORCYCLES

NAME	HANDL	SPEED	ACCEL	BODY	ARMOR	PILOT	SENS	SEATS	AVAIL	COST	REF
Cocotaxi HT	4/2	3	2	5	4	1	1	3	—	4,000¥	p. 139, *Hard Targets*
Cyclops	4/4	4	2	4	4	1	1	1	—	6,500¥	p. 43
Falcon-EX	3/5	2/3	1/2	7	9	1	1	2	—	10,000¥	p. 43
Growler	4/5	3/4	1	5	5	1	1	1	—	5,000¥	p. 462, *SR5*
Horseman	3/1	3	2	4	3	2	2	1	—	12,000¥	p. 41
Kaburaya	5/3	6	3	5	4	1	2	1	—	17,000¥	p. 44
Mirage	5/3	6	3	5	6	1	2	1	—	8,500¥	p. 462, *SR5*
Mustang	4/4	3	2	8	6	1	1	2	3	11,000¥	p. 46
Nightmare	4/3	5	2	8	8	2	3	2	—	22,000¥	p. 45
Nodachi	4/3	5	2	8	9	2	2	2	12R	28,000¥	p. 45
Revolution	5/3	4	3	6	9	2	2	1	4	8,000¥	p. 42
Scoot	4/3	3	1	4	4	1	1	1	—	3,000¥	p. 462, *SR5*
Scorpion	4/3	4	2	8	9	1	2	1	—	12,000¥	p. 462, *SR5*
Spartan	3/4	4	2	7	6	2	2	1	—	11,500¥	p. 44
Terrier	5/2	2	1	2	2	2	2	1	—	4,500¥	p. 42
Zip	3/2	3	1	6	4	1	2	1	—	3,500¥	p. 44

CARS

NAME	HANDL	SPEED	ACCEL	BODY	ARMOR	PILOT	SENS	SEATS	AVAIL	COST	REF
Americar	4/3	3	2	11	6	1	2	4	—	16,000¥	p. 463, *SR5*
Comet	4/4	3	2	11	6	2	2	4	—	20,000¥	p. 49
Artemis	4/2	3	3	9	6	1	1	4	—	17,000¥	p. 187, *Stolen Souls*
Chameleon	4/2	4	1	10	4	1	1	4	—	14,000¥	p. 47
Concordat	5/4	5	2	12	12	2	4	4	10	65,000¥	p. 463, *SR5*
Dynamit	5/1	9	3	10	3	2	3	2	8	98,000¥	p. 50
Equus	3/3	4/3	2	12	10	2	3	4	—	40,000¥	p. 51
FunOne	3/1	3	1	6	4	2	1	2/1	—	8,500¥	p. 47
Gladius	7/3	9	4	10	5	3	5	2	14	154,000¥	p. 49
Jackrabbit	4/3	3	2	8	4	1	2	2	—	10,000¥	p. 462, *SR5*
Journey	4/3	3	3	9	5	1	1	4	—	17,000¥	p. 187, *Stolen Souls*
Longboard	4/3	3	2	12	6	1	2	6	—	31,000¥	p. 52
MetaWay	4/2	4	1	10	4	1	2	1	—	24,000¥	p. 47
Phoenix	4/2	6	3	10	6	2	3	4	—	32,000¥	p. 50
Shin-Hyung	5/4	6	3	10	6	1	2	4	—	28,500	p. 463, *SR5*
Spirit	3/2	4	2	8	6	1	2	2	—	12,000¥	p. 463, *SR5*
Westwind 3000	6/4	7	3	10	8	3	5	2	13	110,000¥	p. 463, *SR5*
Xenon	3/2	4/3	2	8	6	2	2	4	—	18,000¥	p. 47

LIMOS

NAME	HANDL	SPEED	ACCEL	BODY	ARMOR	PILOT	SENS	SEATS	AVAIL	COST	REF
Nightsky	4/3	4	2	15	15	3	5	8	16	320,000	p. 463, *SR5*
Phaeton	5/3	5/3	2	16	12	3	4	2/8	18	350,000¥	p. 52

TRUCKS

NAME	HANDL	SPEED	ACCEL	BODY	ARMOR	PILOT	SENS	SEATS	AVAIL	COST	REF
Armadillo	3/4	4	2	13	10	1	2	2/4	—	22,000¥	p. 54
Escalade	3/3	4	2	16	10	3	4	6	10	125,000¥	p. 57
Gopher	5/5	4	2	14	10	1	2	3	—	25,000¥	p. 463, *SR5*
Hauler	3/3	4/3	1	16	8	2	2	4/4	—	30,000¥	p. 56
Hotspur	4/5	6	3	16	12	2	2	2	8	60,000¥	p. 53
Minotaur	4/5	5	2	14	8	4	4	4	—	45,000¥	p. 53
Morgan	3/5	4	3	14	6	—	—	2	8	7,500¥	p. 52
Northstar	5/3	6	2	12	8	3	5	4	12	115,000¥	p. 56
Percheron	3/3	3	2	15	6	4	3	6	—	39,000¥	p. 54
Sidewinder	4/3	3	2	10	6	2	2	6	—	33,000¥	p. 187, *Stolen Souls*
Talon	4/3	4	2	12	6	2	2	5	—	30,000¥	p. 55
Trailblazer	3/4	3	2	12	6	1	2	4	—	32,000¥	p. 54
Watcher	3/3	3	3	9	8	1	3	5	4	40,000	p. 187, *Stolen Souls*

VANS

NAME	HANDL	SPEED	ACCEL	BODY	ARMOR	PILOT	SENS	SEATS	AVAIL	COST	REF
Bulldog	3/3	3	1	16	12	1	2	6	—	35,000¥	p. 463, *SR5*
Caravaner	3/2	4	1	12	8	2	2	7	—	28,000¥	p. 58
Chuck Wagon	2/2	3	1	16	5	2	2	2	—	40,000¥	p. 59
Econovan	3/2	4	1	14	8	2	2	10	—	30,000¥	p. 58
Endurance	3/3	4	3	14	6	1	2	8	—	35,000¥	p. 187, *Stolen Souls*
Roadmaster	3/3	3	1	18	18	3	3	8	8	52,000¥	p. 464, *SR5*
Rover Model 2072	5/5	4	2	15	12	2	4	6	10	68,000¥	p. 464, *SR5*
S-K LT-21	2/1	2	1	15	7	2	2	2	—	31,000¥	p. 187, *Stolen Souls*
Universe	3/3	4/3	1	14	8	3	2	2/14	—	30,000¥	p. 59

RVS

NAME	HANDL	SPEED	ACCEL	BODY	ARMOR	PILOT	SENS	SEATS	AVAIL	COST	REF
Chinook	3/2	4/3	1	14	12	2	2	10	—	145,000¥	p. 59
Outback	3/4	3/4	1	14	12	2	4	8	—	158,000¥	p. 59
Preserve	3/3	4/4	1	16	12	2	3	10	—	134,000¥	p. 59

TRACTOR/TRAILERS

NAME	HANDL	SPEED	ACCEL	BODY	ARMOR	PILOT	SENS	SEATS	AVAIL	COST	REF
Conestoga Trailblazer	2/1	2	1	14	6	2	1	2	4	75,000¥	p. 187, *Stolen Souls*
Hellhound	3/2	4/3	1	20	15	3	3	2	16R	150,000¥	p. 60
Trailer (Trailblazer)	1/1	1	1	20	6	2	1	—	—	20,000¥	p. 187, *Stolen Souls*

BUSES

NAME	HANDL	SPEED	ACCEL	BODY	ARMOR	PILOT	SENS	SEATS	AVAIL	COST	REF
Camellos HT	3/2	3	1	16	5	1	2	200	—	150,000¥	p. 139, *Hard Targets*
Omnibus	2/2	3	1	18	10	2	2	53	12	296,000¥	p. 62

COMMERCIAL

NAME	HANDL	SPEED	ACCEL	BODY	ARMOR	PILOT	SENS	SEATS	AVAIL	COST	REF
Commercial D-Compact	2/2	3	1	12	8	2	2	2	12	196,000¥	p. 63
Commercial D-series	2/2	3	1	16	10	2	2	2	12	248,000¥	p. 63
Commercial DD	2/2	3	1	20	12	2	2	2	12	312,000¥	p. 63
Commercial G—series	2/2	3	1	18	12	2	3	2	14	287,000¥	p. 62
Konstructors	2/2	3	1	24	18	4	3	2	16	365,000¥	p. 64
Ram Industrail Narrow	3/1	1	1	16	8	2	4	2	4	49,000¥	p. 187, *Stolen Souls*
Ram Industrial Large	2/1	1	1	16	8	2	4	2	4	51,000¥	p. 187, *Stolen Souls*

HOVERCRAFT

NAME	HANDL	SPEED	ACCEL	BODY	ARMOR	PILOT	SENS	SEATS	AVAIL	COST	REF
KVP—28	2/2	3	1	18	12	4	3	2	16	87,000¥	p. 64
Minnesota	4/4	4	2	14	9	3	3	2/12	12R	130,000¥	p. 65
Minsk	2/2	3	1	16	10	4	3	2	16	77,000¥	p. 65
Vodyanoy	3/3	4	3	16	16	1	2	3(10)	12F	84,000¥	p. 65

SECURITY/POLICE/MILITARY

NAME	HANDL	SPEED	ACCEL	BODY	ARMOR	PILOT	SENS	SEATS	AVAIL	COST	REF
Blitzkrieg	4/3	4	2	10	8	3	4	2	14R	46,000¥	p. 66
Charger	4/3	5	2	12	12	4	4	5	16R	65,000¥	p. 67
Command (General)	3/3	4	1	20	16	5	7	10	18R	344,000¥	p. 74
Goliath	3/2	4	2	16	16	3	3	8	20R	120,000¥	p. 70
i8 Interceptor	5/3	8	4	12	8	4	4	3	16R	114,000¥	p. 68
Luxus	5/5	5	3	18	16	5	6	8	14R	398,000¥	p. 73
Rhino	4/4	4	2	17	18	4	4	9	18R	225,000¥	p. 77
Stallion	3/4	5	3	16	12	3	3	4	16R	78,000¥	p. 71
Stürmwagon	5/4	4	2	17	18	4	5	10	20R	145,000¥	p. 75
Teufelkatze	5/4	5	3	16	16	3	3	7	16F	76,000¥	p. 71
Trailer (General)	3/3	3	1	20	16	3	7	1	18R	54,000¥	p. 74
Wolf II	3/3	3	2	24	12	2	2	6	20F	330,000¥	p. 77

WATERCRAFT

NAME	HANDL	SPEED	ACCEL	BODY	ARMOR	PILOT	SENS	SEATS	AVAIL	COST	REF
AirRanger	4	4	3	10	6	1	1	6	6	25,500¥	p. 92
AirRanger Heavy	4	4	3	12	6	1	1	5	8	35,500¥	p. 92
Aquavida 1	2	1	2	20	16	1	3	2/8	10	115,000¥	p. 90
Aquavida 2	2	1	2	20	16	1	3	4/8	12	135,000¥	p. 90
Classic 111	3	4	2	24	14	4	4	14	16	14,870,000¥	p. 88
Cottonmouth	5	7	4	8	4	3	3	4	12	120,000¥	p. 80
Cutlass	5	4	2	16	10	3	5	6	14R	96,000¥	p. 464, SR5
Electronaut	3	3	1	12	10	4	4	2	10	108,000¥	p. 464, SR5
Elysium	1/3	1/4	1/2	14	10	2	3	6	12	78,000¥	p. 85
Kingfisher	3	3	2	16	12	3	4	6	12	61,000¥	p. 92
Lake King	2	3	2	14	8	1	1	8	—	35,000¥	p. 90
Lamprey	3	2	1	6	6	1	3	4	—	14,000¥	p. 464, SR5
Manta Ray	4	5	3	9	6	1	1	3	—	16,000¥	p. 81
Mobius	3	3	2	36	14	6	5	22	36	84,985,000¥	p. 89
Nightrunner	5	6	3	12	6	3	4	6	10	56,000¥	p. 81
Otter	4	3	2	12	6	2	2	8	—	21,000¥	p. 464, SR5
Panther	1/3	2/5	1/3	18	10	2	3	8	12	135,000¥	p. 85
Riverine Military	5	5	2	20	20	6	6	8	20F	225,000¥	p. 92
Riverine Police	4	5	3	16	14	4	5	8	15R	154,000¥	p. 92
Riverine Security	4	5	3	16	12	4	4	8	15R	100,000¥	p. 92
Stingray	5	5	3	8	6	1	1	2	—	13,000¥	p. 81
Trident	1/3	4/5	2/3	16	10	2	3	6	12	125,000¥	p. 87
Trinity	5	6	3	10	6	1	1	3	8	37,000¥	p. 464, SR5
Triton	1	6	2	16	10	2	3	6	—	104,000¥	p. 88
Water Strider	3	2	1	8	5	2	2	1	16	11,000¥	p. 84
Waterbug	6	3	2	8	4	1	—	2	—	8,000¥	p. 83
Waterking	3	3	2	14	8	3	2	12	12	74,000¥	p. 79
Waveskipper	5	3	2	10	4	1	—	1	—	10,000¥	p. 84
Zodiac Scorpio	4	4	2	10	6	1	1	2/6	8	26,000¥	p. 82

AIRCRAFT

NAME	HANDL	SPEED	ACCEL	BODY	ARMOR	PILOT	SENS	SEATS	AVAIL	COST	REF
Agular GX-2	5	7	5	20	16	4	5	2	28F	500,000¥	p. 97
Agular GX-3AT	4	6	4	22	20	4	4	10	28F	550,000¥	p. 97
Banshee	6	8	4	20	18	4	6	12	24F	2,500,000¥	p. 465, *SR5*
Cessna C750	3	5	3	18	4	2	2	4	8	146,000¥	p. 464, *SR5*
Commuter	3	3	3	16	8	3	3	30	10	350,000¥	p. 465, *SR5*
Dragon	4	4	3	22	8	3	3	18	12	355,000¥	p. 464, *SR5*
Gryphon	5	8	7	24	24	4	5	2	28F	3,200,000¥	p. 103
Hound	5	4	3	16	16	2	4	12	13R	425,000¥	p. 464, *SR5*
"Krime Wing"	4	6	5	22	18	4	5	10 (20)	24F	2,275,000¥	p. 105
"Lift-Ticket" ALS-669	5	3	3	16	12	3	4	5	14	325,000¥	p. 102
LZP-2070	4	2	3	12	6	5	4	6	12	85,000¥	p. 106
"Mothership" LAVH	3	3	3	10	5	3	4	1	24R	50,000¥	p. 108
Nightwing	6	3	1	4	0	1	1	1	8	20,000¥	p. 464, *SR5*
PBY-70 Catalina II	4	3	3	22	14	3	4	16	12	250,000¥	p. 100
Sea Sprite	5	4	3	18	12	3	5	14	18R	400,000¥	p. 99
SKA-008	6	5	8	16	18	4	4	12	24R	525,000¥	p. 98
Stallion	5	5	4	16	16	4	4	8	12	440,000¥	p. 95
Tundra-9	3	4	3	20	10	3	3	24	12	300,000¥	p. 464, *SR5*
Venture	5	7	4	16	14	4	4	6	12F	400,000¥	p. 465, *SR5*
Wasp	5	5	3	10	8	3	3	1	12R	86,000¥	p. 465, *SR5*

DRONES

NAME	HANDL	SPEED	ACCEL	BODY	ARMOR	PILOT	SENS	SEATS	AVAIL	COST	REF
Ares KN-Y0											
Deimos	3	2G	1	6(0)	18	5	3	—	20F	220,000¥	p. 143
Eris	3	2G	1	6(0)	18	5	3	—	24F	270,000¥	p. 143
Phobos	3	2G	1	6(0)	18	5	3	—	16F	250,000¥	p. 143
Avenging Angel	3	6J	2	6(0)	12	6	6	—	40F	1,000,000¥	p. 145
Bloodhound	3	1G	1	2(0)	0	2	4	—	8	10,000¥	p. 136
Castle Guard	4/2	1G	1	2(0)	6	3	2	—	8R	10,000¥	p. 133
Cheetah	4	6G	2	2(0)	6	3	2	—	12R	14,000¥	p. 138
Condor	2	0R	0	1(1)	0	2	4	—	6R	4,000¥	p. 129
Crawler	4	1G	1	3	3	4	3	—	4	4,000¥	p. 466, *SR5*
Criado Juan	2	2G	1	2	0	2	2	—	2	8,000¥	p. 145
Dalmatian	5	5	3	5	5	3	3	—	6R	10,000¥	p. 466, *SR5*

DRONES, CONT.

NAME	HANDL	SPEED	ACCEL	BODY	ARMOR	PILOT	SENS	SEATS	AVAIL	COST	REF
Direktionssekretar	4	4G	2	4	3	4	4	—	12R	40,000¥	p. 148
Doberman	5	2G	1	4	4	3	3	—	4R	5,000¥	p. 466, *SR5*
Dragonfly	4	2R	1	1(0)	3	3	2	—	12R	4,000¥	p. 129
Duelist	3	1G	1	4	4	3	3	—	5R	4,500¥	p. 466, *SR5*
Evo Krokodil	3	2G/3W	1	3(1)	6	2	2	—	8R	12,000¥	p. 139
F-B Kull	3	4R	2	3(3)	0	3	2	—	4	10,000¥	p. 140
Ferret RPD-5X	4/2	1G	1	2(1)	3	3	3	—	8R	4,000¥	p. 132
Fly-Spy	4	1R	2	1	0	3	3	—	8	2,000¥	p. 466, *SR5*
Flying Eye	4	1R	2	1	0	3	3	—	8	2,000¥	p. 466, *SR5*
Garuda	6	3J/6J	2/4	2	2	4	3	—	20F	8,500¥	p. 149
Gerbil	4/2	2G	1	1(1)	0	2	2	—	4	2,000¥	p. 130
Goldfish	2/4	1W	1	0	0	2	2	—	6	500¥	p. 128
Gun Turret	—	—	—	2(0)	6	3	2	—	4R	4,000¥	p. 133
Hedgehog	3	1G	1	1(0)	0	2	3	—	8F	8,000¥	p. 129
Horizon CU^3	4	1R	1	1(1)	0	2	3	—	4	3,000¥	p. 130
Jardinero	2/4	1G	1	2(1)	0	2	2	—	4	2,000¥	p. 136
Job-a-Mat	—	—	—	2(2)	0	2	2	—	4	3,000¥	p. 137
Juggernaught	3	4G	1	6	12	3	3	—	14R	100,000¥	p. 147
Kanmushi	4	0G	1	0	0	3	3	—	8	1,000¥	p. 465, *SR5*
Kenchiku-Kikai	2	2G	1	5	3	2	2	—	8R	20,000¥	p. 146
Knight Errant P5	4/2	6G	2	2(1)	0	3	2	—	10R	8,000¥	p. 133
Kodiak	2/4	2G	1	6(2)	12	2	2	—	12R	40,000¥	p. 145
Krake	5	3W	4	2(0)	2	4	3	—	18F	10,000¥	p. 134
LEBD-2	4	2R	1	3(0)	9	4	4	—	12R	20,000¥	p. 140
Little Buddy	2	1G	1	1	0	2	2	—	4	2,000¥	p. 146
Lynx	5	4	2	6	12	3	3	—	10R	25,000¥	p. 466, *SR5*
Malakim	3	6R	2	4(0)	9	4	4	—	20F	40,000¥	p. 143
Matilda	1	2G	1	8	8	2	1	—	12R	18,000¥	p. 141
MediCart	5	5G	1	6(2)	5	4	4	—	6	10,000¥	p. 142
Microskimmer	3	1R	1	0	0	3	3	—	6	1,000¥	p. 465, *SR5*

DRONES, CONT.

NAME	HANDL	SPEED	ACCEL	BODY	ARMOR	PILOT	SENS	SEATS	AVAIL	COST	REF
Mini-Zep	2	0R	0	2(4)	0	2	2	4	4	2,000¥	p. 132
Mule	4	1G	1	4(3)	6	2	2	—	4	8,000¥	p. 141
Neptune	2	3W	1	5(0)	3	4	3	—	10R	17,500¥	p. 143
NoizQuito	4	3R	2	1	0	3	3	—	10R	2,000¥	p. 128
Optic-X2	4	4R	3	2	2	3	3	—	10	21,000¥	p. 466, SR5
Paladin	5	4G	1	5(0)	18	3	2	—	8R	5,000¥	p. 142
Pelican	4	2R	1	2(1)	0	2	2	—	2	4,000¥	p. 137
Pigeon 2.0	4	2R	1	1(1)	0	2	2	—	8	3,000¥	p. 129
Prairie Dog	2/4	2G	1	2(0)	3	3	4	—	12F	8,000¥	p. 134
Proletarian	4/2	2G	1	2(1)	0	2	2	—	6	4,000¥	p. 131
Remote Cyberhand	n/a	n/a	n/a	n/a	n/a	n/a	—	—	8	8,000¥	p. 130
Renraku Dove	4	2R	1	2(1)	0	2	2	—	4	5,000¥	p. 136
Roto-Drone	4	2R	2	4	4	3	3	—	6	5,000¥	p. 466, SR5
Sentry V	4/—	1G	1	2(0)	6	3	2	—	4R	4,000¥	p. 130
Seven											
Wheelie	4/2	2G	1	1(3)	0	1	1	—	—	2,000¥	p. 133
Treads	3	2G	1	1(3)	0	1	1	—	2	2,000¥	p. 133
Dirty	2/4	2G	1	1(3)	0	1	1	—	2	2,000¥	p. 133
Quad	4	1G	1	1(3)	0	1	1	—	4	2,000¥	p. 133
Swims	3	2W	1	1(3)	0	1	1	—	4	1,000¥	p. 133
Hovers	4	1P	1	1(3)	0	1	1	—	6	4,000¥	p. 133
Soars	3	2J	1	1(3)	0	1	1	—	8	4,000¥	p. 133
Sewer Snake	3	1G/1W	1/1	2(1)	0	2	2	—	10	6,000¥	p. 132
Shamus	3	3G	1	4(0)	4	3	8	—	10	30,000¥	p. 137
Shiawase i-Doll	3	3G	1	3	0	3	3	—	4	20,000¥	p. 148
Smoke Generator	3	1G	1	2(0)	0	2	2	—	8	4,000¥	p. 130
Steed	4/2	1G	1	3(1)	0	2	2	—	2	4,000¥	p. 140
Sundowner	3	4P	1	2(0)	0	2	2	—	8	10,000¥	p. 134
Tower	2	1P	1	4(0)	6	2	2	—	8	10,000¥	p. 143
Tunneler	3	0P	0	3(2)	6	2	2	—	8R	10,000¥	p. 140
Wolfhound	3	2J	1	2(1)	0	2	4	—	12	30,000¥	p. 131